Bridging the Cultural Divide

A Report on Aboriginal People and Criminal Justice in Canada

Royal Commission
on Aboriginal Peoples

Canadian Cataloguing in Publication Data

Main entry under title:
Bridging the cultural divide:
a report on Aboriginal people and criminal justice in Canada

Issued also in French under the title: *Par-delà les divisions culturelles :*
un rapport sur les autochtones et la justice pénale au Canada

ISBN 0-660-16283-0
Cat. no. Z1-1991/1-41-8E

1. Native peoples – Canada – Legal status, laws, etc.
2. Criminal justice, Administration of – Canada.
3. Native policing – Canada.
I. Canada. Royal Commission on Aboriginal Peoples.
II. Title: A report on Aboriginal people and criminal justice in Canada.

E78.C2B74 1995   971'.00497   C95-980296-7

Cover photo: Fred Cattroll

© Minister of Supply and Services Canada 1996

Available in Canada through
your local bookseller
or by mail from
Canada Communication Group – Publishing
Ottawa, Canada K1A 0S9

Cat. no. Z1-1991/1-41-8E
ISBN 0-660-16283-0

Canada	Groupe
Communication	Communication
Group	Canada
Publishing	Édition

Royal Commission on
Aboriginal Peoples

CANADA

Commission royale sur
les peuples autochtones

**To His Excellency
the Governor General in Council**

May It Please Your Excellency

We have the honour to submit to you, pursuant to paragraph 9 of Order in Council
P.C. 1991-1597, dated 26 August 1991, a report of the Royal Commission on
Aboriginal Peoples concerning the recognition and establishment of Aboriginal justice
systems.

Respectfully submitted,

René Dussault, j.c.a.
Co-Chair

Georges Erasmus
Co-Chair

Paul L.A.H. Chartrand
Commissioner

J. Peter Meekison
Commissioner

Viola Robinson
Commissioner

Mary Sillett
Commissioner

Bertha Wilson
Commissioner

February 1996
Ottawa, Canada

Contents

Members of the Royal Commission on Aboriginal Peoples

René Dussault, j.c.a.
Co-Chair

Georges Erasmus
Co-Chair

Paul L.A.H. Chartrand
Commissioner

J. Peter Meekison
Commissioner

Viola Marie Robinson
Commissioner

Mary Sillett
Commissioner

Bertha Wilson
Commissioner

Preface

It is rare today to read a newspaper, listen to the radio or watch television without being confronted with issues of crime and punishment, whether in news reports, documentaries or dramatizations. However, the criminal justice system and its effects on the Aboriginal people of Canada reveal themselves in places far removed from the glare of television cameras and reporters' microphones. For Aboriginal people the criminal justice system is not the stuff of drama, real or imagined, but a system in which they, more than any other Canadians, are more likely to become involved, both as victims of crime and as offenders. The over-representation of Aboriginal people in federal, provincial and territorial court systems and prisons casts a long shadow over Canada's claim to be a just society.

Over the last seven years, commissions of inquiry from coast to coast have reviewed the experiences of Aboriginal people with the criminal justice system and have concluded that the system is failing them. Far from redressing the problems they face in their nations, their communities and their personal lives, it is aggravating them. In large measure these problems are themselves the product of historical processes of dispossession and cultural oppression. As we explained in our special report on suicide, *Choosing Life*, the legacy of these historical policies for today's generation of Aboriginal people is high rates of social disorganization, reflected in acts such as suicide and crime.

In this report we review the historical and contemporary record of Aboriginal people's experience in the criminal justice system to secure a better understanding of what lies behind their over-representation there. Our mandate requires us to do more, of course, than provide a framework of understanding. It also charges us with providing a framework for change. That framework has two distinctive yet inter-related dimensions. The first dimension is the reform of the existing criminal justice system to make it more respectful of and responsive to the experience of Aboriginal people; the second dimension is the establishment of Aboriginal justice systems as an exercise of the Aboriginal right of self-government.

The first dimension is one that has been the subject of literally hundreds of recommendations by task forces and commissions of inquiry that have preceded ours.

At an early stage we determined that it would make little sense for this Commission to replicate the work of these inquiries or recite all their recommendations. Instead, we have sought to provide a framework for implementing these recommendations with a view to reforming the existing criminal justice system.

Our primary focus in this report, however, is the second dimension of reform, the recognition and establishment of Aboriginal justice systems. This recognition is an integral part of the right of self-government. The development of such systems, based upon Aboriginal concepts and processes of justice, will, in the long term, enable Aboriginal peoples to address crime and the social disintegration associated with it in ways that promote responsibility and healing for victims, offenders and communities. In this report we have tried to provide a framework that offers both conceptual and constitutional space for the development of Aboriginal justice systems, as well as grappling with the challenging issues raised by the inclusion of Aboriginal justice systems within Canadian federalism.

Readers should also bear in mind that many of the issues raised in this report will be explored in greater detail in our final report, particularly the scope of the right of self-government and how we envisage Aboriginal government as one of three orders of government within Canada. We say this not to suggest that readers should suspend judgement on our recommendations until our final report; rather we offer them in this form at this stage because we believe them to be central to the achievement of a real and enduring justice for Aboriginal peoples in this country.

René Dussault
Co-Chair

Georges Erasmus
Co-Chair

Introduction

The first challenge in writing a report on justice is that "the overall perspective of an Aboriginal person towards Canadian legal institutions is one of being surrounded by injustice without knowing where justice lies, without knowing whether justice is possible."[1]

The voices of Aboriginal people, as they have been expressed to the justice inquiries held over the past few years from Nova Scotia to British Columbia and to this Commission in our community hearings, have described the myriad ways they experience the injustice of a system they view as alien and oppressive.

The Aboriginal Justice Inquiry of Manitoba captured that experience of injustice in its summary of what it heard from the Aboriginal people of Manitoba. They spoke of policing that is at times unresponsive and at times over-zealous, usually insensitive and often abusive. They spoke of a system of laws and courts that ignores significant cultural factors and subjects them to incomprehensible proceedings and inordinate delays in the disposition of their cases. They spoke of a penal system that is harsh and unproductive. They spoke of parole procedures that delay their release from the penal system. They spoke of child welfare and youth justice systems that isolate young people from their families and their communities. They spoke too of historical wrongs, of betrayals and injustice, and of a vision for restoring social harmony to their communities.

---

[1] P.A. Monture-OKanee and M.E. Turpel, "Aboriginal Peoples and Canadian Criminal Law: Rethinking Justice", *U.B.C. Law Review* (1992, Special Edition: Aboriginal Justice), p. 249.

Chief Allan Ross, of Norway House, described how his people saw the face of "lady justice" to the Aboriginal Justice Inquiry of Manitoba as follows:

> Anyone in the justice system knows that lady justice is not blind in the case of Aboriginal people. She has one eye open. She has one eye open for us and dispenses justice unevenly and often very harshly. Her garment is rent. She does not give us equality. She gives us subjugation. She makes us second class citizens in our own land.[2]

An Anishnabe elder, Art Solomon, writes of the continuing suffering of the Aboriginal men, women and young people caught under "the wheels of injustice".

> They say that
> The wheels of "Justice",
>   They grind slowly.
>
> Yes we know.
> But they grind
>   And they grind
>   And they grind
>
> And they grind.
> It seems like they grind
> Forever...[3]

The fundamental question this report poses for all Canadians is, are Aboriginal people to live their lives within a circle of justice, or are they to continue to have their lives broken on the wheel of injustice?

The second challenge in writing about justice issues is that non-Aboriginal Canadians have come to think of the administration of justice as a highly specialized and professionalized aspect of society. The most intrusive and coercive part of that system – the criminal justice system – involves the practices of police officers, lawyers, judges, probation officers, prison administrators and parole board members. In many cases the specialized language that accompanies professional training and the labyrinthine organization that have become the hallmarks of modern bureaucracy are difficult to penetrate by those outside the system. It is not only that justice is a specialized field but that it contains further subdivisions. The curriculum of Canadian law schools mirrors the specialized practices of the legal profession, where the field of law is made up of commercial transactions, family law, the law of succession, criminal law, property law and, more recently, human rights law and environmental law, to name just a few specialties.

---

[2] *Report of the Aboriginal Justice Inquiry of Manitoba*, Volume 1: The Justice System and Aboriginal People (Winnipeg: 1991), p. 6 (cited hereafter as AJI, volume 1).

[3] A. Solomon, "The Wheels of Injustice", in *Songs for the People: Teachings on the Natural Way* (Toronto: W.C. Press, 1990), p. 126.

Aboriginal perspectives on justice are different. That difference is a reflection of distinctive Aboriginal world views and in particular a holistic understanding of peoples' relationships and responsibilities to each other and to their material and spiritual world.

The Assembly of First Nations, in its brief to the Commission, explained this holistic approach:

> Even though First Nations do not adhere to a single world view or moral code, there are nonetheless commonalties in the approach of all First Nations to justice issues. A justice system from the perspective of First Nations is more than a set of rules or institutions to regulate individual conduct or to prescribe procedures to achieve justice in the abstract. 'Justice' refers instead to an aspect of the natural order in which everyone and everything stands in relation to each other. Actions of individuals reflect the natural harmony of the community and of the world itself. Justice must be a felt experience, not merely a thought. It must, therefore, be an internal experience, not an intrusive state of order, imposed from the outside, and separate from one's experience of reality.
>
> Justice for First Nations has traditionally been the daily, shared experience of citizens of the community, part of general teachings, values and traditions that sustain the people as a people. In short, it has been part of the overall fabric of First Nation lives, and part of the sense of responsibility felt by every community member for the other and for the creatures and forces that sustain all human life. Justice is not a concept easily separable from other concepts that make up the ways by which First Nations have come to know themselves and the world. Nor is it static. It evolves as a First Nation grows and adapts to changing circumstances, so that harmony and balance are maintained.[4]

Aboriginal conceptions of justice must be understood as part of the fabric of social and political life rather than as a distinct, formal legal process. The Gitksan and Wet'suwet'en First Nations of British Columbia, in a proposal to the British Columbia ministry of the attorney general entitled "Unlocking Aboriginal Justice", outlined the conceptual framework of their view of justice:

> For a Gitksan and Wet'suwet'en there is no such thing as a purely legal transaction or a purely legal institution. All events in both

---

[4] Assembly of First Nations, "Reclaiming Our Nationhood, Strengthening our Heritage", brief to the Royal Commission on Aboriginal Peoples prepared under the Intervener Participation Program (Ottawa: 1993), p. 65 (referred to hereafter as IPP brief to RCAP).

day-to-day and formal life have social, political, spiritual, economic as well as legal aspects.[5]

For the Gitksan and Wet'suwet'en (along with many other First Nations on the
west coast of British Columbia) the feast (or potlatch) is the fulcrum of their
system. Although it operates as a formal affirmation of the resolution of disputes,
its purposes are much broader, reflecting and encapsulating the holistic way many
Aboriginal institutions function. The hereditary chiefs, as part of their continuing struggle to obtain recognition and respect from the courts of Canada for their
Aboriginal rights, described to the Supreme Court of British Columbia (in
Delgamuukw v. *B.C.*) how their principal institution fulfils functions that in non-
Aboriginal society require a multiplicity of separate institutions, only one of which
is labelled the justice system.

> When today, as in the past, the hereditary chiefs of the Gitksan
> and Wet'suwet'en Houses gather in the Feast Hall, the events
> that unfold are at one and the same time political, legal, eco-
> nomic, social, spiritual, ceremonial and educational. The logistics
> of accumulating and borrowing to make ready for a Feast, and the
> process of paying debts in the course of the Feast have many
> dimensions; they are economic in that the Feast is the nexus of the
> management of credit and debt; they are social in that the Feast
> gives impetus to the ongoing network of reciprocity, and renews
> social contracts and alliances between kinship groups. The Feast
> is a legal forum for the witnessing of the transmission of chiefs'
> names, the public delineation of territorial and fishing sites and
> the confirmation of those territories and sites with the names of
> the hereditary chiefs. The public recognition of title and author-
> ity before an assembly of other chiefs affirms in the minds of all,
> the legitimacy of succession to the name and transmission of
> property rights. The Feast can also operate as a dispute resolution
> process and orders peaceful relationships both nationally, that is,
> within and between Houses, and internationally with other neigh-
> bouring people.
>
> The Feast is charged with the power of the spirit world in the form
> of the crests used in the Feast and in songs and dances performed.
> Furthermore, the public and ceremonial emphasis upon giving,
> paying debts, recognizing and legitimizing the status and author-
> ity of the chiefs and the ownership of territories, and maintaining
> the etiquette of reciprocity – all of these aspects of feasting are
> highly educational. By means of their practice, their repetition and

---

[5] Gitksan and Wet'suwet'en First Nations, "Unlocking Aboriginal Justice: Alternative Dispute
Resolution of the Gitksan and Wet'suwet'en People", proposal submitted to the British Columbia
Ministry of the Attorney General (1987).

recombination through the course of the Feast, the essential values of the culture are both given expression and transmitted from generation to generation.

The hereditary chiefs also cautioned the court not to be misled by the lack of specifically 'legal' signposts in understanding the nature of Aboriginal law.

> In the course of this trial, you will hear repeated references by Gitksan and Wet'suwet'en witnesses to their laws. Yet you will not hear evidence locating the power to legislate in any Gitksan legislature; you will not hear of any Wet'suwet'en Supreme Court House inhabited by a specialized judiciary charged with the duty of interpreting and applying the law; nor will you see any Gitksan policemen or Wet'suwet'en bailiffs who make their living enforcing Gitksan and Wet'suwet'en law. What the court will hear about our principles and rules which entrench fundamental Gitksan and Wet'suwet'en values, establish a basis for social order, and provide for the peaceful resolution of conflict.[6]

In this report we endeavour to keep the holistic Aboriginal perspective on justice at the forefront, in both the form of our analysis and the shape of our recommendations.

The third challenge we faced in writing a report about justice issues is very much related to the first and second. What happens in one discrete area like 'criminal justice' cannot be separated from the broader context of Aboriginal experiences in Canadian society and under the Canadian legal and political regimes. At our National Round Table on Aboriginal Justice Issues, Mary Ellen Turpel elaborated on this important insight:

> For example, in attempting to understand what happened in the Helen Betty Osborne tragedy [one of the specific cases that led to the Aboriginal Justice Inquiry of Manitoba], one cannot just look for procedural or substantive legal or professional error in the police investigation or the trials. We have also to look at why this young 19-year-old woman who desired a formal education had no choice but to attend high school in The Pas instead of her own community, Norway House. We have to consider why the fact that she was an Aboriginal woman made her the chosen target of an abduction, violent rape and murder by four white males. We also have to consider why the Aboriginal community and the non-Aboriginal community in The Pas did not press for the arrest of Helen Betty Osborne's murderer, some of whom were brought to justice only 16 years after the offence. These dimensions to the

---

[6] Opening statement of the Gitksan and Wet'suwet'en Chiefs in *Delgamuukw* v. *B.C.*, reproduced in Gisday Wa and Delgam Uukw, *The Spirit in the Land* (Gabriola, B.C.: Reflections, 1989), pp. 31, 35.

Osborne case defy classification as 'criminal justice' problems – they reveal dysfunctional relationships between Aboriginal peoples and non-Aboriginal peoples at many levels, including among governments and citizens.

I would suggest that when we carefully take apart Aboriginal experiences and perspectives on the criminal justice system – or for that matter any other 'issue' – a tangled and overarching web gets spun. From economic and social disempowerment to problems in the criminal justice system, Aboriginal peoples' issues are seemingly indivisible – one crosses over to another in an interconnected and almost continuous fashion. Alcoholism in Aboriginal communities is connected to unemployment. Unemployment is connected to the denial of hunting, trapping and gathering economic practices. The loss of hunting and trapping is connected to dispossession of land and the impact of major development projects. Dispossession of land is in turn connected to loss of cultural and spiritual identity and is a manifestation of bureaucratic control over all aspects of life. This oppressive web can be seen as one of disempowerment of communities and individual Aboriginal citizens.

There are no satisfactory isolated solutions to each of these problems – the fundamental uniting dilemma is that of control and power and the structural inability of Aboriginal peoples to take control of their lives in communities. This is what I see as the experience of colonization. Subjugation and loss of control premised on conceptions of Aboriginal peoples and their cultures as inferior, needing protection or direction, and requiring supervision.

...Today, Aboriginal peoples are legally and politically surrounded in Canada – they are fenced in by governance they did not discuss, design or desire. It is only as part of a realization of the totalizing and confining nature of the situation that a discrete area like criminal justice can be approached.[7]

Conceived in this way, our recommendations on Aboriginal justice issues must be seen as part of an integrated whole in which the root causes of high Aboriginal crime rates and over-representation in prisons are recognized as intimately related to our overall analysis and recommendations in our other reports. For this reason, our

---

[7] M. E. Turpel, "On The Question of Adapting the Canadian Criminal Justice System for Aboriginal Peoples: Don't Fence Me In", in Royal Commission on Aboriginal Peoples, *Aboriginal Peoples and the Justice System, Report of the National Round Table on Aboriginal Justice Issues* (Ottawa: Supply and Services, 1993), pp. 166-167.

approach in this report is designed to reflect the principles that we recommended as the foundation for a new relationship between Aboriginal and non-Aboriginal people in our earlier constitutional report, *Partners in Confederation*.[8]

We believe that it is essential to frame our discussion of Aboriginal justice issues in the broadest possible context and we have sought to do that. From what we have heard and from what we have read in the reports of the many other justice inquiries, understanding the contemporary realities facing Aboriginal people in the justice system must occur in a historical context of the relationship between Aboriginal and non-Aboriginal people. The sense of oppressiveness, the sense of illegitimacy that has come to characterize Aboriginal peoples' perception and experience of the justice system has deep historical roots.

The trial and execution of Louis Riel for his actions in seeking recognition and respect from Canadian authorities for a Métis homeland have left indelible scars on the collective memory of the Métis people. The perceived injustice of the trial has been compounded by the history of dispossession of Métis people. The trial and execution of eight Cree chiefs who allied themselves with Riel and the Métis, and who were hanged on a single scaffold in the North West Mounted Police court-yard at Battleford, Saskatchewan, on 27 November 1885, continue to cast a long shadow over the descendants of those who were executed for treason for the 'crime' of defending their land.

However, the trials of Louis Riel, of Poundmaker and Big Bear, and of the other Métis and Indian 'criminals' were not unique. Many other episodes that have rarely penetrated the history books of Canada remain alive in the oral histories of Aboriginal peoples and provide not simply a backdrop but the bedrock of Aboriginal peoples' experience of 'justice' according to Canadian law. The importance of understanding this historical experience and recognizing that it is a history whose epilogue has not yet been written – and indeed cannot be written until a new relationship is forged – has been underlined by the most recent of the justice inquiries carried out from one end of the country to the other. Judge Sarich, in his report on the Cariboo-Chilcotin Justice Inquiry in British Columbia, identified the historical context of contemporary expressions of injustice in this way:

> It became apparent early in the course of the inquiry that the Native people of the Cariboo-Chilcotin area were complaining not only about the police and justice system, but also about all non-Native authority structures bearing on their lives. These complaints are long standing and insistent. They are a product of a conflict of cultural values and beliefs and are driven by the past and present conduct of non-Native authority figures. And these complaints go back to the first contact with Europeans.

---

[8] Royal Commission on Aboriginal Peoples (RCAP), *Partners in Confederation: Aboriginal Peoples, Self-Government, and the Constitution* (Ottawa: Supply and Services, 1993).

> In every community west of the Fraser River, there was still barely concealed anger and resentment about the trickery that led to the hanging of the Chilcotin Chiefs in 1864 at Quesnel. The village Chiefs spoke with passion about the desecration of their graves, the spread of smallpox that killed so many of their people, and the brutish conduct of Waddington's road builders.
>
> In accusatory tones the Chiefs also spoke about how their land was taken by government agencies, particularly those lands now used by the Canadian army as a weapons proving ground. They railed as well against the many fenced ranches carved from what they considered their traditional lands, and the forced move of a whole village to accommodate a ranching enterprise.[9]

In this passage Judge Sarich refers to the hanging of the Tsilhqot'n chiefs in 1864. That event, like the hanging of Louis Riel and the Cree chiefs in the North West Territory 21 years later, remains etched in the oral history of the Tsilhqot'n as the clearest demonstration of injustice. Although these events took place 130 years ago, they symbolize for the Tsilhqot'n the attitudes that have characterized their relationship with British Columbians for the past century. They are worth recalling.

The hanging of the Tsilhqot'n chiefs followed the killing of non-Aboriginal road workers. The historical record suggests that the motivations for the attack on the road workers were complex, and although there were undoubtedly a number of grievances arising from the treatment of the Aboriginal people employed by the road party, one of the underlying causes was the intrusion into Tsilhqot'n territory by colonial authorities without any prior treaty to obtain Aboriginal consent. The response by colonial society to the killings has been described by the historian Robin Fisher.

> At first settlers could hardly believe that a party of 'strong, robust, fearless' white men could be nearly all murdered by a dozen 'cowardly savages.' But as the facts of the matter were established, the settlers made it clear that they were not going to treat lightly any threat to their presence in the colonies. *The murders were a flash point in the history of race relations that revealed the attitudes of many of the settlers to Indians who might impede development.* Throughout May 1864 the Victoria newspapers clamoured for retribution against the murderers... On June 1 the British Colonist described the killing of the packers, noted the folly of waiting for the tardy actions of the authorities, and called for citizens to take matters into their own hands. There were, pointed out the editorialist, hundreds of men who would volunteer and who would not rest

---

[9] *Report on the Cariboo-Chilcotin Justice Inquiry* (British Columbia), Judge Anthony Sarich, Commissioner (1993), p. 26.

until "every member of the rascally murderous tribe is suspended to the trees of their own forests." That evening, in a manner typical of the American west, the people of Victoria held a public meeting at which 129 men volunteered to take up arms against the Indians responsible for the killings. Men such as Amor De Cosmos revealed publicly their 'antipathy and hatred' for the Indians... One man, C. B. Young, did remind the audience that justice should be even-handed and that the fencing off of Indian potato patches by Europeans was not justice, nor was it justice when a cricket pitch was taken out of the Indian reserve at Nanaimo. But most Victorians at the meeting were not interested in such logic, and the proposal that the Indians responsible for the murders should be hanged on the spot was greeted with 'general cheers'... The offer of volunteers was declined by the authorities, although the leaders of the Indians held responsible for the murders were later captured, tried, and hanged. Their fate was a signal to the Indians that it was not advisable to object to the presence of Europeans with violence and that vigorous punitive measures would be taken against those who attacked settlers.[10]

Judge Sarich, in his report, wrote about the perception of injustice that the Tsilhqot'n people felt about the hanging of their leaders, from that day to this:

In every village, the people maintained that the Chiefs who were hanged at Quesnel Mouth in 1864 as murderers were, in fact, leaders of a war party defending their land and people. Much has been written but little is known with any certainty of the facts that led to the trial of those Chiefs before Judge Matthew B. Begbie. The people of the Chilcotin have long memories. They hold the memory of those Chiefs in high esteem and cite the effects of smallpox on their ancestors, the incursions onto their land, and the treatment of their people by the road builders hired by Alfred Penderill Waddington as justification for the war. *Many Natives considered the trial and subsequent hanging as a political event in a deliberate process of colonization.*[11]

The Tsilhqot'n people also maintained that the trial was unfair even when judged by the rules of British common law. As Judge Sarich wrote:

It appears that even Judge Begbie was concerned about the fairness of the trial of the Chilcotin Chiefs of Quesnel Mouth in 1864. There was genuine concern that the Chiefs were induced

---

[10]Robin Fisher, *Contact and Conflict: Indian-European Relations in British Columbia, 1774-1890* (Vancouver: University of British Columbia Press, 1977), pp. 108-109 (emphasis added).

[11]Cariboo-Chilcotin Justice Inquiry, cited in note 9, p. 8 (emphasis added).

to surrender and give inculpatory statements on a promise of immunity by Magistrate Cox. Many Natives still feel that the trial and hangings were more a show piece to impress the Natives than an honest search for the truth. Whatever the correct version, that episode of history has left a wound in the body of Chilcotin society. It is time to heal that wound.[12]

1864 may seem a long time ago. But as Judge Sarich found, the attitudes of assumed Indian inferiority and government policies over the last century have had a cumulative impact that is reflected in contemporary relationships between the Aboriginal peoples of the Tsilhqot'n and the agents of the justice system. Addressing allegations of racism by the Tsilhqot'n people against the police, Judge Sarich had this to say:

There is also an attitude problem among the non-Native population from which nearly all police officers are recruited. The Indian Act of Canada is premised upon the postulate that Native people are incapable of managing their own lives, that they cannot make their way in non-Native society and that they are inferior to non-Natives. These concepts have been advanced for so long by the Government of Canada through the Department of Indian Affairs, and so uncritically accepted for so many decades by the non-Native population, that there has come to be an unconscious acceptance of these so-called truths. The dependency, the poverty, the self-destruction to which the Natives were reduced by a conscious policy of government were unspoken confirmation of this 'truth.' This was demonstrated in many ways: from the spontaneous condescension of calling Native people by their first names in a formal situation, to a demeaning and disrespectful attempt at humour in a poem, to a thoughtless comment by an otherwise good and sensitive police officer to grade school children that his job was to 'arrest drunken Indians and put them in jail.' There

---

[12] Cariboo-Chilcotin Justice Inquiry, p. 30. At a symposium on the Tsilhqot'n War of 1864 and the Cariboo-Chilcotin Justice Inquiry of 1993 (sponsored by the University of British Columbia Museum of Anthropology and the First Nations House of Learning and held on 19 November 1994), Judge Cunliff Barnett suggested that the historical evidence raised serious doubts about the fairness of the trial in terms of the Tsilhqot'n chiefs' legal representation. Their court-appointed lawyer was also a principal in a road construction company that was attempting to build a road through the Tsilhqot'n territory, and his business interests had foundered as a result of the unrest engendered by the actions of the Tsilhqot'n. As Judge Barnett commented, "One suspects he may have been less than totally enthusiastic in his last-minute defence of [the Tsilhqot'n Chiefs]." Judge Barnett also questioned the fairness of the subsequent trial, in New Westminster, of two Tsilhqot'n men, who were tried and convicted of murdering the road builders. The person presiding at these trials was the attorney general of the province, Henry Crease, who was given a special commission for this purpose. As the attorney general, Crease was the colony's chief prosecutor and thus could hardly have been an impartial judge.

were other manifestations of that attitude, particularly by those casually inquiring about the purpose and work of the Commission.

It was clear that many officers had brought this attitude with them into uniform by their manner of dealing with Native people. In the business of policing, it explains these officers' readiness to unquestioningly accept allegations made against Natives while keeping a closed mind to anything they raise in answer. It tends to explain the apparent disrespect for any rights of Native people and the aggression and arrogance to which they are often subjected.[13]

The Tsilhqot'n people, like other Aboriginal peoples who spoke to our Commission, made it very clear to Judge Sarich not only that their experience of injustice had to be understood in its widest historical context, but also that their taking back control over their own lives is part of their struggle for justice in its widest meaning.

They demand control over their own lives. They are looking for justice as they understand it and they want to be the architects of their own process. But to them justice is an integrated process involving not only their agencies of social control within their communities, but also control of their own lands and resources.[14]

That larger vision of justice, one that is linked to recognition of the Aboriginal right of self-government and to the resolution of treaty and Aboriginal rights based on claims to lands and resources, is one that our Commission shares and endorses, and it is one that forms the backbone of our recommendations in this report.

---

[13] Cariboo-Chilcotin Justice Inquiry, p. 11. These observations parallel those of the Australian Royal Commission into Aboriginal Deaths in Custody with regard to the experience in that country flowing from the historical role of the police as agents of colonization:

Police officers naturally shared all the characteristics of the society from which they were recruited, including the idea of racial superiority in relation to Aboriginal people and the idea of white superiority in general; and being members of a highly disciplined centralist organization their ideas may have been more fixed than most; but above and beyond that was the fact that police executed on the ground the policies of government and this brought them into continuous and hostile conflict with Aboriginal people. The policeman was the right hand man of the authorities, the enforcer of the policies of control and supervision, often the taker of the children, the rounder-up of those accused of violating the rights of the settlers. Much police work was done on the fringes of non-Aboriginal settlement where the traditions of violence and rough practices were strongest. (Australia, Royal Commission into Aboriginal Deaths in Custody, *National Report: Overview and Recommendations* (Canberra: Australian Government Publishing Service, 1991), p. 10.)

[14] Cariboo-Chilcotin Justice Inquiry, p. 27.

1

Aboriginal Concepts of Law and Justice – The Historical Realities

Non-Aboriginal Canadians pride themselves on the fact that they live in a country governed by the rule of law and that their relationships with each other and their rights and responsibilities are not subject to the arbitrary determination of despots. Today's Canadian laws and legal institutions trace their origins to two broad historical streams, the common law of England and the civil law of France. Going back yet further, we find that many of the concepts underpinning the western idea of law found earlier expression in Roman and Greek legal thought.

The development and entrenchment of the western idea of law is seen as one of the significant contributions of western civilization; it has, however, an underside less worthy of celebration. Indeed, it has been described as one of the tragedies of western history that the culture-specific nature of western systems of law has blinded it to the existence of law in other societies. In the case of Aboriginal peoples, not only in Canada but in other places in the world, this has led to a dismissal of complex Aboriginal cultural systems as not being 'legal' and to a denigration of societies bound only by 'primitive custom'. The same dismissive approach has characterized western views of Aboriginal governance, despite the clearest evidence to the contrary. Francis Jennings, a scholar who has studied the early historical record of relationships between Aboriginal peoples and colonial governments, has well described the origins of European dismissal of Aboriginal legal and political traditions, which pre-dated those of Rome and Athens.

> Europeans' pronouncements that Indians had no government
> were contradicted by their practice of dealing with Indian chiefs

through the protocol of diplomacy with sovereign states. The bulk of evidence about Indian communities implies structures of political association irreconcilable with assumptions of anarchy. From anthropology comes the root conception of 'kinship state', a community of families and clans in which some of the ordering functions of society are performed by the kin groups individually while others are assigned to officers and counsellors chosen cooperatively.

In this structure, as European observers were quick to notice, there was no law in the European sense, and no specialized apparatus of law enforcement. Binding decisions were made by legitimate officers, however, and before the intervention of Europeans eroded the Chiefs' authority there were forceful sanctions for both occasional decisions and enduring customs. In a community where every man bore arms no need existed for a corps of specialized police; any man could be appointed to act guard or do executioner's duty. Early 17th century observers reported that the paramount Chiefs of the tribe sometimes inflicted corporal punishment upon criminals with their own hand.

Families also bore responsibility for protecting kinsfolk, and the accompanying threat of vengeance sanctioned by custom proved an effective deterrent to potential wrongdoers. Such sanctions in the social context were more effectual than European procedures of criminal justice; Adriaen Van der Donck wonderingly noticed 'how uncommon' crimes were among the Hudson River Indians. 'With us,' he continued, 'a watchful police is supported, and crimes are more frequent than among them.' Not recognizing the sanctioning functions formed by means that he had himself described, he was baffled to understand how there could be so little crime 'where there is no regard paid to the administration of justice.' *Van der Donck could recognize due process only when it appeared in the forms to which he had been trained. That fault was shared by other Europeans contemporary with himself and in following generations.*[15]

Although early European accounts of Aboriginal justice are replete with references to its "savagery" and "barbarity", Aboriginal responses to serious disturbances in the peace of their people were, in fact, far more restrained than the "bloody codes" of England and Europe. Francis Jennings' comparative account of how Aboriginal and European societies dealt with the crime of murder illustrates some of the different assumptions that European and Aboriginal legal traditions bring to bear on the role of law and the process of peace-keeping.

---

[15] Francis Jennings, *The Invasion of America: Indians, Colonialism and the Cant of Conquest* (New York: W.W. Norton, 1976), pp.111-112 (emphasis added).

Of crimes common to both societies, murder requires special notice. It was conceived of differently by Indian and European and was therefore punished by different processes. In Europe murder was an offence against the state; among Indians it was an offence against the family of the victim. European law demanded the murderer's life as atonement to the state; Indian custom made his life forfeit to his victim's family. In Europe the state apprehended the murderer; among Indians it was the family's obligation to do so. European observers tagged the Indian custom "revenge" and blathered much about the savagery revealed by it. Yet, as compared to the state's relentlessness, the tribe provided an institution carefully and precisely designed to staunch the flow of blood. The obligation of blood for blood quickly commuted into a payment of valuable goods by the murderer's own kin-folk to the relatives of his victim. This custom (which had been known centuries earlier in Anglo-Saxon England as *wergild*) was a widespread stabilizer of Indian societies, forestalling the development of obligatory revenge into exterminating feuds. Although the term feud has been used freely by the condemners of savage society, Marion W. Smith has been unable to find the phenomena properly denoted by it. 'True feud,' he remarks, 'in its threat of continued violence between particular groups, is surprisingly rare in the New World.'

Europeans understood the *wergild* custom and used it themselves in their dealings with Indians, but only unilaterally. Europeans would pay blood money to avert Indian revenge for the killing of an Indian, but Indians were not permitted to buy absolution for the killing of a European. In the latter case the Europeans demanded the person of the accused Indian for trial in a European court. In the event of non-apprehension of the suspected culprit, mass retribution might be visited upon his village or tribe. *The savagery of revenge, therefore, was simply a semantic function of its identification with an Indian; European revenge was civilized justice.*[16]

Cultural blindness has not only limited western understanding of Aboriginal justice systems; the mischaracterization of those systems as 'uncivilized' has provided a moral justification for imposing western concepts of law and justice in ever-widening geographical and conceptual arcs. The conjunction of moral, cultural and economic imperialism involved in the imposition of western law and western justice was stated as clearly as it could be in 1917, the first time that Inuit ever faced trial in a Canadian court.

---

[16]Jennings, *The Invasion of America*, pp. 147-149 (emphasis added).

Two Inuit hunters, Sinnisiak and Uluksuk, were charged with the murder of two Roman Catholic priests. The two hunters claimed that they acted in self-defence, fearing that the priests, armed with rifles, were going to kill them. In his opening address to a jury trial in Edmonton, counsel for the Crown, after praising the Royal North West Mounted Police for apprehending the accused following a "thrilling story of travel and adventure in lands forlorn", explained why this trial, which he described as "absolutely unique in the history of North America", was so important.

> It is important particularly in this. The Indians of the Plains, the Blackfeet and the Crees, and the Chippeweyans and the Sarcees and the Stoneys have been educated in the ideas of justice. They have been educated to know that justice does not mean merely retribution, and that the justice which is administered in our courts is not a justice of vengeance; it has got no particle of vengeance in it; it is an impartial justice by which the person who is charged with crime is given a fair and impartial trial....

> *These remote savages, really cannibals, the Eskimo of the Arctic regions, have got to be taught to recognize the authority of the British Crown, and that the authority of the Crown and of the Dominion of Canada, of which these countries are a part, extends to the furthermost limits of the frozen north.* It is necessary that they should understand that they are under the Law, just as in the same way it was necessary to teach the Indians of the Indian Territories and of the North West Territories that they were under the Law; that they must regulate their lives and dealings with their fellow men, of whatever race, white men or Indians, according to, at least, the main outstanding principles of that law, which is part of the law of civilization, and that this law must be respected on the barren lands of North America, and on the shores of the Arctic Ocean, and on the ice of the Polar Seas, even as far as the Pole itself. They have got to be taught to respect the principles of Justice, and not merely to submit to it, but to learn that they are entitled themselves to resort to it, to resort to the law, to resort to British Justice, and to take advantage of it the same way as anybody else does. *The code of the savage, an eye for an eye, a tooth for a tooth, a life for a life must be replaced among them by the code of civilization.* They must learn to know, whether they are Eskimo or not, that death is not the only penalty for a push or a shove, or a swear word, or for mere false dealing; that for these offences our civilization and justice do not allow a man to be shot or to be stabbed, to be killed or murdered. They have got to learn that even if slight violence is used it will not justify murder, it will not justify killing, and they must be made to understand that Death is not 'the only penalty

that Eskimo know' or have got to know. If that is their idea, their notion of justice, I hope when the result of this trial is brought back to the Arctic regions that all such savage notions will be effectually dispelled.

This is one of the outstanding ideas of the Government, and the great importance of this trial lies in this: *that for the first time in history these people, these Arctic people, pre-historic people, people who are as nearly as possible living today in the Stone Age, will be brought in contact with and will be taught what is the white man's justice.* They will be taught that crime will be swiftly followed by arrest, arrest by trial, and if guilt is established, punishment will follow on guilt. You, gentlemen, can understand how important this is: white men travel through the barren lands; white men live on the shores of Bear Lake; white men go to the shores of the Arctic Ocean; and if we are to believe the reports of the copper deposits near the mouth of the Copper Mine River, many white men more may go to investigate and to work the mines. The Eskimo must be made to understand that the lives of others are sacred, and that they are not justified in killing on account of any mere trifle that may ruffle or annoy them.

Just as it is possible today for any white man to travel through the country of the Blackfeet, or the country of the Crees, or the country of any of our own Indians, under the protection of the aegis of justice, so it becomes necessary that any white man may travel in safety among the far tribes of the North.[17]

Not all western-trained jurists have been so blinded by assumptions of cultural and moral superiority in their characterization of Aboriginal justice. A powerful antidote to the cultural myopia of earlier descriptions of Aboriginal justice can be found in the work of some of the most distinguished lawyers and anthropologists of this century. In one of the classics of modern jurisprudence and anthropology, *The Cheyenne Way*, published in 1941, Karl Llewellyn and E. Adamson Hoebel demonstrated the sophistication of Cheyenne law and legal process. Writing some 20 years later, in *The Cheyennes, Indians of the Great Plains*, Hoebel summarized some of the achievements and important features of the Cheyenne legal system:

As an operating system, Cheyenne law is remarkable for the degree of juristic skill that is manifest in it. By juristic skill we mean the creation and utilization of legal forms and processes that efficiently and effectively solve the problems posed to the law and in

---

[17] R.G. Moyles, *British Law and Arctic Men: The Celebrated 1917 Murder Trials of Sinnisiak and Uluksuk, First Inuit Tried Under White Man's Law* (Burnaby, B.C.: Simon Fraser University for the Northern Justice Society, 1989), pp. 38-39 (emphasis added).

such a way that the basic values and purposes of the society are realized and not frustrated by rigid legalism. Juristic skill implies the ability to define relations between persons, to allocate authority, and to clear up conflicts of interest (trouble cases) in ways that effectively reduce internal social tensions and promote individual well-being and the maintenance of the group as a group. [In an earlier work, we commented] on this outstanding quality of the Cheyenne: "It is not merely that we find neat juristic work. It is that the *generality* of the Cheyennes, not alone the 'lawyers' or the 'great lawyers' among them...worked out their nice cases with an intuitive juristic precision which among us marks a judge as good; that the *generality* among them produced indeed a large percentage of work on a level of which our rarer and greater jurists could be proud."[18]

This description of the Cheyenne way accords with the principles of recognition and respect that we set out as a critical part of the framework for understanding and reshaping the relationship between Aboriginal peoples and the rest of Canadians. It is, however, a recognition and respect which Aboriginal peoples continue to have difficulty in wresting from Canadian courts, as the experience of the Gitksan and Wet'suwet'en demonstrated recently. In response to the assertions by the hereditary chiefs of these two First Nations, located in British Columbia, that they "govern themselves according to their laws, maintain their institutions and exercise their authority over the territory through those institutions", Chief Justice McEachern of the Supreme Court of British Columbia concluded:

I have no difficulty finding that the Gitksan and Wet'suwet'en people developed tribal customs and practices relating to Chiefs, clans and marriages and things like that, but I am not persuaded their ancestors practiced universal or even uniform customs relating to land outside the villages...

The plaintiffs have indeed maintained institutions but I am not persuaded all their present institutions were recognized by their ancestors... I do not accept the ancestors 'on the ground' behaved as they did because of 'institutions.' Rather I find they more likely acted as they did because of survival instincts which varied from village to village.[19]

---

[18] E. Adamson Hoebel, *The Cheyennes, Indians of the Great Plains* (New York: Holt, Rinehart and Winston, 1960), p. 50 (reference omitted).

[19] *Delgamuukw* v. *British Columbia*, [1991] 3 W.W.R. 97, pp. 372-373. The British Columbia Court of Appeal reversed the trial judge's finding that Aboriginal rights had been extinguished in British Columbia by pre-colonial legislation ([1993] 5 W.W.R. 97).

The Chief Justice's dismissive approach to Gitksan and Wet'suwet'en laws and institutions has been the subject of critical commentary. The United Nations Special Rapporteur for the Study on Treaties wrote in his interim report that statements such as these show "that deeply-rooted western ethnocentric criteria are still widely shared in present-day judiciary reasoning vis-à-vis the indigenous way of life."[20]

Before we consider some of the submissions to this Commission and to several of the justice inquiries regarding the nature of Aboriginal justice systems within Canada, we believe that it is helpful to look at another comparative description. Along with the Aboriginal peoples of Canada, the Maori have been among the most vigorous, both within New Zealand/Aotearoa and in the international arena, in asserting their Aboriginal and treaty rights to maintain and develop their own systems of governance, including their distinctive systems of justice. The importance of this comparative work is that it is powerful evidence in support of the existence and survival of distinctive indigenous processes of justice that demand both recognition and respect along with the major tributaries of western legal tradition – the common and the civil law. Put another way, it is powerful evidence in support of the need to expand the horizons of legal pluralism in Canada to find the rightful and honourable place for Aboriginal law and Aboriginal processes of justice.

In a report written for the New Zealand department of justice, Moana Jackson, a Maori lawyer, provides this account of the Maori system of justice:

> Although the Maori system shared with the *Pakeha* [the Maori term for non-Maori settlers] a clear code of right and wrong behaviour, its philosophical emphasis was different. The system of behavioral constraints implied in the law was interwoven with the deep spiritual and religious underpinning of Maori society so that *Maori people did not so much live under the law, as with it....*
>
> The traditional Maori ideals of law have their basis in a religious and mystical weave which was codified into oral traditions and sacred beliefs. They made up a system based on a spiritual order which was nevertheless developed in a rational and practical way to deal with questions of *mana* [authority], security, and social stability. Like all legal systems, it covered both collective and more specifically individual matters. They were thus precedents embodied in the laws of Tangaroa. There were also specific but interrelated laws dealing with dispute settlement, and the assess-

---

[20] Miguel Alphonso Martinez, Special Rapporteur, "First Progress Report on the Study on Treaties, Agreements and Other Constructive Arrangements Between States and Indigenous Populations" (United Nations document number E/CN4/Sub.2/1992/32), 25 August 1992, para. 130. See also Michael Asch, "Errors in Delgamuukw: An Anthropological Perspective", in *Aboriginal Title in British Columbia:* Delgamuukw v. The Queen, ed. Frank Cassidy (Lantzville, B.C.: Oolichan Books and the Institute for Research on Public Policy, 1992), pp. 221-243.

ment and enforcement of community sanctions for offences against good order.

The particular reasons why certain people might act in breach of social controls, the 'causes' of 'offending', were understood within the same philosophical framework which shaped the laws themselves. Anti-social behaviour resulted from an imbalance in the spiritual, emotional, physical or social well-being of an individual or *whanau* [extended family or clan]; the laws to correct that behaviour grew from a process of balance which acknowledged the links between all forces and all conduct. In this sense, the 'causes' of imbalance, the motives for offending, had to be addressed if any dispute was to be resolved – in the process of restoration, they assumed more importance than the offence itself.

This belief led to an emphasis on group rather than individual concerns: the rights of the individual were indivisible from the welfare of his *whanau*, his *hapu* [sub-tribe], and his *iwi* [tribe]. Each had reciprocal obligations tied to the precedents handed down by shared ancestors. Although oral, the precedents established clear patterns of social regulation....

The explanations for these rights and obligations, their philosophy, grew out of, and was shaped by, ancestral thought and precedent. The reasons for a course of action, and the sanctions which may follow from it, were part of the holistic interrelationship defined by that precedent and remembered in ancestral genealogy or *whakapapa*. The *whakapapa* in turn tied the precedents to the land through tribal histories, and so wove together the inseparable threads of Maori existence....

The system imposed responsibility for wrongdoing on the family of the offender, not just the individual, and so strengthened the sense of reciprocal group obligation. The consequences of an individual or group action could therefore rebound on the *whanau*, the *hapu*, or even the *iwi*, since the ancestral precedents which established the sanction also established the kinship ties of responsibility and duty.... Thus the use of *muru* [payment of compensation] enabled justice to not only be done, but to manifestly be seen to be done by all members of both the offenders' and victim's *whanau*. The ever-present influence of *tapu* [the concept that each life was a sacred gift] created a group consciousness about the behaviour which was *tika* or correct because everyone was linked to its source.... These concepts were not 'foul superstitions,' as the missionaries claimed, but a consistent body of theory and sanction upon which the society depended. They incorporated and reflected the Maori ideals of group control and responsibility within a weave of kinship obligation. Rules of conduct were not divided into civil and criminal laws since a 'criminal' act of violence or a 'civil' act of negligence influenced the same basic order: the balance between the individual, the group, and the ancestors.

Sanctions imposed for any infringement aimed to restore this balance. Thus the *whanau* of the offender was made aware of its shared responsibilities, that of the victim was given reparation to restore it to its proper place, and the ancestors were appeased by the acceptance of the precedents which they had laid down....

The precedents were refined over time and their application clearly proceeded on a different basis to that of western jurisprudence. However, they provided a sense of legal control which was effective because it had a unifying basis that recognized the need for social order and the value of balancing community affairs.[21]

Turning from the Maori and the Cheyenne to a consideration of the systems of law and justice of Aboriginal peoples in Canada, in the past few years we have seen First Nations and Aboriginal communities articulating the nature and elements of those processes in their submissions to this Commission and to other justice inquiries. From reviewing some of those submissions we can discern both the distinctiveness and the common elements of Aboriginal justice systems within Canada.

The report of the Osnaburgh/Windigo Tribal Council Justice Review Committee provides this overview based on submissions from four communities of the Ojibwa Nation in northern Ontario.

Aboriginal societies had their own ideas of justice and dispute resolution. Aboriginal law was concerned with maintaining social harmony since interdependency was necessary in order to meet the exigencies of a hunting and gathering existence. Disputes would be solved by a person known to both of the disputants, in contrast to the impersonalized machinery adopted by the Euro-Canadian justice system. When a dispute arose, it tended to involve other members within the same community and a well-understood system existed to resolve it. What the common law is to the Euro-Canadian justice system so customary law, based upon an oral rather than a written tradition, was to Aboriginal justice systems.

Crimes were seen as a hurt against a community of people, not against an abstract state. Community meetings of 'calling-

---

[21] Moana Jackson, *The Maori and the Criminal Justice System, He Whaipaanga Hou, A New Perspective*, part 2 (New Zealand Department of Justice, 1988), pp. 36-44 (emphasis added).

to-account' therefore played an important part in investigation, evaluation, sentencing and even, through the shame they could inspire, punishment. The judicial system itself was viewed in a fundamentally different light than is the European system by non-Natives. Its primary goal was to protect the community and further its goals. To this end it placed much more emphasis on modifying future behaviour than on penalizing wrong-doers for past misdeeds. Counselling, therefore, was far more important than punishment. Punishment, in fact, was often only a last resort used to safeguard a community against extremely disruptive activity, when rehabilitative efforts had failed.[22]

The Blood Tribe in Alberta explained its traditional concept of justice to the Task Force on the Criminal Justice System and its Impact on the Indian and Metis People of Alberta, headed by Mr. Justice Cawsey.

Traditional approaches to justice were based upon the principle that every person should be given his due. This involved a reference to the tribal moral standard of the tribe. Acceptable behaviour was ascertained in light of the competing interests of the tribe. However, individual and group interests, if the occasion arose, would be sacrificed in favour of the greater tribal interest in such totality. As a result, social sanctions developed to protect individual interests as well as tribal interests, along with the appropriate machinery to enforce social sanctions. For the Blood Tribe this instrument was the *Ikunuhkahtsi* which was called upon to settle disputes, carry out punishments, maintain order and tribal equilibrium, and to guard against/or expel external aggression. The *Ikunuhkahtsi* were normally composed of tribal chiefs or headmen, religious leaders, elders and/or respected warriors.[23]

The Cawsey task force also heard submissions from the Federation of Metis Settlements regarding Métis dispute resolution.

The traditional way of [administering justice] was to bring the offender before the whole community to be confronted by elders and the leaders of the village. The offender was then lectured and reprimanded in front of the whole community. When this type of system was used there were very few repeat offenders. This

---

[22] Report of the Osnaburgh/Windigo Tribal Council Justice Review Committee, prepared for the Attorney General (Ontario) and Minister Responsible for Native Affairs and the Solicitor General (Ontario) (July 1990). Quotation is from the submission of the New Saugeen Nation to the committee.

[23] *Justice on Trial: Report of the Task Force on the Criminal Justice System and Its Impact on the Indian and Metis People of Alberta* (1991) volume 1, p. 3 (cited hereafter as *Justice on Trial*).

system could work today if the Métis communities became totally involved, with minimal or no interference from the provincial and federal governments.[24]

At our round table on justice, Zebedee Nungak, chairman of the Inuit Justice Task Force for Nunavik, outlined the traditional justice system of the Inuit of Nunavik.

> The radical transformation of Inuit life in the Arctic which has transpired in the past forty years can lead the uninformed to the erroneous conclusion that Inuit did not possess any semblance of a justice system before contact with European civilization. That our people led a nomadic existence in a harsh unforgiving Arctic environment may lead Qallunaat [literally, persons with pale or white faces, that is, Caucasians] or others to conclude that Inuit did not have a sense of order, a sense of right and wrong, and a way to deal with wrong-doers in their society. Inuit did possess this sense of order and right and wrong. The way it was practised and implemented may never have been compatible with European civilization's concepts of justice, but what worked for Inuit society in their environment was no less designed for conditions of life in the Arctic than that of Qallunaat was for conditions of their life.
>
> In the pre-contact period, Inuit lived in camps dictated according to seasons and availability of life-sustaining wildlife. Their leadership consisted of elders of the camp, as well as hunters who were the best providers and were followed for their ability to decide for the clan or group where the best areas were to spend the seasons. The overriding concern was the sustenance of the collective. Any dispute among the people was settled by the elders and/or leaders, who always had the respect and high regard of the group....
>
> The bulk of disputes handled by the traditional ways pre-contact mostly involved provision of practical advice and persuasive exhortation for correct and proper behaviour, which was generally accepted and abided by. In more serious cases, offenders were ostracized or banished from the clan or group. In these cases, the ostracized or banished individuals were given no choice except to the leave the security and company of the group which imposed this sentence. The social stigma of having such a sentence imposed was often enough to reform or alter behaviour which was the original cause of this measure, and people who suffered this indignity once often became useful members of society, albeit with another clan in another camp. Our oral traditions also abound with stories of such people who went on to lead lives useful to their

---

[24] *Justice on Trial*, volume 1, p. 31.

fellow Inuit as providers, and in some cases, leaders of their own groups or clans....

In the rare cases...where an offender refused to obey the sanctions imposed by the leadership, extreme measures were taken. If the offence was serious enough to disrupt the constant struggle for life, and the person who was the cause of that disruption made clear his refusal to obey what was imposed on him, the leadership often resolved to kill the offender. Our oral traditions are rich with stories of such episodes... It should be said immediately that such cases were the exception and not the rule. Then again, everything humanly possible was done to advise the culprit to amend his ways or to follow the decision of the leadership before such a radical measure was carried out.[25]

The Independent First Nations Alliance (IFNA), which represents four First Nations communities in northwestern Ontario, in an intervener participation brief to this Commission, described how social control was maintained within their communities in the 1920s and 1930s before the intrusion of the Euro-Canadian justice system. Their description is based on the accounts of elders who remember when problems within the community were resolved by the community, not by those wielding authority that originates in a government not of the people's making. The following account describes the process in Big Trout Lake:

Big Trout Lake First Nations signed treaty in 1929. Two of the elders interviewed by IFNA were alive at the time of the treaty and remember the events.... Big Trout Lake was one of the summer gathering places. From Big Trout Lake, people fanned out to their winter hunting and trapping territories in the surrounding land. Many of the communities in the area surrounding Big Trout Lake were once winter hunting and trapping territories for groups who spent their summers together in Big Trout Lake.... Elders Jeremiah McKay and Maryanne Anderson described how order was kept amongst the Big Trout Lake peoples in the early days of contact. Social order was maintained through the use of 'Circles'. In the summer community, the community leaders met in these Circles to review what had happened in the winter groups and to maintain order in the summer settlement. Circles were made up of representatives of the smaller winter groups along with the leaders of the summer community and the spiritual leaders.

In addition, each of the winter groups had one or more 'designated keepers' whose role was also to oversee the matters in the winter

---

[25] Zebedee Nungak, "Fundamental Values, Norms, and Concepts of Justice", in *Aboriginal Peoples and the Justice System*, cited in note 7, pp. 86-87.

groups and report to the Circle upon the return of the summer gathering place. There is no exact English term for these designated persons. The term used by Jeremiah McKay combined to express the role they played in the community. He uses three terms: *oganawengike*, the keeper, *odibaajimoog*, the reporter and, *onagachecheka*, the person who watches. The most frequently used term is *oganawengike*. These roles might be the responsibility of a number of different persons or they might be combined as a responsibility of a single person. Jeremiah McKay describes how they operated:

> If anything went wrong in the little settlements in winter time, the *odibaajimoog* [the reporter] would be holding the meetings there. And his role was to keep things going well. If anything not too serious happened, he would keep the incident to himself rather than try to resolve it immediately. And he would not discuss what he was doing. When the group went back to Big Trout Lake in June, the chief of the band would meet with the *oganawengike* [the keeper] to discuss what had happened over the winter. The *oganawengike* would report to the chief and that is how the chief would find out what had happened in other groups.

> The chief would start working on problems right away. They would call a Circle to discuss the cases. The chief would bring the person who had been reported into the Circle and would say to him, 'What do you say? Is it true you did this thing?'

> The person who was being asked would usually reply, 'Yes, it is true.'

> And at that time the chief would usually start talking to him. After the chief finished talking to him, the others would follow. The spiritual leader would be the last person to talk to the person. The process worked when it was applied.

What is described here is a very formal process of policing and adjudicating individual behaviour. The object is to impress upon the person being talked to the importance of right behaviour rather than the imposition of any sanction.[26]

As the submission of the Independent First Nations Alliance makes clear, there have been dramatic changes in the life of Big Trout Lake people since the times described by Jeremiah McKay.

---

[26]Independent First Nations Alliance (IFNA), "Genowin Disomin/Gunowen Disomin – Keeping Ourselves: A Comparison of Justice in Four First Nations", IPP brief to RCAP (1993), pp. 18-20.

In living memory, Big Trout Lake First Nation has gone from being a peaceful community, self-governing in justice, to a troubled community forced into increasing reliance on a justice system which was not designed for it, which functions poorly and which undermines the traditional norms and values of the Big Trout Lake people.

Instead of the Circle process, Big Trout Lake First Nation is now served by the Euro-Canadian justice system through the Ontario Provincial Courts and the Ontario Provincial Police.... The Ontario Provincial Court flies in from Kenora and holds court in the community on a regular basis. Figures are not readily available but anecdotal information indicates a rising crime rate with alcohol an element in the majority of the offences committed.... Elders and leaders within the community are all too aware of the tragedy that they are living through. They recognize that their community is under threat from increasing encroachment from outside. The full meaning of the very recent loss of control of the social control in the community is very clearly understood....[27]

The people of Big Trout Lake, like many other Aboriginal people who made presentations to this Commission, emphasized the vital importance, in their struggle to regain control of their lives and their communities, of building upon and revitalizing the values and the institutions that have sustained them. The final statement of the Independent First Nations Alliance makes it very clear that Aboriginal peoples, in looking to the past, are not engaged in romanticism and nostalgia but are drawing deep upon their strengths in charting paths for their future.

We do not wish to finish looking backwards. Like elder Albert Peters, indeed like all the elders, we would rather end on a note which looks forward with hope. Let us finish with these, the closing words of Albert Peters, spoken on a beautiful summer's day in his home by Pikangikum Lake where his people have gathered for as long as is remembered:

Thank you for letting me talk about the past. I know something of what happened in the past. First Nations people looked after themselves in the past without anyone telling them what to do. Nobody told us what to do in the past. Now we are trying to get back what we have lost. We lost it because someone told us there was a better, a right way. Now we are trying to keep ourselves, to govern ourselves: we are trying to get back what we have lost and what we know is right.[28]

---

[27] IFNA, "Genowin Disomin/Gunowen Disomin", pp. 32-33.

[28] IFNA, "Genowin Disomin/Gunowen Disomin", p. 62.

2
Current Realities

More than in any other area of our mandate, the Commission had the benefit of a large number of inquiries, reports and conferences addressing the current realities of Aboriginal people and the justice system. Some of these were federal and nation-wide, addressing broad issues of criminal justice,[29] while others had a narrower focus on the corrections system.[30] Others were provincial in scope, in some cases addressing particular issues or focusing on the experience of specific Aboriginal peoples.[31]

From our reading of these reports and from what we learned through our research and our hearings, we drew two principal conclusions. The first is that there is a remarkable consensus on some fundamental issues and, in particular, on how the

---

[29]Canadian Corrections Association, *Indians and the Law* (Ottawa: 1967); *Native People and Justice*, reports on the National Conference and the Federal/Provincial Conference on Native People and the Criminal Justice System (Ottawa: Solicitor General of Canada, 1975); Law Reform Commission of Canada, *Aboriginal Peoples and Criminal Justice*: *Equality, Respect and the Search for Justice*, Report No. 34 (Ottawa: 1991).

[30]Task Force on Aboriginal People in Federal Corrections, *Final Report* (Ottawa: Solicitor General of Canada, 1988); *Creating Choices*, Report of the Task Force on Federally Sentenced Women (Ottawa: 1990).

[31]Royal Commission on the Donald Marshall, Jr., Prosecution (Nova Scotia: 1989); Report of the Osnaburgh/Windigo Tribal Council Justice Review Committee (Ontario: 1990); *Justice on Trial*, Report of the Task Force on the Criminal Justice System and its Impact on the Indian and Metis People of Alberta (1991); *Report of the Aboriginal Justice Inquiry of Manitoba* (1991); *Report of the Saskatchewan Indian Justice Review Committee* (1992); *Report of the Saskatchewan Metis Justice Review Committee* (1992); *Report on the Cariboo-Chilcotin Aboriginal Justice Inquiry* (British Columbia: 1993);

justice system has failed Aboriginal people; the second conclusion is that notwithstanding the hundreds of recommendations from commissions and task forces, the
reality for Aboriginal people in 1996 is that the justice system is still failing them.

The Failure of the Justice System

The opening paragraphs of the report of the Aboriginal Justice Inquiry of Manitoba
is unequivocally dark in its condemnation.

> The justice system has failed Manitoba's Aboriginal people on a
> massive scale. It has been insensitive and inaccessible, and has
> arrested and imprisoned Aboriginal people in grossly dispropor-
> tionate numbers. Aboriginal people who are arrested are more
> likely than non-Aboriginal people to be denied bail, spend more
> time in pre-trial detention and spend less time with their lawyers,
> and, if convicted, are more likely to be incarcerated.
>
> It is not merely that the justice system has failed Aboriginal people;
> justice also has been denied to them. For more than a century the
> rights of Aboriginal people have been ignored and eroded.[32]

Our three-day round table on Aboriginal justice came resoundingly to the same
conclusion. The rapporteur, James MacPherson, summarized the presentations of
participants from federal, provincial, territorial and Aboriginal governments.

> The first theme I would identify was a particularly powerful one.
> Moreover, it may well be a unanimous one. The current Canadian
> justice system, especially the criminal justice system, has failed the
> Aboriginal people of Canada – Indian, Inuit and Métis, on-reserve
> and off-reserve, urban and rural, in all territorial and govern-
> mental jurisdictions. The principal reason for this crushing failure
> is the fundamentally different world view between European
> Canadians and Aboriginal peoples with respect to such elemen-
> tal issues as the substantive content of justice and the process for
> achieving justice.[33]

In a brief to this Commission, Robert Mitchell, who as attorney general and minister of justice of Saskatchewan has directed his mind to these issues as much as
any minister has, underscored a conclusion that the evidence clearly compels:

Justice for and by the Aboriginals, Report and Recommendations of the Advisory Committee on the
Administration of Justice in Aboriginal Communities, submitted to the Minister of Justice and the
Minister of Public Security (Quebec), 17 August 1995.

[32] AJI, cited in note 2, volume 1, p. 1. See also, Law Reform Commission of Canada, *Aboriginal Peoples
and Criminal Justice*, cited in note 29, p. 16.

[33] James MacPherson, "Report from the Round Table Rapporteur", in *Aboriginal Peoples and the Justice
System*, cited in note 7, p. 4.

> The current criminal justice system has profoundly failed Aboriginal people. It has done so in failing to respect cultural differences, failing to address overt and systemic biases against Aboriginal people, and in denying Aboriginal people an effective voice in the development and delivery of services. This must end.[34]

Robert Mitchell is not alone in this political admission of the failure of the justice system. At the federal-provincial-territorial justice ministers conference held in Ottawa on 23-24 March 1994, ministers agreed "...that the justice system has failed and is failing Aboriginal peoples and agree that a holistic approach including the healing process is essential in Aboriginal justice reform."[35]

The federal minister of justice, Kim Campbell, added her voice to the consensus in a presentation to our justice round table:

> It has not been easy for me to accept that, for some, our laws and our courts are viewed as instruments of oppression, rather than as mechanisms for the preservation of justice.... I have come to learn that the administration of justice, despite the good intentions of most of the people who work within it, has often failed to meet the needs of Aboriginal people who, all too frequently, come into contact with our courts as offenders, as victims, and as communities.... I have learned that Aboriginal people are too often alienated by, and from, the existing justice system, and that many feel powerless even to participate in determining what will happen to people from their communities who have found themselves in conflict with the law.[36]

Injustice Personified – Aboriginal Over-Representation

The justice inquiries that preceded our work documented extensively how this failure has affected the lives of Aboriginal men, women and young people. The clearest evidence appears in the form of the over-representation of Aboriginal people in the criminal justice system. This was first documented in 1967 by the Canadian Corrections Association report, *Indians and the Law*, and in 1974 by the Law Reform Commission of Canada in *The Native Offender and the Law*. **Reports and inquiries since then have not only confirmed the fact of over-**

---

[34] Robert Mitchell, QC, Minister of Justice and Attorney General of Saskatchewan, submission to RCAP (7 March 1994), p. 2.

[35] Quoted in Richard Gosse, "Charting the Course for Aboriginal Justice Reform Through Aboriginal Self-Government", in *Continuing Poundmaker and Riel's Quest, Presentations made at a Conference on Aboriginal Peoples and Justice*, comp. Richard Gosse, James Youngblood Henderson and Roger Carter (Saskatoon: Purich Publishing, 1994), p. 29.

[36] *Aboriginal Peoples and the Justice System*, cited in note 7, pp. 432-433.

representation but, most alarmingly, have demonstrated that the problem is getting worse, not better.

The over-representation of Aboriginal people in Canadian prisons has been the subject of special attention and appropriately so, because the sentence of imprisonment carries with it the deprivation of liberty and represents Canadian society's severest condemnation. The Canadian Bar Association focused its attention on Aboriginal imprisonment in 1988, arguing that lawyers have a particular responsibility to bring these issues to the forefront of the public and governmental agenda.

> As Members of the Bar we see the people that lie behind the statistics. We see them in the courts and prisons of this country and are witnesses to the continuing injustice towards them which we as a society practice in the name, paradoxically, of a criminal justice system.[37]

The Association provided this bleak overview of the measure of this injustice:

> Statistics about crime are often not well understood by the public and are subject to variable interpretation by the experts. In the case of the statistics regarding the impact of the criminal justice system on Native people the figures are so stark and appalling that the magnitude of the problem can be neither misunderstood nor interpreted away. Government figures which reflect different definitions of 'Native' and which probably underestimate the number of prisoners who consider themselves Native show that almost 10 per cent of the federal penitentiary population is Native (including about 13 per cent of the federal women's prisoner population) compared to about 2 per cent of the population nationally. In the west and northern parts of Canada where there are relatively high concentrations of Native communities, the over-representation is more dramatic. In the Prairie region, Natives make up about 5 per cent of the total population but 32 per cent of the penitentiary population and in the Pacific region Native prisoners constitute about 12 per cent of the penitentiary population while less than 5 per cent of the region's general population is of Native ancestry. Even more disturbing, the disproportionality is growing. Thus, in 1965 some 22 per cent of the prisoners in Stony Mountain Penitentiary were Native; in 1984 this proportion was 33 per cent. It is realistic to expect that absent radical change, the problem will intensify due to the higher birth rate of Native communities.

---

[37] Michael Jackson, *Locking Up Natives in Canada*, Report of the Canadian Bar Association Committee on Imprisonment and Release (1988); reprinted in *U.B.C. Law Review* 23 (1989), p. 220. The report was adopted by the Canadian Bar Association at its annual meeting in 1989.

Bad as this situation is within the federal system, in a number of the western provincial correctional systems, it is even worse. In B.C. and Alberta, Native people, representing 3-5 per cent of the province's population constitute 16 per cent and 17 per cent of the admissions to prison. In Manitoba and Saskatchewan, Native people, representing 6-7 per cent of the population constitute 46 per cent and 60 per cent of prison admissions.

[A] Saskatchewan study brings home the implications of its findings by indicating that a treaty Indian boy turning 16 in 1976 had a 70 per cent chance of at least one stay in prison by the age of 25 (that age range being the one with the highest risk of imprisonment). The corresponding figure for non-status or Métis was 34 per cent. For a non-Native Saskatchewan boy the figure was 8 per cent. Put another way, this means that in Saskatchewan, prison has become for young Native men, the promise of a just society which high school and college represents for the rest of us. *Placed in a historical context, the prison has become for many young Native people the contemporary equivalent of what the Indian residential school represented for their parents.*[38]

The Association cautioned that "absent radical change, the problem will intensify." The surest evidence that there has been no radical change, and the most damning indictment, is found in the commissions of inquiry appointed since the publication of *Locking Up Natives in Canada*. The Aboriginal Justice Inquiry of Manitoba reported that whereas Aboriginal people accounted for 33 per cent of the population at Stony Mountain Federal Penitentiary in 1984, by 1989 the figure had risen to 46 per cent. In 1983 Aboriginal people accounted for 37 per cent of the population of the provincial Headingly Correctional Institution; by 1989 they accounted for 41 per cent. By 1989 Aboriginal women accounted for 67 per cent of the prison population at the Portage Correctional Institution for Women, and in institutions for young people, the proportion of Aboriginal people was 61 per cent. All together, Aboriginal people made up 56 per cent of the population of correctional institutions (both federal and provincial) in Manitoba in 1989. Aboriginal people account for just under 12 per cent of Manitoba's total population and "thus, Aboriginal people, depending on their age and sex, are present in the jails up to five times more than their presence in the general population."[39]

The figures received by the Task Force on the Criminal Justice System and its Impact on the Indian and Metis People of Alberta also confirmed that Aboriginal over-representation is getting worse in the province of Alberta. Indeed, because Alberta has the second highest rate of imprisonment per person charged in the

---

[38] *Locking Up Natives in Canada*, p. 215 (emphasis added).

[39] AJI, cited in note 2, volume 1, pp. 101-102.

whole country, over-representation has even harsher effects than elsewhere. Aboriginal men now make up 30 per cent of the male population in provincial jails and Aboriginal women 45 per cent of the female jail population. The most alarming conclusion of the task force is that for Aboriginal young offenders, "over-representation in the criminal justice system is even more dramatic" than it is for adults, and future population projections indicate that the situation will get much worse.

> Projections indicate that by the year 2011, Aboriginal offenders will account for 38.5 per cent of all admissions to federal and provincial correctional centres in Alberta, compared to 29.5 per cent of all such offenders in 1989... In some age categories, for example, the 12-18 years of age group, Aboriginal offenders are projected to account for 40 per cent of the admission of population to correctional facilities by the year 2011.[40]

The fact that in some provinces the coercive intrusion of criminal laws into the lives of Aboriginal people and Aboriginal communities is increasing, not receding, is reflected in the most recent figures from Saskatchewan. John Hylton, a human justice and public policy adviser who has kept a close watch on the situation in Saskatchewan, has broken down total and Aboriginal admissions to provincial correctional centres for the years 1976-77 and compared them to the figures for 1992-93. The breakdown reveals several startling findings:

> 1. Between 1976-77 and 1992-93, the number of admissions to Saskatchewan correctional centres increased from 4,712 to 6,889, a 46 per cent increase, during a time when the provincial population remained virtually unchanged. The rate of increase was 40.7 per cent for male admissions and 111 per cent for female admissions.
>
> 2. During the same period, the number of Aboriginals admitted to Saskatchewan correctional centres increased from 3,082 to 4,757, an increase of 54 per cent. Male Aboriginal admissions increased by 48 per cent, while female Aboriginal admissions increased by 107 per cent.
>
> 3. In terms of overall rates of admission, Aboriginals were 65.4 per cent in 1976-77 and 69.1 per cent in 1992-93.
>
> 4. Increases in Aboriginal admissions accounted for 77 per cent of the increase in total admissions between 1976-77 and 1992-93.
>
> *These data indicate clearly that the problem of disproportionate representation of the Aboriginal people in Saskatchewan's justice system is*

---

[40] *Justice on Trial*, cited in note 23, chapter 8, p. 17.

growing worse, not better.... Predictions that were prepared in the early 1980s and that were rejected by some as too extreme, have in some instances proven to be conservative, particularly in the case of female Aboriginal admissions.[41]

Aboriginal over-representation in the country's prisons, while presenting the face of injustice in its most repressive form, is only part of the picture. The Aboriginal Justice Inquiry of Manitoba commissioned a great deal of research on the other parts of a system that from beginning to end treats Aboriginal people differently. The Inquiry reported that

> Aboriginal over-representation is the end point of a series of decisions made by those with decision-making power in the justice system. An examination of each of these decisions suggests that the way that decisions are made within the justice system discriminates against Aboriginal people at virtually every point...
>
> • More than half of the inmates of Manitoba's jails are Aboriginal
> • Aboriginal accused are more likely to be denied bail
> • Aboriginal people spend more time in pre-trial detention than do non-Aboriginal people
> • Aboriginal accused are more likely to be charged with multiple offences than are non-Aboriginal accused
> • Lawyers spend less time with their Aboriginal clients than with non-Aboriginal clients
> • Aboriginal offenders are more than twice as likely as non-Aboriginal people to be incarcerated
>
> The over-representation of Aboriginal people occurs at virtually every step of the judicial process, from the charging of individuals to their sentencing.[42]

---

[41] John H. Hylton, "Financing Aboriginal Justice Systems", in *Continuing Poundmaker and Riel's Quest*, cited in note 35, p. 155 (emphasis added). The most recent figures issued by the Canadian Centre for Justice Statistics shows that in comparison to 1986-87, when Aboriginal prisoners made up 10 per cent of those admitted to federal institutions, the figure for 1993-94 is 12 per cent. According to figures in Correctional Service Canada, Executive Information System, as of 20 February 1995, 13 per cent of federal prisoners were Aboriginal. The figures regarding admissions to provincial institutions vary. While the percentage of Aboriginal prisoners has increased in Saskatchewan (the 1993-94 figure is 72 per cent, up 3 percentage points from that referred to by Hylton for 1992-93), in Manitoba the proportion has dropped from 51 per cent to 47 per cent. In the Northwest Territories the percentage has remained stable, although stability entails 90 per cent of admissions being Aboriginal prisoners; Aboriginal people represent 63 per cent of the total population of the Northwest Territories. (Statistics Canada, Canadian Centre for Justice Statistics, *Adult Correctional Services in Canada, 1993*, pp. 67 and 90.)

[42] AJI, cited in note 2, volume 1, p. 86. The Aboriginal Justice Inquiry of Manitoba relied on a provincial court study, conducted by the provincial justice department in 1986, involving a random sample

In a society that places a high value on equality before the law, documenting the appalling figures of over-representation might seem to be enough, without any further analysis, to place resolution of this problem at the very top of the national human rights agenda. However, as compelling as the figures are, we believe that it is equally important to understand what lies behind these extraordinary figures, which are a primary index of the individual and social devastation that the criminal justice system has come to represent for Aboriginal people. Understanding the root causes is critical to understanding what it will take by way of a national commitment to bring about real change.

Systemic Discrimination and Aboriginal Crime Rates

Over-representation of the magnitude just described suggests either that Aboriginal peoples are committing disproportionately more crimes or that they are the victims of systemic discrimination. Recent justice studies and reports provide strong confirmatory evidence that both phenomena operate in combination.

The Royal Commission on the Donald Marshall, Jr., Prosecution concluded that

> Donald Marshall, Jr.'s status as a Native contributed to the miscarriage of justice that has plagued him since 1971. We believe that certain persons within the system would have been more rigorous in their duties, more careful, or more conscious of fairness if Marshall had been white.[43]

A research study prepared for that commission, *The Mi'Kmaq and Criminal Justice in Nova Scotia*, by Scott Clark, found that

> Systemic factors in Nova Scotia's criminal justice system lead to adverse effects for Aboriginal people because they live in or come from Aboriginal communities. Policing that has been designed specifically for Aboriginal communities is relatively ineffective. Justice processing, including legal representation in courts...[is] often at considerable distance from Native people both physically and conceptually. By the same token, a lack of understanding by many justice system personnel of Mi'Kmaq social and economic conditions and aspirations leads to differential and often inappropriate treatment. Probation and parole services apply criteria that have built-in biases against Natives by failing to allow

---

of Aboriginal and non-Aboriginal cases in Winnipeg, Thompson, The Pas and nine reserves in northern Manitoba. The inquiry engaged Dansys Consultants, a firm specializing in statistical analysis of the justice system, to conduct an independent review of the data generated by the provincial court study. See Dansys Consultants, "Manitoba Aboriginal Justice Study", research paper prepared for the Aboriginal Justice Inquiry of Manitoba (Ottawa: May 1991).

[43] Royal Commission on the Donald Marshall, Jr., Prosecution (hereafter, Marshall inquiry), *Volume 1: Findings and Recommendations* (1989), p. 162.

for their unique social and economic conditions. Indigenous processes are officially by-passed, if not consciously weakened.[44]

The Cawsey report in Alberta also concluded that "systemic discrimination exists in the criminal justice system." The report dealt specifically with the assertion of the police that discrimination on the basis of race did not exist in Alberta.

> In their briefs, policing services in Alberta generally express the same response: we do not treat or police people differently on the basis of race, or: race is not a fact in policing functions. On the surface, this may seem satisfactory. However, it does not address systemic discrimination. Systemic discrimination involves the concept that the application of uniform standards, common rules, and treatment of people who are not the same constitutes a form of discrimination. It means that in treating unlike people alike, adverse consequences, hardship or injustice may result...
>
> It is clear the operational policies applied uniformly to Aboriginal people sometimes have unjust or unduly harsh results. The reasons may be geographical, economic, or cultural. However, it must be acknowledged that the application of uniform policies can have a discriminatory effect.[45]

Before describing some of the ways systemic discrimination contributes to over-representation of Aboriginal people in the criminal justice system, it is important to review the available evidence on the incidence and nature of Aboriginal crime. This is because there is a significant interrelationship between systemic discrimination and crime rates that has powerful implications for the appropriate directions for change.

The available evidence confirms that crime rates are higher in Aboriginal communities than non-Aboriginal communities. Based on 1985 figures, the task force report of the Indian Policing Policy Review concluded that

- crime rates for on-reserve Indians are significantly higher than for off-reserve Indians and than the overall national crime rate; [and that]...
- the rate of on-reserve violent crimes per 1,000 is six times the national average, for property crimes the rate is two times the national average, and for other criminal code offences the rate is four times the national average.[46]

In urban areas, where more than 40 per cent of Aboriginal people live, the available data suggest that Aboriginal people commit more crime and disorder offences

---

[44] Marshall inquiry, *Volume 3: The Mi'Kmaq and Criminal Justice in Nova Scotia* (1989), p. 52.

[45] *Justice on Trial*, cited in note 23, chapter 2, p. 46.

[46] *Indian Policing Policy Review*, Task Force Report (Ottawa: Indian Affairs and Northern Development, 1990), p. 3.

than similar groups of non-Aboriginal people but proportionately fewer violent offences than Indians living on-reserve.[47]

The Aboriginal Justice Inquiry of Manitoba (AJI), using 1989-1990 crime rate figures for areas of Manitoba policed by the RCMP, found that the crime rate on Indian reserves was 1.5 times the rate in non-reserve areas. The AJI also found, based on its study of provincial court data, that on the reserves surveyed, 35 per cent of crime fell into a group of four offences: common assault, break and enter, theft under $1,000, and public mischief. Aboriginal persons were charged with fewer property offences and more offences against the person and provincial statute violations than non-Aboriginal persons.[48]

An extensive study conducted for the Grand Council of the Crees in 1991, based on information obtained from police daily reports, current files, youth and adult court files and community interviews, found a significantly higher crime rate in nine Cree communities compared to both the Quebec and the overall Canadian rate. The assault rate in the Cree communities was more than five times the Quebec average and more than three times the national average. There were, however, significant differences among the Cree communities and, as the study itself noted, there was some difficulty in interpreting these findings, owing to a lack of information about the nature and seriousness of the assaults and their degree of comparability. The Cree research also found that much of the interpersonal violence was directed against family members, often in alcohol abuse situations. The high levels of interpersonal violence, particularly family violence, and the close relationship to alcohol abuse, parallels the findings of other studies.[49]

Having concluded that there was a higher rate of crime among Aboriginal people (but one that varied considerably from community to community), the AJI also concluded that systemic discrimination contributed greatly to this. This was also the conclusion drawn by the Cawsey task force in Alberta. Both reports identified over-policing as one of the sources of systemic discrimination. Tim Quigley has described the phenomenon of over-policing and its impact on higher Aboriginal crime rates.

> Police use race as an indicator for patrols, for arrests, detentions...
> For instance, police in cities tend to patrol bars and streets where
> Aboriginal people congregate, rather than the private clubs fre-

---

[47] Canadian Centre for Justice Statistics, *Aboriginal Crime in Urban Centres* (Ottawa: Statistics Canada, 1991). The body of research on the nature and extent of Aboriginal crime was reviewed for RCAP by Robert Depew. See "Aboriginal Policing: A Research Perspective", research study prepared for RCAP (1994). This study, like others cited in this report, was conducted under the auspices of the Commission's research program and as such will be part of the information base available to scholars, researchers and other interested parties in a variety of forms (published studies, CD-ROM, archival files, etc.) after the Commission completes its work.

[48] AJI, cited in note 2, volume 1, p. 87.

[49] Carol La Prairie, *Justice for the Cree: Communities, Crime and Order* (Grand Council of the Crees of Quebec, 1991), pp. 62-63.

quented by white business people... This does not necessarily indicate that the police are invariably racist (although some are) since there is some empirical basis for the police view that proportionately more Aboriginal people are involved in criminality. But to operate patrols or to allocate police on...[this] basis...can become a self-fulfilling prophecy: patrols in areas frequented by the groups that they believe are involved in crimes will undoubtedly discover some criminality; when more police are assigned to detachments where there is a high Aboriginal population, their added presence will most assuredly detect more criminal activity.

Consider, for instance, the provincial offence of being intoxicated in a public place. The police rarely arrest whites for being intoxicated in public. No wonder there is resentment on the part of Aboriginal people arrested simply for being intoxicated. This situation very often results in an Aboriginal person being charged with obstruction, resisting arrest or assaulting a peace officer. An almost inevitable consequence is incarceration... Yet the whole sequence of events is, at least to some extent, a product of policing criteria that include race as a factor and selective enforcement of the law.[50]

The Aboriginal Justice Inquiry of Manitoba also addressed the systemic effect of police perceptions of Aboriginal people.

Differences in crime statistics between Aboriginal and non-Aboriginal people result, at least in part, from the manner in which the behaviour of Aboriginal people becomes categorized and stigmatized. This may happen because, to a certain extent, police tend to view the world in terms of 'respectable' people and 'criminal' types. Criminal types are thought to exhibit certain characteristics which provide cues to the officer to initiate action. Thus, the police may tend to stop a higher proportion of people who are visibly different from the dominant society, including Aboriginal people, for minor offences, simply because they believe that such people may tend to commit more serious crimes. Members of groups that are perceived to be a danger to the public order are given much less latitude in their behaviour before the police take action. An example might be a group of Aboriginal youth who gather in a park. Because it is believed that their presence may be a precursor to more deviant action, they are subjected to controlling activities by the police.[51]

---

[50] Tim Quigley, "Some Issues in Sentencing of Aboriginal Offenders", in *Continuing Poundmaker and Riel's Quest*, cited in note 35, pp. 273-274.

[51] AJI, cited in note 2, volume 1, p. 107.

Over-policing is not unique to Canadian police forces. A similar point is made in a New Zealand report dealing with the effect on crime control strategies of police perceptions of the high rate of Maori crime.

> Individual police, both as officers and as members of society, are aware of the high rate of Maori offending... Individual police officers, subject to those perceptions, become susceptible to beliefs that Maori men are more likely to be criminal, or that certain types of conduct are more likely to be associated with them. Such beliefs unavoidably, if often unconsciously, affect the exercise of discretionary powers.

> These individual perceptions and stereotypes are reinforced by the intrinsic attitudes of the police institution which is constantly aware of the wider society's concerns and values. Thus, for example, a social perception of increasing gang or street crime, apparently disproportionately committed by Maori offenders, will lead to an increased allocation of police resources to those areas of activity. Such a concentration leads to a greater number of arrests of mainly Maori people who in turn will maintain the perception of Maori criminality. The likelihood that this perception will bias future use of discretionary powers by the police is thereby increased as well. It is a cyclic process of 'deviancy amplification' in which stereotypes and perceptions help stimulate policies in a self-fulfilling weave of unfairness.[52]

Significantly, several of the studies we reviewed concluded that some Aboriginal communities experience the extremes of both over-policing and under-policing. Jean-Paul Brodeur, in his study for the Grand Council of the Crees, provided this review of the research:

> In a joint study for the Government of Canada, the Government of Saskatchewan and the Indian Nations, authors Prefontaine, Opekokew and Tyler found that Native communities complained of an excessively rigorous enforcement of the law in relation to minor or petty offences. In his study on RCMP policing of Aboriginals, Loree also concluded that when compared to non-Aboriginal communities, Aboriginal communities received proportionately greater law enforcement attention and proportionately less peace-keeping and other services. The situation is best described by Depew when he states that:
>
> > Despite some similarities in Native and non-Native offender profiles, the prevalence of minor and alcohol-related offences

---

[52]Jackson, *The Maori and the Criminal Justice System*, cited in note 21, pp. 120-121.

provides the basis for Native over-representation in the correctional system which in many areas of the country is disturbingly high...

Native people also appear to be subject to the extremes of over-policing and under-policing which can lead to disproportionate levels of Native arrests and charges, and under-utilization of policing services, respectively.[53]

Under-policing is an issue identified by Pauktuutit, the Inuit Women's Association of Canada, in its report, *Inuit Women and Justice*, as one of special concern in some smaller Inuit communities where there are no community-based police services. In an appendix documenting the concerns of Inuit women in Labrador, the report demonstrates forcefully how this places women and children at particular risk.

The RCMP has a responsibility to protect and serve our community. Women and elders are major consumers of police services. In order to serve all parts of the communities, the police have to know our communities, they must be a part of our communities. They must also understand what the life of a woman who has been beaten can be like in the community along the Labrador coast where there are no police, or where the police are not very supportive. Without this knowledge and understanding, the RCMP will not be able to respond to the needs of the victims of violence. Until we have the necessary resources in our communities to provide for protection to women on a permanent basis (for example, police based in the community) and to provide a safe place where women can receive counselling, support and protection, many women will not leave and can't leave the violent home....

While we recognize that the realities of violence in the family translate into the need for added resources, it is not acceptable, on the one hand, to tell us that this is a funding problem and that there is not enough money provided by the province to provide adequate policing. Yet on the other hand, the federal government provides enough funds to hire two police officers for Labrador and eight in Newfoundland to respond to cigarette smuggling. The communities of Postville, Rigolet, and Makkovik, like other communities on the coast, require police based in the community. Women in these communities are in a dangerous position.[54]

---

[53] J.-P. Brodeur, *Justice for the Cree: Policing and Alternative Dispute Resolution* (Grand Council of the Crees of Quebec, 1991), pp. 16-17.

[54] Pauktuutit (Inuit Women's Association of Canada), *Inuit Women and Justice: Progress Report No. 1* (Ottawa: 1995), Appendix, Violence Against Women and Children: The Concerns of Labrador Women pp. 5-6.

Brodeur points out that simultaneous under- and over-policing prevail not only in Canadian Aboriginal communities but also have characterized the style of policing in Australian Aboriginal settlements and in inner-city areas in England where there are significant black populations. We were struck by the relevance of the following statement, based on the findings of Lord Scarman, who conducted a public inquiry into the riots in Brixton, a predominately black suburb of London.

> The true nature of police-black relations in the inner-cities of Britain can only be understood in terms of this simultaneous over-policing and under-policing. There is too much policing against the community and not enough policing that answers the needs of the community.[55]

Brodeur concludes that

> In a Canadian context, Aboriginals are submitted to over-policing for minor or petty offences – e.g., drinking violations – and suffer from under-policing with regard to being protected from more serious offences, such as violent assaults against persons (particularly within the family).[56]

The Root Causes of Over-Representation and Aboriginal Crime

Although over-policing and other forms of systemic discrimination undoubtedly play their part in higher crime rates, the evidence available to us leads us to conclude that for many Aboriginal communities, crime and social disorder play more havoc in personal and community well-being than they do in the lives of non-Aboriginal people and communities. Like the figures on over-representation, the statistics on higher crime rates demand further answers to hard questions directed to the root causes. Misunderstanding the roots of the problem can lead only to solutions that provide, at best, temporary alleviation and, at worst, aggravation of the pain reflected in the faces of Aboriginal victims of crimes – in many cases women and children – and in the faces of the Aboriginal men and women who receive their 'just' desserts in the form of a prison sentence.

We are not the first commission to grapple with the question of explaining and understanding the causes of Aboriginal over-representation and high crime rates. As the Aboriginal Justice Inquiry of Manitoba observed, an entire sub-specialty of criminology is devoted to determining the causes of crime, and a great deal of academic attention has been directed to the specific issue of Aboriginal over-representation. From our review and analysis of the research, we have identified three primary

---

[55] C. Ronalds, M. Champman and K. Kitchener, "Policing Aborigines", in *Issues in Criminal Justice Administration*, ed. M. Findlay, S. Egger and J. Sutton (North Sydney, Australia: George Allen and Unwin, 1983), p. 170, quoted in Brodeur, *Justice for the Cree*, cited in note 53, p. 17.

[56] Brodeur, *Justice for the Cree*, cited in note 53, p. 17; see also Depew, "Aboriginal Policing", cited in note 47, p. 31.

explanatory theories; although they have significant points of overlap, they point in different directions regarding what must be changed to stem and turn the tide.

One powerfully persistent explanation for the problems facing Aboriginal people in the justice system is cultural difference between Aboriginal people and other Canadians. This was invoked most recently by Chief Justice McEachern in his judgement in the Gitksan and Wet'suwet'en case, where the following explanation is offered for Indian disadvantage:

> For reasons which can only be answered by anthropology, if at all, the Indians of the colony, while accepting many of the advantages of the European civilization, did not prosper proportionately with the white community as expected... No-one can speak with much certainty or confidence about what really went wrong in the relations between the Indians and the colonists.... *In my view the Indians' lack of cultural preparation for the new regime was indeed the probable cause of the debilitating dependence from which few Indians in North America have not yet escaped.*
>
> Being of a culture where everyone looked after himself or perished, the Indians knew how to survive (in most years) but they were not as industrious in the new economic climate as was thought to be necessary by the new-comers in the Colony. In addition, the Indians were a gravely weakened people by reason of foreign diseases which took a fearful toll, and by the ravages of alcohol. They became a conquered people, not by force of arms, for that was not necessary, but by an invading culture and a relentless energy with which they would not, or could not, compete.[57]

A cultural explanatory model has provided the basis for a number of initiatives, referred to generically as the 'indigenization' of the criminal justice system. The intent of these initiatives is to close the culture gap by adding to the existing system elements that make it more culturally appropriate for Aboriginal people. Thus, on the assumption that one of the important cultural problems facing Aboriginal people is understanding the language and formal processes of Canadian law, the introduction of Aboriginal court workers is designed to provide a cultural bridge within the existing process. Using the same cultural model, we have seen in different parts of Canada the appointment of Aboriginal police officers, probation officers and justices of the peace. We describe some of these developments in more detail in the next chapter.

There is no doubt that cultural conflict explains much of the alienation that Aboriginal people experience in the justice system, and we return to some of the fundamental cultural differences between Aboriginal and non-Aboriginal understandings of justice later in this report. The difficulty, however, with this explanation

---

[57] *Delgamuukw* v. *B.C.*, cited in note 19, pp. 268-269 (emphasis added).

and the uses to which it has been put is that it is often based on an underlying assumption that the problem lies with the limitations of Aboriginal culture to adapt to non-Aboriginal legal culture – an assumption of inferiority reflected in the passage from Chief Justice McEachern's judgement just quoted.

Associate Chief Judge Murray Sinclair, one of the commissioners of the Aboriginal Justice Inquiry of Manitoba, recently addressed the limitations of this approach. After reviewing some of the principal conclusions of the Manitoba inquiry – including findings that Aboriginal people are less likely than non-Aboriginal people to plea bargain or to benefit from a negotiated plea, that they are more likely than non-Aboriginal people to plead guilty, even when they are not or do not believe themselves to be guilty, and that they are more likely to leave the legal process without understanding, and therefore without respecting, what has occurred to them or why – he makes the following comments:

> Many times I have heard people ask: 'What is it about Aboriginal people that causes them to behave like that?' Such a question suggests the problem lies within the Aboriginal person or with his or her community. That, almost inevitably, leads one to conclude that the answer lies in trying to change the Aboriginal person or his or her community. As a result, almost all our efforts at reform have centred on informing or educating Aboriginal people about the justice system, on finding ways to get them to "connect" with the system or on finding ways to make it easier for them to find their way through it.
>
> Establishing and funding more and better Aboriginal court worker or Aboriginal paralegal programs, printing more and better Aboriginally focused information kits, making more and better audio and video tapes in Aboriginal languages about how courts and laws work, establishing Aboriginal law student programs, hiring more Aboriginal court staff with the ability to speak Aboriginal languages and recruiting or appointing more Aboriginal judges, all find their justification in such thinking.
>
> Attempts at reforming the system itself in ways that address other, more significant, issues have not been undertaken. The main reason, I believe, is because the non-Aboriginal people who control the system have not seen the problem as lying within "the system." It is time to question whether at least some of the problem lies in the way we do business within the justice system. Perhaps the question should be restated as "what is wrong with our justice system that Aboriginal people find it so alienating?"[58]

---

[58] Murray Sinclair, "Aboriginal Peoples, Justice and the Law", in *Continuing Poundmaker and Riel's Quest*, cited in note 35, p. 175.

We agree with Judge Sinclair that asking the question in this way allows us to address the fundamental differences that Aboriginal people bring to the meaning of justice as a concept and a process.

As Judge Sinclair argues, theories of culture conflict have been applied in the past in a way that locates the source of the problem within Aboriginal culture. There is, however, a further limitation on the exclusively cultural explanation of over-representation in the criminal justice system that takes us deeper into an understanding of Aboriginal crime. This limitation is that an exclusively cultural explanation obscures structural problems grounded in the economic and social inequalities experienced by Aboriginal people. As described by Carol La Prairie,

> What the early Task Forces and studies failed to recognize or did not want to address, was that the disproportionate representation of Native people as offenders in the system, was not tied exclusively to culture conflict but was grounded primarily in socio-economic marginality and deprivation....
>
> Access to justice by way of indigenization has both strengths and weaknesses. It provides employment to a number of Aboriginal people and it may help to demystify the criminal justice process so that Aboriginal people feel less alienated and fearful. *What indigenization fails to do, however, is to address in any fundamental way the criminal justice problems which result from the socio-economic marginality.* The real danger of an exclusively indigenized approach is that the problems may appear to be 'solved', little more will be attempted, partly because indigenization is a very visible activity.[59]

Cast as a structural problem of social and economic marginality, the argument is that Aboriginal people are disproportionately impoverished and belong to a social underclass, and that their over-representation in the criminal justice system is a particular example of the established correlation between social and economic deprivation and criminality.

We observed in our special report on suicide that Aboriginal people are at the bottom of almost every available index of socio-economic well-being, whether they measure educational levels, employment opportunities, housing conditions, per capita incomes or any of the other conditions that give non-Aboriginal Canadians one of the highest standards of living in the world. There is no doubt in our minds that economic and social deprivation is a major underlying cause of disproportionately high rates of criminality among Aboriginal people.[60]

---

[59]Carol La Prairie, "Native Criminal Justice Programs, An Overview" (1988, unpublished), p. 3 (emphasis added).

[60]RCAP, *Choosing Life, Special Report on Suicide Among Aboriginal People* (Ottawa: Supply and Services, 1995), p. 24.

We are also persuaded that some of the debilitating conditions facing Aboriginal communities daily are aggravated by the distinctive nature of Aboriginal societies. Thus, as Carol La Prairie points out in her study for the James Bay Cree, there is evidential support for a correlation between over-crowded housing conditions and interpersonal conflict and violence, which often takes place between close family members residing together. In the case of the James Bay Cree, traditional concepts of order and the cultural values placed on the way people relate to each other in a social context reflect the legacy of nomadic-hunting settlement patterns. People not only have their distinctive roles but have their distinctive places in relationship to each other. Over-crowded housing where these distinctions cannot be reflected or respected can and does exacerbate an already problematic sedentary existence in contemporary Cree communities. Thus, current housing conditions, not only in Cree but other Aboriginal people, contribute to tensions in kinship relationships that may in turn be linked to problems of interpersonal conflict, violence and crime.[61]

Socio-economic deprivation not only has explanatory power in relation to high rates of Aboriginal crime, but it also contributes directly to the systemic discrimination that swells the ranks of Aboriginal people in prison. The most obvious and well documented example of this is the imprisonment of Aboriginal people for non-payment of fines. In a 1974 report entitled *The Native Offender and the Law*, the Law Reform Commission concluded that a large number of Aboriginal offenders were sent to jail for non-payment of fines. The advent of fine option programs, under which a person can pay off a fine through community work, has not significantly changed the fact that Aboriginal people go to prison for being poor. In Saskatchewan, in 1992-93, Aboriginal people made up almost 75 per cent of those jailed for fine default.[62] The Cawsey report, after observing that the Canadian Sentencing Commission recommended a reduction in the use of imprisonment for fine default, concluded that there was little evidence of that recommendation, made in 1987, being implemented in Alberta. The report stated:

> A number of speakers at our community meeting spoke with disdain about a practice associated with the problem of fine default. They stated that some judges keep a 'black book' on offenders. Apparently, these notations are used in determining whether an accused will be granted time to pay for fines levied. By means of the 'black book' system, a judge keeps a tally on those who have failed to meet the time limits on previous occasions. When appearing in court again, accused persons do not get time to pay if their names have been entered in the 'black book' previously.

---

[61] La Prairie, *Justice for the Cree: Communities, Crime and Order*, cited in note 49; Roger McDonnell, *Justice for the Cree: Customary Beliefs and Practices* (Grand Council of the Crees of Quebec, 1992).

[62] Quigley, "Some Issues in Sentencing of Aboriginal Offenders", cited in note 50, p. 270.

> This practice means that many Aboriginals get an automatic jail sentence. For a person who is not part of the wage-economy and receives welfare, this sentencing is discriminatory. It should not continue.[63]

The Aboriginal Justice Inquiry of Manitoba also confirmed that Aboriginal people are particularly vulnerable to imprisonment for fine default.

> Our research indicates that Aboriginal men who defaulted were twice as likely to be incarcerated as non-Aboriginal men, and Aboriginal women were three times more likely to be incarcerated than non-Aboriginal women. According to our study, the typical fine defaulter is an Aboriginal male between the ages of 22 to 29, who is single, unemployed, has less than grade 12 education and resides in rural Manitoba. Aboriginal offenders were twice as likely to be incarcerated for fine default for one outstanding fine than non-Aboriginal offenders. The average amount of the unpaid fines that led to the incarceration of Aboriginal people was $201.20. Aboriginal inmates incarcerated for defaulting on their fines served an average of 23 days in custody.[64]

Paralleling the findings of the Cawsey task force, Manitoba's Aboriginal Justice Inquiry also concluded that fine option programs had not brought an end to imprisonment for non-payment of fines.

> Despite the fact that the fine option program has been operating in Manitoba for eight years, hundreds of people, more than half of them Aboriginal, are going to jail every year for defaulting on their fines. We believe that for the vast majority this occurs simply because they lack the resources to pay. The archaic practice of putting people in jail because they cannot afford to pay a fine is being perpetuated. While the fine option program has succeeded in reducing somewhat the incarceration of fine defaulters, it has failed to bring this practice to an end.[65]

The failure of fine option programs to reduce imprisonment of Aboriginal people for non-payment of fines itself is attributable to systemic problems. As noted by the Aboriginal Justice Inquiry of Manitoba:

> Single-parent families and families where the mother is the primary care-giver to the children predominate in Aboriginal communities. These situations make participation in a community work program problematic, if not impossible. In cities, the cost of

---

[63] *Justice on Trial*, cited in note 23, chapter 4, p. 35.

[64] AJI, cited in note 2, volume 1, p. 420.

[65] AJI, volume 1, p. 423.

transportation and the need to care for children are further factors that prevent women from participating. There does not appear to be any effort being made to encourage Aboriginal women to participate, or to provide them with viable options to defaulting on fines.[66]

But imprisonment for fine default is only the most obvious example of systemic discrimination built upon socio-economic deprivation. As the Aboriginal Justice Inquiry of Manitoba found, Aboriginal people are more likely to be denied bail and therefore subject to pre-trial detention. While there is certainly no evidence to suggest that judges deliberately discriminate against Aboriginal people, the factors taken into account in determining whether to subject a person to pre-trial detention relate to whether the person is employed, has a fixed address, is involved in educational programs, or has strong links with the community; as a result, social and economic disadvantage can influence the decision in a particular direction, and that direction is toward the doors of remand centres.

Pre-trial detention, once imposed, has a number of effects. It creates additional pressure to plead guilty in order to get the matter over with, it limits the accused's ability to marshal resources, whether financial or community, to put before the court a community-based sentencing plan, and it therefore increases the likelihood of a sentence of imprisonment.

The way apparently neutral and legally relevant criteria applied at various stages of the criminal justice process compound or snowball to produce systemic discrimination against Aboriginal people is described well by Quigley.

> There are also some other factors that might bear on the disproportionate rate of imprisonment and that are more directly related to the sentencing process. Some of these are presently seen as legally relevant criteria – prior criminal record, employment status, educational level, etc.... Prior criminal record as a factor can have an undue influence on the imprisonment rate for Aboriginal people due to the snowball effect of some of the factors listed above. If there are more young Aboriginal people, if they are disproportionately unemployed, idle and alienated, and if they are overly scrutinized by the police, it should not be surprising that frequently breaches of the law are detected and punished. Add to that the greater likelihood of being denied bail (which increases the chance of being jailed if convicted), the greater likelihood of fine default and the diminished likelihood of receiving probation, and there is a greater probability of imprisonment being imposed. Some of the same factors increase the chances of the same person re-offending and being detected once again. After

---

[66] AJI, volume 1, p. 424.

that, every succeeding conviction is much more apt to be punished by imprisonment, thus creating a snowball effect: jail becomes virtually the only option, regardless of the seriousness of the offence.

Socio-economic factors such as employment status, level of education, family situation, etc. appear on the surface as neutral criteria. They are considered as such by the legal system. Yet they can conceal an extremely strong bias in the sentencing process. Convicted persons with steady employment and stability in their lives, or at least prospects of the same, are much less likely to be sent to jail for offences that are borderline imprisonment offences. The unemployed, transients, the poorly educated are all better candidates for imprisonment. *When the social, political and economic aspects of our society place Aboriginal people disproportionately within the ranks of the latter, our society literally sentences more of them to jail. This is systemic discrimination.*[67]

The Aboriginal Justice Inquiry of Manitoba came to the same conclusion. The commissioners wrote:

Historically, the justice system has discriminated against Aboriginal people by providing legal sanction for their oppression. This oppression of previous generations forced Aboriginal people into their current state of social and economic distress. Now, a seemingly neutral justice system discriminates against current generations of Aboriginal people by applying laws which have an adverse impact on people of lower socio-economic status. *This is no less racial discrimination; it is merely 'laundered' racial discrimination.* It is untenable to say that discrimination which builds upon the effects of racial discrimination is not racial discrimination itself. Past injustices cannot be ignored or built upon.[68]

There is no doubt in our minds that economic and social deprivation is a significant contributor to the high incidence of Aboriginal crime and over-representation in the justice system. We believe, however, that a further level of understanding is required beyond acknowledgement of the role played by poverty and debilitating social conditions in the creation and perpetuation of Aboriginal crime. We are persuaded that this further understanding comes from integrating the cultural and socio-economic explanations for over-representation with a broader historical and political analysis. We have concluded that over-representation is linked directly to the particular and distinctive historical and political processes that have made Aboriginal people poor beyond poverty.

---

[67] Quigley, "Issues in Sentencing", cited in note 50, pp. 275-276 (emphasis added).

[68] AJI, cited in note 2, volume 1, p. 109 (emphasis added).

Our analysis and conclusions parallel those set out in our special report on suicide. In that report we identified some of the risk factors that explain, in part, the high rate of Aboriginal suicide. As we have just demonstrated with respect to the high rate of Aboriginal crime, these factors include culture stress and socio-economic deprivation. We concluded, however, that

> Aboriginal people experience [these] risk factors...with greater frequency and intensity than do Canadians generally. The reasons are rooted in the relations between Aboriginal peoples and the rest of Canadian society – relations that were shaped in the colonial era and have never been thoroughly reshaped since that time.[69]

The relationship of colonialism provides an overarching conceptual and historical link in understanding much of what has happened to Aboriginal peoples. Its relationship to issues of criminal justice was identified clearly by the Canadian Bar Association in its 1988 report, *Locking Up Natives in Canada*.

> What links these views of native criminality as caused by poverty or alcohol is the historical process which Native people have experienced in Canada, along with indigenous people in other parts of the world, the process of colonization. In the Canadian context that process, with the advance first of the agricultural and then the industrial frontier, has left Native people in most parts of the country dispossessed of all but the remnants of what was once their homelands; that process, superintended by missionaries and Indian agents armed with the power of the law, took such extreme forms as criminalizing central Indian institutions such as the Potlatch and Sundance, and systematically undermined the foundations of many Native communities. The Native people of Canada have, over the course of the last two centuries, been moved to the margins of their own territories and of our 'just' society.

> This process of dispossession and marginalization has carried with it enormous costs of which crime and alcoholism are but two items on a long list....

> The relationship between these indices of disorganization and deprivation and Canada's historical relationship with Native people has been the subject of intense scrutiny in the last decade. In the mid-1970s the MacKenzie Valley Pipeline Inquiry focused national attention on the implications for the Native people of the North on a rapid escalation of a large scale industrial development. Mr. Justice Berger (as he then was), in assessing the causes for the alarming rise in the incidence of alcoholism, crime, violence and welfare dependence in the North, had this to say:

---

[69] *Choosing Life*, cited in note 60, p. 26.

I am persuaded that the incidence of these disorders is closely bound up with the rapid expansion of the industrial system and with its persistent intrusion into every part of the Native people's lives. The process affects the complex links between Native people and their past, their culturally preferred economic life, and their individual, familial and political respect. We should not be surprised to learn that the economic forces that have broken these vital links, and that are unresponsive to the distress of those who have been hurt, should lead to serious disorders. Crimes of violence can, to some extent, be seen as expressions of frustrations, confusion and indignation, but we can go beyond that interpretation to the obvious connection between crimes of violence and the change the South has, in recent years, brought to the Native people of the North. With that obvious connection, we can affirm one simple proposition: the more the industrial frontier displaces the homeland in the North, the worse the incidence of crime and violence will be.

Important implications flow from this analysis.

The idea that new programs, more planning and an increase in social service personnel will solve these problems misconstrues their real nature and cause. The high rates of social and personal breakdown in the North are, in good measure, the responses of individual families who have suffered the loss of meaning in their lives and control over their destiny.

The principal recommendations which come from the MacKenzie Valley Pipeline Inquiry were that the Native people of the North must have their right to control that destiny – their right to self-determination – recognized and that there must be a settlement of Native claims in which that right is entrenched as a lodestar. Only then could Native people chart a future responding to their values and priorities rather than living under the shadow of ours.[70]

The importance of locating the contemporary problems facing Aboriginal people in the broad context of colonization is also emphasized in the report of the Osnaburgh/Windigo Tribal Council Justice Review Committee. In its overview the committee asserts:

The arrival of Europeans produced a profound effect on [First Nations] societies and their way of life. One need only travel to the four First Nations communities involved in this report to realize that the First Nations people have become dispossessed –

---

[70] *Locking Up Natives in Canada*, cited in note 37, p. 218.

the fourth world.... What Euro-Canadians accept as common-place for themselves and their children are absent from these communities; clean drinking water, proper housing, adequate sewage disposal, effective dental and medical care, relevant education and a viable base for economic activity. Absent too is the hope that, under present circumstances, the First Nations people can share in the economic life of Canada. Above all, they are a people without an adequate land base. As one commentator has noted:

> History demonstrates that there is a strong correlation between the loss of traditional lands and the marginalization of Native people. Displaced from the land which provides both physical and spiritual sustenance, Native communities are hopelessly vulnerable to the disintegrative pressure from the dominant culture. Without land, Native existence is deprived of its coherence and distinctiveness.

Stripped of their land, some First Nations people are forced...[into] existing communities that are not viable and often the only reaction to situations of despair, poverty and powerlessness manifests itself in alcoholism, substance abuse, family violence and suicide to name but a few. Such responses may even be a 'sane' reaction to these oppressive living conditions. It is a national shame and a calamity on our own doorstep.

While this report addresses the justice system it is but a flash point where the two cultures come in poignant conflict. The Euro-Canadian justice system espouses alien values and imposes irrelevant structures on First Nations communities. The justice system, in all of its manifestations from police through the courts to corrections, is seen as a foreign one designed to continue the cycle of poverty and powerlessness. It is evident that the frustration of the First Nations communities is internalized; the victims, faced with what they experience as a repressive and racist society, victimize themselves. In most cases, both victim and offender are First Nations people. They kill and injure each other and may kill and injure themselves, having a suicide rate several times the non-Native average in Canada.

The clash of the two cultures has been exacerbated by the attempts of the Euro-Canadian justice system to address the problems faced by the First Nations people. It lacks legitimacy in their eyes. It is seen as a very repressive system and as an adjunct to ensuring the continuing dominance of Euro-Canadian society....

> Any attempt to reform the justice system must address this cen-
> tral fact; the continuing subjugation of First Nations people.[71]

Building on this analysis, the Osnaburgh/Windigo report, in addition to making
specific recommendations dealing with the criminal justice system, insisted that
these had to be placed in the context of a much broader agenda designed to re-
establish Aboriginal societies as healthy, strong and vibrant. The report saw this
as requiring government recognition that Aboriginal communities must have eco-
nomically viable land bases and powers of self-government, including the power
to develop Aboriginal justice systems.[72]

In its submission to the Cawsey task force, the Blood Tribe also analyzed the
problems from the perspective of colonization:

> The over-criminalization of Aboriginal people in Canada defies
> conventional criminological assumptions. For instance, although
> there is a well known correlation between poverty and crime, as
> well as urbanization and crime, these arguments do not adequately
> explain why Aboriginal people are over-represented in Canadian
> prisons. Furthermore, Aboriginal crime is simply not an extension
> of their alcohol problem, as some authors seem to suggest. It is the
> Blood Tribe's position that the key to ascertaining the antecedent
> causes of Aboriginal incarceration lies in their history of oppres-
> sion, colonization, exploitation of the lands and resources and
> the detrimental policy basis of the past Indian Acts, coupled with
> the fact that the criminal justice system is primarily a white middle-
> class male institution with no concept or understanding of
> Indianness.[73]

The Aboriginal Justice Inquiry of Manitoba, after its review of the various theories advanced to explain the social roots of Aboriginal crime, concluded:

> From our review of the information available to us, including the
> nature of the crimes committed by Aboriginal people, and after
> hearing the hundreds of submissions presented to us in the course
> of our hearings, we believe that the relatively higher rates of crime
> among Aboriginal people are a result of the despair, dependency,
> anger, frustration and sense of injustice prevalent in Aboriginal
> communities, stemming from the cultural and community break-
> down that has occurred over the past century.[74]

---

[71] Report of the Osnaburgh/Windigo Tribal Council Justice Review Committee, cited in note 22,
pp. 4-6.

[72] Report of the Osnaburgh/Windigo Tribal Council Justice Review Committee, p. 72.

[73] *Justice on Trial*, cited in note 23, chapter 8, p. 1.

[74] AJI, cited in note 2, volume 1, p. 91.

The significance of placing the contemporary experience of Aboriginal people in Canada with the criminal justice system in a framework that integrates the distinctive historical, political, cultural and economic influences that have characterized the establishment of colonial governments in their territories is reinforced in reports from other countries whose Aboriginal peoples have shared and continue to suffer the legacies of colonialism. Addressing the argument that the problem of Maori offending could be attributed to the lower socio-economic status of the Maori, Moana Jackson has argued:

> To view Maori offending...in purely socio-economic terms is unnecessarily restrictive and limits any meaningful understanding of the problem.... While many of the burdens of poverty are shared by all people in the lower socio-economic stratum, the difficulty of the Maori poor emanates from specific historic and cultural forces that overlay the purely economic....

> The early *pakeha* settlers ridiculed the efficacy of...[Maori] spiritual powers, the missionaries condemned the philosophy which underpinned them, and the colonial government suppressed the sanctions and institutions which gave force to them.

> Suppression, of course, involved more than the replacement of mere institutions. It involved the removal of one of the major cohesive forces in Maori society and so had a direct effect on the security, values and self-esteem of the people themselves. Increasing alienation of land compounded this sense of loss because it removed the tangible link between those living in the present and those in the past from whom the precedents for behaviour came.

> The story of the combined attacks on the two basic threads of Maori existence is well known in the Maori community and is a source of grievance still expressed...throughout the country. It is a story kept alive not because of the stubborn desire to instill guilt in the *pakeha* community, or even to exact revenge; but simply because of the injustice inherent in the narrative, and the often tragic consequences played out in its present day epilogue.

> The extent of criminal offending is a specific part of that epilogue, and its understanding flows from a realization of how traditional Maori society was affected by colonization.

Relating this analysis to the involvement of young Maori in crime, Moana Jackson concluded:

> The present relationship between young Maori, their families and community has been divorced by inequality from the realities and strengths of its traditional form. In the past, the relationship

was like a fabric design woven from the threads of a vibrant culture.... Those threads have been torn by the history of Maori/*pakeha* interaction and frayed by the contemporary realities of life in a consumer society. They have been re-woven into a new, confusing, and often destructive pattern of existence.

Young Maori, battered in their self-esteem by the effects of cultural deprivation and denigration, are denied access to the Maori ideals of right and wrong, and are thereby weakened in their allegiance to any traditional standards of behaviour. The resentment of economic inequality reduces their willingness to abide by the accepted codes of the wider society so that a developing pattern of behaviour emerges which challenges both of those codes.

This pattern may take many, often inter-related forms, each of which may eventually lead to behaviour that is defined as criminal. Thus the lack of a positive cultural identity may lead to identification with peer groups and an initiation into the solidarity and subculture of a gang.... The lack of emotional security may lead to an identification with behaviours which provide security in drug or alcohol induced escapism. Whatever the scenario, and there are many, the patterns are manifest in the too frequent cost of violence to oneself, to others or to property...

Economic unfairness and cultural loss thus feed off each other in an almost symbiotic relationship shaped by the cycle of social confinement.... Thus if low socio-economic status is the catalyst for much unacceptable behaviour by Maori youth, it is cultural loss which makes the behaviour manifest itself to such a worrying extent. *Since economic and cultural deprivation both exist as the outcome of shared history, it is clear that any disproportionate behavioral consequences of Maori existence issue from that history as well. In this sense, the level of criminal behaviour by young Maori men can be viewed as the cost of the history and policies which have shaped their place in contemporary society.*[75]

We have quoted from this and the other reports at considerable length because we are of the opinion that locating the root causes of Aboriginal crime in the history of colonialism, and understanding its continuing effects, points unambiguously to the critical need for a new relationship that rejects each and every assumption underlying colonial relationships between Aboriginal peoples and non-Aboriginal society.

Locating the root causes of Aboriginal crime and other forms of social disorder in the history of colonialism has other important implications related to the nature

---

[75]Jackson, *The Maori and the Criminal Justice System*, cited in note 21, pp. 44-45, 100, 102-103 (emphasis added).

of the interventions most likely to bring about significant changes and improvements in Aboriginal peoples' lives, rather than provide merely short-term palliative relief of the underlying problems. Kayleen Hazlehurst has captured the nature of this relationship in her description of the work being done by Australian Aboriginal peoples in the State of Queensland.

> We Al-Li has developed a number of workshops for Aboriginal persons suffering from trauma injury (victims), and violent behaviours (perpetrators) arising from historical violence (settler, colonial and paternalistic interventions over several generations) and from contemporary experiences of alcoholism, sexual assault, incest, and other family and community dysfunctions.
>
> The We Al-Li program is community-based and targets those most immediately and urgently in need. Its explanatory context is based upon a belief that contemporary Aboriginal addiction, violence, and related social decline, is grounded in historical experiences which saw the slaughter, dispossession, and social and cultural devastation of the people following European contact. Rather than blaming victims or perpetrators, participants are assisted in understanding how the spirit of their people was broken over time and how the decline into the destructive lifestyles of alcohol dependency and cyclical patterns of violence and self-destructiveness occurred.[76]

As described by Judy Atkinson, the Aborigine woman whose work has underpinned the We Al-Li program,

> The group workshop process enables people to name and own abusive behaviours and attitudes from their own experiences, and to see the connections between physical, mental, emotional and spiritual injury across the generations and cultures. The emphasis is on personal and group responsibility through sharing and healing in heuristic learning situations, as individuals within the group explore behaviours and define strategies for individual, family and community transformation.[77]

Therefore we can see how responding to the historical roots of Aboriginal crime and social disorder points directly to the need to heal relationships both internally within Aboriginal peoples and communities and externally between Aboriginal and non-Aboriginal people.

---

[76] Kayleen Hazlehurst, "Community Healing and Revitalization and the Devolution of Justice Service", paper presented at Putting Aboriginal Justice Devolution into Practice: The Canadian and International Experience, a conference sponsored by the Centre for Criminal Law Reform and Simon Fraser University, Vancouver, 5-7 July 1995, p. 6.

[77] Quoted in Hazlehurst, "Community Healing and Revitalization", p. 9.

The Right of Self-Government and the Authority to Establish Aboriginal Justice Systems

Justice and its Relationship to Self-Government

We have already stated that at the core of a new relationship between Aboriginal and non-Aboriginal people must be recognition of Aboriginal peoples' right of self-government. It is our conclusion that this right must encompass the authority to establish Aboriginal justice systems. We are not the first to draw it.

Since 1988, when the Canadian Bar Association released its report, *Locking Up Natives in Canada*, which linked the development of Aboriginal justice systems to the right of self-government and urged recognition of legal pluralism in the context of Aboriginal justice, there has been a developing acceptance by non-Aboriginal people experienced in the justice system of the legitimacy and urgency of moving in this direction.

As attorney general and minister of justice of Saskatchewan, Robert Mitchell came to understand the challenges involved in Aboriginal peoples' struggle for justice. He participated in our round table on justice and presented a thoughtful brief setting out the government of Saskatchewan's position on justice reform. In that brief and in comments to the Saskatchewan Conference on Aboriginal Justice in 1993, he clearly articulated the relationship between justice reform and self-government.

> I believe that justice reform has to be built upon and has to develop within the framework of self-government. You can't go very far with many of the ideas that relate to justice reform without running smack up against the idea of self-government. For that reason, I believe that as we continue to work on these concepts, we must keep right in front of us the idea that they are part and parcel of the inherent right of Aboriginal peoples to govern themselves.[78]

Ted Hughes, whose experience with the criminal justice system includes serving as a judge in the Saskatchewan Court of Queen's Bench and as deputy attorney general of British Columbia, has explained how his thinking on the issue of Aboriginal justice systems has evolved over the last few years. In 1987 he chaired the B.C. Justice Reform Committee, and although the committee's mandate was not concerned primarily with Aboriginal justice, its report did address the issue. This is what the report said:

> Native groups spoke about cultural barriers that have alienated them from the Canadian justice system. For many Natives

---

[78] Robert W. Mitchell, "Blazing the Trail", in *Continuing Poundmaker and Riel's Quest*, cited in note 35, p. 304.

Canadian justice can seem like a foreign system, imposing a value system which is at odds with their own culture. This conflict poses problems that non-Natives do not experience.[79]

In the report, the chair and the seven other committee members came to this conclusion:

> The concept of an Aboriginal justice system was presented to the Committee as one that is receiving a great deal of interest and attention; however, the Committee favours a mainstream system for all British Columbians which serves the needs of the people of this province. At the same time, it is recognized that Native people have traditions, values and customary ways that the justice system can and should accommodate.[80]

Ted Hughes reflected on that conclusion when he spoke at the Aboriginal Justice Conference in Saskatoon in 1993 and described how his thinking had changed:

> That was five years ago. That would not be my conclusion today... Experiences I have had over the last five years, which have built upon my previous experiences, have convinced me that an exclusive mainstream system of justice is not the answer. Perhaps I should be a little ashamed about associating myself with that statement made five years ago.... *These five years that have just passed, in my view, have been very significant years in the struggle of Aboriginal peoples for a justice system that honours and respects their culture, their values, their heritage and their aspirations. I am fully on side with the achievement of such a system....* I have had other experiences within the justice system over the last five years, besides exposure to [the various criminal justice] reports, instances that tell me that racism, often of a systemic nature, continues to surface within the justice system of this country against Aboriginal people. It is not enough to say that this is unacceptable.[81]

The Aboriginal Justice Inquiry of Manitoba, after its extensive review, recommended that

> ...the federal and provincial governments recognize the right of Aboriginal people to establish their own justice systems as part of their inherent right to self-government [and] assist Aboriginal peoples in the establishment of Aboriginal justice systems in their communities in the manner that best conforms to the traditions,

---

[79] Quoted in Ted Hughes, "The Crown's Responsibility for Policing and Prosecution", in *Continuing Poundmaker and Riel's Quest*, cited in note 35, p. 343.

[80] Quoted in Hughes, "The Crown's Responsibility", p. 343.

[81] Hughes, "The Crown's Responsibility", pp. 343-344 (emphasis added).

cultures and wishes of those communities, and the rights of their people.[82]

Without seeking to define the full scope of Aboriginal self-government, the inquiry commissioners were unequivocal on this point: "It includes the right to establish and maintain their own forms of justice systems in their own territories."[83]

The basis for the inquiry's recommendations is set out in the following passages. We quote them at some length because they not only reflect the conclusion of many of those who made submissions to us, but are, in our judgement, the right conclusions.

> There must be a drastic shift in thinking about power and authority. The federal and provincial governments and their officials have to accept that Aboriginal people must have the necessary power and authority to govern themselves in this area. Impediments to the exercise of such power and jurisdiction must be removed....

> Aboriginal people have a right to their own cultures.... Culture is more than the values, traditions or customary practices of Aboriginal people. Culture is also the laws, customary or contemporary, of the people who belong to a distinct society. Culture is the social and political organization of the people who constitute a distinct society. Culture also includes the administration of justice as a fundamental component of every organized society.

> The right of Aboriginal people to control their own pace and direction of development must be retained. The use of Aboriginal social and cultural institutions, such as the Aboriginal family and the role of elders in maintaining peace and good order in their communities, and in transmitting knowledge about acceptable and unacceptable behaviour is, we believe, the proper road to Aboriginal recovery and development....

> It is wrong, in our view, simply to maintain the status quo on the assumption that eventually Aboriginal people will learn to accept the justice system as it presently exists.... It is wrong to assume that changes to the existing system will enable it to provide fully adequate services to Aboriginal people. To think in this manner is to ignore the impact of the past human experience of Aboriginal people. Their self-determination has been denied and suppressed, social disorganization has been the consequence, and they are unable to accept the 'white man's solution' any longer.

[82] AJI, cited in note 2, volume 1, p. 266.

[83] AJI, volume 1, p. 262.

The reality is that approaches taken by a non-Aboriginal justice system in Aboriginal communities will not address the social needs, development, culture, or the right to self-determination of those communities. A court system that is not seen as an institution that belongs to them, and that is unable to adapt to their indigenous concepts and mechanisms of justice, will not work in Aboriginal communities.

An important principle for change and for bringing about changes in Aboriginal communities is that Aboriginal people must be seen as having control. This principle, we discern, is gaining greater and greater acceptance in Canadian society.

Clearly, the maintenance of law and order on Aboriginal lands is an integral part of Aboriginal government jurisdiction. This means that in establishing the system of justice for Aboriginal people, the laws enacted by Aboriginal people themselves, or deliberately accepted by them for their purposes, must form the foundation for the system's existence.[84]

The Law Reform Commission of Canada, in *Aboriginal Peoples and Criminal Justice*, also endorsed the right of Aboriginal peoples to establish their own justice systems.

Aboriginal communities identified by the legitimate representatives of Aboriginal peoples as being willing and capable should have the authority to establish Aboriginal justice systems. The federal and provincial governments should enter into negotiations to transfer that authority to those Aboriginal communities.[85]

The Case for Aboriginal Control of Justice

It has been through the law and the administration of justice that Aboriginal people have experienced the most repressive aspects of colonialism. Ovide Mercredi, National Chief of the Assembly of First Nations, made this point in a presentation to the Aboriginal Justice Inquiry of Manitoba:

In law, with law, and through law, Canada has imposed a colonial system of government and justice upon our people without due regard to our treaty and aboriginal rights. We respect law that is fair and just, but we cannot be faulted for denouncing those laws that degrade our humanity and rights as distinct peoples.[86]

---

[84] AJI, volume 1, pp. 264-265.

[85] Law Reform Commission of Canada (LRCC), "Minister's Reference: Aboriginal Peoples and Criminal Justice", Report No. 34 (1991), p. 16.

[86] AJI, cited in note 2, volume 1, p. 1.

It is in Aboriginal law, with Aboriginal law and through Aboriginal law that Aboriginal people aspire to regain control over their lives and communities. The establishment of systems of Aboriginal justice is a necessary part of throwing off the suffocating mantle of a legal system imposed through colonialism. It is difficult and disturbing to realize that Aboriginal people see the non-Aboriginal justice system as alien and repressive, but the evidence permits no other conclusion. As the Law Reform Commission found in its report, *Aboriginal Peoples and Criminal Justice*,

> From the Aboriginal perspective, the criminal justice system is an alien one, imposed by the dominant white society. Wherever they turn or are shuttled throughout the system, Aboriginal offenders, victims or witnesses, encounter a sea of white faces. Not surprisingly, they regard the system as deeply insensitive to their traditions and values: many view it as unremittingly racist.

> Abuse of power and the distorted exercise of discretion are identified time and again as principal defects of the system. The police are often seen by Aboriginal people as a foreign, military presence descending on communities to wreak havoc and take people away. Far from being a source of stability and security, the force is feared by them even when its services are necessary to restore a modicum of social peace in the community.

> For those living in remote and reserve communities, the entire court apparatus, quite literally, appears to descend from the sky – an impression that serves to magnify their feelings of isolation and erects barriers to their attaining an understanding of the system.[87]

The report of the Aboriginal Justice Inquiry of Manitoba, based on its extensive hearings, came to the same conclusion:

> For Aboriginal people, the essential problem is that the Canadian system of justice is an imposed and foreign system. In order for a society to accept a justice system as part of its life in its community, it must see the system and experience it as being a positive influence working for that society. Aboriginal people do not.[88]

Aboriginal people's alienation from the justice system is partly a result of the fact that justice – far from being the blind, impartial arbiter – has been the handmaiden to their oppression. But equally important, this alienation is a product of the fundamental differences Aboriginal people bring to the concept and process

---

[87] LRCC, "Minister's Reference", cited in note 85, p. 5.

[88] AJI, cited in note 2, volume 1, p. 252.

of justice. Recognition of the right of Aboriginal peoples to establish and control their own justice systems is an essential and integral part of recognizing and respecting cultural difference. It is to these cultural differences and how they contribute to alienation of Aboriginal people and discrimination against them that we turn now.

As one of the first Aboriginal lawyers appointed to the Canadian bench, and as one of the two commissioners in the Aboriginal Justice Inquiry of Manitoba, which remains the most extensive inquiry of its kind yet conducted in Canada, Judge Murray Sinclair has brought to bear his own experience and understanding and that of the many Aboriginal people with whom he has had contact in his work as a member of the judiciary and as a commissioner. We therefore quote at some length Judge Sinclair's reflections on the meaning of justice to Aboriginal people and the highly significant ways it is different from Euro-Canadian conceptions. In large measure they mirror the views we heard in our round table on justice, our hearings in Aboriginal communities, and the research we commissioned.

Judge Sinclair starts with the proposition that conceptions of justice in any society are integrally related to that society's world views and life philosophies. Building differences in world view and philosophy and recognizing that there is no universalized Aboriginal conception of justice, Judge Sinclair offers this description of some of the differences between Aboriginal and non-Aboriginal understandings of the substance and process of justice:

> At a basic level, justice is perceived differently by Aboriginal society. In the dominant society, deviant behaviour that is potentially or actually harmful to society, to individuals or to perpetrators, is considered a wrong that must be controlled by interdiction, enforcement and correction designed to punish and deter harmful deviant behaviour. The emphasis is on punishment of the deviant to make him or her conform to socially acceptable forms of behaviour or to protect other members of society.
>
> The primary meaning of 'justice' in an Aboriginal society would be that of restoring peace and equilibrium to the community through reconciling the accused with his or her own conscience and with the individual or family that is wronged. This is a fundamental difference. It is a difference that significantly challenges the appropriateness of many of the ways in which the present legal and justice systems deal with Aboriginal people in the resolution of their conflicts, in the reconciliation of the accused with their communities and in maintaining community harmony and good order.
>
> Aboriginal cultures approach problems of deviance and non-conformity in a non-judgmental manner, with strong preferences for non-interference, reconciliation and restitution. The principle

of non-interference is consistent with the importance Aboriginal peoples place on the autonomy and freedom of the individual, and the avoidance of relationship-destroying confrontations.

In the past, smaller populations and larger areas of uninhabited land made it possible for non-conformists, either voluntarily or under pressure from the community, to leave the community where their deviance was unacceptable or dangerous to the collective. The Canadian justice system frequently deals with people who misbehave by removing them from society for a period of time. We call this incarceration. To this extent banishment and incarceration appear to have the same objective. However, there is an underlying value of punishment attached to the principle of incarceration that is not associated with the concept of banishment.

While during either a period of incarceration or banishment, the accused cannot repeat his or her offences in the community and may, at some point, be allowed back, restitution and atonement are issues that still apply when the Aboriginal community banishes someone and decides to let him or her return. The established principle surrounding incarceration, on the other hand, is that after completing his or her sentence, the accused has 'paid the price' and should be seen as having atoned to society for what he or she has done. The principles of restitution to the victim and reconciliation with the community do not mark the manner in which the accused is dealt with at any point in the process. While they may be referred to, such principles are not accorded the importance they receive in Aboriginal societies.

Rehabilitation is not a primary aim of the Euro-Canadian justice system when dealing with an offender, with the possible exception of very young offenders. It is only one of several factors taken into account by sentencing judges, and it is often undermined by lack of public support. Institutionalized support is rarely and only minimally offered to victims. Restitution is ordered generally as a form of financial compensation and usually only if the offender has the financial resources to do so. Thus, retribution is often the primary thrust of action taken against deviance.

Most Aboriginal societies value the inter-related principles of individual autonomy and freedom consistent with the preservation of relationships and community harmony, respect for other human (and non-human) beings, reluctance to criticize or interfere with others, and avoidance of confrontation and adversarial positions. When the dominant society's justice system is applied to Aboriginal individuals and communities, many of its principles are clearly at odds with the life philosophies that govern the behaviour of the people.[89]

Judge Sinclair goes on to illustrate how differences in world views and philosophies between Aboriginal and non-Aboriginal people infuse such concepts as truth, law and justice. He also highlights significant differences in the objectives of justice systems and how they should go about achieving those objectives. He illustrates this with reference to the process for determining the 'truth' of what happened.

> According to the Aboriginal world view, truth is relative and always incomplete. When taken literally, therefore, the standard courtroom oath – to tell the truth, the whole truth and nothing but the truth – is illogical and meaningless, not only to Aboriginal persons but, from the Aboriginal perspective, to all people. The Aboriginal viewpoint would require the individual to speak the truth "as you know it" and not to dispute the validity of another viewpoint of the same event or issue. No-one can claim to know the whole truth of any situation; every witness or believer will have perceived an event or understood a situation differently. It would be rare for an Aboriginal witness to assert that another witness is lying or has gotten his facts wrong.

> Our justice system frowns upon an individual who appears uncertain about his or her evidence, and failing to assert the superiority of one's own evidence over that of another is often seen as uncertainty. Given the Aboriginal world view, where the relativity of truth is well understood, one can readily perceive that it would be virtually impossible for an Aboriginal witness to comply with the strictures of the court in the manner of truth-telling. In a system where one's credibility is determined to a large extent by how well one's testimony stands up to cross-examination, the Aboriginal view of the relativity of truth can give the erroneous perception that the witness is changing his or her testimony, when in reality all that may be happening is that the witness is recognizing or acknowledging that another view of the events, no matter how far-fetched or different from his or her reality, may be just as valid as his or hers.

In many respects the way the Aboriginal and Euro-Canadian systems approach the issue of guilt or innocence is a paradigm of their different conceptions of what is involved in doing justice.

> The fundamental thrust of the Euro-Canadian justice system is the guilt-determination process. The principle of fairness in deter-

---

[89]Sinclair, "Aboriginal Peoples, Justice and the Law", cited in note 58. This quotation and those that follow in the next few pages, come from pp. 178-184 of that article.

mining whether the accused is guilty is of the utmost importance to what we do as judges. This arises, one could easily conclude, because our criminal justice system developed from a society where wrongdoers were placed in stocks and chains, or flogged, or whipped, or drawn and quartered, or put to death, all in public, for any one of a large number of offences. This orientation led to concerns over ensuring that only those who were "truly guilty" of the charges brought against them should be subject to the punishments being imposed, for they were considered so severe. The adage "better a guilty man go free than an innocent man be convicted" finds its justification in this history.

As Judge Sinclair goes on to explain, within this framework it is not seen as perverse for a non-Aboriginal person to plead not guilty to a charge for which he or she is in fact responsible.

In western tradition, the plea is not seen as dishonest; it is understood as a conventional response to an accusation, based on the doctrine that people are innocent until proven guilty, on the principle that accused are not required to incriminate themselves, and on the practice of requiring the prosecution to prove guilt beyond a reasonable doubt in open court. In Aboriginal cultures, to deny a true allegation is seen as dishonest and such a denial would be a repudiation of fundamental, highly valid, though silent, standards of behaviour...

In Aboriginal cultures, the guilt of the accused will be secondary to the main issue. The issue that arises immediately upon allegation of wrongdoing is that 'something is wrong and it has to be fixed.' If the accused, when confronted, admits the allegation, then the focus becomes 'what should be done to repair the damage done by the misdeed?' If the accused denies the allegation, there is still a problem and the relationship between the parties must still be repaired. Because punishment is not the ultimate focus of the process, those accused of wrongdoing are more likely to admit having done something wrong. That is why, perhaps, we see so many Aboriginal people pleading guilty. At the same time, to deny an allegation which is 'known' by all to be true, and then to go through the 'white man's court' is often seen as creating more damage.

The concepts of adversarialism, accusation, confrontation, guilt, argument, criticism and retribution are not in keeping with Aboriginal value systems. Adversarialism and confrontation are antagonistic to the high value placed on harmony and the peaceful co-existence of all living beings, both human and non-human, with one another and with nature... The idea that guilt and innocence can be decided on the basis of argument is incompatible with the firmly rooted belief in honesty and integrity that does not permit lying. Retribution as an end in itself and as an aim of society is a meaningless notion in an Aboriginal value system that emphasizes reconciliation of the offender with the community and restitution for the victim.

The same contradictions between the Aboriginal values and the dominant justice system result in a heavy burden being placed on Aboriginal accused and witnesses when they enter the justice system. Accusation and criticism (giving adverse testimony), while required in the Canadian justice system, are antagonistic to an Aboriginal value system that makes every effort to avoid criticism and confrontation.

As [Rupert] Ross has pointed out, 'refusal or reluctance to testify, or when testifying, to give anything but the barest and most emotionless recital of events, appears to be the result of deeply rooted cultural behaviour in which giving testimony face to face with the accused is simply wrong... [and] where in fact every effort seems to have been made to avoid such direct confrontation.' In Aboriginal societies, it may be ethically wrong to say hostile, critical, implicitly angry things about someone in their presence, precisely what our adversarial trial rules have required.

A final example [of culturally driven contradictions] is the implicit expectation of lawyers, judges and juries that accused will display remorse and a desire for rehabilitation. Because their understanding of courage and their position in the overall scheme of things includes the fortitude to accept, without protest, what comes to them, Aboriginal people may act contrary to the expectations of non-Aboriginal people involved in the justice system. Many years of cultural and social oppression, combined with the high value placed on controlled emotion in the presence of strangers or authority, can result in an accused's conduct in court appearing to be inappropriate to his plea....[90]

---

[90]Judge Sinclair's reference to a cultural reluctance to show emotion to strangers, particularly those in authority, is one that a number of anthropologists have observed. (See, for example, Hugh Brody, *The People's Land: Eskimos and Whites in the Eastern Arctic* (Harmondsworth: Penguin Books, 1975).) This should not be seen, however, nor did Judge Sinclair intend to suggest, that a lack of emotion is a cultural trait of Aboriginal people; the subject is socially appropriate ways of displaying emotions and inner feelings to others. The public hearings of this Commission and of others that have endeavoured to understand the experience of Aboriginal people have provided a forum for Aboriginal people to express the emotional depth of their experiences with the non-Aboriginal systems that have caused them so much pain and damage, both individually and collectively.

To require people to act in ways contrary to their most basic beliefs is not only a potential infringement of their rights; it is also, potentially, a deeply discriminatory act. Witnesses who do not testify directly, complainants who do not complain vociferously and accused who do not behave 'appropriately' or who show little emotion may find that they are 'dealt with' differently or achieve different results than those who react in ways expected by the system. Such culturally induced responses can easily be misunderstood. Sometimes they are wrongly treated as contempt for the courts. Sometimes they result in a hearing that is less than fair and, far too often, they result in inappropriate sentencing.

The Aboriginal focus on restorative justice means that a non-Aboriginal sentencing process that gives such a concept little, if any, weight may conflict with and undermine the expectations of Aboriginal societies in the achievement of justice.

Because 'justice' is achieved in Aboriginal societies only when harmony is restored to the community, not only the accused but also other people who have been or might be affected by the offence, particularly the victim, would have to be considered as well. In the Ojibwa concept of order, when a person is wronged, it is understood that the wrongdoer must repair the order and disharmony of the community by undoing the wrong done. In most cases, responsibility is placed on the wrongdoer to compensate the persons wronged...

Reparation or restitution to the victim or the community in a way that restores balance and harmony to the people involved would therefore be a primary consideration... In the eyes of the community, sentencing the offender to incarceration, or worse still, placing him or her on probation, without first addressing the issue of reconciliation, would be tantamount to completely relieving the offender of any responsibility for restitution of the wrong. But such is 'justice' in the western sense – at least from the Aboriginal perspective. Such action is viewed by them as an abdication of responsibility and a total exoneration of the wrongdoer.

Judge Sinclair's reflections led him to the following conclusions:

Clearly something must be done. Not only must we undertake reforms to the existing system to change the way we 'do business' where Aboriginal people are concerned, but it seems clear to me as well – as it became clear to my colleague, Associate Chief Justice A. C. Hamilton, during the course of the work we did together on the Aboriginal Justice Inquiry of Manitoba – that we must also undertake reforms that allow and empower Aboriginal people to do justice for themselves.

We have reached the same conclusions.

It is impossible to read or listen to Judge Sinclair's – views and those of many other Aboriginal people, describing their conceptions of justice in the context of their distinctive history, culture and experience of the non-Aboriginal justice system – without becoming acutely aware that the pursuit of justice is an integral part of the pursuit of self-government. We are not the first commission to come to this conclusion, and it is hardly a revolutionary one. The inter-generational transfer of the values that bind social groups together, the principles by which people order their relationships with each other and the world around them, and the processes by which they maintain their well-being, their peace and their security are the defining framework for communities, for peoples and for nations. Why would it be any different for Aboriginal peoples seeking recognition of their right of self-government within the framework of Canada? The very fact that we are forced to ask this question demonstrates the extent to which colonialism has been the pervasive ideology and practice of Canadian relationships with Aboriginal peoples. In making this point we are not ignoring the fact that the exercise of the right of self-government in the context of a federal state such as Canada requires a commitment to co-existence and accommodation, issues we address later in this report.

When Aboriginal people point out that before the arrival of Europeans, they had their own distinctive laws and legal tradition, that they have never given these up voluntarily, and that they assert the right to take back control of their communities through the instrumentality of their own laws and their own vision of justice, they are not trying to turn back the clock and ignore the realities and challenges of the contemporary world. Mary Ellen Turpel, who has, like Judge Sinclair, thought long and hard about these issues, has this to say about the process of making the distinctive Aboriginal legal traditions a contemporary reality of Aboriginal self-government:

> I find it a great challenge to chart the differences between the Canadian and Aboriginal systems because I am suspicious of simplistic anthropological inquiries, and I am increasingly aware of how dynamic, interacting and undivorced culture is from history, politics and economics. Should we strive to describe a pre-colonial state of affairs? What is the point anyway? Can the pre-colonial regime ever be resurrected? My own view is no, not except as a relic of the past. It cannot be resurrected because we have all been touched by imperialism and colonialism, and there is no simplistic escape to some pre-colonial history except a rhetorical one. In my view, we need to regain control over criminal justice, indeed all justice matters, but in a thoroughly post-colonial fashion....

> One cannot erase the history of colonialism, but we must, as an imperative, undo it in a contemporary context... We have to accept

that there are profound social and economic problems in Aboriginal communities today that never existed pre-colonialization and even in the first few hundred years of interaction. Problems of alcohol and solvent abuse, family violence and sexual abuse, and youth crime – these are indications of a fundamental breakdown in the social order in Aboriginal communities of a magnitude never known before. A reform dialogue or proposals in the criminal justice field have to come to grips with this contemporary reality and not just retreat into a pre-colonial situation.[91]

In charting a critical path for that reform dialogue, Turpel urged us not to create unnecessary dichotomies, in particular, that in calling for the recognition of distinctive Aboriginal justice systems we not abandon the need to reform the non-Aboriginal justice system, because there will remain important links between the two, and the process of re-establishing Aboriginal systems will necessarily be an evolutionary one.[92]

Aboriginal control over the substance and process of justice, flowing from the Aboriginal right of self-government, and the right to have a justice system that respects the cultural distinctiveness of Aboriginal peoples, are not only issues of principle. Based on the evidence we have considered, it is our view that the contemporary expression of Aboriginal concepts and processes of justice are likely to be more effective than the existing non-Aboriginal justice system, both in responding to the wounds that colonialism has inflicted, which are evident in a cycle of disruptive and destructive behaviour, and in meeting the challenges of maintaining peace and security in a changing world.

The strengths of the distinctive Aboriginal vision of justice are not something that Aboriginal people alone can understand. We have been impressed by the way practitioners in the non-Aboriginal criminal justice system who have had extensive contact with Aboriginal people have been able to overcome assumptions of cultural superiority and have been able to listen and learn from the people to whom they dispense justice. Rupert Ross, a Crown attorney, is one of these people, and his writings have been influential in educating judges, lawyers, and royal commissioners across the country. In a presentation to a conference on Aboriginal justice held in Saskatoon in 1993, he described how he perceived the approach of the community of Hollow Water, Manitoba to dispensing justice – an initiative we discuss in greater detail in the next chapter. This initiative speaks clearly to the different perspective on justice that an Aboriginal community brings when it draws on the strengths of its legal traditions to address and redress the problems that threaten to overwhelm many Aboriginal communities and for which the non-Aboriginal

---

[91] M. E. Turpel, "Reflections on Thinking Concretely About Criminal Justice Reform", in *Continuing Poundmaker and Riel's Quest*, cited in note 35, pp. 208-209.

[92] Turpel, "Reflections on Thinking Concretely", p. 215.

criminal justice system has but one ineffective answer – longer and longer imprisonment.

> [Aboriginal people] seem to be speaking about a picture of justice that is very different from the one I've been trained in. Indeed, many who speak from within this perspective don't even seem to begin their analysis of justice where we do. For them, the exhaustive dissection of justice issues contained in the reports of numerous Royal Commissions and task forces, with their focus on judges, Crown attorneys, lawyers, police, prisons and so forth, seems almost beside the point.

> They look first toward very different kinds of players, people like alcohol and family violence workers, traditional healers, mental health workers, sexual abuse counsellors and the like. They then speak of creating (or recreating) very different processes, ones which are conciliatory, bridging and educational as opposed to adversarial. Finally, they seem to focus on very different goals as well, discarding the retroactive imposition of punishment for things that have already happened in favour of trying to bring people, families and communities into health and wholeness for the future.[93]

Writing about his experience with another Aboriginal justice initiative in northern Ontario, Rupert Ross makes the important point that what lies behind increasing demands by Aboriginal people for greater control of the administration of justice are the critical issues of community respect and legitimacy.

> The cries for local control over community justice are growing. It is tempting to conclude that they spring only from political claims of sovereignty, incidental only to the larger issue of political autonomy. While that may indeed form part of the background, it appears that much more is at stake in their eyes: the contribution which local control over justice would make, directly and indirectly, to the very goal of peaceful co-existence to which our system aspires. In this connection, a proposal submitted by the Sandy Lake Band in Northwestern Ontario to the Ministry of the Attorney General provides as clear an articulation of the issue as I have yet encountered. In that proposal, they requested a number of experiments, including the formation of a salaried Elders Panel to "co-judge" during sentencing, the establishment of a community lock-up for less serious offences, and exploration of a youth diversion court. It was their explanation of

---

[93] Rupert Ross, "Duelling Paradigms?: Western Criminal Justice Versus Aboriginal Community Healing", in *Continuing Poundmaker and Riel's Quest*, cited in note 35, p. 242.

the reasons behind such requests which began to explain what they perceive as a central failing of our system. Their own words cannot be improved upon:

> The element of community respect must be instilled in the court in order for any meaningful changes in attitude (of the offender) to occur. The court does attempt to cause respect in a formal sense, however, the factors of deep-seated respect are absent. Respect for Elders occurs over a lifetime of familiarity and trust in their wisdom. It is therefore expedient that the court be perceived as part of a *community process* and that the offender is not only before the court but *before the community*.
>
> In earlier days the community practiced public courts wherein a person was confronted in the presence of the whole community with his misbehaviour. This caused great shame because the community as a whole was respected by all. This shame and remorse laid the groundwork for the teaching that would occur... An important ethic...is the use of shame to teach and rehabilitate. *Since a person can only be shamed by someone who is respected and looked up to, this cannot be effected by a travelling court.*[94]

Ross suggests there are several issues involved here:

> The first is the more obvious: because "we" are outsiders, we are incapable of making the accused feel truly ashamed... Removal to an outside jail, in their view, permits an offender to *escape* being held accountable to the community. It is not, as we tend to see it, the ultimate punishment, because it enables offenders to avoid the very people whose presence is most likely to give rise to shame and remorse.[95]

The second issue has to do with the restoration to Aboriginal peoples of their legitimate forums of dispute resolution.

> The very presence of our courts has taken away a critical forum in which wisdom can be demonstrated and respect earned. There can be no doubt that it was respect for elders which was the social glue holding people together in relatively peaceful obedience to commonly accepted rules. People accepted their guidance because

---

[94] Rupert Ross, "Cultural Blindness and the Justice System in Remote Native Communities", paper presented to the Sharing Common Ground Conference on Aboriginal Policing Services, Edmonton, May 1990, pp. 11-12 (emphasis in original).

[95] Ross, "Cultural Blindness", p. 12 (emphasis in original).

they had observed their wisdom. The arrival of the court took away the critical arena of dispute-resolution from the Elders. With a grossly diminished opportunity to demonstrate wisdom, there was a corresponding diminishment of heart-felt respect. The same dynamic took place as we introduced our education, our health care, a bureaucratic Band Council structure, our policing, etc. The Elders arena shrank, and the glue that held each small society intact began to dry and crack.

Viewed from this perspective, the cry for "local control" is more than a grab for power. It comes from more than an assertion that we do a poor job. Instead, it aims at a restoration of forums within which wisdom can be developed and demonstrated, and respect can once again be earned. Absent that rebuilding of respect within the community, they see only a continuing slide into social anarchy...

As long as we appropriate such forums as dispute-resolution to ourselves we will only aggravate the problem of diminishing respect of the community leaders and community wisdom, thereby putting the possibility of effecting remorse even further out of reach.[96]

In his discussion of the Hollow Water initiative, Ross makes specific reference to three features of the approach to the process of Aboriginal justice that distinguish it from the approach of the non-Aboriginal system. The first is that decision-making influence is dispersed among many people as part of the search for consensus. The second is that Aboriginal women are primary participants at every stage of the process. The third feature is that the people involved, whether the offender, the victim or the families affected, can be neither understood nor assisted as long as they are seen as isolated individuals. Instead people must be seen as participants in a large web of relationships. This is intimately connected to Aboriginal world views, in which the philosophy of interrelationship informs people's understanding of who they are and their responsibilities to each other, their ancestors and the generations yet to come. An important part of the strength of this philosophy is that behaviour that is characterized as criminal – and in particular the behaviour that is the most disruptive and destructive in Aboriginal communities (and Aboriginal people see family and sexual assault as a central part of this) – is itself intertwined in a larger web of the destructive historical experiences of Aboriginal people.

---

[96] Ross, "Cultural Blindness", pp. 13-14. The Norwegian criminologist, Nils Christie, has written about how, in the modern criminal justice system, state professionals 'steal' conflicts from ordinary citizens and in the process undermine the social fabric on which public order ultimately depends. Nils Christie, "Conflict as Property", *British Journal of Criminology* 17 (1977), p. 1.

In our final report we will deal with the damage done by government agents and missionaries in efforts to assimilate Aboriginal people by undermining Aboriginal institutions and cultural values. The relationship between these practices – and the attitudes underlying their planning and implementation – and the contemporary problems in Aboriginal communities with the justice system is something Aboriginal people brought forward to this commission and to the various justice inquiries. In his report on the Cariboo-Chilcotin Justice Inquiry, in a chapter entitled "What the People Said", Judge Sarich wrote:

> One of the common threads that ran through the litany of complaints was the effect of the residential school – St. Joseph's Mission – on the lives of the Native people... There was no admission by any of the people that the education they received at that school prepared them in any way for life in non-Native society. On the contrary, experiences at the Mission led to very serious social and psychological injury to generations of Native people in the Cariboo-Chilcotin. It is not surprising that rampant alcoholism, family violence and distrust of authority are part of the mix they bring into the equation of their relationship with the justice system.[97]

The non-Aboriginal criminal justice system was never designed to address and redress the impact of the accumulated injustices of colonialism – nor do those involved in it, whether as police officers, lawyers, judges or correctional administrators, see this as their mandate. The principle of individual responsibility, which lies at the heart of western concepts of criminal law, requires that the system deal with the individual accused who is before the court, and the focus of the process is on his or her actions in the context of specific definitions of what constitutes a crime.

The concept of legal guilt requires a voluntary act and, broadly speaking, a state of mind in which the accused intended to cause the harm or, being aware that harm might result, recklessly disregarded that possibility. Usually absent from determinations of legal guilt are considerations such as the fact that the accused's formative years were spent in state institutions where physical and sexual abuse were a regular part of life. The non-Aboriginal criminal justice system does not permit an allocation of legal guilt between individuals and the society in which they live. If the accused is found legally guilty, the principles governing sentencing do not focus on providing a structure and resources to enable and empower either the offender or the victim to recover or, in many cases, find for the first time a sense

---

[97] Report on the Cariboo-Chilcotin Justice Inquiry, cited in note 9, pp. 17-18. In our special report on suicide we described the experience of members of the Shuswap First Nation of Canim Lake, B.C. at the St. Joseph's Residential School and how for them, "suicide is seen as just one expression of the pain accumulated by Aboriginal people over many generations, as a result of their experiences as objects of British and Canadian government policy." See *Choosing Life*, cited in note 60, pp. 56-60.

of well-being and strength to become a healthy person and member of the community.

What the Aboriginal approach and process seek to do lies not simply at the periphery of the non-Aboriginal system; it lies outside the framework entirely. How often in the courts of this country have sensitive judges lamented the fact that an Aboriginal accused, being sentenced as an abuser – of drugs or family members – is himself or herself the victim of an abusive upbringing and an intolerant society? How often have they been forced to say, "Unfortunately the problems that have brought this accused before the court lie outside the ability of this court to resolve." For Aboriginal people this lamentation is not acceptable. They demand that through their own processes of justice they be able to deal with victimizer and victim in the context of their continuing relationships, in the context of their place in their communities, in the full understanding of the forces that have turned family members into victims and victimizers, and in the conviction that through their own justice systems they can do more than simply fuel the cycle of violence. To do that they need not only the strength of their own philosophies and, the skills of their healers, but also a share of the enormous resources consumed by the non-Aboriginal system in a manner that has failed the Aboriginal people of this country. Those resources must include the legal resource of recognized jurisdiction in relation to justice, as part of the right of self-government, and the fiscal resources to make that jurisdiction an effective one.

Joanne Barnaby, executive director of the Dene Cultural Institute, spoke at our round table on justice of a case she had observed; in a poignant and compelling way, the case highlights how the specific and limited focus of the Canadian criminal justice system fails to address the underlying and fundamental causes of personal and community disintegration.

> I was subpoenaed to attend a sentence hearing that involved an elder who had been charged and convicted of assault. I went a couple of days ahead to the community where the case was going to be heard and [talked] to the defendant, the elder.

> What I learned in a couple of days in sitting with him and listening to him was that he was really depressed. He felt worthless. He felt unneeded. He felt no respect for himself... He had spent about 40 years living on the land, living a very traditional life and he was in the community. He had moved to town about 20 years ago and his life began to fall apart. He lost his role as an educator, as a teacher. He lost his role as a leader. He was displaced by the Chief and band council system. He didn't feel he had anything to give in the community life context and he was striking out. He was striking out in anger and he had no hesitation about acknowledging his actions and his guilt. He had no hesitation about facing the sentencing hearing.

The kinds of questions that were asked of the defendant, of the elder, were totally irrelevant and didn't address the real problem, didn't address his depression, didn't address his need for healing, didn't address his need to gain a sense of place, a sense of self-respect once again and to contribute to community life... Because the question that the sentencing hearing was focusing on was whether or not he should be allowed to carry firearms given he had been convicted of assault, the lawyer asked him, 'How much do you depend on hunting and trapping?' The elder said, 'Not very much at all.' Very sadly he said that. In fact, he still spends about half of the year in total out on the land but his own lawyer didn't understand the elder's context. He didn't understand that relative to what he wanted to do, relative to his full life experience, he was not spending much time on the land at all from his perspective. Of course, if the defence lawyer knew anything about our culture, he would have probed further and found out exactly the extent of his continued dependence on firearms for hunting.[98]

Even with an Aboriginal lawyer who understood the context, the sentencing process in a criminal case is not intended to address or redress the problems facing this elder. Within the non-Aboriginal system the issue is the assault and the assaulter; it is not how we as a society and as a community respond in a sympathetic, supportive and healing way to a person searching for meaning in his life. While an Aboriginal justice system will not be a panacea for this elder's problems, endeavouring to resolve them within the context of the collective strength of the community would be at the centre of its mandate rather than lying beyond the scope of the court's responsibilities.

The limits of indigenizing the existing justice system by increasing the participation of Aboriginal lawyers and judges was graphically revealed to us at our round table. Vina Starr, an Aboriginal lawyer practising in Vancouver, described how entering the legal profession has required her and her Aboriginal brothers and sisters in law to become culturally schizophrenic:

I want to compare the kind of acculturation that those of us who are Aboriginal lawyers have to be prepared to accept in order to survive and excel in your system. It required a deliberate decision – a very private personal decision – long before the initial act which entailed deciding on wiping clean our Indian brains and our Indian hearts of every value that had been taught to us and that we hold and will always hold dear, but in order to have that white-washed brain and that whitewashed heart receptive to the new system of common law values, it was necessary. So today we stand

---

[98] RCAP, National Round Table on Aboriginal Justice Issues, 26 November 1992, transcript, p. 376; summarized in *Aboriginal Peoples and the Justice System*, cited in note 7, p. 454.

here because we have been successful at being deliberate schizophrenics on a daily basis. On the one hand, I know that my right foot is very firmly planted on the white justice side of the fence and yet, at the same time, I know that my left foot was born on the Indian side of the fence and will be buried on that side of the fence.[99]

A number of judges with long experience in the criminal justice system have come to the point where they realize that there has to be a better way to respond to the social and personal disorganization of many Aboriginal societies and that Aboriginal justice systems hold a promise that the criminal justice system has failed to fulfil. Judge Fafard of the Provincial Court of Saskatchewan, who has some 20 years' experience of the fly-in circuit court in northern Saskatchewan, summed up his feelings, and we think those of many other judges, when he stated:

I believe we have an offender-processing system, but I am not sure we have a criminal justice system... I feel we have to take an about turn away from the case processing punitive system – the Euro-Canadian system, under which we now operate and turn in the direction of a social-justice healing process, such as is happening in the Hollow Water Reserve in Manitoba. It is the only thing that I have seen that might be able to deal with the maelstrom of dysfunction that is occurring in some communities. I don't need to try to list here the reasons for the dysfunction... but you cannot deal with these problems by punishing people. You can't punish a community into functioning as a community, as a peaceful community. It's got to be a healing process. There's been a lot of harm done and there is a lot of hurt out there.[100]

Judge Jean-Charles Coutu is another non-Aboriginal judge who has had extensive experience in operating a circuit court in northern communities separated by many hundreds of miles. Reflecting on his experience with the Cree and Inuit peoples of the James Bay region, he has written:

Our system is one of confrontation. In the Native tradition the main objective of legal systems is to try and restore harmony between individuals or between an individual and the community. This harmony is usually achieved by the adhesion of both parties to a solution, whereas under the Euro-Canadian system, someone must be condemned whether it be for rehabilitative, deterrent or punitive purposes. Any conflict, be it private or public in nature, disrupts harmony in the community. The ultimate aim of a jus-

---

[99] Round Table, transcript, 25 November 1992, pp. 223-224.

[100] Claude Fafard, "On Being a Northern Judge", in *Continuing Poundmaker and Riel's Quest*, cited in note 35, pp. 403-404.

tice system should be to help restore order, which gives rise to notions of conciliation and reparation. In order to restore harmony, the judge should be able to go beyond the conflict which is put before him... Our system rarely allows for such an extension of a judge's power. In light of these facts, it seems evident if we apply our system as is, in Native communities, we will continue to offer a sort of justice, which would lack the ingredients needed to achieve a positive effect and inspire the respect that it should.[101]

At our round table we had the advantage of hearing from the chief judge and from a lawyer in the Navajo tribal court system. In their presentations, advising us of both the strengths and the limitations of the Navajo experience (discussed later in this report), they suggested that Canada has an enormous opportunity if governments are prepared to seize the moment and acknowledge both the legitimacy and the necessity of Aboriginal justice systems. James Zion, a lawyer with extensive experience in the Navajo and other tribal court systems in the United States, told us:

> Traditional Indian justice rules and methods are not 'alternative dispute resolution'; they are the way things are done... They provide lessons for general methods of alternative dispute resolution... Canada has the opportunity to foster and nourish Native laboratories for change. In doing so, it will give its nation and the world the advantage of seeing other approaches to justice, law and government. A half-hearted or stingy approach to the human rights of Natives to have their own law will only repeat the mistakes of the past. 'Thou shalt not ration justice.'[102]

The opportunity and advantage to which Zion refers are important. What a new partnership between Aboriginal and non-Aboriginal peoples could do in the broad field of justice could be of enormous significance in ending the history of injustice that has so far characterized the experience of Aboriginal peoples in Canada. This partnership could also provide the impetus for significant new directions in the conceptualization of justice for Aboriginal people beyond the borders of Canada. By taking concrete steps consistent with the evolving international human rights standards for indigenous peoples, our collective efforts may become part of the engine of change for justice for indigenous peoples in other parts of the world.

The power of the precedent that would be set by recognizing and implementing Aboriginal justice systems should not be underestimated. Some of the criticisms

---

[101] J.-C. Coutu, "Native Justice Committees: A Proposal for a More Active Participation of Native Peoples in the Administration of Justice" (1985, unpublished); quoted in *Locking Up Natives in Canada*, cited in note 37, pp. 259-260.

[102] Round Table, transcript, 27 November 1992, p. 346; summarized in *Aboriginal Peoples and the Justice System*, cited in note 7, p. 474.

of the non-Aboriginal criminal justice system voiced by Aboriginal people have also been raised by non-Aboriginal critics. Over the past decade, in some ways paralleling the Aboriginal justice inquiries, a series of major commissions and inquiries have addressed the directions that reform of the criminal justice system should take. Large questions have been raised regarding Canada's heavy reliance on imprisonment compared to many other countries and about the need to redefine the purposes of the criminal justice system so that the traditional emphasis on retributive goals is balanced with restorative goals. Some of these critics have argued for the articulation of a new paradigm of criminal justice, based on a restorative model. One of the research studies commissioned by the Law Reform Commission as part of the minister of justice's Reference on Aboriginal Peoples and Criminal Justice reviewed the body of research (much of it done under the auspices of the Law Reform Commission) advancing alternative models of criminal justice. In the research study, Michael Jackson summarized that work:

> Over the past 20 years in Canada a growing understanding has developed regarding the limitations on the traditional criminal justice process and its reliance on imprisonment to further retributive and deterrent objectives. Furthermore, a consensus is emerging on the need to develop community based sanctions and non-adversary processes which balance the interests of the victim, the offender and the community. There is also a significant and growing body of opinion that restorative justice principles should play a far more important role in criminal justice policy and practice.

> It should also have become apparent that these initiatives to reshape the criminal justice process share many principles and elements which characterize traditional Aboriginal justice systems. It should be a salutary reminder of the indifference we have paid to Aboriginal legal, political and cultural institutions to realize that, using the words of the Minister of Justice's Reference to the Commission, 'The development of new approaches to and new concepts of the law' in relation to alternative dispute resolution leads to the discovery and recognition of the indigenous approaches and conceptions of Canada's First Nations which pre-date the *Penitentiary Act* and the building of Kingston Penitentiary by many centuries.'

The significance of this discovery and recognition in the context of the Minister's Reference is that a consideration of the proposals of Aboriginal communities to achieve a greater accommodation between their systems of justice and the larger Canadian system and in some cases to make over and take over the administration of justice should be seen not only as reforms necessary to achieve real justice for Native people but also as opportunities from which our criminal justice system can learn from the experience and accumulated wisdom of Canada's First Nations.[103]

As to the importance of Canadian developments in the realm of contemporary Aboriginal justice systems, it is instructive to look at the United Nations Draft Declaration on the Rights of Indigenous Peoples, which has been completed by the Working Group on Indigenous Populations and is now working its way through the United Nations system. Article 33 of the Draft Declaration provides as follows:

> Indigenous peoples have the right to promote, develop and maintain their institutional structures and their distinctive juridical customs, traditions, procedures and practices, in accordance with internationally recognized human rights standards.[104]

Clearly, recognition under Canadian law of the right of Aboriginal peoples to develop Aboriginal justice systems would be an implementation of the Draft Declaration, and in so doing Canada would advance the struggle of other indigenous peoples who, like the Aborigines of Australia, the Maori of New Zealand/Aotearoa, and the Indian nations of the Americas, have lived under the "long and terrible shadow" of European colonization.[105]

Changing the Realities – Directions for the Future

It is the view of this Commission that recognizing the right of Aboriginal peoples to re-establish their own justice systems and providing the resources to exercise that right is a necessary part of the new relationship we have proposed. This is clearly a long-term goal, although, as we describe in the next chapter, important steps have already been taken by some Aboriginal communities in charting these future directions for their nations. We do not underestimate the enormous challenge this represents for Aboriginal peoples, involving as it does addressing the destructive and dislocating legacies of the laws and policies of the past. The problems that bring Aboriginal people into the courts and prisons of this country do

---

[103] Michael Jackson, "In Search of the Pathways to Justice: Alternative Dispute Resolution in Aboriginal Communities", *U.B.C. Law Review* (1992, Special Edition: Aboriginal Justice), pp. 187-188. There is a growing international literature on the principles of restorative justice. See, for example, Howard Zehr, *Changing Lenses* (Scottsdale: Harold Press, 1990); Jim Consedine, *Restorative Justice: Healing the Effects of Crime* (Lyttleton, New Zealand: Ploughshares Publications, 1995). We refer further to international developments in restorative justice in Chapter 3, in our review of the New Zealand experience with young offenders, beginning on page 121.

[104] Commission on Human Rights, Sub-Commission on Prevention of Discrimination and Protection of Minorities (United Nations document number E/CN.4/Sub.2/1994/2/Add.1) 20 April 1994; see also Report of the Working Group on Indigenous Populations on its Eleventh Session (E/CN.4/Sub. 2/1993/29) 1993.

[105] Thomas R. Berger, *A Long and Terrible Shadow: White Values, Native Rights in the Americas, 1492-1992* (Toronto/Vancouver: Douglas & McIntyre, 1991).

not lend themselves to easy solutions. As we have been told over and over again, there is a great need for healing, which can be provided only by Aboriginal people themselves to replace "the great Canadian lockup."[106]

It is the Commission's position that Aboriginal peoples' right of self-government as an existing Aboriginal and treaty right within section 35 of the *Constitution Act, 1982* must encompass the jurisdiction to establish Aboriginal justice systems. In Chapter 4 we set out the contours of what that jurisdiction might look like, the shape of some of the institutional arrangements through which it might be exercised, and the nature of the challenges that jurisdiction would have to meet, particularly the protection of fundamental human rights.

The Commission is also of the view that Aboriginal jurisdiction in relation to justice is the responsibility of each Aboriginal nation. That is to say, it is the right and will be the responsibility of each nation to create and design the nation's justice system. This is in accordance with our general position that Aboriginal self-government as one of three orders of government should reside with each nation, a principle we will be elaborating on in our final report. The recognition of jurisdiction at the level of the nation does not, however, preclude sharing that authority at the community level. Indeed, as we describe in the next chapter, the majority of the ground-breaking work done thus far has been the product of community initiatives.

Our reasons for recognizing that jurisdiction over justice is a responsibility of each nation are several and reflect a blend of principle and pragmatism. As a matter of principle the legitimacy of a system of justice rests on its being an expression of a society's basic values, expressed in the rules that govern people's rights and responsibilities and the way peace and order are maintained when disputes arise. In light of the diversity of Aboriginal nations, recognition of jurisdiction over justice at the nation level allows each nation to give concrete expression to its values and preferred systems of dispute resolution. It is, of course, for the people of each nation to decide how this jurisdiction is to be exercised between the nation and its communities.

As a practical matter, recognition of Aboriginal jurisdiction at a nation level will ensure that there is greater access to the human and financial resources necessary for the effective development and management of justice systems than would be the case if jurisdiction rested with each Aboriginal community. In Chapter 4 we discuss further how recognition of jurisdiction at the nation level can contribute to practices and policies that ensure that decisions are made fairly, are free from undue political interference, and are responsive to the needs of vulnerable groups.

What we have in mind – not only in the area of justice but in all aspects of relationships between Aboriginal peoples and other Canadians – is a transformation

---

[106] This phrase is from the submission of Darryll Bretton of the First Nations Freedom Network, who addressed the Commission at our hearings in Edmonton, 11 June 1992.

from the assimilationist policies of the past to policies and constitutional arrangements based on recognition and respect.

Until this transformation (in effect, the decolonization of the Canadian justice system) takes place, the wheels of injustice grind on. As Tony Mandamin reminded us at the round table, fine words are all well and good, but if our recommendations do not bring about change in the lives of Aboriginal people, we will have accomplished nothing. **For this reason, in approaching an agenda for reform, although we have focused most of our attention on the broad recommendation to establish Aboriginal justice systems, we have also made other recommendations directed to ensuring implementation of the many proposals in the justice reports preceding ours, whose primary focus was reform of the existing Canadian justice system. We believe this is necessary not only to address the harsh realities facing Aboriginal people today but also because the non-Aboriginal justice system is likely to continue to play a significant part in the lives of Aboriginal people.**

There are several reasons for this. First, for Aboriginal nations that choose to reestablish their own justice systems, there will be a transition period before they assume the full scope of their jurisdiction. Second, some nations may decide that certain cases are beyond their collective ability to resolve and may wish those cases to be referred to the non-Aboriginal system. A third reason relates to the challenges of establishing Aboriginal justice systems in urban areas. The commission considers that in the cities, where almost half of Aboriginal people live, there is a place for such systems (and we address this issue later in the report), although the intersection between the Aboriginal and non-Aboriginal systems is obviously an important part of that urban reality. The connections between the establishment of Aboriginal justice systems and necessary changes to the non-Aboriginal system should be seen in a holistic framework of reform. In the area of justice – perhaps more than any other, because of the impact on the lives of Aboriginal people – constructive partnership and dialogue are critical.

Many of the submissions made to us referred to a two-track approach to reform – the first track being the reform of the non-Aboriginal system, the second the establishment of Aboriginal justice systems. As helpful as this may be in terms of identifying long-term and short-term changes, the necessary bridge between the two tracks must be understood clearly to be a new partnership, based on the foundation of Aboriginal self-government. That message resonated in all the submissions and presentations made to the commission. It is the same message delivered to the other justice inquiries. In the conclusion of the Cariboo-Chilcotin inquiry, Judge Sarich wrote:

> One constant drum beat that followed the commission from reserve to reserve was the message that native people want to control their own lives and manage their own affairs. That means a process of justice that is comprehensible and culturally accept-

able to them. To achieve these ends some of the communities will institute their own justice process and others will experiment with an adaptation of the non-native process. But because any process they adopt will be closely connected to all other aspects of the development of their societies, including economic development and the provision of services, there will inevitably come an interrelationship of their justice process with that of non-native society... In their own good time, they will develop a justice system suitable to themselves.[107]

The need to proceed within a framework of intercultural dialogue on justice reform at the federal, provincial and territorial levels is far more important than endless debate about whether a particular initiative fits within a track-one or track-two agenda. This point is effectively made by Mary Ellen Turpel:

> We spent several years in a distracting debate over whether justice reform involves separate justice systems or reforming the mainstream justice system. This is a false dichotomy and a fruitless distinction because it is not an either/or choice. The impetus for change can better be described as getting away from the colonialism and domination of the Canadian criminal justice system. Resisting colonialism means a reclaiming by Aboriginal peoples of control of the resolution of disputes and jurisdiction over justice, but it is not as simple or as quick as that sounds. Moving in this direction would involve many linkages with the existing criminal justice system and perhaps phased assumption of jurisdiction...
>
> What I learned from meeting community justice workers in 1993 is that public security and a gradual process of criminal justice reform is what people are looking for, not a sudden break and some completely isolated regime. Community members want lots of time for discussion, training (including training on the relevant aspects of the Canadian legal system) and a phased-in process of criminal justice reform implementation. They also require fiscal resources. There might be some aspects of the current criminal justice system that will never be taken on by Aboriginal justice systems. There will be many points of convergence between Aboriginal justice systems and the Canadian criminal justice system....[108]

Although the challenges facing Aboriginal peoples in reclaiming control over justice are enormous, they are not theirs alone. Aboriginal people have clearly articulated that these challenges must be met within the framework of a new rela-

---

[107] Report on the Cariboo-Chilcotin Justice Inquiry, cited in note 9, p. 28.

[108] Turpel, "Reflections on Thinking Concretely", cited in note 91, pp. 208-209.

tionship. In his presentation at our hearings in Saskatoon, Alphonse Janvier made the point as clearly as anybody:

> The next question is: what can we do, as Métis people, to deal with the justice and social issues that face us on a daily basis?
>
> Again, the answer is simple. We have been telling governments and bureaucracies that the mainstream system that deals with the so-called Métis problem pertaining to justice and social issues does not work. The legislative/policy environment in which justice and social development takes place does not properly reflect the unique Métis traditions and values. It is time that government and their administrative bureaucracies hear the voices of Métis people.
>
> We have been telling governments that the Métis want to take responsibility for the so-called problems and attack these issues from the viewpoint of Métis people. We are prepared to legislate, develop policies, design and implement programs and services that are unique, designed for the Métis people wherever they may live in tackling justice and social issues.
>
> To accomplish such a goal, the Métis and other governments must develop a new relationship; one that harbours mutual trust, respect as well as generally harmonious and supportive relationships.
>
> It is now time to stop blaming one another and start discussing some of the issues at a partnership level. The Métis communities are prepared to take ownership of the responsibilities for the so-called problems pertaining to justice and social issues.
>
> We now need the support, trust and respect of the institutions that historically exercised so much control over us and above all the Métis nation must be given the opportunity to heal itself and become a productive and meaningful nation within the federation of Canadian nations.[109]

As stated so clearly here, the challenges facing Métis people and other Aboriginal peoples require and demand the "support, trust and respect" of non-Aboriginal participants in the justice system. In his report on the Cariboo-Chilcotin Justice Inquiry, Judge Sarich framed the challenge of Aboriginal aspirations and the implications of their rejection:

---

[109] Alphonse Janvier, transcripts of the hearings of the Royal Commission on Aboriginal Peoples (hereafter, RCAP transcripts), Saskatoon, 12 May 1993. Verbatim transcripts of the Commission's hearings are available in electronic and hard copy form and will be part of the CD-ROM released along with the Commission's final report.

Those working in the current non-native justice system – partic- ularly provincial court judges – have a choice. They can assist in the evolution of an emerging native justice system or stand back and condemn it on strict constitutional interpretation. If they choose the latter course, that court will be excluded entirely from participation in the evolution of the native justice process and become less than a full provincial court. If judges choose the first course, they will be required to become familiar with the cultural imperatives of each of the native peoples with whom they will be in contact. In all areas of development, a sensitive and knowl- edgeable approach by judges can directly influence the evolution of the native process. Such an approach can be instrumental in expanding and articulating a more flexible and uniquely Canadian common law of benefit to both processes.

But this development will not be quick or easy. In the meantime, the non-native court system must be made more accessible and responsive to natives.[110]

---

[110] Report on the Cariboo-Chilcotin Justice Inquiry, cited in note 9, p. 28.

3

Current Aboriginal Justice Initiatives

Over the past twenty years, Aboriginal communities across the country have begun to take back a measure of control over various aspects of the justice system. These initiatives are a testament to the determination of Aboriginal peoples to assert their right of self-government and also of the readiness of some federal, provincial and territorial judges, politicians and public servants to allow for a degree of flexibility in the way justice is delivered to Aboriginal people. These initiatives, more pronounced over the past five years, have taken place in a jurisdictional vacuum. For the most part they exist at the level of official sufferance. They rarely have either the level or the security of funding assumed to be prerequisites for critical parts of the criminal justice system administered by non-Aboriginal governments and agencies. Nevertheless, in this not particularly hospitable ground, several initiatives have established a footing and even flourished.

In this chapter we review some of these initiatives, together with other steps taken by non-Aboriginal governments and the judiciary to make the justice system more responsive to the experiences and needs of Aboriginal people. The initiatives include Aboriginal policing, the appointment of Aboriginal justices of the peace and Aboriginal judges, Aboriginal court worker programs, and efforts to increase the understanding of non-Aboriginal participants in the justice system through Aboriginal awareness and cross-cultural training programs. We also look at the experience of the few Aboriginal courts that have been established under the *Indian Act* and consider a number of diversion projects that have sought to create alternative pathways of conflict resolution. We examine more recent developments as well, particularly the use of elders panels and sentencing circles, which have become important in northern Canada, and we look at some of the work done with young offenders to provide greater community control over what happens to young people in conflict with the law. The final part of this overview focuses on the experiences of Aboriginal prisoners, both men and women, and the remarkable journey some of them have made toward healing through the teachings of Aboriginal spirituality.

In providing this review we have endeavoured to offer some insights into several common features of these initiatives. We have also attempted to identify the factors that have enabled some initiatives to develop successfully and the impediments that have caused others to falter. In addition, we have looked at how some of these initiatives, although introduced initially as reforms to the non-Aboriginal justice system, may be able to assist Aboriginal nations and communities in the transition to Aboriginal control of justice. As well, we have tried to identify initiatives that may, over time, become integral elements of Aboriginal-controlled justice systems.

Following this broad review of Aboriginal justice initiatives, we present two detailed case studies. The initiatives examined are the community council project of Aboriginal Legal Services of Toronto and the community holistic circle healing project of the Hollow Water First Nation community in Manitoba. These programs were selected because they respond to two of the most difficult issues facing the development of Aboriginal justice systems. The Toronto initiative addresses the crucial issue of creating an Aboriginal justice system in an urban context, where almost half of Aboriginal people now live. The Hollow Water initiative addresses the equally important issue of how Aboriginal communities can deal with the potentially socially divisive problem of sexual abuse of women and children. In addition, both initiatives have been operating for a sufficient length of time to have generated some statistical case data and have been the subject of outside evaluations and assessments.

Aboriginal Policing

Until the early 1970s, policing services were provided to Aboriginal communities in large part by the RCMP, who discharged this responsibility as part of their role in enforcing the *Indian Act*, consistent with the view, then current, that the federal government was responsible for all aspects of Aboriginal affairs. In 1967, a report of the Canadian Corrections Association, *Indians and the Law* (which was the first of many Aboriginal justice reports), made recommendations dealing with, among other things, improvement of policing services for Aboriginal communities, including expansion and improvement of the band constable system. The Department of Indian Affairs and Northern Development (DIAND) – which during this period and until 1992 was the federal department overseeing policing arrangements – obtained Treasury Board approval to develop a more elaborate program to increase the number of band constables. This led ultimately to what is known as Circular 55, issued on 24 September 1971, which provided that the objective of the band constabulary, over and above matters of band jurisdiction (for example, enforcing the band by-laws) was to supplement the senior police forces at the local level, but not supplant them.

In 1973, a second, broader study by DIAND, *Report of the Task Force: Policing on Reserves*, focused on the employment of Aboriginal people in a comprehensive policing role and proposed expansion and improvement of the band constable program. The task force examined three basic options; the first two were based on band council policing (the existing Circular 55 concept) and municipal policing, that is, contracting local municipalities for policing services. Option 3(a) proposed the establishment of autonomous Aboriginal police forces, while option 3(b) proposed the development of a special constable contingent within existing police forces. The task force concluded that option 3(b) should be made available to interested bands. Following the task force report, DIAND obtained approval to establish an experimental program for an Indian special constable contingent and was authorized to negotiate, in consultation with the Solicitor General, cost-sharing agreements with the provinces to support the development of an Indian special constable contingent within provincial/territorial policing services.

The 1990 federal task force report, *Indian Policing Policy Review*, described the policing programs then in place:

> Current Indian policing programs have a total authorized complement of 708 Indian Constables.... The majority are employed under the RCMP 3(b) program and the Ontario Indian Special Constable Program with essentially full police officer status. Band Constables (Circular 55) performed varying police functions, but usually of a more limited nature.[111]

In addition to the band constables appointed under Circular 55 and the special constable program operated under 3(b), there are various other policing arrangements for what have been characterized as Indian police forces operating pursuant to a variety of federal and provincial agreements, *Indian Act* band by-laws, and provincial legislation.

In Quebec, several programs have existed since 1978 relating to the administration of police services in various Aboriginal communities. In that year, the Amerindian Police Council, a non-profit corporation with a federal charter, was established, originally to provide policing in some 23 Quebec First Nations communities. In 1978, the Sûreté du Québec also set up an Aboriginal police program for communities falling within the scope of the James Bay and Northern Quebec Agreement and the Cree and Naskapi Northeastern Agreement. This program covers Cree communities, the Inuit, and the Naskapi of Kawawachikamach. In early 1995, nine Aboriginal communities withdrew from the Amerindian Police Council,

---

[111] *Indian Policing Policy Review*, cited in note 46, p. 8.

leaving fourteen in its jurisdiction.[112] Aboriginal constables employed by the Amerindian Police Council enjoy full peace officer status under Quebec's *Police Act*,[113] although their jurisdiction is restricted to Indian reserves.

Since 1990, some Aboriginal communities in Quebec have preferred to negotiate tripartite agreements – involving the federal department of the solicitor general, the provincial public security ministry and their own band councils – for the administration of their communities' police services. Recent amendments to the *Police Act* gave peace officer status to all members of these Aboriginal police forces, following the signing of an agreement with the province.[114] The community of Kahnawake recently concluded such a tripartite agreement.[115] Since 1979, it had operated its own peacekeeper force pursuant to band council resolutions. Its constables did not have police officer status under provincial legislation, but had been sworn in by a justice of the peace under the *Indian Act*.[116]

In June 1991 the federal government announced a new on-reserve First Nations policing policy; 'on-reserve' includes not only Indian reserves but certain Indian communities on Crown lands and Inuit communities. Under the new policy, responsibilities previously discharged by DIAND were transferred to a single First Nations policing program under the authority of the federal Solicitor General. The new program committed an extra $116.8 million over a five-year period.[117]

At our public hearings and our round table on justice, we heard from some of the most experienced Aboriginal police officers in the country. They told us of the achievements of Aboriginal police forces but also of the problems they face and the impediments to development of Aboriginal police services as part of integrated Aboriginal justice systems. Frank McKay is the chief of police of the Dakota Ojibway Tribal Council (DOTC) police department in Manitoba. The DOTC police force was established in 1978 to deliver locally-controlled police services to eight Dakota and Ojibwa reserves. It was the first tribal police force of its kind. The DOTC police force of 25 constables is administered by a chief of police who reports to the

---

[112] These Aboriginal communities are the Mi'kmaq of Maria; the Montagnais of Saint-Augustin, La Romaine, Natqashquan, Mingan, Escoumins, and Pointe-Bleu; the Algonquin of Timiskaming, Kipawa and Winneway; the Abenaki of Odenak; and the Attikamek of Weymontachie and Manawan. See letter to RCAP from the Office of the Aboriginal Affairs Co-ordinator, Department of Public Security (Quebec), 10 May 1995.

[113] The *Police Act*, R.S.Q., chapter P.13, sections 80 and 83.

[114] *An Act to amend the Police Act and the Act respecting police organization as regards Native police*, S.Q. 1995, chapter 12.

[115] Agreement respecting police services in the Kahnawake Territory between the Mohawks of Kahnawake, the government of Quebec and the government of Canada, signed 11 September 1995.

[116] Indian Policing Policy Review, cited in note 46, pp. 32-34.

[117] The tripartite First Nations policing agreements that have been signed can be found in User Reports No. 1992-10 and No. 1994-03, published by the Solicitor General of Canada. The RCMP-First Nations Community Policing Service Agreements are collected in User Report No. 1995-08.

police commission, whose members include the chiefs of the participating reserves as well as representatives of the provincial justice department, the federal government, the RCMP and the Manitoba Police commission. The DOTC constables have peace officer status and authority to enforce all legislation and statutes, but their jurisdiction is limited, under the terms of the federal/provincial/DOTC agreement, to DOTC reserves. The force shares investigative responsibilities with the RCMP for minor criminal code offences, while major offences are turned over to the RCMP in accordance with a written protocol. The DOTC police force also enforces band by-laws at the request of individual chiefs and band councils. The police force receives its training at the RCMP training academy in Regina, although Chief McKay informed us that future plans include the establishment of an Indian police training academy either in Manitoba or centrally located where other First Nations police departments can have access.

One of the major problems that has faced the DOTC is one that many other Aboriginal justice initiatives have encountered; it has been referred to as the 'pilot project mentality'. Chief McKay highlighted the continuing problems caused by funding uncertainty that no non-Aboriginal police department would or could ever tolerate.

> We have always experienced funding problems. It was always on a year-to-year basis. Further, we could not make plans for anything.... There could be no long term operations and programs because of the year-to-year funding. The attrition rate is very high because there is no long term funding. Usually the Constables that are very good in their work seek other employment with other police departments. The salaries are very low and there is no payment for overtime. There is no ongoing training for senior Constables. There is no proper detachment offices or housing.[118]

Wally McKay, chair of the Ontario First Nations Police commission, made a submission at our hearings in Toronto. The commission plays a supervisory and advisory role for the First Nations constable programs operated by more than half of Ontario bands, pursuant to a tripartite agreement between the major Ontario First Nations associations and the federal and provincial governments. The submission particularly addressed what McKay sees as the limitations of indigenizing police authorities without addressing the substantive issue of jurisdiction and Aboriginal concepts of peacekeeping.

> It is twenty years since the first Special or "Band" Constable positions were created. It is ten years since the current type of tripartite policing agreements took hold. There has been much progress in understanding and in action on the part of federal and provincial government officials. First Nations policing officials, myself

---

[118] Chief Frank McKay, RCAP transcripts, Brandon, Manitoba, 10 December 1992.

included, have learned much to help us respond to the challenges of adapting to contemporary situations. As well, it is necessary that there be stages of transition. This stage, however, is now close to a generation in duration and a generation is too long. The indigenization of on-reserve policing is in clear danger of becoming entrenched in the minds of authorities on all sides, federal, provincial and even First Nations.... The goal of the young men and women who undertake the process of becoming First Nations Constables is to serve their people. In all my years as Chair of the First Nations Police commission that is what most impresses me. The courses these young people begin are designed specifically to prepare them for work on First Nations territories in actual contemporary conditions.... They know, too, they have options in policing careers. When they choose then to enter First Nations Constable programs, the huge majority of these young people want to combine the police training that they will receive with their knowledge of and commitment to their communities. They want to be more effective than the RCMP or the provincial policing presence they have experienced during the course of their lives. They want to be one of a complex of community resources that help our people heal. By peace making and peace keeping as key figures in restoring social harmony, they want to make a real difference.

This is a perfectly legitimate goal. It is the goal of all institutions which focus on ensuring social regulation and control for the purpose of social harmony, whatever the society. It was the goal of the first modern police forces in 19th century England, as much as our traditional warrior societies of the Plains – to use only one example – the peace keeping methods developed by our nations in North America. Enabling our young people to actually achieve that goal should be, equally, perfectly realistic.

However, they are doomed to frustration. It is not, as it turns out, realistic for them to expect to be able to make that kind of a contribution.... That is because they function still within another society's system. They have been indigenized.... The job of these recruits becomes subject to two separate authorities representing two different world views, not to mention differences in specific laws, relationships, goals and expectations. Has it not been said in times of old that no-one can serve two masters? Yet First Nations Constables must meet the expectations of the community while reporting to the local detachment. The present rigid hierarchical police system puts at risk Constables wanting to support a First Nations perspective on policing matters. There has been great progress in cross-cultural appreciation and understanding in many of these forces. However, in a rigid hierarchy, systems which do not complement it cannot be accommodated. First Nations Constables apply a model of peace keeping which precludes the integration of their position into the ways which are traditional to and still effective within the communities they are supposed to serve. Their policing system is adversarial. They have to charge and arrest. They have to isolate....

The focus of the policing model which our First Nations Constables are required to apply at this time is not that of peace keeping, the focus of our tradition, but rather of controlling crime. Police must search out acts that can be identified as criminal and the individuals who commit them. All parts of this process are fundamentally adversarial in nature. Specific arrest quotas may or may not be officially in place but the reward system is such that police persons excelling in these activities are reinforced, especially but not only through promotion. Furthermore, police funding agencies rely on crime and enforcement statistics. Rather than rewarding decreasing crime rates, police forces are cut back.

The crime control model has resulted in the peculiar phenomenon by which First Nations communities are both under- and over-policed. As statistics of Canadian society's definitions of social despair, we fill Canadian correctional institutions but should our communities call for help to keep peace and restore social harmony, it will take much longer, often years longer, to get the money for a Constable. Our complement in Ontario, for example, is hugely inadequate, a point which the commission, the Ontario Provincial Police and the Federal Government all understand.

....Meanwhile [First Nations constables] are perceived as being more or less junior or subsidiary forces limited to a narrow range of policing activity. They are not paid equally to their counterparts in the regular forces, without recognition of precisely the aspect of education that counts most in their work, language and community living knowledge. They are not appropriately trained in many respects, neither in the crime control model nor in the techniques of peace keeping and peace making that would be of utmost relevance to realizing their actual potential.[119]

In addition to submissions from representatives of Aboriginal police forces, we had the benefit of a commissioned study by Robert Depew, which throws some impor-

---

[119] Wally McKay, Ontario First Nations Police Commission, RCAP transcripts, Toronto, 4 June 1993.

tant historical light on why the indigenization approach to Aboriginal policing within the overall framework of a non-Aboriginal policing model has been problematic and has given rise to the kinds of concerns voiced by Wally McKay. Depew's study describes the history of police organization in Great Britain, its influence in shaping policy throughout the old British empire, and their important implications for models of Aboriginal policing applied in Canada. Referring to the work done by Philip Stenning, he contrasts the 'London Met' and the Royal Irish Constabulary models and the reason why the one rather than the other came to be applied in Canada.

> The first [model] generally historically known as the 'London Met', has provided an organizational charter for non-urban, small-scale municipal and regional policing in Canada. The key organizing principle of this model is the notion of 'local responsibility fulfilled through locally-controlled institutions.' Generally speaking, this has meant that in non-urban and small town settings the police have developed as an integral part of the community which they serve... The corresponding form of police organization has a number of distinctive features or characteristics: it usually has a simple, decentralized management and control structure and a reactive, discretionary and informal policing style which emphasizes order maintenance. Not surprisingly, these police departments continue to show low arrest and charge rates. In summary, the main orientation of the police under the 'London Met' model is that of peace keeping which, together with the reactive, responsive and informal operational style, reflects the organization and structure of the small scale communities of which they are a part and, to some extent, a product.[120]

This policing model has similarities to the principles of a peacekeeper force, described by Wally McKay as being the model that is more consistent with traditional Aboriginal approaches to maintaining order and social harmony. The London Met has not, however, been the operational model generally applied by federal, provincial or municipal police forces to policing Aboriginal communities. The model that has been applied finds its prototype in the Royal Irish Constabulary (RIC), and under this model the police are seen as part of 'crime control'. As described by Depew:

> In contrast to the ruralized 'London Met' model's more informal organization and operational style, the 'RIC' model is characterized, above all else, by a military-type organization, a formal

---

[120] Depew, "Aboriginal Policing", cited in note 47. The quotation here and those in the next few pages are from that commissioned study. See also Philip Stenning, "Police Governance in First Nations in Ontario", report prepared for the negotiators of the Ontario First Nations Policing Agreement (1992), pp. 19-34.

policing style of intervention and law enforcement and a central-ized management and control structure.... In line with the particular characteristics and principles of the 'RIC' model of polic-ing, the more general crime control model focuses on the detection of offences, apprehension of criminals and the laying of charges. The resultant policing style is frequently adversarial in its approach to intervention and investigation and is supported by a centralized para-military bureaucracy. The division of labour within the police force is specialized and distinguished by rank, order and hierar-chical authority. The performance of specialized police roles is based on rule-governed responsibilities and obedience to superi-ors in the police hierarchy.

The RIC model was inherited in various forms by federal and provincial police forces, including the RCMP, the Ontario Provincial Police (OPP) and the Sûreté du Québec (SQ). More important, it is this model rather than the more community-based London Met model that has generally been applied by federal and provincial police forces to policing Aboriginal people. As Depew points out, "Why this should be so, historically, is not difficult to comprehend considering the role of the RCMP and other colonially-administered police in the colonization, 'pacification' and administration of Aboriginal populations." Depew goes on to make the point that

the RIC model of policing does not, and for many Aboriginal com-munities manifestly cannot, change the structure of interaction between the police and the community. This is partly because it restricts police-community interaction and partly because the interaction it does foster is usually far too narrow or ambiguous to be effective or appropriate.

On the other hand, "the 'London Met' policing model would seem to have far more in common with the structural parameters and requisites of Aboriginal policing in so far as it is more a part and product of the nature of community organization and structure itself."

Aboriginal people have, however, been exposed mainly to the RIC concept and model, which underlies most RCMP, OPP and SQ Aboriginal policing programs. As Depew concludes,

It would appear then that conventional models of policing cur-rently available to Aboriginal peoples are far too limited structurally and psychologically to meet the variable and chang-ing policing needs of many diverse Aboriginal communities.

Depew's analysis reinforces what Wally McKay told us about the limited benefits likely to flow from indigenizing the policing function in the absence of structural changes in the organizational model under which a police force operates.

> Substituting Aboriginal police for non-Aboriginal police within existing police structures has little impact on policing problems, especially in small scale rural and remote Aboriginal communities.

There is a further important point of convergence between our commissioned research and what we heard at our public hearings. That point is the very direct relationship between the development of new approaches to Aboriginal policing and Aboriginal self-government. Depew referred to recent developments in the non-Aboriginal policing climate in the direction of community-based policing.

> As a concept and philosophy, community-based policing is an organizational and service delivery initiative that is designed to address and solve underlying community problems rather that rely exclusively on reactive responses to specific incidents or calls for service. Accordingly, it focuses on a number of key principles of organization and service delivery but involves a more broadly defined mandate that highlights a multi-purpose role oriented to pro-active policing and related community crime prevention strategies. This is intended to facilitate a partnership and inter-dependency with the community which rely on local mechanisms of responsibility and accountability for the police and policing.

Community-based policing – involving as it does a more holistic approach to policing in so far as the duties, responsibilities and activities of the police become part of and integrated with other public and social institutions – shares some of the features advanced by Aboriginal people in their peacekeeping concept. Depew draws the link between community-based policing and Aboriginal self-government in this way:

> The desire to participate in both the development and operation of policing institutions and services has been articulated by Aboriginal people in conferences, research reports and justice inquiries, both provincial and federal. At the root of this is the belief on the part of Aboriginal people that long-lasting solutions to policing programs are grounded in the people and the communities themselves. Obviously, Aboriginal self-government offers the greatest scope for community involvement in policing. This is not simply because it is the most promising – although not the only – avenue to change in existing arrangements, but because it promises a coherent and comprehensive foundation for community governmental structure, decision making and law making authority, all of which are prerequisites for the development, implementation and operation of truly autonomous Aboriginal police forces.

The overarching importance of Aboriginal self-government in the development of effective policing arrangements for Aboriginal nations and communities was urged upon us by Wally McKay in his presentation to the commission.

> To bring relevance to policing in First Nations communities necessarily implies legitimizing and restructuring the justice system as a whole within the revitalization of self-government, our inherent and never extinguished right, that is currently in progress....
> *Jurisdiction is the central crux of self-government.* The first essential and immediate priority is that we must have jurisdictional framework agreements in place and I would like to qualify that... we are not talking about delegated responsibilities. It is a federal responsibility, a provincial responsibility and a First Nations responsibility.[121]

The importance of recognizing the necessary link between Aboriginal self-government and Aboriginal policing is underlined when we consider the federal First Nations Policing Policy of 1991. Two of the objectives of the policy are "to support and encourage evolving self-government in First Nations communities" and "to ensure on-reserve police services are independent of the First Nation or Band governance authority, yet accountable to the communities they serve."[122]

In a report entitled "Justice for the Cree: Policing and Alternative Dispute Resolution", Jean-Paul Brodeur points out that these objectives are not only inherently contradictory but also reflect the narrow vision of self-government that non-Aboriginal governments apply in the policing context. Referring to the objective that on-reserve police services be independent of First Nations community or band governance authority, yet accountable to the communities they serve, Brodeur writes:

> Applied literally within the Canadian context, this principle is obviously absurd; it states that the police must be both independent of Parliament and accountable to the community. In other words, police should be accountable to the community, but not to its elected representative. The difficulty of applying this principle in a Canadian political context is again indicative of the narrow concept of Aboriginal self-government that underlies government literature. It is also indicative of something else. One can make sense of the principles stated above by interpreting it as meaning that politics should not interfere with policing.... Yet, if the federal and provincial governments were to make their support of autonomous Aboriginal policing conditional on inescapable guarantees that Aboriginal political authorities would never inter-

---

[121] Wally McKay, testimony cited in note 119 (emphasis added).

[122] "First Nations Policing Policy" (Ottawa: Supply and Services, 1992), p. 2.

fere with policing, they will be demanding what they have always failed to guarantee within Canadian society. If uncompromisingly made, such a request would only be a covert way of refusing to grant policing autonomy. One of the outstanding traits of colonialism is to ask of the colonized peoples virtues that were never practised by their colonizers.[123]

We would also point out with respect to these objectives that it has sometimes been difficult to achieve balance between police forces' accountability to elected politicians and their capacity to conduct day-to-day operations free from political interference in a *non*-Aboriginal context. Moreover, this goal may also be at odds with traditional Aboriginal practices in which community leadership is directly involved in the peacekeeping process. Ensuring fair and even-handed administration of justice is, of course, vital in demonstrating and maintaining the legitimacy of any justice system, and we therefore return to the issue later in the report. The point here is that to establish these kinds of pre-conditions as part of federal Indian policing policy can be subversive of the ultimate objective of providing conceptual and legal space for Aboriginal peoples to revitalize their own systems of justice, including peacekeeping.

Indigenization

Some programs developed to serve the needs of Aboriginal people involved with the justice system are based on the notion of indigenization. These programs attempt to make the current justice system – particularly but not exclusively the criminal justice system – more hospitable to Aboriginal people. These programs do not attempt to change substantively the way Aboriginal people are dealt with by the justice system. They do, however, attempt to lessen the feelings of alienation experienced during this interaction. Philosophically, these programs start from the premise that all people living in Canada should be subject to the same justice system, but that special measures may have to be taken to make that system understandable and comfortable to Aboriginal people who come to it from a different perspective.

In terms of government spending on Aboriginal justice programs, by far the bulk of expenditures has been in the area of indigenization. For example, of the $3,874,500 spent annually by the province of Ontario on Aboriginal justice programs and projects, almost 90 per cent goes to indigenization programs.[124] This

---

[123] Brodeur, *Policing and Alternative Dispute Resolution*, cited in note 53, p. 10.

[124] The combined annual budgets of the three alternative justice programs operating in the province – in Toronto, Sandy Lake and Attawapiskat – is $300,000. By contrast, the annual budget of the Native Justice of the Peace program is $900,000, and the province spends more than $1.4 million per year on Aboriginal court worker programs. (S. Jolly, *Information on Federal and Provincial Contributions to Aboriginal Justice Projects and Programs in Ontario* (Toronto: Ministry of the Attorney General, May 1994), p. 1.

figure is particularly significant, as Ontario spends more money than any other province on Aboriginal community justice projects.

One possible explanation for this development is that indigenization programs tend to lie within the exclusive domain of government and thus cannot be seen as presenting any sort of challenge to existing judicial and bureaucratic control over operation of the justice system. This does not mean, however, that these programs are weak or irrelevant.

Several indigenization programs have been undertaken in Canada. The three reviewed here are the appointment of Aboriginal justices of the peace and Aboriginal judges; the Aboriginal court worker program; and cross-cultural awareness programs.

Appointment of Aboriginal Justices of the Peace and Aboriginal Judges

One approach to making the current justice system more accommodating of Aboriginal people is to have Aboriginal faces present throughout the court process in roles other than that of accused persons. Seen in a broader framework, this type of initiative falls within the employment equity concept. In particular, the programs discussed here emphasize seeing that Aboriginal accused people have the opportunity to come before Aboriginal judges or justices of the peace. It is hoped that the presence of Aboriginal people on the bench, in what would otherwise be an alien environment, will put Aboriginal people appearing the court more at ease and make the point that what is being dispensed is not solely 'white man's justice'.

Aboriginal judges are appointed on the same basis as other judges and through the same channels. Their caseload is identical to that of other judges, and the number of Aboriginal persons they see depends primarily on the geographic location of their court and its level in the judicial hierarchy. At present there are at least 13 federally and provincially appointed Aboriginal judges.

In some provinces, Aboriginal justices of the peace (JPs) are appointed on the same basis as other JPs. Essentially they are JPs who happen to be Aboriginal. In other provinces and territories, however, special programs have been established to appoint Aboriginal JPs. In Ontario, for example, Aboriginal JPs are appointed where government statistics indicate that the number of Aboriginal people in the community warrants such appointments. There is a separate application process for Aboriginal JPs, and they face unique qualification and hiring processes.

In more remote communities, where courts are often held on a fly-in basis, the role of the JP is quite significant. In these cases, most people coming before the court will be Aboriginal. In urban settings, the Aboriginal JP will see only those Aboriginal people who move through her or his court.

One of the crucial roles of JPs is to hold bail hearings. As noted in the previous chapter, whether a person gets bail has a great bearing on the ultimate disposition of the case. In cases involving Aboriginal accused persons, particularly where the offence occurs in a predominately Aboriginal community, Aboriginal JPs may have greater sensitivity in striking a balance between the protection and safety of the community on one hand and, on the other, the right of the individual to avoid pre-trial detention unless clearly warranted. This sensitivity may best be exhibited in the creative use of bail conditions that take into account the contemporary realities of Aboriginal people and communities.

There have been few independent assessments of the strengths and weaknesses of Aboriginal JP programs or the appointment of Aboriginal judges. There is no question, however, that the appointment of Aboriginal people to positions of power and prestige in the justice system has engendered pride among Aboriginal people. At the same time, the limitations of these programs must be recognized. Given their philosophical starting point – that one justice system is adequate for all Canadians – there is a limit to the substantive changes that can be expected from such appointments.[125] There are also significant limits on the extent to which the justice system can be made subjectively amenable to Aboriginal people. Take, for example, the question of language.

Many Aboriginal languages have no words corresponding to 'guilt' or 'innocence'. This causes real problems for people attempting to provide interpretation services in the courts. Although one of the recommended skills required of Aboriginal JPs in Ontario is the ability to speak an Aboriginal language, this skill cannot be used where it might well do the most good – in the courtroom itself. The use of languages in court is governed by provincial or territorial legislation. In Ontario, as in much of the rest of the country, the only languages permitted in court are English and French.[126] Under the provisions of the *Criminal Code*, individuals who wish to speak in court in a language other than one of the country's two official languages must do so through an interpreter.[127] Thus even if the JP and the Aboriginal person before the court both speak Cree, for example, they are not permitted to speak to each other in court in that language.

---

[125] Don Auger, executive director of Nishnawbe-Aski Legal Services, pointed out the limitations of this aspect of indigenization when he told the Commission:

> ...the simple fact of the matter is that, when an Indian person comes to court and the judge is sitting in front of him, it doesn't matter whether it is a white face, a yellow face or a brown face; he is still in a black robe administering the same type of system that was there. So nothing has changed. All that has changed is that the players that are in it have a brown face. (RCAP transcripts, Thunder Bay, Ontario, 27 October 1992.)

[126] In civil matters, the language of the court is restricted to English in some provinces. In criminal matters, every accused has the right, everywhere in Canada, to have a trial conducted before a judge or a judge and jury in either French or English as prescribed in section 530 and 530.1 of the *Criminal Code*.

[127] These provisions are found in sections 530 and 530.1 of the *Criminal Code*.

In the Northwest Territories, the accused and his or her counsel can present writ-ten and oral pleadings in any of the six Aboriginal languages recognized by the territorial *Official Languages Act*, in addition to English and French. In general, the Northwest Territories has been innovative in terms of using justices of the peace to address the needs of Aboriginal communities. These initiatives have been part of an overall orientation to community-based justice.[128] Given that the communi-ties in the Territories are, for the most part, multi-racial, although with a significant Aboriginal component, the programs developed are not seen as exclusively Aboriginal programs. Currently more than 100 justices of the peace are active in the Territories, the majority of them being Aboriginal people.[129]

The *Justices of the Peace Act* sets out a community process for identifying potential justices of the peace. Those selected undergo training in a variety of areas. In particular, JPs are encouraged to reinforce dispute resolution practices in com-munities where they still operate, and to be receptive and flexible to alternative justice arrangements such as circle sentencing and elders councils. At the same time, JPs are reminded to remain aware of the realities of the power dynamics at play in small communities.[130]

The experience in the Northwest Territories indicates that a great deal that can be done within the current system to make it more responsive to the community in general and to Aboriginal people in particular. The lessons learned from the expe-rience in the Territories with justices of the peace, and with other aspects of their community justice initiatives, deserve wider recognition and attention through-out the country.

Aboriginal Court Workers

The Native Criminal Courtworker Program is a federal-provincial cost-shared pro-gram currently in operation in most provinces. The role of the court worker is to help Aboriginal accused persons understand their rights in the criminal justice process and to explain the process as it unfolds. Court workers also perform a wide variety of other roles, including helping accused persons find counsel; interpret-ing for counsel; assisting with preparations for bail hearings; writing pre-sentence reports; providing recommendations for probation orders; and a host of other services.

The importance of the role of court workers was emphasized to us in presentations from individuals and groups across the country. For example, Paul Turmel, exec-utive director of Aboriginal para-judicial services of Quebec (the Quebec court worker program) stated:

---

[128] Samuel Stevens, "Northwest Territories Community Justice of the Peace Program", in *Aboriginal Peoples and the Justice System*, cited in note 7, p. 386.

[129] Chief Judge R.W. Halifax, Territorial Court, letter to RCAP, 10 May 1995, p. 2.

[130] Chief Judge R. W. Halifax, letter, pp. 2-3.

> The operation of our program has meant that Aboriginal accused are better informed of their rights and responsibilities, and they have better access to legal services in the criminal justice system through the assistance provided by the court workers. It is therefore vitally important...that this program be maintained...[131]

There is a very real sense that without the presence of court workers, people might plead guilty to charges on which they might not have been found guilty (for example, if they had a valid legal defence) and that relevant sentencing options might not be presented to the court. A study undertaken by Obonsawin-Irwin Consulting on behalf of the Native Canadian Centre of Toronto in 1989 revealed that judges in that city felt that Aboriginal people were not as willing as other accused persons to avail themselves of possible defences. As one judge stated in the study,

> Unfortunately, Indians are the ideal accused in the courts. They are quick to accept blame for their offences and they accept their punishment very passively. In many ways they appear to be the victims of the system.[132]

There may be a number of explanations for this behaviour. For one thing, participation in the criminal justice system is a particularly alienating experience for Aboriginal people. As well, Aboriginal cultures emphasize the importance of a person taking responsibility for his or her actions. Thus even if a person charged with a particular offence has a valid legal defence, he or she may nevertheless plead guilty out of a wider, culturally based, sense of responsibility than is recognized in law. An example might be where evidence from a police search did not meet the standards set out in the *Canadian Charter of Rights and Freedoms*, where the individual is charged with an offence more serious than the one he or she has actually committed, or where the individual committed the act but acted without criminal intent. Unfortunately, the other aspects of Aboriginal culture that accompany the willingness to accept responsibility for one's actions are absent from the non-Aboriginal criminal justice system; thus, an individual may be imprisoned for an act that, while morally blameworthy, is not in law a criminal offence.

Whatever the reason for this phenomenon, the court worker plays an important role in seeing that Aboriginal accused persons understand the criminal justice system and are aware of their rights. Aboriginal court workers provide a friendly, familiar face and an explanation of the judicial process in terms that the accused person can understand. Court workers can also be a gateway to alternative justice programs. As they are in court regularly, court workers have the best opportunity to locate clients for diversion or other programs.

---

[131] Paul Turmel, RCAP transcripts, Wendake, Quebec, 18 November 1992 [translation].

[132] Obonsawin-Irwin Consulting Inc., *A Review of Justice Services to Native People in Metropolitan Toronto* (Toronto: 1989), p. 36.

Aboriginal court workers' associations have, over the past few years, developed an increasingly broader vision of their mandates. This is hardly surprising in light of the fact that the men and women who fulfil these important roles see first-hand, on a daily basis, the pain and distress of Aboriginal people caught up in the cycle of crime and imprisonment. They have also come face to face with the realization that the immediate client is at the centre of an ever-widening circle of cause and effect that began long before the client first appeared in court. Aboriginal women and children are most often those caught up in the cycle of violence. Extending even further, the underlying causes of this violence virtually ensure that patterns of violence will be passed on. It is for these reasons that some court workers' associations have identified as a priority the issues of sexual and domestic violence. The Native Court Worker and Counselling Association of British Columbia, in the introduction to a pamphlet addressed to victims of family and domestic violence, clearly signalled the reasons for giving this high priority.

> Often we hear Aboriginal politicians and others talk about self-government. Many people hope that self-government will occur soon. What many people fail to realize is that Aboriginal governments will only be as strong as the people who support them. As long as Aboriginal children go to bed at night crying because of violence in their homes, there can be no authentic self-government.

> Violence in the home is like a contagious disease. It moves from one victim to another spreading fear, distrust and pain. Children who grow up exposed to the disease of domestic violence may themselves later fall victim to it.

> The Native Court Worker and Counselling Association of British Columbia believes in the right of Aboriginal women and children to live their lives free from fear and free from violence.... We are ready to help stop the violence and begin the healing.[133]

The Native Court Worker and Counselling Association of B.C. is currently involved in a proposal to provide Aboriginal counsellors with extensive training in dealing with Aboriginal sex offenders, their victims and communities, an initiative intended to contribute to stopping the violence and beginning the healing. It shares many of the features of initiatives discussed at greater length in the next chapter.

While the role of the court worker may well change in Aboriginal nations and communities that develop their own distinct justice systems, the need for such individuals will likely remain. In addition, the experience that court workers have gained in the non-Aboriginal justice system gives them a unique and vital perspective on justice in general that will be of great benefit in the development of Aboriginal alternatives.

---

[133] Native Court Workers and Counselling Association of British Columbia, "A Safer Place", information pamphlet (1993), p. 3.

Cultural Awareness Training Programs

The third major initiative in the area of indigenization is the development of cultural awareness training programs. Unlike the appointment of Aboriginal JPs and judges or Aboriginal court worker programs, the focus of Aboriginal awareness training programs is the non-Aboriginal actors in the justice system. The idea behind this training is that if people working in the justice system are more familiar with Aboriginal cultural norms and values, Aboriginal people will find the judicial process less threatening and more accommodating of their concerns. As Gordon McGregor, chief of police for the Kitigan Zibi Anishnabeg Council, said of this type of training, "Although this may seem to be a band-aid solution to existing problems, it can be an immediate step in the right direction to changing the perception of Native justice issues by justice officials."[134]

The need for cultural awareness training grew out of a number of circumstances. Rupert Ross's articles and book, *Dancing With a Ghost*, illustrated the need for awareness of Aboriginal culture on the part of Crown attorneys and judges. Ross noted that his cultural biases when prosecuting Aboriginal people led to serious misperceptions about the veracity of witnesses. For example, for many of the Cree people of northern Ontario, it is a sign of disrespect to look a person in the eye. Ross noted that in the trial context, this reluctance to look directly at the Crown attorney during cross-examination is often interpreted by non-Aboriginal people as evidence of the witness's evasiveness and thus diminishes the person's credibility. As well, ignorance of Aboriginal cultural practices can lead to inappropriate and counter-productive strategies in attempts to resolve conflicts through the criminal justice system.[135]

Training to improve awareness of Aboriginal culture has become a regular part of training for many RCMP officers and municipal police forces as well. Police representatives appearing before us spoke about the importance of these courses in allowing police to understand better how to deal with Aboriginal people. This increased understanding has led not only to better police-community relations, but also to new co-operative ventures.[136]

Cross-cultural education has also been initiated in the federal correctional system and in some provincial correctional systems as well. With the advent of specific programming for Aboriginal inmates, correctional officers and staff needed to learn

---

[134] Gordon McGregor, RCAP transcripts, Maniwaki, Quebec, 2 December 1992.

[135] Rupert Ross, *Dancing With a Ghost* (Markham, Ontario: Octopus Publishing Group, 1992), p. 4.

[136] We heard about a number of Aboriginal justice projects that got their start as a result of cultural awareness training programs. Three such examples are the South Island Tribal Council justice program; the Aboriginal component of the Battlefords Adult Diversion Program in North Battleford, Saskatchewan; and the alternative sentencing and supervision programs in Fort St. John, British Columbia. See *Aboriginal Peoples and the Justice System*, cited in note 7, p. 425; David Arnot, RCAP transcripts, North Battleford, Saskatchewan, 29 October 1992; Sergeant Randy Munroe, RCAP transcripts, Fort St. John, British Columbia, 20 November 1992.

about Aboriginal culture. As part of these programs (described in more detail later in this chapter), Aboriginal elders visit inmates in institutions in their capacity as teachers, counsellors and spiritual advisers, bringing with them medicine bags, bundles and other spiritual items necessary for their work. On occasion, these items have been subjected to intrusive and insensitive searches, showing the need for staff to learn more about Aboriginal culture in order to understand how to treat visiting elders and the importance of Aboriginal-specific programs in general. These types of incidents continue to occur today; a number of cases were described to us, and those raising the issue felt that more Aboriginal cultural awareness training for correctional staff was required.

Such training is not a panacea, however. As with the other programs discussed in this chapter, it proceeds from the basis that the current system is appropriate for everyone but that a bit more work is required to make the system function properly for Aboriginal people. Aboriginal cultural awareness training nevertheless has the potential to open the eyes of non-Aboriginal people to even more innovative and dramatic change in the system.

At the commission's round table on justice, a cautionary note regarding cultural awareness training was sounded by Carol Montagnes, executive director of the Ontario Native Council on Justice, an organization that has done a great deal of this type of training, particularly with correctional staff. In light of the council's experience, she felt she had to ask whether this approach leads to genuine change or, in her words, "Are we just creating culturally aware racists?"[137]

Indian Act Provisions

The *Indian Act*, the law under which the lives of status Indians living on-reserve have been controlled since 1876, contains provisions that have allowed First Nations to begin to exercise significant control over some aspects of the justice system.[138] Sections 81 and 83 of the act give bands a wide range of by-law making powers, while section 107 allows for justices of the peace to hear cases on reserve lands. Neither of these provisions was envisaged initially as an engine of self-government or self-determination, but the creativity of First Nations in British Columbia, Quebec and Ontario has seen the act put to such uses.

By-Law Making Powers Under Sections 81 and 83

Under sections 81 and 83, bands can enact by-laws dealing with the health of residents, 81(a); traffic, 81(b); the observation of law and order, 81(c); fish and game management, 81(o); the licensing of businesses, 83(1)(a)(ii); and the raising of money from band members to support band projects, 83(1)(f), among other sub-

---

[137] *Aboriginal Peoples and the Justice System*, cited in note 7, p. 427.

[138] S.C. 1876 (39 Victoria), chapter 18, section 70.

jects. A significant restriction on these powers is that their exercise requires the approval of the minister of Indian affairs.

The Spallumcheen First Nation of British Columbia used these by-law making powers to enact a comprehensive child welfare by-law in 1980. The by-law, entitled A By-Law for the Care of our Indian Children, gave the Spallumcheen exclusive jurisdiction over child welfare matters involving members of the band both on- and off-reserve. The by-law does not merely give the Spallumcheen band the powers of a local children's aid society; rather it proposes a distinctly Aboriginal way to address child welfare matters. The by-law is an example of how traditional Aboriginal concepts of the family can be merged with modern child welfare concerns. The by-law recognizes the child as an equal member of the band whose wishes must be taken into account in any decision. As well, the by-law dispenses with narrow notions of standing by allowing any member of the band to ask for a reconsideration of a decision made under the by-law.[139] Ultimately, a party dissatisfied with decisions made under the by-law can request a general band meeting to resolve the matter. This option has not been taken up since the program began operation.[140]

When first presented with the by-law, the minister of Indian affairs, apparently acting on legal advice, disallowed it. After extensive lobbying, however, he changed his mind.[141] As the by-law dealt with child welfare concerns, which constitutionally are a matter of provincial jurisdiction, another round of lobbying and political action was required at the provincial level before the by-law could come into force.[142]

Although the by-law envisages broad responsibilities being exercised, the strictures of sections 81 and 83 have prevented the by-law from having as much of an effect as was hoped. Given that the by-law draws its authority from the *Indian Act*, it has power only over Spallumcheen living on-reserve. Thus, despite the intentions of the by-law, it cannot be applied off-reserve. On the other hand, where band members off-reserve would rather use the services of the Spallumcheen program than that of the local child welfare system, the by-law gives the band the authority to intervene. As well, where foster parents live off-reserve, the by-law allows for

---

[139] J. MacDonald, "Child Welfare and the Native Indian Peoples of Canada", *Windsor Yearbook of Access to Justice* 5 (1985), pp. 294-295. Some of the implications of this by-law are discussed in greater detail later in this chapter.

[140] Monique Godin-Beers and Cinderina Williams, "Report of the Spallumcheen Child Welfare Program", research study prepared for RCAP (1994).

[141] J. MacDonald, "Child Welfare", cited in note 139, p. 293. The minister at the time, John Munro, did not disallow the by-law when it was put before him a second time, nor did he accept it or approve it. Spallumcheen First Nation, *Spallumcheen Family Services Policy Manual* (1994), p. 2.

[142] The lobbying consisted of, among other things, having 1,000 supporters of the by-law demonstrate outside the home of the human resources minister on Thanksgiving. MacDonald, "Child Welfare", cited in note 139, p. 294.

staff to undertake home visits.[143] Legal opinions prepared for the band indicate that the by-law cannot apply to children who are not members of the Spallumcheen First Nation but who are living on-reserve, even if the children are members of other First Nations.[144]

Ultimately, despite the creativity displayed by the Spallumcheen First Nation, it is hard to see the by-law powers of the *Indian Act* playing any major role in the development of Aboriginal justice systems. As noted, by-laws apply only to the reserve itself; where reserve lands are small, this can present a real problem.[145] As well, only status Indians living on-reserve can make use of the by-law provisions. The most important problem with the by-law making powers, however, is that all but a few relatively insignificant by-laws are subject to the approval of the minister of Indian affairs. The minister has total discretion in this regard, and there are no guidelines on when consent may or may not be given. Clearly, Aboriginal self-determination in the justice field cannot become a reality where any attempted exercise of the right must first be approved by the federal government and where no guidelines exist to structure the exercise of the minister's discretion.

Section 107 Courts

Section 107 of the *Indian Act* provides for the appointment of special justices of the peace with jurisdiction over matters arising on the reserve.[146] The creation of the post of special justices of the peace for reserves pre-dates Confederation and did not spring from the government's concern to maintain the distinctiveness of Aboriginal societies in communities within a pluralistic Canada. Historically, those appointed to this position were Indian agents – government appointees whose job it was to see that matters ran smoothly once Aboriginal people were located on reserves. In this way the special justices of the peace were intended to act as yet

---

[143] Funding constraints on the program mean that home visits to foster parents in Vancouver and Winnipeg are difficult to do on a regular basis. The program hopes to have liaison staff in these two cities to perform this role in the near future. Godin-Beers and Williams, "Report of the Spallumcheen Child Welfare Program", cited in note 140, 433.

[144] D. James, "Legal Structures for Organizing Indian Child Welfare Resources", *Canadian Native Law Reporter* 2 (1987), p. 11.

[145] *Locking Up Natives in Canada*, cited in note 37, p. 245.

[146] R.S.C. 1985, chapter I-5. The section reads as follows:

> 107. The Governor in Council may appoint persons to be, for the purposes of this Act, justices of the peace and those persons have the powers and authority of two justices of the peace with regard to
>
> (a) any offence under this Act; and
>
> (b) any offence under the *Criminal Code* relating to the cruelty to animals, commons assault, breaking and entering and vagrancy, where the offence is committed by an Indian or relates to the person or property of an Indian.

another engine of assimilation; it was never intended that these roles would be filled by Aboriginal people appointed by the bands themselves.[147]

The most extensive use of section 107 courts has been by the Mohawk communities at Kahnawake and Akwesasne. In Kahnawake the section 107 court hears all types of traffic cases as well as many criminal offences punishable on summary conviction. The court has also dealt with hybrid offences under the *Criminal Code*, hearing them as summary conviction cases. Owing to the wording of some provisions of section 107, the court also has jurisdiction to hear break and enter cases – cases classed as indictable in the *Criminal Code*. Approximately 90 per cent of the traffic offences are committed by non-Aboriginal people driving through the reserve, while approximately 90 per cent of the *Criminal Code* offences are committed by Aboriginal people living on the reserve.[148] The operation of the court is aided by the fact that policing functions on the reserve are maintained by the reserve's own force – the Peacekeepers, although this has not been without its difficulties.[149]

In their current incarnation section 107 courts have been operating in Kahnawake since 1974. In that time they have established themselves as a vital part of the community. Expansion of the program is limited in two ways, however. First, the federal government has put the further development of these programs on hold and has made no new appointments of section 107 justices of the peace. Thus, although the Court of Kahnawake has requested the federal government to make two additional appointments, none has been made.[150] Second, even if the government were receptive to these requests, the restrictive nature of the *Indian Act* minimizes the extent to which these courts can deal with the range of legal issues facing Aboriginal society. In addition, recognition of the jurisdiction of section 107 courts is often problematic. We heard during our public consultations that outside police forces and lawyers have not always respected the decisions of these courts.

The Aboriginal Justice Inquiry of Manitoba discussed the possibility of using section 107 courts as the basis for new Aboriginal justice initiatives. They wrote:

> The section 107 court remains in the...[*Indian Act*] as a vestige of the ignominious past of federal colonization and domination of reserve life. It has been seized upon by...First Nations who wish to assert

---

[147] *Locking Up Natives in Canada*, cited in note 37, pp. 242-243. We return to this issue in our final report.

[148] Winona Diabo and Joyce King Mitchell, "Court of Kahnawake", *Aboriginal Peoples and the Justice System*, cited in note 7, p. 404.

[149] See *Guy Favreau* v. *Cour de Kahnawake* (1993), R.J.Q. 1450. Steinberg J. of the Quebec Superior Court, sitting in appeal, held that the appellants had reasonable grounds to refuse to enter the Kahnawake reserve to attend court and ordered a new trial before a court of the province of Quebec. The appellants had invoked sections 7 and 24(1) of the *Canadian Charter of Rights and Freedoms* because, in their view, they were not given free and secure access to the territory where the court was situated. This decision was confirmed by the Quebec Court of Appeal on 30 August 1995 (see (1995), R.J.Q. 2348). Note that the *jurisdiction* of the Court of Kahnawake was not at issue.

[150] Diabo and Mitchell, "Court of Kahnawake", cited in note 148, p. 403.

some level of control over the local justice system. The restrictions that exist in the Act are such that it offers little promise for the long-term future and is unlikely to satisfy current demands from First Nations to establish their own justice system. At most, it offers a short-term interim measure and an indication that a separate court system can function readily in Indian reserves without causing grave concerns within the rest of society or the legal community.[151]

Diversion Programs and Related Initiatives

Diversion programs are best understood as alternatives to the judicial process. In general, a person must accept responsibility for the offence with which he or she is charged before having access to the program. Diversion programs do not determine guilt or innocence. In some jurisdictions in Canada matters are diverted before a charge is laid; in others, diversion occurs after the charge but before a plea is entered. Where a matter is diverted from the courts, the offender has no criminal record for the particular offence, since the court has made no finding of guilt.

Adult diversion programs exist in several provinces for a variety of criminal offences. These programs are usually available to first offenders charged with what can best be categorized as minor criminal offences – theft under $5,000 (shoplifting), transportation fraud (not paying for a taxi), and similar non-violent offences. Assaults are rarely diverted; nor are cases where the accused is likely to receive a jail sentence if convicted of the offence. Those accepted into diversion programs generally are required to write letters of apology, make restitution, or attend some type of class. The specific action required of the offender is usually determined by the Crown attorney.

Aboriginal diversion programs move beyond this model in two ways. First, these programs generally take in a wider range of offences than do non-Aboriginal diversion programs. Thus the programs are available to offenders who might have received jail sentences if the case had proceeded through the court system. The second distinction is that these programs have culturally appropriate deliberative bodies to determine what actions the offender is required to take. Since these programs operate outside the court system, there is no role for a judge in the process. Although the programs have a great deal of freedom once a matter comes into their hands, they continue to operate within the non-Aboriginal justice system.

The decision to have a case diverted to an Aboriginal program is ultimately the responsibility of a Crown attorney. Thus diversion is not seen as a right of Aboriginal peoples, but as an exercise of prosecutorial discretion in favour of Aboriginal-specific programs. As with the sentencing projects described in the next section, the fact that these programs exist at all is a tribute to the hard work of Aboriginal communities and the willingness of Crown attorneys, police and provincial and federal justice officials to look for alternatives to the current system.

---

[151] AJI, cited in note 2, volume 1, p. 309.

Aboriginal diversion programs have been operated at different times in a number of provinces and territories across the country, including Nova Scotia (at Shubenacadie), Ontario (in Toronto and Attawapiskat), Saskatchewan (at Onion Lake), British Columbia (South Vancouver Island Justice Project and the Gitksan and Wet'suwet'en Unlocking Aboriginal Justice Project), and the Yukon (the Kwanlin Dun Justice Project in Whitehorse). Most of the Aboriginal diversion programs are operated on a reserve basis, the principal exception being the community council of Aboriginal Legal Services of Toronto, discussed in greater detail later in this chapter. Despite their relatively small geographic base (Toronto excepted), some programs have cast a wider net and take in members of First Nations communities who come into conflict with the law outside reserves. Thus the program operating on the Shubenacadie reserve in Nova Scotia can divert cases involving members of the reserve arrested anywhere in the province.[152] Since the decisions of these programs are beyond the scrutiny of the courts, they can develop under the control of the community itself.

In some diversion programs, the Crown adjourns the case for disposition by the Aboriginal body and agrees to withdraw the matter only after being satisfied that the individual has met the conditions imposed by the body. Failure to abide by the decision of the deliberative body or, theoretically, a perception by the Crown that the actions required by the body are insufficient, can lead to the charges being proceeded with.[153] In the community council program in Toronto, charges against the individual are generally withdrawn rather than adjourned once it has been decided that the matter will be diverted. The question of what to do with those who do not comply with the council decision is up to the council itself.

The significance of Aboriginal diversion projects that use traditional processes in coming to grips with seemingly intractable problems that have thus far resisted the corrective action of the non-Aboriginal justice system is reflected in an example drawn from the South Island Tribal Council justice initiative on Vancouver Island. It is described by Mary Ellen Turpel, who visited various justice projects across the country in the summer of 1993.

> The one individual I spoke with at length was a 28 year old man who had left the reserve when he was about 10 with his mother... They had moved to an urban centre where he was raised on skid row... and he became an alcoholic at a very early age.

> He had been before the courts repeatedly for assaults, always stemming from his drinking. His violence was directed at everyone around him: police, friends, family... This young man, his wife, indeed his entire family, was out of control. He had profound prob-

---

[152] Such a diversion has not yet occurred, but the protocol documents establishing the project acknowledge explicitly that such an event can take place.

[153] We are not aware of a case where a Crown attorney has insisted on proceeding with a charge after the individual has successfully completed the terms of a diversion.

lems in his life, which were escalating with each offence... The court had ordered him to anger management classes. Social workers were involved. He had no success in changing his behaviour. The Canadian criminal justice system did not reach this young man.

[His case was then diverted to the South Island initiative.] The young man had been working with the elders for over a year when I met him. He was a man who had obviously changed quite fundamentally in his behaviour. The elders, particularly the elders from his clan, took time to explain his place in his community, his family and clan.

They told him, "You have been in an urban centre, you have been away. Welcome home. Here is your family, let's go, we are going to introduce you to everybody in your family." He was introduced to everybody in his family again. He was integrated into the community. The elders spent every single day for four months meeting with him, and they still meet with him on a weekly basis. They involved non-Aboriginal social workers in part of his healing because they believed they did not have all the answers, and they saw that neither did the social workers.

The elder that was working with this young man had himself been an alcoholic for fifteen years in his youth. He had been out of control and had moved to an urban centre to drink... This elder knew what the young man was going through. He did not have to preach to him, to shame him or punish him. He told him his own story and explained to him in the way elders do, how he had to assume his responsibilities for himself and his family.

Through their compassion, teaching and family reintegration, the elders have assisted this young man to gain control of his life for the first time... I asked him what he learned from his experiences in the Canadian justice system. He said he just wanted to get out of jail and drink again. It was nothing more. I asked him what he saw for the future. He said he wanted to raise his children right. I listened very carefully to this story because what was happening with this man's life was nothing short of a miracle. He had changed because the elders running the justice project were committed to healthy families and rebuilding their community.[154]

---

[154]Turpel, "Reflections on Thinking Concretely", cited in note 91, pp. 217-219. See also the discussion of the South Island Tribal Council initiative in *Aboriginal Peoples and the Justice System*, cited in note 7, pp. 390, 393-394, 425-427. As we will see, however, this initiative had to be suspended after encountering serious problems (see text accompanying note 159).

One of the first, if not the first, Aboriginal adult criminal diversion programs was located in Attawapiskat – a Cree community on the western shore of Hudson Bay. The diversion program was developed in response to a request from the community to the Ontario ministry of the attorney general for more control over justice issues.[155] The project, funded by the attorney general, saw the appointment of a panel of elders to hear cases involving residents of the reserve that had been diverted from the non-Aboriginal court system.

When it was active, the Elders Court sat monthly to hear cases. Since the court held its hearings after matters were diverted from the non-Aboriginal justice system, proceedings could be carried out totally in Cree. Sittings of the court attracted many community members. Ralph Carr, a Timmins lawyer with experience in remote northern Ontario courts, had an opportunity to visit the Attawapiskat Elders Court and reported the following to the Ontario Legal Aid Plan:

> As you are aware, I have attended in the Northern Courts as Duty Counsel for the past six or seven years and as such am well acquainted with the various Courts in the Northern communities. I have seen on many occasions the veiled and often open contempt with which the natives hold the judicial system which is obviously viewed by many as a continuing aspect of white supremacy and dominance. This lack of respect for the Court is quite apparent from the demeanour of witnesses, onlookers and Defendants in many of the cases.
>
> However, during the Elders Court, it became quite apparent to me that the Elders took their job very seriously. They conducted the Court in a manner that was totally unique and foreign to my experience as an Ontario lawyer. They did not ask for example the Defendants how they pleaded but simply asked them as to whether or not they did what was alleged. This direct confrontation elicited from most what I perceive to be an honest answer (in all the cases that I observed the answer was in the affirmative) and the Elders proceeded to lecture the accused as to how they had embarrassed the community at large, their families in particular and themselves, i.e., the Defendants, even more specifically. The accused obviously held the Elders in respect and certainly displayed shame and remorse that I had not observed in my other experiences in the Courts in the North generally and this one in particular.[156]

---

[155] D. W. Fletcher, *Attawapiskat Justice System – A Diversion Court Method – Prepared for the People of Attawapiskat* (March 1989).

[156] Letter from Ralph Carr, Barrister and Solicitor, to the Ontario Legal Aid Plan, Office of the Area Director, Timmins, 13 February 1991, p. 3.

According to an independent evaluation of the program, on the days when it was sitting, the Elders Court heard approximately 20 cases per day. Almost 70 per cent of the cases heard dealt with violations of band by-laws against the use of intoxicants on the reserve. Cases involving mischief to property or break and enter made up 16 per cent of cases. The most common disposition of an offence coming before the court was the imposition of a fine. Fines alone were relied upon in 45 per cent of the cases, and fines in conjunction with a form of probation were relied upon in an additional 23 per cent of cases. At the beginning of the program a relatively serious assault charge was diverted, but neither the elders nor the community felt particularly comfortable dealing with the matter, so such cases were no longer diverted.[157]

The independent evaluation of the program noted that co-operation was not forthcoming from the local police on the reserve. This reluctance to participate harmed the image of the program and raised questions among community members about its legitimacy.[158] The Elders Court is not hearing cases formally at present, although it continues to be involved in dispute resolution activities. Community members are currently discussing how they would like to see the program re-established.

We will return to the question of community consultation and involvement in the development of diversion and similar projects later in the report. At this point it is sufficient to note that without adequate time for extensive consultation, diversion and related projects will lack the community support necessary to allow them to work. The effects of insufficient consultation are felt particularly when a controversial issue comes to the fore.

A graphic example of this phenomenon occurred when the South Island Tribal Council initiative, referred to earlier, was suspended because of concerns on the part of women within and outside the community that inappropriate cases were being diverted and that victims' consent to diversion was not being properly obtained. A review of the South Island project, completed in the wake of such an occurrence, concluded that Aboriginal justice initiatives should be preceded, at both the development and the implementation stage, by extensive community consultation involving all members of the community, including victims, offenders, advocacy groups and service providers.[159] As the South Vancouver initiative demonstrates, without extensive prior consultation, programs can easily founder. Specific issues related to ensuring the safety of women in Aboriginal justice systems are discussed in the next chapter.

---

[157] Obonsawin-Irwin Consulting Inc., *An Evaluation of the Attawapiskat First Nation Justice Pilot Project* (Toronto: Ministry of the Attorney General, June 1992), pp. 11-12, 14, 47.

[158] Obonsawin-Irwin, *An Evaluation*, p. 52.

[159] Sheila Clark & Associates, *Building the Bridge, A Review of the South Vancouver Island Justice Education Project* (Vancouver: February 1995).

As diversion projects become more sophisticated and gain more expertise, it is to be expected that obtaining consent from Crown attorneys will become more and more routine, and the programs can be expected to take on a greater number and range of cases. As useful as they are in their own right, diversion and related initiatives are best seen as evolutionary steps toward the development of distinct Aboriginal justice systems.

Elders Panels and Sentencing Circles[160]

Over the past five years much progress has been made in opening up the sentencing of Aboriginal people to greater Aboriginal input. This advance has come about through the initiative of Aboriginal communities and the support of judges concerned about the problems the justice system causes for Aboriginal people. The development of these initiatives sprang originally from the Yukon and Northwest Territories.

The small size and remoteness of many northern Aboriginal settlements mean that it is literally often months before a judge or a justice of the peace arrives to deal with outstanding criminal offences. When court officials arrive in these settlements they generally fly in, hear cases for a day or two, and then fly out again. Accompanying the judge or JP are a Crown attorney, defence counsel and other relevant parties.[161] The idea behind fly-in (or in some cases drive-in) courts was to deliver justice to remote communities. Despite the best intentions of all those involved, however, the notion that a judge, Crown, and defence counsel – none of whom live anywhere near the settlements they are visiting, none of whom have more than a passing knowledge or acquaintance with it, and none of whom, in most cases, are Aboriginal or speak the local language[162] – can provide any sort of real justice strains all notions of common sense.[163]

What makes the task facing the court even more difficult is that the offence will likely have occurred months earlier. Given the proximity of the parties to each other

---

[160] In this report we refer on occasion to the role of elders. The term elder should not be considered synonymous with 'an older person'. Rather, elders are people who set an example by living their lives in a good way and who have wisdom that they share with other members of the community. These ideas will be elaborated on in our final report, in a chapter devoted to the role of elders.

[161] Concerns about the appearance of fairness have now started to change the practice of having the judge, the Crown attorney and the defence counsel all arrive on the same airplane. While all parties may still arrive and leave at the same time, they now try to use more than one plane.

[162] Even if all parties did speak that language, however, this would not necessarily help those coming before the court. As noted earlier in our discussion of Aboriginal JPs, legislation at the provincial and territorial level often restricts the languages that can be spoken in Canadian courts without the mediating influence of an interpreter to English and French.

[163] Rupert Ross, *Dancing With a Ghost*, cited in note 135, provides several examples of how the losers in culture clashes between Aboriginal and non-Aboriginal societies in the context of the non-Aboriginal justice system are, almost inevitably, the Aboriginal accused person and his or her community.

and the need to find a way of co-existing pending the arrival of the court, the community often manages to find a mutually satisfactory way of dealing with lesser criminal matters before they are dealt with formally by the justice system. In some cases, not only has a solution been worked out, but the offending party may have done all the community feels is required before the court sits to consider the case.

Faced with these realities, Judges Heino Lilles and Barry Stuart in the Yukon looked to the communities themselves for alternative ways of dispensing justice. Discussions with community leaders and elders led to a decision to return, in a fashion, to the way justice was done before the arrival of the non-Aboriginal legal system. The return to more traditional approaches led to an opening up of the sentencing process to greater community input.[164] The precise manner in which each community would provide this input was chosen by the community.

Generally speaking, these initiatives have come in two forms – elders panels and sentencing circles.[165] In the case of elders panels, elders or clan leaders sit with the judge and provide advice about the appropriate sentence in a case. This advice may be given in open court or in private. In a sentencing circle, individuals are invited to sit in a circle with the accused and discuss together what sentence should be imposed. In both cases, the ultimate decision about the sentence rests with the judge.

Regardless of the precise mechanism established, the purpose behind the process is the same – to give the court meaningful input from the people who know and understand the offender and who are most directly affected by his or her conduct. The experience of these programs is that the offender responds more deeply to concerns and suggestions expressed by members of the community than by a judge who is removed in all ways from the offender's world.[166]

The notion of obtaining community input to the sentencing process has spread from the far North to other areas as well. Similar initiatives are in place in Ontario, British Columbia, Quebec, Manitoba and Saskatchewan. Many people appearing before us indicated that they felt that greater community input in sentencing decisions involving Aboriginal offenders is needed.

---

[164] The Yukon program, in its many facets, is described by Judge Lilles in "Tribal Justice: A New Beginning", a paper delivered to a conference entitled Achieving Justice: Today and Tomorrow, Whitehorse, Yukon, 3-7 September 1991, and by Judge Barry Stuart, "Alternative Dispute Resolution in Action in Canada: Community Justice Circles", a paper presented at a National Symposium on Restorative Justice, Aylmer, Quebec, 5-7 February 1995. The Quebec experience in the development of sentencing circles is described in P. Allard, "Le cercle de consultation", *National* 3/7 (October 1994), p. 32 (a Canadian Bar Association publication).

[165] These distinctions are not rigid, and initiatives have taken on aspects of both approaches.

[166] While observing that recidivism among offenders who have been through the circle sentencing process is lower and generally involves less serious crimes and less frequent criminal activity, Judge Stuart has also pointed out, based on his experience in the Yukon, that the success of any circle or community-based initiative should not be measured solely in terms of what happens to the offender:

The question of what criteria are appropriate for holding sentencing circles has been discussed in a number of court decisions. In *R. v. Alaku*,[167] Judge Jean-L. Dutil of the Court of Quebec examined the decisions of the Saskatchewan Court of Queen's Bench in *R. v. Cheekinew*,[168] the Yukon Territorial Court in *R. v. Moses*,[169] and an earlier Court of Quebec case, *R. v. Naappaluk*.[170] After a review of the cases Judge Dutil stated:

> When deciding whether to hold a circle, the court could consider two criteria, which, in our opinion, are absolutely essential. It is not easy to imagine a consultation circle being held unless these two conditions are met.
>
> Criterion I
> The accused must have the firm and clear intention to rehabilitate himself and become a good citizen; this is, without a doubt, the absolutely essential condition or the first criterion to be met to hold a circle. ...
>
> Criterion II
> Another criterion or essential condition which must be considered is the desire of the community to become involved for the sake of one its members.[171]

The impact of community-based initiatives upon victims, upon restoring relationships injured by crime, upon fostering harmony within the community, upon the self-esteem of others working in the Circle, on strengthening families, on building connections within the community, on establishing, communicating, and enforcing community values, or mobilizing community action to reduce factors causing crime, to prevent crime – and ultimately to make the community safer – are perhaps not readily visible results of community processes, but in the long run they are significantly more important than the immediate impact on offenders. (Judge Barry Stuart, "Circles into Squares: Can Community Processes be Partnered with the Formal Justice System?" (draft paper, 1 May 1995), p. 1.)

[167] *R. v. Alaku* 112 D.L.R. (4th) 732 (1994) (Court of Quebec).

[168] *R. v. Cheekinew*, 80 C.C.C. (3d) 148 (Saskatchewan Court of Queen's Bench).

[169] *R. v. Moses* 71 C.C.C. (3d) 347 (1992) (Yukon Territorial Court).

[170] *R. v. Naappaluk* 25 C.R. (4th) 220 (1993) (Court of Quebec).

[171] *R. v. Alaku*, cited in note 167, pp. 734-735 [translation]. Judge Dutil went on to list six factors that should come into play after the initial criteria were met in order to determine finally whether a circle is appropriate: (1) the nature of the crime; (2) the degree to which the community was affected by the crime; (3) whether the accused pleaded guilty or was found guilty following a trial; (4) where there was an identifiable victim of the crime, whether that victim should participate in the circle; (5) the role to be assumed by the community; and (6) whether the circle would be held in a small community, a town or a city (pp. 736-740).

The highest court in the country to address this issue is Saskatchewan Court of Appeal in the case of *R. v. Morin.*[172] It concluded that judges should not agree to a sentencing circle's recommendation for a reduction of a sentence where the accused shows little remorse or demonstrates little chance for rehabilitation. In a 3-2 decision, this court overturned the sentence imposed by Judge Milliken of the Saskatchewan Court of Queen's Bench following the deliberations of a sentencing circle held in Saskatoon to deal with the case of a Métis man charged with robbery and assault. The request for the circle came from the accused but was supported from the outset by members of the Saskatoon Métis community. The sentencing circle recommended a period of incarceration of approximately twelve months and a follow-up treatment program. Judge Milliken followed the circle's recommendations and noted that without the benefit of the circle's advice, he would have imposed a longer custodial sentence.[173]

The appeal did not call into question the legitimacy of sentencing circles. The Crown noted in its factum that more than 100 circles had been held in Saskatchewan and that it had appealed the decisions of judges in these cases on only two occasions.[174] The Crown did ask, however, for the court to provide some principles or criteria for judges to follow when they considered the appropriateness of holding circles. While the majority cited with approval the criteria for holding circles set out by the trial judges in *Cheekinew* and *R. v. Joseyounen,*[175] they stated:

> ...given the wide latitude accorded to judges as to the sources and types of evidence and information upon which to base their sentencing decisions, it is doubtful that this Court should attempt to lay down guidelines in respect of a decision whether or not a sentencing circle should be used in a given case.[176]

---

[172] *R. v. Morin* (1995), 101 C.C.C. (3d) 124, appeal from *R. v. Morin* (1994), 114 Sask. R. 2 (Saskatchewan Court of Queen's Bench).

[173] *R. v. Morin*, Judgement of Sherstobitoff J.A., p. 134, speaking for the majority.

[174] *R. v. Morin*, Judgement of Sherstobitoff J.A., p. 130. Since this case was argued, the Crown has launched another appeal in the case of *R. v. Taylor* (unreported judgement of Judge Milliken, June 9, 1995, Q.B.C. No. 112). In this case, the court accepted a sentencing circle's recommendations in Lac LaRonge to banish a man convicted of sexual assault for one year, followed by a three-year period of probation on specific terms.

[175] *R. v. Joseyounen*, [1995] 6 W.W.R. 438 (Saskatchewan Court of Queen's Bench).

[176] *R. v. Morin*, cited in note 172, Judgement of Sherstobitoff J.A., p. 134. Writing for the minority, Bayda C.J.S. set out two mandatory criteria for the holding of a sentencing circle: the willingness of the offender and the existence and willingness of a community. Chief Justice Bayda went on to state that, after reviewing all the relevant criteria, the judge must then answer the question, "Is a fit sentence for *this* accused who has committed *this* offence better arrived at by using the restorative [justice] approach or the ordinary [justice] approach?" *R. v. Morin*, Judgement of Bayda C.J.S., pp. 157-159 (emphasis in original).

The court did say that it would be futile, in their opinion, to use circles in cases where the custodial aspect of the sentencing circle's recommendation was two years or more. Such cases would not be suitable for circles because under the *Criminal Code*, a sentence of two years or longer, which must be served in a federal penitentiary, cannot be accompanied by conditions following completion of the sentence. Thus, no probation or follow-up treatment orders can be part of the sentence imposed.[177]

The main reason given by the majority for overturning the decision of the circle was that in this particular case – given the circumstances of the offence, the prior record of the offender, and an assessment of the offender's true interest in changing his life[178] – it was not appropriate to depart from the usual range of sentencing for such an offence.[179] The court did make it clear, however, that in suitable cases, the existence of sentencing guidelines for particular offences should not preclude a sentencing circle from recommending an alternative that included less time in jail.[180]

As the use of sentencing circles and elders panels becomes more common and more experience is gained on their operation, we can expect that the criteria seen as prerequisites for holding circles will evolve. Indeed, the use of such innovations in the Yukon over the past few years has led to just such changes.

For example, Judge Lilles called upon an elders panel for advice in a case involving a non-Aboriginal offender living in a predominately Aboriginal community. The judge felt that as the offence occurred in the community, the community should be heard on the question of an appropriate sentence. The particular racial or ethnic origin of the offender was not a determining factor for him. The offender in this case did not like the idea of an elders panel and voiced his concern and displeasure.[181] The matter was not appealed, however.

There is no doubt that sentencing circles and elders panels perform a useful but limited role. They provide a good example of how the current system can be made significantly more responsive to Aboriginal concerns without a radical restructuring of the process. It must be noted, however, that determinations of guilt and innocence are still made by the court in these cases, and the bases for making these determinations remain the standard ones of the non-Aboriginal justice system. As well, the actual sentencing decision is the judge's. The judge is under no obligation

---

[177] *R. v. Morin*, Judgement of Sherstobitoff J.A., pp. 134-135.

[178] The court was able to comment on this aspect of the case, as the transcript of the sentencing circle was made available to them.

[179] *R. v. Morin*, Judgement of Sherstobitoff J.A., p. 136. The Saskatchewan Court of Appeal has stated that the starting point for sentences for robberies of commercial establishments such as convenience stores and gas bars should be three years' imprisonment. *R. v. Morin*, Judgement of Sherstobitoff J.A., p. 139.

[180] *R. v. Morin*, Judgement of Sherstobitoff J.A., p. 137-138.

[181] Judge Heino Lilles, "Tribal Justice", cited in note 164.

to follow the suggestions of the elders panel or the sentencing circle. Sentencing guidelines set down by courts of appeal and maximums sentences enshrined in the *Criminal Code* take precedence over any suggestions from the community.[182] Judge Lilles has noted that there have been occasions when an elders panel has recommended a term of incarceration for an offender that exceeded what even the Crown felt was appropriate. In one such case he asked the clan leaders to explain their decision. While he did not fully accede to the clan leaders' wishes, he tried to accommodate them as best he could within existing sentencing guidelines.[183]

For programs such as these to work, it is important that the entire community have an opportunity to determine the level of participation it wishes to have. Concerns have been expressed that in their enthusiasm to solicit community input, judges may have recruited people to participate in elders panels or sentencing circles without real community involvement in the selection process. In some cases the individuals chosen were ill-suited to this role, as they had serious personal problems that needed to be resolved before they could properly comment on the conduct of others. These initiatives cannot succeed if the members of the panel advising a judge are handpicked by the court or by a few members of the community with whom a judge has happened to develop a comfortable relationship. This issue was brought home at a talking circle on justice, held by the commission in Saskatoon in January 1994. At the circle a participant from the North stated:

> I know we have had experiences...where these tinkering approaches have not worked very well... When you live in the north or in an isolated community, there are unique problems that you have to look at... For example, because communities are small there are unique power structures involving dominant families that can often lead to protectionist attitudes [toward particular offenders] that overlook the community as a whole... [This does] not result in healing for the community, for the perpetrator, or for the victim.[184]

---

[182] See, for example, the decision of the Alberta Court of Appeal, sitting in its capacity as the Northwest Territories Court of Appeal, in a case of sexual assault. An elders panel and community members recommended a sentence of 90 days' imprisonment, to be served intermittently in the community of Arctic Bay, and this was the sentence imposed by the trial judge. The appeal decision replaced that sentence with a sentence of 18 months' imprisonment, on the grounds that the original sentence did not adequately take into account the Court of Appeal's 'starting point' of 3 years for crimes of sexual assault. *R. v. Naqitarvik* (1986), 25 C.C.C. (3d) 193. For a comment on this decision, see *Locking Up Natives in Canada*, cited in note 37, pp. 261-266.

This approach is in conflict with the view expressed by the Saskatchewan Court of Appeal in *Morin*, discussed earlier. The issue does not arise with Aboriginal diversion programs, since they operate outside the court's purview.

[183] Lilles, "Tribal Justice", cited in note 164, pp. 11-12. Judge Lilles also makes the point that this scenario illustrates that it cannot be assumed that Aboriginal people will somehow be more lenient with each other than if the matter proceeded before a judge sitting alone.

[184] Joan Mercredi, transcripts, RCAP Talking Circle on Justice, Saskatoon, January 1994, pp. 182-183.

Because we see this issue as critical to the success of any Aboriginal justice initiative, we return to a discussion of what it means to have general community input to the development of these initiatives later in this chapter and again in Chapter 4, where we address the need to ensure that Aboriginal justice systems protect the interests of women and children.

Other aspects of the justice system lend themselves quite easily to increased input from Aboriginal communities. These opportunities are best recognized when the system is seen as a collection of discrete processes – bail, plea discussion, trial and sentencing – that are all part of a continuum. One of the advantages of looking at the system in such a way is that it reduces the emphasis now placed on the trial process, since the great majority of criminal cases are disposed of without trial as a result of guilty pleas. Rupert Ross, who developed this conceptual approach in a paper entitled "Managing the Merger", points out that effective Aboriginal involvement in the bail, plea discussion and sentencing processes could make the trial component even less significant than it already is. Ross points out that few initiatives have targeted the bail and plea discussion processes, although there is great scope for community involvement at these stages.

In terms of bail hearings, Ross sees a greater role for community participation in the presentation of relevant information at the bail hearing, as well as for community members in setting bail conditions. Increased community control over the bail process could result in the following:

- quicker response to accused persons – particularly in remote settlements;
- a more powerful response, coming as it does from the community itself;
- a more thorough response drawing upon a wider group of people with relevant information and insight;
- a more culturally appropriate response; and
- a head-start on the creation of long-term healing strategies.[185]

With regard to the plea discussion phase, Ross sees a role for the development of pre-trial circles. In the non-Aboriginal system, plea discussions are carried out at pre-trial hearings involving only defence and prosecution counsel and, on some occasions, a judge. The purpose of the pre-trial is usually to assess how strong the prosecution's case is and to explore sentencing options in the event of a guilty plea. However, since pre-trial discussions are not governed by the same rules of evidence that apply to trials, they present an opportunity to hold a pre-trial circle. At such a circle, community members would have a chance to present their views on the matter at hand – whether in terms of the facts of the case or in terms of an appropriate sentence. Since the circle would be held as part of the pretrial process, it could

---

[185] Rupert Ross, "Managing the Merger: Justice-as-Healing in Aboriginal Communities", draft discussion paper (Kenora: August 1994), pp. 7, 12.

proceed in a non-adversarial setting.[186] Ross sees the use of such circles as leading to a reduction in the number of full-scale trials held.

An example of how this approach could be used to develop new ways of obtaining Aboriginal input can be seen in the development and evolution of the sentencing circle in the Yukon. Those familiar with the circle concept believe it has the potential to do much more than simply provide advice for judges on the disposition of a particular case. In a paper entitled "Alternative Dispute Resolution in Action in Canada: Community Justice Circles", Judge Barry Stuart and Barbara Hume, a justice of the peace for the Yukon and one of the founders of the Community Circle Sentencing Project, outlined how community circles can act as an informal diversion project as well.

In this model, a healing circle is convened as soon as possible following the commission of an offence. Members of that circle usually include the victim, the offender, elders, clan leaders, and other interested parties. If the matter can be resolved to everyone's satisfaction at this circle, it will go no further. If necessary, additional circles may be held with a wider range of participants. Following the circles, the matter may be resolved without judicial intervention, or it may be referred to court. Serious criminal offences may go directly to court. In such a case the judge may still wish to have the guidance of a formal sentencing circle. This approach to circle sentencing is currently functioning in a limited capacity in the Yukon.[187]

Sentencing circles and elders panels should not be seen as ends in themselves. Rather, as with diversion and related initiatives, they are perhaps best seen as stages in an evolutionary process. The idea of community circles in the Yukon has recently been expanded, so that they now act as an alternative to the courts. These initiatives must be allowed to grow and develop on their own. They are helpful, not only in continuing reform of the existing system, but as useful models in the development of distinct Aboriginal justice systems.

Young Offender Initiatives

The *Young Offenders Act*, passed by Parliament in 1982 to replace the *Juvenile Delinquents Act* of 1908, sought to bring about a new balance between the rights and interests of young persons and the protection of society. While extending to young persons the same rights as adults with regard to due process of law and fair and equal treatment, the act recognized that special measures were required to reflect the needs of young persons in conflict with the law. In its declaration of principle the act states that "The rights and freedoms of young persons include a

---

[186] Ross, "Managing the Merger", pp. 12-13.

[187] For a discussion of the various types of circles being used in the Yukon, see Barry Stuart and Barbara Hume, "Alternative Dispute Resolution in Action in Canada: Community Justice Circles", paper presented to a conference of the Society of Professionals in Dispute Resolution, Toronto, 23 October 1993.

right to the least possible interference with freedom that is consistent with the protection of society."[188] In furtherance of this principle, the legislation makes provision for "alternative measures". Section 4(1) provides that

> Alternative measures may be used to deal with a young person alleged to have committed an offence instead of judicial proceedings.

Alternative measures must be part of a program authorized by a province, and the young person must accept responsibility for the offence allegedly committed. The promise of innovative initiatives for young Aboriginal offenders – which the young offenders legislation intended to encourage – like so many promises of our "just society", has not been fulfilled in the case of Aboriginal people.

The Cawsey task force found that in Alberta, custody dispositions for non-Aboriginal convicted young offenders **declined** by 8 per cent between 1986 and 1989, while custody dispositions for Aboriginal young offenders **increased** over the same period by 18.2 per cent. The task force also found that there was a "persistent lack of involvement" of Aboriginal young offenders in the alternative measures program. More than 33 per cent of new cases involving non-Aboriginal young offenders used the program, compared to only 11.1 per cent of new cases involving Aboriginal young offenders. Based on the experience in Alberta, the Cawsey report concluded:

> Aboriginal young offenders appeared to be under-represented in the more favourable dispositions and over-represented in the more disfavourable dispositions. The result is a significant over-representation in the incarcerated young offender population.[189]

The Aboriginal Justice Inquiry (AJI) of Manitoba also concluded that young Aboriginal offenders in Manitoba received open custody sentences that were, on average, twice as long as those given to non-Aboriginal young offenders. In addition, 18 per cent of Aboriginal offenders received closed custody sentences, compared to 11 per cent of non-Aboriginal offenders.

In an otherwise grim picture of the way young Aboriginal offenders experience the justice system, the AJI identified one area in the implementation of alternative measures that offered some real prospects for change. The province of Manitoba relies on alternative measures more than any province in Canada, and many of the cases dealt with under these measures are handled by volunteer youth justice committees. These committees derive their mandate from section 69 of the *Young Offenders Act*, which provides that

> The Attorney General of a province...may establish one or more committees of citizens, to be known as Youth Justice Committees,

---

[188] *Young Offenders Act*, R.S.C. 1985, chapter Y-1, section 3(1)(f).

[189] *Justice on Trial*, cited in note 23, chapter 6, p. 7.

to assist without remuneration in any aspect of the administration of this Act or in any program or services for young offenders and may specify the method of appointment of committee members and the functions of the committees.

Ten Aboriginal youth justice committees were operating in Manitoba in 1991. The AJI described how these committees become involved in the justice system:

> They become involved with youth in one of two ways. If a youth is causing trouble in the community, the Band Constable or another police officer, a member of the Band Council, the parents or any concerned person can ask the Youth Justice Committee to become involved in the case before a charge has been laid. If a charge has been laid, the youth can still be referred to a Youth Justice Committee by the Crown Attorney or, later in the process, by a Judge.
>
> Once a young person agrees to participate, the Youth Justice Committee meets with the youth to discuss the problem and the options that are available.... The range of measures is limited only by the resources and imagination of program administrators and the consent of the youth.
>
> Some Youth Justice Committees provide bail supervision, others supervised probation orders, while still others are involved in victim-offender reconciliation and other forms of alternative dispute resolution. Some make representations to the court on behalf of young offenders.[190]

The report of the AJI also provided examples of the work done by some Aboriginal youth justice committees. The St. Theresa Point youth justice committee grew out of the efforts of a group of parents, who lobbied for the establishment of the committee to deal with the growing number of young people engaged in gas sniffing and truancy.

> The committee was established by the community and is based on the traditions and customs of the tribe. The committee began calling young people who were sniffing gasoline and not attending school to appear at meetings where they were lectured by elders about their inappropriate behaviour. Generally, the rebuke took place in public meetings with others from the community in attendance. Soon, the parents were also called to account. In this way, the committee functioned as a true diversion program. Eventually, young people who faced criminal charges were being

---

[190] AJI, cited in note 2, volume 1, p. 576.

referred to the committee as an alternative to formal court processing.

The Band Council then took a further step by appointing a community "magistrate." While this position has no status under either provincial or federal laws, the individual is considered by the community to be acting upon authority stemming from known tribal customs. There does not appear to have been any instance were a person in the community has questioned the authority of the community magistrate.

The RCMP have been supportive of the program. They have found it so effective that they too refer young people to the program, rather than laying a charge, as they would likely have done before the program was instituted.

We were advised that the number of young offender crimes in the community has been reduced dramatically.[191]

In its review of the experience of successful Aboriginal youth justice committees, the AJI was troubled by several features of the *Young Offenders Act* (YOA) provisions regarding alternative measures and the establishment of these committees. The first troubling aspect was the lack of financial support.

We do not understand why Youth Justice Committees, some of which are becoming quite sophisticated, should be required to operate without the financial and administrative support that is accorded to other components of the justice system. Nor do we understand why section 69 of the YOA stipulates that members of the Youth Justice Committees must serve without remuneration.[192]

The issue of the level of service that volunteers alone can provide to a justice initiative is an important one. While community support for such activities is vital, it is unrealistic to expect that all the necessary work to establish and maintain these initiatives can be accomplished by volunteers. Lack of resources for initiatives as demanding as those dealing with young people in conflict with the law leads inevitably to volunteer burn-out. Eventually, initiatives that begin with great promise may end up abandoned. This does not serve the needs of those requiring the services and acts as a deterrent to the development of new initiatives. This holds true for all justice initiatives not just those developed for young offenders.

---

[191] AJI, volume 1, pp. 576-577. The report also describes the successful experience of the Wi Chi Whey Wen youth justice committee, which operates in Winnipeg, and the Roseau River Tribal Council justice committee.

[192] AJI, volume 1, p. 576.

A second problematic feature identified by the Aboriginal Justice Inquiry of Manitoba is that the YOA leaves it up to the attorney general of the province to develop guidelines for alternative measures programs. In Manitoba the guidelines specified that young persons can be referred to alternative measures only if they have committed less serious offences and do not have a history of serious offences. Thus, young persons charged with serious driving offences, crimes of violence or threatened violence, and crimes resulting in a total loss of more than $1,000 were excluded from the programs. The AJI recommended that new guidelines be established to provide that alternative measure programs be available to all offenders, particularly where an offender has never been offered an opportunity to participate in an alternative measures program.

Building on the success of the current Aboriginal youth justice committees, the Aboriginal Justice Inquiry recommended that the provincial government establish Aboriginally focused diversion and alternative measures programs and that adequate administrative and financial support be provided to youth justice committees.

Many of the recent justice inquiries have made recommendations designed to further the principles of the *Young Offenders Act* and to increase provincial governments' commitment to alternative measures programs. As we have seen, Aboriginal young offenders are over-represented in the young offender system yet are under-represented when it comes to alternative measures. Therefore, recommendations like those of the Aboriginal Justice Inquiry of Manitoba, which called for more Aboriginally focused diversion and alternative measures programs, make sense. However, over the past several years government attention has focused increasingly on changing the *Young Offenders Act*, to shift the balance away from its rehabilitative purpose in the direction of punitive objectives.[193] The apparent mood of the country, fuelled by widely publicized crimes of random violence perpetrated by both adults and young offenders, has given rise to calls for the system to be 'toughened up'. These calls are not directed specifically to Aboriginal offenders, but because of the already great over-representation of Aboriginal young offenders in the corrections system, measures designed to tighten the correctional screws have a disproportionate impact on Aboriginal youth, placing the promise of alternatives to imprisonment even further out of reach.

In the context of a chilly Canadian climate, where demands for more punishment occupy headlines and parliamentary agendas, it is appropriate to review some recent developments in other jurisdictions that are moving in a different direction. We have found the experience in New Zealand in relation to young offenders particularly relevant in the crafting of creative Canadian initiatives in relation to youth justice. There are several reasons for this. As we have observed, Aboriginal people in New Zealand have experienced the same over-representation in the criminal justice system as Aboriginal people in Canada. The recent changes introduced in New Zealand trace their inspiration in some measure to principles and

---

[193] See *An Act to Amend the Young Offenders Act and the Criminal Code*, S.C. 1995, chapter 19.

processes of restorative justice, based in Maori traditions. While the New Zealand legislation applies to all young offenders, Maori and non-Maori alike, Maori young offenders have been the majority of those involved in proceedings under the new legislation.

In 1989 New Zealand introduced the *Children, Young Persons and Their Families Act*. This legislation bears some similarities to the *Young Offenders Act* in so far as it establishes a separate youth court to handle offences by young persons, provides for the full panoply of due process protections in cases where a young offender pleads not guilty, and provides for young persons to be dealt with in adult court for really serious offences. Where the New Zealand legislation differs from the YOA is that alternative measures are built into the system as a pivotal, rather than discretionary, feature. The New Zealand version of alternative measures focuses on what is referred to as the family group conference (FGC). The New Zealand scheme is described by Judge McElrea of the Auckland District Court.

> The FGC is attended by the young person, members of the family (in the wider sense), the victim, a youth advocate (if requested by the young person), a police officer (usually a member of the specialist Youth Aid Division), a social worker (in certain cases only), and anyone else the family wishes to be there....
>
> Where the young person has not been arrested, the FGC recommends whether the young person should be prosecuted and if not so recommended, how the matter should be dealt with, with a presumption in favour of diversion. All members of the FGC (including the young person) must agree as to the proposed diversionary program, and its implementation is essentially consensual. Where the young person has been arrested the court must refer all matters not denied by the young person to a FGC which recommends to the court how the matter should be dealt with. Occasionally an FGC recommends a sanction to be imposed by the court. Usually it puts forward a plan of action, for example, apology, reparation (in money or work for the victim), community work, curfew and/or undertaking to attend school or not to associate with co-offenders. The plan is supervised by the persons nominated in the plan, with the court usually being asked to adjourn proceedings, say for three to four months, to allow the plan to be implemented.
>
> The Youth Court nearly always accepts such plans, recognizing that the scheme of the Act places the primary power of disposition with the FGC. However, in serious cases the court can use a wide range of court imposed sanctions, the most severe being three months residence in a social welfare institution followed by six months supervision; or the court may convict and refer the

young person to the District Court for sentence under the
Criminal Justice Act 1985 which can include imprisonment for up
to three years.[194]

Judge McElrea suggests that the practice of youth justice under the 1989 legislation has three distinctive elements: the transfer of power from the state, principally the court's power, to the community; the family group conference as a mechanism for producing a negotiated, community response; and the involvement of victims as key participants, making possible a healing process for both offender and victim. It is these elements of restorative justice that link the New Zealand initiatives with Maori concepts of justice based on restoration of harmony within a network of family, community and tribal relationships. In many cases involving Maori young offenders, the participation of the offender's and the victim's extended family and tribal group are the key to the development of a negotiated community response.[195]

John Braithwaite and Steven Mugford, two Australian criminologists, have written about how the New Zealand experience with family group conferences has provided avenues for Maori communities to redress the disempowerment and oppression they have experienced through the imposition of the criminal justice system.

> The structure of laws and the daily routines of the police and the courts contribute mightily to that oppression. Thus, to alter the police-court process is an important step, even if it is not a sufficient step... The philosophy of the New Zealand reforms is that when families are in deep trouble, a social worker from the State is not likely to be the best person to straighten out their problems. However big a mess the family is in, the best hope for solving the problems of families resides within the families themselves and their immediate communities of intimate support. What the State can do is empower families with the resources.... In New Zealand, where the Maori community contribute half the cases processed by the New Zealand juvenile justice system, conferences offer an important redress in a criminal justice system that is otherwise not a peripheral but a central source of their disempowerment.... Conferences will never usher in revolutionary changes; they do, however, give little people chances to strike little blows against oppression.... The theory of the conference is not really that what is said at the conference will change lives in an instant and irreversible way – a conference is a social activity, not a genie from a

---

[194] F.W.M. McElrea, "Restorative Justice – The New Zealand Youth Court: A Model for Development in Other Courts?", *Journal of Judicial Administration* 4 (1994), pp. 35-36.

[195] The links between the Maori restorative justice tradition and recent developments in New Zealand with respect to youth justice are reviewed in Consedine, *Restorative Justice*, cited in note 103.

bottle. Rather the hope for the conference is that it will be a catalyst for community problem solving.... There are no criminal justice utopias to be found, just better and worse directions to head in. The New Zealand Maori have shown a direction for making reintegration ceremonies work in multi-cultural metropolises such as Auckland, a city that faces deeper problems of recession, homelessness and gang violence than many cities in western Europe.[196]

As Braithwaite and Mugford point out, although family group conferences reflect Maori concepts of restorative justice, incorporation of this process into the juvenile justice system has been received favourably by non-Maori communities in New Zealand. The reasons seem to be that the process breaks the control of professionals, empowers the community, particularly victims, and is oriented to flexible community problem solving.

> Indeed, flexibility and participant control of the process are the reasons why this strategy can succeed in a multicultural metropolis like Auckland. This is not a communitarian strategy for the nineteenth century village, but for the twenty-first century city. Flexible process, participant control – these are keys to delivering the legal pluralism necessary for the metropolis.[197]

In contrast with the experience in Canada, where implementation of the *Young Offenders Act* has seen an increase in the rate of young people sentenced to custody, in New Zealand since 1988 the rate of institutionalization of young offenders has dropped by more than half, resulting in closure of most of the social welfare homes to which young people had been remanded in the past.[198] The New Zealand reform also commands public support across a broad spectrum and is seen in particular by the police in a positive light. As reported by Braithwaite and Mugford,

> The Australian and New Zealand Police Federation carried a resolution at its 1991 conference supporting the New Zealand

---

[196] John Braithwaite and Steven Mugford, "Conditions of Successful Reintegration Ceremonies: Dealing with Juvenile Offenders", *British Journal of Criminology* 34/2 (Spring 1995), pp. 156, 157, 158, 162, 168. Family conferencing, first introduced in New Zealand, has also been used successfully in Australia. In its Australian version the police have a more central role in the process and, unlike the situation in New Zealand, more non-Aboriginal than Aboriginal young persons have participated in family conferences. Joy Wundersitz, "Family Conferencing in South Australia and Juvenile Justice Reform", in *Family Conferencing and Juvenile Justice: The Way Forward or Misplaced Optimism*, ed. Christine Adler and Joy Wundersitz (Canberra: Australian Institute of Criminology, 1994), pp. 87-102.

[197] Braithwaite and Mugford, "Conditions of Successful Reintegration Ceremonies", p. 159.

[198] Braithwaite and Mugford, "Conditions of Successful Reintegration Ceremonies", p. 162. See also Gabriel Maxwell and Allison Morris, *Family, Victims and Culture: Youth Justice in New Zealand* (Wellington: Social Policy Agency and Institute of Criminology, Victoria University, 1993).

juvenile justice reforms. In New Zealand, 91 per cent of the time police report that they are satisfied with the outcomes of the conferences in which they participate.... Perhaps this should not surprise us. The approach appeals to the common sense of police. On balance, it cuts their paperwork and economizes on criminal justice system resources; they often feel empowered by the capacity the conference gives them to make practical suggestions to the family on what might be done about the problem (an opportunity they are rarely given by courts); they like to treat victims with the decency that they believe courts deny them (in particular they like to see the victims actually getting compensation); and they find that the program builds good will towards the police in communities that are empowered through the process. Most critically, they find participation in community conferences more interesting, challenging and satisfying work than typing up charges and sitting around in court houses for cases that are rushed through in a matter of minutes.[199]

Despite its demonstrated successes, the family group conference system, like alternative measures in Canada, does not receive the level of funding necessary to build on those successes. Indeed, in its submissions to Parliament's Social Services Select Committee, the New Zealand Police Association referred to the "woeful under-funding of the system."[200] Nor should the FGC system be seen as a sufficient response to persistent demands by the Maori for recognition of their right of self-determination. Although many Maori see the New Zealand reforms as significant improvements offering a measure of empowerment, these reforms have not stilled demands for the re-establishment and revitalization of a Maori-controlled justice system.

In a recent paper, Carol La Prairie, a Canadian researcher who has done extensive work in Aboriginal communities on the impact of the criminal justice system, considered some of the advantages offered by family conferencing. La Prairie's views on how the concept could apply in Canada are informed by her observations of family conferencing in South Australia:

There are a number of ways in which conferencing of crime and disorder offences may be useful to Aboriginal communities. One of the most obvious is that it could provide more options for police and other institutional personnel. This is important for communities where few resources exist. Police presently have the option of cautioning or charging, removing offenders from the

---

[199] Braithwaite and Mugford, "Conditions of Successful Reintegration Ceremonies", pp. 165-166.

[200] McElrea, "Restorative Justice", cited in note 194, p. 53.

home for short periods of time, providing services such as assisting in obtaining medical help, counselling, or doing nothing.

Conferences may provide the opportunity for communities and individuals to re-claim private and informal (or customary) practices where these have been eroded by public institutions. The lament of many people in communities, particularly the middle and older age groups, is the erosion of traditional values and authority structures. Modernization and mass communication have created roles for public institutions in communities which were formerly the responsibility of kin and other groups.

Conferences may also provide a 'safe' place for people to air their opinions and concerns without undue fears of gossip and retribution, which many see as a concern about speaking out in a public forum such as a court. Bearing witness against fellow community members or kin may be another source of gossip, scorn and/or retribution, and it also has the potential to complicate and create strains for people living together year round and in close physical proximity.

In the area of family violence, some research suggests that victims might be more amenable to conferencing than to charging. Taking offenders away or charging them is of little value when victims simply want the behaviour to change and the relationship to improve. In many Aboriginal communities the lack of resources makes marriage and other kinds of counselling unlikely so 'widening the circle' by expanding the roles of extended family members and other conference participants may provide support and assistance to victims and reduce the use of violence by offenders. In situations involving abuse against mothers and/or fathers by youth or young adults, the shame partners feel about exposing it may be more usefully dealt with in the confines of the conference than in the police station or court.[201]

The Commission believes that recognition of the jurisdiction of Aboriginal nations in the area of justice will necessarily encompass the administration of youth justice in their communities. We cannot ignore the fact that, at the time this report was being written, the Parliament of Canada was engaged in reviewing the *Young Offenders Act* to consider what future amendments should be made. This would have been an excellent opportunity to consider including provisions such as family group conferencing, which, in the transition to self-governing Aboriginal justice systems, would have addressed existing over-representation of Aboriginal youth

---

[201] Carol La Prairie, "Conferencing in Aboriginal Communities in Canada: Finding a Middle Ground in Criminal Justice?", *Criminal Law Forum* (forthcoming, 1996).

, institutions and paved the way for Aboriginal nations and their com-
.ddress the problems facing their most precious gifts, their children
people. Parliament should return to this issue at the first available
.y.

Aboriginal Initiatives in Canadian Prisons

The initiatives described thus far take place outside prison; indeed, most are
designed to explore and implement alternatives to imprisonment. This is both a
response to over-representation of Aboriginal people in prison and a reflection of
the fact that Aboriginal people did not historically build "iron houses".

Nevertheless, among the most remarkable Aboriginal justice initiatives in the last
decade are those that have taken place inside Canadian prisons. During this period
Aboriginal prisoners and organizations working with them became increasingly critical of the lack of recognition by correctional authorities of the distinctive cluster
of problems facing Aboriginal prisoners and the lack of relevance for those prisoners of many correctional programs. Aboriginal prisoners maintained that they
had the right to practise their spirituality, including participation in spiritual and
healing ceremonies, and that this was not only an existing Aboriginal right under
section 35 of the *Constitution Act, 1982*, but also a right protected by the *Canadian
Charter of Rights and Freedoms* in relation to freedom of religion. Beyond these arguments, they also maintained that practising culturally relevant ceremonies directed
to healing was more appropriate in their journey toward rehabilitation and reintegration into the community than programs that lacked any Aboriginal cultural
content. The report of the Canadian Bar Association, *Locking Up Natives in Canada*,
identified the powerful influence of Aboriginal spirituality in the lives of Aboriginal
prisoners.

> Native prisoners who learn the ways of Native spirituality discover,
> often for the first time, a sense of identity, self-worth and com-
> munity. Because the path is one which must be taught by those
> who have special knowledge and who are respected for their spir-
> itual strength and wisdom, the practice of Native spirituality
> requires that prisoners communicate with Elders in the outside
> Native community. Some prisoners, by virtue of their prior train-
> ing or the training they undergo in prison, are able to lead certain
> ceremonies and provide spiritual counselling to other prisoners.
> There develops, therefore, a continuum in which those who are
> more experienced in spiritual ways are able to help those less
> experienced. In this way a sense of community emerges based
> not on the common element of criminality, but rather on a search
> for spiritual truths. In place of the alienation which prison typi-
> cally engenders, Native prisoners are able to experience a sense
> of belonging and sharing in a core set of values and experiences
> which link them with the outside Native community. Native pris-

oners are able to experience feelings of value and self-worth not only through their spiritual training but also in the work they are able to do in helping other prisoners along the same path. Native spirituality, therefore, provides Native prisoners not only with constructive links to each other but also with Native people outside of prison and with their collective heritage. Native spirituality is seen by many Native people, both inside and outside the prison, as an important element in dealing with problems of alcohol and drug dependency, violence and other forms of anti-social behaviour. Some of the alternative responses to crime which are being fashioned by Native communities on the outside, whether in the form of diversion or community counselling, have built into them an element of exposure to Native spirituality.[202]

The report commented on the difficulties of Aboriginal prisoners in having their spiritual practices taken seriously and given the appropriate respect by correctional officials.

The distinctiveness of Native spirituality makes it difficult for non-Natives to accord due respect to Native spiritual beliefs and practices. Although there are Native men and women who have special powers and responsibilities in spiritual matters, they are not distinguished by clerical collars or degrees from schools of divinity. Native spirituality has its own ceremonies and rituals which are not those familiar to Judeo-Christian orthodoxy. There are places of special spiritual significance, but churches and temples of worship are not part of the architecture of Native spirituality. This is not to say that the practice of Native spirituality has no specific form in the particular context of the prison system. The ceremony of the sacred pipe and the sweat lodge are two of the distinctive ways in which Native prisoners have sought to express their spiritual traditions. The sacred pipe ceremony is one common to many Indian nations and represents the unifying bonds of the Indian ethos. Through smoking the pipe within a ritual circle, the prayers of Indian supplicants rise with the smoke and mingle with all living creatures. The Great Spirit evoked by the pipe enters and connects Native people with all their relations in the living world. The pipe contains animal, vegetable and mineral matter. The different materials used in the ceremony – sweetgrass, sage, red willow and cedar bark – all have symbolic importance. In the same way, the use of eagle feathers and certain articles of personal adornment are integrally related to matters of the spirit. The sweat lodge ceremony, like the pipe, is widely dis-

---

[202] *Locking Up Natives in Canada*, cited in note 37, pp. 287-288.

tributed across Native cultural and geographic lines and it is primarily an act of purification. Each component of the sweat lodge structure symbolizes the elemental forces of the universe and the cycles of nature.[203]

In response to these problems of lack of recognition and respect, Parliament incorporated specific provisions dealing with Aboriginal offenders in the 1992 *Corrections and Conditional Release Act*.[204] This legislation obligates the Correctional Service of Canada to "provide programs designed particularly to address the needs of Aboriginal offenders" (section 80), authorizes the solicitor general to enter into agreements with Aboriginal communities for the provision of correctional services to Aboriginal offenders (section 81), mandates the establishment of a national Aboriginal advisory committee, and authorizes regional and local Aboriginal advisory committees to advise the Correctional Service of Canada on the provision of correctional services to Aboriginal offenders (section 82). Section 83 provides that

1. For greater certainty, Aboriginal spirituality and Aboriginal spiritual leaders and elders have the same status as other religions and other religious leaders.

2. The Service shall take all reasonable steps to make available to Aboriginal inmates the services of an Aboriginal spiritual leader or elder...

Legislating respect and recognition is one thing. Its achievement in the reality of every-day prison life is another. Although advisory boards of elders have been appointed and the Correctional Service has hired elders on a contract basis, the struggle for respect and recognition continues, and in some institutions the translation of legislation and official policy into respect at the front gate of the prison when elders bring in their medicine bundles and sacred pipes is an imperfect one.

As part of our public consultations process, the Commission convened special hearings consultations in the Saskatchewan Penitentiary in Prince Albert, Stony Mountain Institution in Winnipeg, and the Prison for Women in Kingston. At the Saskatchewan Penitentiary, Warden O'Sullivan informed us that 48 per cent of the prisoners in the institution were of Aboriginal ancestry. A number of them spoke

---

[203] *Locking Up Natives in Canada*, pp. 288-289.

[204] *Corrections and Conditional Release Act*, S.C. 1992, chapter 20, sections 79-84. The situation in the provinces and territories varies with regard to formal recognition of the need for Aboriginal-specific programming. Some provinces and territories recognize the role of Aboriginal elders explicitly, but others do not. Even in provinces with published guidelines, experience has shown that, as in federal institutions, policy and practice often diverge. At the provincial level, the availability of Aboriginal programming varies from one institution to another. As well, even if a correctional facility has Aboriginal-specific programs, Aboriginal offenders may not necessarily be sent there to serve their sentences.

to us about the strength they had gained from practising Aboriginal spirituality and working with the elders. Keith Bruno told us:

> There are a lot of brothers in here. They learn how to be sweat holders. They learn how to be pipe carriers. When they get on the street it's my belief that they have something to give to the younger generations who are in institutions right now. They understand what those young people are dealing with, the separation from the family, the separation from their own spirit... When you hold the pipe and you walk with that pipe, you are walking with strength. You look at that and it carries you. It helps you understand what your purpose is because you now have a purpose to live for. It is not being thrown back out in the street, going into a circle to come back in here.[205]

Other prisoners at the penitentiary described how their lives in foster homes – where contacts with family, language and culture were severed – and their experiences in juvenile detention facilities virtually assured their eventual incarceration in a federal penitentiary. Ken Noskiye of the Prince Albert Native Awareness Group told us that the group surveyed the Aboriginal prisoners at Prince Albert and discovered that more than 95 per cent had been in either a foster home or a group home.[206]

Pat McCormick described his long and painful journey. Before the age of ten his life had become a succession of group homes, receiving homes and foster homes from which he ran away to live on the streets of Winnipeg, "sniffing solvents, gasoline, glue, whatever I could get my hands on." Eventually he was placed in a youth detention centre, and his history of institutionalization began in earnest. He spent his eighteenth birthday in the Headingly Jail, and between the ages of 18 and 20 he spent only seven months in the outside world. Shortly after he turned 20 he was convicted of first degree murder. As he told us, "Now I had done something and taken something that I could never give back." In the first year of his sentence his mother died, and McCormick determined that he wanted to change his life. He told the commission that in the penitentiary he had begun the arduous task of discovering his Aboriginal culture. As he put it:

> In the penitentiary today I have taken programs and participated in the culture and I still struggle today as I try to develop a value system, to understand where I've come from and where I am today and how to pick up the pieces and learn from my past. Yet, I hear this voice and it's the voice of a child and no-one seems to be listening. I wondered what I might say to you people today... I don't know the number of people in this institution, but I know it's

---

[205] Keith Bruno, RCAP transcripts, Prince Albert, Saskatchewan, 27 May 1992, p. 121.

[206] Ken Noskiye, RCAP transcripts, Prince Albert, Saskatchewan, 27 May 1992.

high, who have gone through that road, that pattern through child welfare. I know it is necessary to deal with that while we are here and now, but as I told you earlier I hear this voice and I hear them pleading for someone to come and help. As we speak, there are children all across this country who need to come home to their people, so I said a prayer that this commission would help them.[207]

Little research has been done on the effects of Aboriginal spirituality on Aboriginal offenders in Canada, although the subjective experience of many offenders suggests that it is a major factor in rediscovering Aboriginal identity and pride and that it has paved the way for healing, which in many cases, given long histories of abuse and institutionalization, will be life-long.[208] One of the few researchers to examine the question, James Waldram of the department of Native Studies at the University of Saskatchewan, concluded on the basis of interviews with Aboriginal prisoners who have participated in spirituality and awareness programs, that they have a significant effect on the mental health and well-being of offenders. Waldram observes that corrections has received considerably less attention than other aspects of the justice system with respect to the integration of traditional approaches. His research suggests that although recognition of Aboriginal spirituality in Canadian law and policy is based primarily on its religious aspects, its principal benefits may well be those that flow from the healing and therapeutic effects, particularly of working with respected elders and participating in ceremonies that provide avenues for individual and collective discovery and growth.

Waldram confirmed what we heard at Saskatchewan Penitentiary – that for many Aboriginal offenders their exposure to elders and to the ceremonies of Aboriginal spirituality marked their first experiences with the strengths and power of Aboriginal culture. Waldram also found that many offenders said they could talk more openly with Aboriginal elders than with non-Aboriginal correctional staff and that elders demonstrated much more empathy with their life situations, particularly because some of the elders had themselves led troubled lives, often involving alcohol and drug abuse and even periods of incarceration. As one of the prisoners observed,

> Talking to an elder is very easy for me, because a lot of the elders experience that same type of thing I have gone through, and I could relate to them in that respect, and they could understand me more than a person that has got a degree could understand me in

---

[207] Pat McCormick, RCAP transcripts, Prince Albert, Saskatchewan, 27 May 1992, p. 47.

[208] It is not only prisoners who have commented on the changes brought about by a commitment to Aboriginal spirituality. In a recent article, Peter Moon reported the observation of the warden of Stony Mountain Penitentiary, Art Majkut, that he has seen Aboriginal inmates who have participated in spiritual activities completely changed by the process. Peter Moon, "Natives Find Renewal in Manitoba Prison", *The Globe and Mail*, 20 July 1995, p. A1.

my point of view, because they haven't experienced that lifestyle that I have experienced.[209]

Another prisoner explained his experience with the elders in this way:

> I talk about myself and the problems I have, and they give me advice, you know, how to have a better life out there. That's something that I've learned so much from these elders... Like I go out there for a one-on-one when I'm depressed, then I ask him why I feel like this? Why am I having so much guilt? What can I do to get rid of these feelings and that's where they come in. And they make sense when they say something to me, because I can relate to these guys. They've been through what I'm going through, and how they've changed their life is something that I want so bad for myself. And I admire these people turning their lives around and becoming somebody.[210]

A Métis prisoner described his introduction to the sweat lodge ceremony and what he saw it providing for himself and other prisoners.

> I've seen a lot of people go into the sweats and it seemed like it was changing them, that they were becoming different because of it. I watched their attitude, whether they were in prison, or whatever they are and I didn't at first just jump right into it. But I watched how, because I was always sceptical. I watched the change... They weren't as bitter, they weren't full of bitterness and...hate. They seemed to have more compassion, more caring after practising it for a while... It's been like a cleansing. It has given me a chance to cleanse my insides, my thoughts and spiritual learning process.[211]

In a compelling case study of Aboriginal spirituality as a healing process, Waldram describes the journey of one Aboriginal offender – a journey very similar to those described to us by prisoners at the Saskatchewan Penitentiary, and one that demonstrates the great potential for healing Aboriginal offenders through cultural awareness and spirituality programs.

> 'Jack' was an individual of mixed ancestry. His father was Aboriginal, his mother Euro-Canadian and he grew up mostly in the city. I first met him at a meeting of the Native brotherhood. My first impression of Jack was that he was an intensely angry man, who seemed suspicious of everyone and who spewed venom with

---

[209] James Waldram, "Aboriginal Spirituality: Symbolic Healing in Canadian Prisons", *Culture, Medicine and Psychiatry* 17 (1993), p. 351.

[210] Waldram, "Aboriginal Spirituality", p. 350.

[211] Waldram, "Aboriginal Spirituality", p. 353.

every comment. He shouted angrily, denouncing the police, the judges, the [correctional] staff and finally me... At the time he was interviewed by me he was in his early 30s and was doing a long sentence for a violent offence. At the time of that offence, he had been on the street just one day since completing an earlier sentence. His criminal convictions began at age sixteen, and he had at least seven convictions between the ages of sixteen and twenty-one. His most serious offences include armed robbery, hostage takings and gun battles with police. He had been in institutional care since the age of twelve.

His prison record showed many incidents of violence, escape, and other problems. He had also been involved in prison hostage taking incidents, and had spent more than two years 'in the hole' (segregation) and in the special handling unit... designed to handle the most dangerous offenders. According to his file, 'up to approximately one year ago his behaviour in prison was disruptive, rebellious and often a threat to institutional security.' As a result, he had served time in most Canadian prisons capable of handling him. He let it be known that he hated anyone in authority, especially prison guards... He was diagnosed as having a 'personality disorder' including a substance abuse problem, 'difficulty coping with stress resulting in aggressive behaviour, and difficulty interacting with authority.' Indeed, many prison staff were fearful of him....

Jack's father had grown up on a reserve, but Jack had spent relatively little time there as a child. His formative years were spent in the city, and he never learned his Aboriginal language. He had very little cultural knowledge of his people. It is evident that his childhood was quite disturbing, filled with alcohol abuse and violence:

> My dad was an alcoholic and my mom, she used to take lots of beatings, lots of screams, stuff like that. And I saw my father rape one of my sisters. And then I said, 'fuck that shit,' and I ran away from home.'

His description of his prison experiences was considerably more graphic than what his record described:

> I found the time I spent in the jail wasn't easy, either, I watched a few hostage takings, took part in a riot... I spent six years in the special handling unit out of fourteen years... Did lots of pipings, stabbings... When I arrived at [one prison], [the guards] tried to torture me, tried to hang me, smashed three of my ribs. I got nineteen stitches in the back of my head.

They really did put a number on me. And all those friends that I had when I first came in when I was sixteen, most of them today are dead... I got a hatred.'

Despite his relatively weak links to his Aboriginal heritage and his pale complexion, he was subjected to racism and taunting as a child. His response was to fight, and he was cajoled by his father if he appeared to have lost any such encounter. After witnessing his father rape his sister, on two occasions, he attempted to kill his father but was charged only once, with assault.

The most pleasant memories of his childhood were the brief times he spent on the reserve, ironically often the result of trouble he had encountered while in the city. He stayed primarily with his aunt and uncle, and received a cursory introduction into Aboriginal culture and spirituality. On the reserve he found a refuge from the racism of the city.

Despite his early exposure to an Aboriginal culture, by the time he entered prison as a young adult he knew very little and he would ultimately experience a personal and spiritual awakening. He explained his reasons for becoming involved in the prison's Aboriginal awareness and spirituality programs:

> I see some of my friends, they were there before me – they were in the special handling unit and when I hit [the prison] I don't know, I saw a change in those guys... I couldn't understand how come they were changing like that. And they used to tell me, 'you try this, you listen, you see. You try this and you see.' So I put myself into it, and I believe it today.

It was in prison that Jack experienced his first sweat, and began to learn more about Aboriginal culture. But his real awakening came when he entered the Regional Psychiatric Centre and began to work with the elder:

> When I started to talk to that guy it was easy to relate to him. He knew a few of my friends. That was our first conversation there, of a couple of people we knew and we talked about that. And then we talked about myself. And I was sitting in my cell one day and I said, 'fuck, that's not my dad. That's what I would like to have fucking had my dad for.' So to me he is a friend, he is a dad. He's everything, that guy. And that was the first person to come along and be willing to put everything on the line for me, so that means a lot to me. That was the first person that came along, crossed my road and asked me if I wanted help, and was willing to give me a hand...

And you know, for me that means a lot, because I never had anybody come along and ask me those things before. I wish somebody did, but it never happened.'

One particular incident seems to have been the turning point for Jack. Despite having been abused by his father, Jack was particularly troubled when news of his father's death reached him, followed by news that he would not be allowed to attend the funeral. Indeed, he was so upset that the security staff became nervous that he might become violent. The elder was there to assist:

I asked [the elder] for a special sweat, then he made a special sweat. He made two rounds instead of three. And it was for me and my father. And I was sitting down and I asked him for more, more understanding. I went through what basically I went through when I was a kid. I talked basically about all my life... the pain and the hurt. And he showed me how to pray, how to get a better understanding of myself. And since I did that, I do feel better, because when you grow up like that, you just keep those things inside you. That's why you become so bitter.

Jack's story was corroborated in a separate interview with the elder. The elder explained that Jack broke down and cried in the sweat as he related his story and particularly his difficult relationship with his father. Because of his image in prison as a tough 'con' this was something he simply could not let himself do; but in the security of the sweat lodge, alone with the elder, his true pain came out. The elder saw this as a turning point.

Jack's relationship with the elder was quite different from that he had established with the nurses and the other staff at RPC. He suggested that there was a great deal he could not bring up in his counselling sessions with the nurses, and chastised them for always looking at their watches to gauge session time. As Jack said, 'It's hard to trust when you see a person act this way.' In his estimation, he had obtained some benefits from the group therapy sessions, but his lack of trust of the staff clearly inhibited his participation. In contrast his work with the elder was built upon a foundation of trust. His respect for the elder stemmed, in part, from his respect for the knowledge the elder had gained over the course of his life, and he contrasted this with the knowledge of the nurses.

How can somebody twenty-four years old, twenty-five years old, sit down in front of you and talk to you about life when you're a lot older?... To me it's hard to understand. If someone is able to talk to me about life, somebody is going to be older than me, somebody that has seen more than me... I can learn from that person. Somebody younger than me didn't even go through half what I've gone through. How can I learn from that person?'

Jack was subsequently transferred to another prison to await his release on mandatory supervision. His release plans at the time centred on continuing his work with the elder. In fact, the elder had invited Jack to work with him as his helper, an opportunity which Jack initially could not resist. He had been in prison since the age of sixteen... However, he also recognized how seriously institutionalized he had become, and that he still required treatment in order to adjust on the outside:

> I seriously believe I have hurt a lot of people and I have to try to make up for it. More sweats to go through. More suffering I have to give for the people that I made suffer all my life. I wish to help some other people like [the elder]... I want to be working with some kids, try to give them understanding, talk with them. Because I remember when I was a kid, that was one of my dreams. To see somebody come along, sit down, kind of talk with me and tell me what's wrong. I never had that happen when I was a kid, and I know when I was a kid I was needing that. So maybe this is the way I will pay back... But I am not going to go home until I am strong. Until I can walk on my two legs without no worry. That is a time I am going to go there.[212]

Several aspects of the experience with Aboriginal spirituality in the prisons are likely to be of importance in the development of contemporary Aboriginal justice systems. The first is that the use of Aboriginal spirituality has evolved in the prison setting and has been able to respond to the needs of Aboriginal people from a diversity of cultural and in some cases acultural backgrounds. Because of the location of federal correctional institutions and the policies regarding transfer, an institution in southern Saskatchewan may have prisoners not only from the Prairie region but also from the east and west coasts, as well as from the northern part of the prairie provinces and the Territories. The elders offering services at this institution usually come from a prairie cultural tradition in which the pipe and the sweat lodge are important ceremonies. These ceremonies may or may not exist in other Aboriginal cultural traditions. On the west coast, for example, longhouse ceremonies occupy a central place in the spiritual life of many of the Aboriginal nations, and other distinctive spiritual ceremonies are specific to other Aboriginal nations. Of necessity the practitioners of Aboriginal spirituality within the prison setting have sought to develop ceremonies and teachings that go to the heart of

---

[212] James Waldram, "Aboriginal Spirituality in Corrections: A Canadian Case Study in Religion and Therapy", *American Indian Quarterly* 18 (1994), pp. 201-207.

Aboriginal spirituality and provide a framework for healing that unites rather than divides Aboriginal prisoners.

Some may criticize this development as a form of pan-Aboriginalism that fails to reflect the cultural diversity of Aboriginal peoples. There is no denying, however, that the form in which Aboriginal spirituality has developed in the prison context has provided a powerful magnet for Aboriginal people who had hitherto remained outside any constructive circle in which they could share both their pain and their dreams. In his interviews with prisoners at a prairie institution, who came from very many different cultural backgrounds, Waldram found they were not troubled by the nature of the spirituality being offered, including those with the firmest roots in an Aboriginal culture. It would seem that both prisoners and elders understand that in the contemporary situation in which they find themselves, there must be a search for some common denominators linking their distinctive cultures and experiences so that they can address the critical issue of healing. That the specific ceremonies and forms of spirituality differ from those of any particular Aboriginal tradition does not negate their essential character.

Indeed, what appears to be happening in prisons is an example of the contemporary expression of Aboriginal traditions in a way that responds to current needs and experiences of Aboriginal prisoners. The convergence of Aboriginal people from different nations and distinctive cultures is not, of course, confined to prisons. It is also a contemporary fact of life in the urban centres of Canada. The experience of Aboriginal spirituality in the prisons may provide one of the models for the development of an urban Aboriginal justice system that would seek to build on the common denominators between different Aboriginal traditions to respond to the issues facing urban Aboriginal people on the brink of the twenty-first century. It is a model that while celebrating the cultural diversity of Aboriginal nations looks to a common framework for their expression. The experience of Aboriginal prisoners and their work with elders demonstrates that the achievement of a common framework is not only a laudable but an achievable objective.

Although federal legislation now provides a legal framework for recognition of Aboriginal spirituality, we are impressed by the fact that it was Aboriginal prisoners and their support networks in the community who provided the inspiration and the energy to make this most important correctional initiative available to Aboriginal prisoners. As we observed at the beginning of this report, the criminal justice system has long been the preserve of criminal justice professionals, an observation that extends to the correctional field, particularly as regards program development and evaluation. By insisting on recognition of their Aboriginal rights, Aboriginal prisoners have struggled successfully to regain a measure of control over their lives by reclaiming their heritage and building on its strengths at the point in their lives when they are in most need of its sustenance.

We were told at the Saskatchewan Penitentiary that it is ironic that Aboriginal offenders have to come to a federal penitentiary to experience the benefits of their traditional healing ceremonies. This points to the urgent need to move into the future with an integrated and holistic approach to Aboriginal justice. We were also told that when Aboriginal prisoners are released from prison, and particularly when they return to an urban environment, they encounter difficulty finding the places and people to continue the path they discovered inside the prison. As Waldram has noted,

> Not only are they faced with the many problems associated with their past (such as their criminal record and old friends still following a criminal lifestyle), but they are also ill-equipped to pursue spiritual activities outside the heavily regulated prison environment.[213]

Given the enormous problems facing Aboriginal offenders who have served long terms, there is a need for community-based and community-controlled Aboriginal programs that build on the work done inside the prisons. A small handful of Aboriginal halfway houses, operated under the auspices of Aboriginal organizations and societies, exist but they operate on very limited budgets and are overloaded with Aboriginal applicants seeking a place to stay as the basis of a viable community plan to support a parole application or provide reintegration during statutory release. Like other voluntary sectors of the criminal justice system, halfway houses operate on a contract basis, depend on governmental largesse and, increasingly these days, face cutbacks.

Organizations working with Aboriginal prisoners have sought in recent years to bridge the gap between prison and the community with a number of initiatives. The Native Counselling Services Association of Alberta has a long history of working with Aboriginal offenders in the community and in prisons. In 1988, under an agreement with the federal solicitor general, Native Counselling Services assumed responsibility for managing a community correctional centre previously known as the Grierson Community Correctional Centre and now called the Stan Daniels Community Correctional Centre. The mandate of the Stan Daniels Centre is to provide community support to Aboriginal offenders conditionally released from federal and provincial institutions to the Edmonton area. The philosophy of the centre is premised on a holistic approach in which the offender's physical, emotional, psychological and spiritual needs are addressed. The centre offers programs that include a family life improvement program (FLIP), art therapy, a spiritual and cultural program and a work-related program. An internal evaluation of the centre, conducted in 1993, provides useful descriptions of some of these initiatives and the views of present and former residents on the extent to which the centre has lived up to its mandate.

> The underlying emphasis of the FLIP program is Native spirituality and tradition. As such, participants are provided with an

---

[213] Waldram, "Aboriginal Spirituality in Corrections: A Canadian Case Study in Religion and Therapy", p. 212.

opportunity to re-connect themselves to their cultural heritage. Often participants have little knowledge and understanding of their roots. Participants are provided with an opportunity to participate in a variety of traditional practices and ceremonies such as fasts, sundances, sweats, sweetgrass, and others. An elder remains on site three days per week to provide residents with support and counselling. Native tradition and spirituality are interwoven throughout FLIP.

Throughout the seven week program, participants explore topics that include self-identity, relationships, family dynamics, sexuality, family violence, suicide, addictions, and substance abuse. Although prescribed content has been developed, in practice, the content delivered is based upon the needs of the participants. Therefore, each group is unique in terms of its participants and content.

Program trainers are selected on the basis of their life and work experience, familiarity with Native tradition and spirituality, and positive and accepting attitudes towards Native offenders. Program trainers often come from similar dysfunctional families and have had similar experiences and feelings as the participants. Program trainers have experienced their own healing and personal growth and therefore, act as positive role models for participants to help normalize participants' experiences.[214]

Residents and former residents were asked how the Stan Daniels Centre staff compared with the staff at other correctional centres. The evaluators found that

the positive treatment of residents was the primary factor which differentiated SDC staff from staff at other correctional centres. Staff sensitivity and respect for Native spirituality was also identified as another difference.[215]

Residents and staff were asked to compare programs at the Stan Daniels Centre with those they had experienced at other centres. According to the evaluation,

A review of [residents'] responses suggests that the atmosphere in the group is different in that one can open up and express his feelings. Their responses also indicate that they felt comfortable in the programs at SDC, did not feel confined and did not worry about how the information revealed in group could be used against them. In essence, they reported feeling a degree of comfort that allowed them to be themselves. Another positive aspect of the pro-

---

[214] Nancy Davis-Patsula and Marilyn Mogey, "Evaluation of the Stan Daniels Correctional Centre" (Edmonton: Native Counselling Services of Alberta, November 1993), p. 12.

[215] "Evaluation of the Stan Daniels Correctional Centre", p. 44.

grams at SDC noted by the respondents was that the programs were Native-oriented. FLIP focused on the history of Native spirituality and offered sweats and pipe ceremonies.

A review of [staff] responses suggests similarities to the residents and ex-residents. The Native focus of the programs was identified as one difference. In particular, staff reported that the programs are Native-oriented, facilitated by Native staff, have a spiritual foundation, fit with Native traditional values, and deal with culture....

Staff identified several differences between working at SDC and other correctional centres. Their responses fell into five categories that include atmosphere, staff, spirituality, treatment of residents, and contact with residents. Staff indicated that the atmosphere at SDC is different in that it is more open, trusting, caring, warm, and like a family. They also identified the treatment of the residents as unique. Residents were reported as being treated with dignity, respect, and as individuals. Staff also talked about the presence of spirituality at the centre. In contrast to other correctional centres, staff reported an emphasis on Native culture at SDC. They also indicated that the entire foundation of the centre was premised on Native spirituality and tradition.[216]

One of our commissioned research studies looked at the provision of social services to Aboriginal people in Edmonton in general and at the Stan Daniels Centre in particular. After interviewing a number of men at the centre, the researchers concluded that the success of the program was owed, in large part, to the emphasis on Aboriginal spirituality, the use of elders and programs such as the family life improvement program. The men interviewed in the study felt that they had developed more effective coping strategies while at SDC and now wanted to lead more productive lives following their release.[217]

The Stan Daniels Correctional Centre is clearly an important and ground-breaking initiative. It demonstrates that given the authority and the resources, Aboriginal communities can change the nature of institutional experience and can offer hope where before there was only alienation.

The critical importance of transforming alienation into hope and the fulfilled promise of a better future was nowhere made clearer to us than in our special consultation at the Prison for Women in Kingston. The experiences of Aboriginal women prisoners are of special significance, not only because of their triple disadvantage – they are prisoners, they are women, they are Aboriginal – but also because developments and events within the Correctional Service of Canada in just

---

[216] "Evaluation of the Stan Daniels Correctional Centre", pp. 44-45.

[217] Heather Harris and Marcelle Gareau, "Edmonton Social Service Agency Case Study – Native Counselling Services of Alberta", research study prepared for RCAP (1993).

the last year reveal both the alienation that has symbolized the oppressive nature of prison regimes and the hope that healing within an Aboriginal perspective can offer women whose lives have been characterized by violence and abuse.

Sandy Paquachon described the horrific journey that culminated in her incarceration in the Prison for Women.

> I lived on a reservation when I was a young kid. My dad used to beat my mother up. He was an alcoholic. There were 14 of us in the family. He beat my mother up. He beat her up and he beat her up. So finally they put us in foster homes and then from foster homes, I went to a convent from the age of 6 to the age of 16.... I ran away from there after the nun beat me up so bad my ears were ringing. I called it a convent. It was like a residential school, but we prayed on our knees right around the clock....
>
> From there I started doing all kinds of things in that year and then ended up in prison. I had one break, a 14 month break, but I have been in prison for 14 years steady.... A lot of things happened in my life. Believe me, I am no angel but I am not as bad as they put me out to be.... I was sexually abused. I was mentally abused. I was physically abused. I was raped from just about everything. The nuns beat us and stripped us naked. The scars will always be there, but I am healing. When I was a little kid, I couldn't laugh or smile. I learned how to laugh and smile in prison, believe it or not. Still, sometimes, I get a hard core face, but even my friends tell me sometimes, 'You should smile a little bit. It is not going to crack your face'...
>
> I am so perceptive that I know where everybody is at all times on the range, in every room, at every move, because my dad used to beat us up and we used to hide in the bushes on the reserve and peep around for him. He would be on horseback running and screaming, 'I am going to murder you – you and the kids, Georgina. I will kill you', and he would shoot at us. We would hear the bullets going by our heads. One time I thought I was shot. I said, 'Oh, God! He shot me!' I was laying there and my mom said, "Get up! Get up! Get up!' and I couldn't get up because I could still hear the ringing of the bullet in my ear. I will always remember this until the day I die.... So we were running and we hid in the bushes for days on end and we could hear him yelling around, 'Georgina, I'm going to kill you'.... There were many times I fought with him. The scars that I have may not show now, but it has been a while. I had a 10 stitch mark on my forehead here, a cut here. I always threw myself on my mother each and every time my dad beat her up and this would go on for days on end when he would drink.

...The abuse went on. My mother died in my arms. She died in my arms and I remember the words she said. She said, 'Be good, my girl.' I went crazy after that and ended up in here, but at least I could cry and I could laugh and I could feel like a human being with my sisters....

I have to watch what I say or I will end up in seg, and I don't like that place. It doesn't help me. It doesn't help anybody. I have seen people go crazy in there, stir crazy, and starting hanging and slashing themselves because they couldn't handle being locked up like that....

There is a lot of heartache and pain in here that a lot of us wouldn't want to talk about.... I know deep down inside that there is a lot of pain and hurt within each individual in this institution.[218]

The women who appeared before us at the Prison for Women, at great emotional cost to themselves, were prepared to share with us some of that pain. They did so that we could understand and, through our report, enable other Canadians to understand that, in the words of Bev Auger,

Even though we are in prison, we are human and there are reasons why we ended up in prison, and a lot of it goes back to our upbringing, our abusive backgrounds, lack of traditional teachings because our communities are so deep into alcoholism that even they have lost their traditional way of life, their values. So I think when people start recognizing that there are reasons why we end up here, we weren't born like this. We weren't born to come to jail. It is everything that took place within our lives, all the struggles we have endured, all the hardships we have travelled. It all comes down to this. This is where we end up.[219]

The women at Prison for Women described how for Aboriginal women prisoners, the path to healing is anchored in the bedrock of their Aboriginal spirituality and, paralleling what we were told by Aboriginal men at the Saskatchewan Penitentiary and Stony Mountain Institution, how many of them first discovered that path within the prison. As Bev Auger told us,

One of the biggest things in here is our spirituality, our Native way. This is what makes the women in here a lot stronger and more able to deal with their time and to heal themselves. It all goes back to that: being able to heal yourselves.

---

[218] Sandy Paquachon, RCAP transcripts, Prison for Women, Kingston, Ontario, 31 March 1993, pp. 76-77, 84-90.

[219] Bev Auger, RCAP transcripts, Prison for Women, Kingston, Ontario, 31 March 1993, pp. 142-143.

141

> Over the years, with women who have come here, including
> myself, this is the only place that I have been really able to rec-
> ognize my own heritage, my own spirituality and it is sad because
> it is being in prison that I was able to really appreciate being
> Native or being proud that I am a Native woman.[220]

Since our special consultation at the Prison for Women, events have occurred that
highlight our earlier point that although there are no criminal justice utopias,
there are clearly better and worse directions to follow. For women prisoners, and
particularly Aboriginal women prisoners, we have some clear examples of both
directions.

As described in a special report by the federal correctional investigator, Ron
Stewart, events at the Prison for Women in April 1994 provide the clearest demonstration of the wrong direction.[221] Following a series of incidents in the segregation
unit at the prison, for women an emergency response team (ERT) composed of male
correctional officers from the Kingston Penitentiary was deployed against a number
of women prisoners, including Aboriginal prisoners. A video tape of the intervention
was provided to the correctional investigator together with an internal report
completed by staff of the Correctional Service of Canada. The following excerpt
from the correctional investigator's report reflects what appeared on the tape and
his findings.

> The video tape of the deployment of the ERT shows a massive dis-
> play of force being exercised in the face of virtually no resistance.
> Even if one could accept legitimacy of the initial decision to
> deploy the ERT, it is difficult to accept the continuation of this exer-
> cise given the obvious level of cooperation displayed by the
> inmates. The task of the ERT was to remove one woman at a time
> from her cell, strip the cell of all effects, and return that woman
> to her cell.
>
> In the first case depicted, the woman's clothing was forcibly
> removed and given that the film starts during this process, it is not
> clear if she was initially offered the opportunity remove her own
> clothes. In each case after that, the ERT members entered the cell
> and if the woman was not already naked, ordered the woman to
> remove her clothes. In all but one of these instances, the women
> complied, and in the case where one woman did not comply
> quickly enough, her clothing was also forcibly removed. Each

---

[220] Bev Auger, RCAP transcripts, pp. 24-25.

[221] R. L. Stewart, "Special Report of the Correctional Investigator pursuant to section 193, *Corrections
and Conditional Release Act*, Concerning the Treatment of Inmates and Subsequent Inquiry Following
Certain Incidents at the Prison for Women in April 1994 and Thereafter" (14 February 1995).

woman was then told to kneel, naked, on the floor of her cell, surrounded by ERT members while restraint equipment was applied.

After the restraint equipment was applied, each woman was helped to her feet, backed out of the cell naked, then given a flimsy paper gown, and marched backwards by the ERT from her cell to the shower area.

The woman was then directed by the ERT, with the assistance of their batons and shields, to stand facing the wall, one member holding the woman's head against the wall, presumably so that she could not see what was going on while another member held a baton close to her head.

While in the shower area, the cell was stripped of everything including the bed. Once the cell was stripped, the woman was marched backwards back to her cell, each was placed in her cell, asked to lie or kneel on the floor, the ERT members exited, the door was locked and the woman was left without a blanket or mattress in the stripped cell with the restraint equipment still on, contrary to sections 68, 69 and 70 of the CCRA [*Corrections and Conditional Release Act*]. However, in one case the woman was returned to her cell, made to kneel naked on the floor surrounded by ERT members for in excess of ten minutes, while team members fumbled with the restraint equipment.

This procedure was repeated for each of the eight women involved and it took in excess of two and a half hours to complete. Over the course of this time period, there was evidence of physical handling of the women by the ERT members and a number of women were poked or prodded with batons.

These incidents appeared in part to result from the women not understanding the mumbled directions given through the security helmets worn by ERT members.

This exercise was, in my opinion, an excessive use of force and it was without question degrading and dehumanizing for those women involved....[222]

The report also addresses the conditions under which the women were held in the segregation unit following the deployment of the emergency response team.

The women were held, in some cases, for up to eight months, in segregation cells, essentially stripped of all amenities, subject to 24 hour a day camera surveillance and the wearing of restraint equipment whenever they left their cells. They were denied for

---

[222] "Special Report of the Correctional Investigator" (emphasis added).

extended periods of time bedding, clothing, including underwear, basic hygiene items, personal address books, writing material, contact with family and daily exercise. The unit was not cleaned for over a month following the April incident and senior management was not visiting the segregation unit on a daily basis to meet with offenders as required by the legislation (section 36(2) of the CCRA). In fact this office noted a month period where there is no record of the unit manager attending the area. The level of insensitivity displayed following the 26 April ERT intervention is difficult to comprehend and indefensible.

The extended period of time spent in segregation and the conditions under which the women were forced to live were punitive and inconsistent with the legislative provisions governing administrative segregation.[223]

One of the prisoners involved in the events of April 1994 was Sandy Paquachon, who just a year earlier had spoken to us about the years of emotional and physical abuse she had suffered. The dehumanizing and degrading events described by the correctional investigator were for Sandy Paquachon yet another example of her abuse as an Aboriginal woman; for Aboriginal people they were a dark reflection of abuse by a system of which they are unjustly and disproportionately the victims.

If the events of April 1994 convey the darkest vision of a non-Aboriginal system of justice, it must be contrasted with another vision that is in the process of taking shape. This different and, we hope, ultimately more compelling vision of justice for Aboriginal women was given expression in the report of the Task Force on Federally Sentenced Women, published in 1990. The task force, made up of federal government representatives, community service agencies, and women's organizations, including Aboriginal women's organization, reviewed the experience of women in the federal prison system and charted a new direction for change. As set out in a preface to the report,

> The recommended plan contained in this report must be seen within the context of a long-term goal where incarceration will not be the intervention of choice, where harm done to victims, to federally sentenced women, to communities and to society will be repaired to the highest extent possible, and where Aboriginal people will have self-determination in their pursuit of justice.[224]

---

[223] "Special Report of the Correctional Investigator". Following release of this report, the solicitor general established an independent inquiry into the events at the Prison for Women in April 1994, conducted by Madam Justice Louise Arbour of the Ontario Court of Appeal (Order in Council, P.C. 1995-608).

[224] *Creating Choices*, cited in note 30, p. 2.

The task force added its voice to the long list of those who had called for the closure of the Prison for Women and its replacement with smaller regional institutions to enable federally sentenced women to be closer to their communities and families. It also recommended that a healing lodge be created for Aboriginal women. The task force recommendations were accepted by the solicitor general, and the Prison for Women is scheduled to close in 1996. The new regional institutions are being built; of particular significance for Aboriginal women, the healing lodge opened this year in Maple Creek, Saskatchewan.

Although the healing lodge is a federal institution governed by the *Corrections and Conditional Release Act* and its regulations,[225] the development and implementation of the Aboriginal vision of healing has reflected an unprecedented partnership between the Correctional Service of Canada and Aboriginal people. The healing lodge

> ...will recognize the unique disadvantaged position of Aboriginal women in the justice system, and will attempt to redress that disadvantaged position through a culturally sensitive setting which will respond to their needs. The Healing Lodge will provide the opportunity...through Aboriginal teachings, spirituality, and culture to recover from histories of abuse, to regain a sense of self-worth and hope to rebuild families, and to gain skills for 'walking in the new forest' (urban, non-Aboriginal society).[226]

To translate the vision into a physical space and an operational reality, a healing lodge planning circle was formed, composed of Aboriginal and non-Aboriginal representatives from government and non-governmental organizations. Twenty-three communities, both Aboriginal and non-Aboriginal, submitted proposals for the healing lodge, and these were evaluated against culturally sensitive Aboriginal and correctional criteria by a committee of correctional staff, Aboriginal women and elders. The most important criteria were those related to land, water and the availability of a supportive Aboriginal community, including elders and medicine people.[227] A proposal submitted by the communities of Maple Creek-Nekaneet in southwestern Saskatchewan was chosen because their submission demonstrated a strong tradition of Aboriginal and non-Aboriginal co-operation, an offering of sacred rural land, a sincere interest in making the healing lodge part of their communities, and a strong sense of responsibility to Aboriginal women under sentence. The site for the healing lodge, chosen by elders, is the northeastern part of the Nekaneet reserve in the Cypress Hills. The women will live in small, home-like lodges, and there are larger spaces for programs, spiritual ceremonies and gath-

---

[225] *Corrections and Conditional Release Act*, chapter 20.

[226] "Federally Sentenced Women Initiative, The Healing Lodge", information bulletin (Correctional Service Canada, 1994), unpaginated.

[227] 'Medicine people' is a term used by Aboriginal people to designate individuals who have healing powers and who act as community leaders in spiritual and other matters.

erings. The land surrounding the buildings is extensive enough that sweat lodges can be private and relocated yearly and will allow for gardens to be planted.

Not only is the physical space at the healing lodge quite different from other federal institutions; reflecting the underlying philosophy of 'healing', as opposed to 'correction', the training of staff for the lodge, many of whom are Aboriginal people drawn from the local communities, is much more intensive and directed to different goals than those that underpin other correctional training. It is designed to allow

(a) Self-knowledge. The staff must know themselves and acquire a thorough awareness of self and of the issues that have affected their lives in order to be effective in encouraging the women in their journey towards healing;

(b) Equality. The staff must acquire the knowledge and ability to empower the women as equals. There must be a breakdown of the us/them dynamic which exists in traditional correctional settings;

(c) Aboriginal spirituality and traditions. The entire training plan incorporates the all-important elements of Aboriginal Teachings, Traditions and Spirituality to allow staff to acquire and/or deepen their understanding of these in order to encourage a holistic approach to life skills with the women at the lodge.[228]

Reflecting the different philosophy of the healing lodge, the first part of the staff training is a 28-day practicum at the Poundmaker Treatment Centre where staff participate as clients in the treatment program. The Poundmaker Centre was one of the first Aboriginal-run treatment centres in the country to adapt a holistic approach to treating substance abuse. The objective of this part of the training is to give staff first-hand experience in the approaches that will provide the foundation for the healing lodge's programs. Subsequent phases of the training program are designed to give staff theoretical and practical knowledge of the counselling approaches best suited to the issues facing the women who will be living at the healing lodge, as well as examining these issues as they apply to themselves.[229]

In addition to the planning circle, the healing lodge is also supported by an elders circle whose members provided advice and counsel during the planning stage. The role of elders and medicine people is also deeply embedded in the operation of the healing lodge. Healing will be facilitated by elders who will conduct the ceremonies and medicine people who will help with the holistic healing of mind, body and spirit.

---

[228] "Training Plan Summary for the Healing Lodge" (Correctional Service Canada, June 1994).

[229] "Training Plan Summary".

146

Present plans anticipate that about thirty Aboriginal women will be accommodated at the healing lodge, and the policies will allow for some of their young children to be at the lodge with them.

A critical part of the healing lodge concept, and one recommended explicitly by the Task Force on Federally Sentenced Women, is links between the community and the institution. Those involved in the healing lodge see its ultimate success as linked to the support and assistance that the lodge and the women living there will receive from neighbouring communities. The people of the Nekaneet reserve are sharing their traditional lands with the women, and that sharing is intended to embrace a sharing of a mutual journey toward strength and renewal.

The healing lodge has been established and will be operated under the legislative framework of the *Corrections and Conditional Release Act*. Provisions in that law authorize the solicitor general to enter into agreements with Aboriginal communities to provide correctional services to Aboriginal offenders. There is clearly potential for developments along these lines in terms of the operation of the Maple Creek Healing Lodge and the local Aboriginal communities from whom many of the staff are being drawn and whose elders and medicine people will be associated with the lodge. It is not difficult therefore to see how the healing lodge concept, as it is evolving at Maple Creek, could become a model for how Aboriginal and non-Aboriginal society can respond to women like Sandy Paquachon and her sisters in the Prison for Women – a model that mends the damage done to their lives, that helps prevent the damage they in turn have done to the lives of others, and that contributes to a safer society in ways that respect the women's dignity and humanity. As Valerie Desjarlais, a former prisoner at the Prison for Women, reminded us,

> The women who will enter the healing lodge are women like me, lost in the society who degrades us, not recognizing that we are the victims of society's teachings, society's way of life.
>
> We are the children of you, who told us it was okay to drink ('go open mommy/daddy a beer'). We are the children of you, who told us violence was okay (we saw you beat mommy or other people up). We are the children of you, who told us racism was okay (those low, good for nothing, drunken bums).
>
> We are the children of you, that beat us up. We are what you made us. No, we're not a risk to society, society is a risk to us. We no longer want your teachings, nor your way of life. We followed your way of life, and your teachings, and you stripped us of our dignity and humanity.
>
> So you ask, 'Who are the women?' We are the children of society.[230]

---

[230] Quoted in "Federally Sentenced Women Initiative, The Healing Lodge", cited in note 226.

Two Case Studies

Community Council Project, Aboriginal Legal Services of Toronto

History and development

Although nearly half the Aboriginal people in Canada live in urban areas,[231] most Aboriginal justice initiatives are designed for people living on reserves or in rural communities. Toronto, home to more than 40,000 Aboriginal people,[232] hosts the only urban Aboriginal justice program in Canada – Aboriginal Legal Services of Toronto's (ALST) community council.[233] ALST is a comprehensive one-stop legal services centre for Aboriginal people. Founded in 1991, it operates an Aboriginal court worker program (two criminal court workers, one family court worker and one young offender court worker), inmate liaison programs (at the Guelph Correctional Centre, the Ontario Correctional Institute, the Vanier Centre for Women, and the Syl Apps Treatment Centre for Young Offenders) and a legal clinic, in addition to the community council. For the past two years, it has also offered an Aboriginal justice court worker training program.

In 1990, the founding board of directors of ALST wrote to Ian Scott, then attorney general of Ontario, requesting funds for the development of an adult Aboriginal criminal diversion project in Toronto. The board was concerned that urban Aboriginal people were not seen as having the cohesiveness necessary to develop justice initiatives.[234]

Expanding on this theme in testimony before this commission in 1993, Joy Fontaine, then president of the board of ALST, said,

> We are often asked whether it is fair to describe the Native population in Toronto as a community. After all, it is widely dispersed across the city and there is no one place that Native people live or congregate. But communities are not just defined by streets and blocks – communities, particularly in the urban context are defined by a sense of association and belonging. Native people in the city

---

[231] M.J. Norris et al., "Projections of the Population with Aboriginal Identity in Canada, 1991-2016", prepared by Statistics Canada for RCAP (February 1995).

[232] Statistics Canada, *1991 Aboriginal Census*, Table 3, p. 15 (1993, catalogue number 94-327). This figure is based on persons reporting Aboriginal origins in the Census. For persons who identify with their Aboriginal origins, the total is 14,205. These figures are not adjusted to account for undercoverage. Agencies providing services to Aboriginal people in Metropolitan Toronto estimate the population at between 60,000 and 70,000 people.

[233] As there do not appear to be any specific justice programs for urban Aboriginal people in the United States either, the community council is likely the only urban Aboriginal justice program operating in North America.

[234] Aboriginal Legal Services of Toronto, *Native Community Councils – An Alternative Measures Program for Toronto's Native Community* (Toronto: Aboriginal Legal Services of Toronto, 1990).

acknowledge themselves as Native and wish to be acknowledged and recognized as Native by others in their community as well. They have a wish to be served by people who understand their needs, their culture and their way of life. So even if there is no neighbourhood that can be seen as a Native neighbourhood there is a very real Native community in Toronto.[235]

In early 1991, ALST received funding from the ministry of the attorney general to develop the project. The development phase of the project lasted eleven months and was roughly divided into four stages: (1) discussions with justice system personnel regarding the parameters of the project; (2) consultation with elders and traditional teachers; (3) community consultations; and (4) selection and training of council members.[236]

Discussions with justice system personnel involved talks with the Toronto Crown attorney's office regarding how the project would function. As a result of these discussions, a protocol was signed between ALST and the Crown attorney's office. The preamble to the protocol sets out some of the key notions behind the project:

> The rationale behind the Community Council project is that the Native community best knows how to reach Native offenders. It is the expectation of ALST that this project will be more relevant and meaningful to both offenders and victims and thus will ultimately reduce the recidivism rate among Native offenders.

> The concept of the Community Council is not new – it is the way justice was delivered in Native communities in Central and Eastern Canada for centuries before the arrival of Europeans to North America and also the way that disputes were resolved in many reserve communities across the country...[237]

Under the terms of the protocol, no offences are inherently ineligible for diversion, nor is any individual inherently ineligible for the program by virtue of his or her prior criminal record. As well, once agreement from all parties has been reached with regard to diversion, charges against the individual are withdrawn or stayed. If the individual fails to appear at his or her hearing, the charges can be brought back. If the person does attend the hearing, however, charges cannot be brought before the courts in other than exceptional circumstances.

The community council program differs quite significantly from other diversion programs, both Aboriginal and non-Aboriginal. The open-ended nature of offences

---

[235] Joy Fontaine, RCAP transcripts, Toronto, 2 June 1993.

[236] Sharon Moyer and Lee Axon, "An Implementation Evaluation of the Native Community Council Project of the Aboriginal Legal Services of Toronto" (Toronto: Ontario Ministry of the Attorney General, 1993), pp. 17-21.

[237] "Protocol Between Aboriginal Legal Services of Toronto and the Toronto Crown Attorney's Office With Regard to the Community Council Project" (1992), p. 1.

eligible for diversion is one major difference, as is the fact that the program is open to people regardless of their criminal record. To date, 33 per cent of those diverted to the program have more than 10 previous convictions, while only 24 per cent have no prior convictions.[238]

The other significant difference is that charges against the individual are withdrawn when the person enters the program. In many diversion programs, charges are withdrawn only after the individual has successfully completed the diversion. In these programs, failure to complete the tasks assigned means that the diversion does not continue and charges are proceeded with. In the case of the community council, such an approach was considered counter-productive. One of the goals of the project is

> to encourage offenders to accept more responsibility for their criminal behaviour and to instil in them a greater degree of accountability for their conduct by more active involvement in undoing the wrong they have done.[239]

It was felt that even if holding the threat of reinstatement of charges over the offender might encourage compliance with the council's decisions, compliance would not result from a desire on the part of the individual to address the wrong they had done or move toward changing their behaviour, but rather from a wish to avoid punishment. Removing the threat of reinstated charges means that those who comply with council decisions will be doing so because they want to, because they feel it is important for them.

Following successful negotiation of the protocol, the next step in the development process was consultation with elders and traditional teachers. In July of 1991, more than 20 elders, traditional teachers, and faithkeepers met in Toronto to discuss, among other things, the community council project. It was the consensus of this gathering that a smaller group should gather for a few days to consider the project in greater detail.[240] The second gathering took place on 27-30 August 1991 on Birch Island. The substance of the gathering was reported in a three-page summary document. The gathering envisaged a process very different from that of the criminal courts:

> At the heart of the Community Council must be a real, conscious feeling of kindness and respect for both the offender and the victim. When the offender and victim realize that the Council members actually care about them and respect them, then the message of the Council has a better chance of getting through...

---

[238] "Demographic and Cases Statistics – Quarterly Report to the Ministry of the Attorney General of the Community Council Program for the Period October 1 to December 31, 1994" (Toronto: Aboriginal Legal Services of Toronto, 1995).

[239] Moyer and Axon, "An Implementation Evaluation", cited in note 236, p. 5.

[240] Moyer and Axon, "An Implementation Evaluation", p. 18.

The most important characteristic of those sitting as Council members should be a sense of kindness...

It must always be remembered that changing a person's lifestyle can only be done by the person him or herself. While a person can be ordered to stop certain actions and to start doing other things, whether or not the person will respond is in their hands alone... even if a person is not yet ready to make the changes in their life that are necessary, they may be taking steps in the right direction and those steps should be encouraged. [Council decisions] therefore should be realistic and should motivate the person to look at their life and re-examine it...

...the Council should always keep in mind that some of its most important resources are the elders and teachers of the community... Professional agencies can help an offender, but sometimes the most meaningful help an offender can receive comes from a person who is spending time with them because they want to, not because they are paid. This... is one of the strong points of the Council, those people hearing the cases will not be judges pulling down large salaries, but members of the community, volunteering their time.[241]

Following the elders gatherings, two community consultations were held in Toronto with representatives of Aboriginal agencies operating in the city. Toronto has a very active network of Aboriginal agencies providing social services and other programs. In addition to these consultations, a presentation on the project was made to the annual general meeting of the Native Canadian Centre of Toronto, and the program was discussed on a number of radio programs – both Aboriginal-specific and of general interest.

The purpose of the consultation phase was to determine what concerns the Toronto Aboriginal community had about the project as it was designed. While overall support for the project was high, the consultations revealed a great concern for the safety of victims of violence. In particular, concerns were raised about the possible diversion of cases of family violence. Those participating in the consultations made it clear that they felt that family violence cases should not be diverted until (a) the safety of victims could be assured and (b) Aboriginal-specific programs had been established to provide services to abusers. In light of these concerns, cases of family violence were not diverted to the council when it began operations.[242]

---

[241] "Elders and Traditional Teachers Gathering on Birch Island" (Toronto: Aboriginal Legal Services of Toronto, 1991), pp. 1-2.

[242] This issue has not been abandoned. A Family Violence Working Group was set up in December 1992 to discuss how the council might eventually be in position to hear family violence cases. This issue is discussed more fully later in this report.

The final phase of project development involved the selection of the initial group of men and women to serve as volunteer council members. It was ALST's concern that the project be seen as one belonging genuinely to the Aboriginal community, not as the project of one agency. As a result, ALST played no role in vetting the selection of people to sit as council members. Council members were recruited by sending a letter to a number of Aboriginal agencies inviting them to recommend people as council members. The letter contained the summary of the Birch Island gathering to assist the organizations in making recommendations. All those recommended were invited to a day and a half orientation session in February 1992. Those who attended the orientation learned more about the project and discussed their hopes and concerns for the project. At the end of the session, those attending were asked whether they wished to sit as council members. In their evaluation report of the project, Sharon Moyer and Lee Axon noted:

> The...Project Coordinator observed...that in keeping with the goal of the Project that it was to be a community-directed program, he was not certain until the very end – that is, after the Community Council members' orientation – whether the community was willing to continue with the Project. This was significant in the sense that this was not a program that was being foisted upon the Native community, but was something which right up to the point of going operational, the community had the final decision with respect to ...implementation... without the support and agreement of the Community Council members there would be no project.[243]

As it turned out, all 16 people – 7 men and 9 women – who attended the orientation agreed to volunteer as council members. The council heard its first case in March 1992.

Project operation

All Aboriginal people charged with a criminal offence who are willing to accept responsibility[244] for their actions are eligible for the community council project.[245] The protocol with the Crown attorney's office gives ALST sole responsibility for identifying Aboriginal people for entry to the program. As with all other programs at ALST – and at other Aboriginal social service agencies in Toronto as well – the

---

[243] Moyer and Axon, "An Implementation Evaluation", cited in note 236, p. 28.

[244] Accepting responsibility does not require the individual to admit guilt before a court, nor does accepting responsibility mean that the person necessarily agrees that she or he has committed all the offences with which he/she is charged.

[245] In practice, in addition to family violence cases, the only cases in which Crown attorneys will not consent to diversion are sexual assault (as the result of a directive from the ministry of the attorney general to all diversion projects), impaired driving, and firearms offences in which a firearms prohibition will be sought.

community council is a status-blind program and is therefore open to all Aboriginal people.[246] Status plays a role only after the council hearing, in terms of programs and services available to Aboriginal people from government bodies. For example, Health Canada's Medical Services Branch will pay for the transportation of status Indians to alcohol or drug treatment centres outside Toronto, or even outside Ontario, but will not do the same for non-status individuals.

At the gathering of elders and traditional teachers at Birch Island, the issue of selecting people for the program was raised. The gathering made it clear that

> It is the role of the Court workers to make the initial selection of those to go before the Council. In making these choices however, the Court workers cannot try to guess what offenders will be more likely than others to 'get something positive' from the program. It is not the Court worker's job to judge who will likely benefit or not benefit from the Council. How can anyone know the answer to such a question? The Council should be open to any offender. The only restriction to offender participation in the Council should be the lack of resources in the community, either in terms of the ability to help a certain number people at any one time, or the ability to help that particular individual.[247]

Following the eleven-month development phase, the program began hearing cases in March 1992. To the end of December 1994 the program had heard 214 cases. In the 1993/94 fiscal year, the program heard 115 cases. Attendance at council hearings by offenders is high – 89 per cent. This figure is particularly significant because 41.5 per cent of those diverted have had previous convictions for failure to appear in court.[248]

Overall, 86.1 per cent of those attending their hearings have either completed the terms of the council decision or are in the process of doing so. Non-compliance with council decisions is only 13.9 per cent. It should also be noted that many of those who do not comply fully with the council decision comply with a portion of it; very few people attend a council hearing and simply walk away with no intention of doing any of what they have agreed to do.

The council has a range of dispositions available to it. Essentially it can do anything but send a person to jail. Generally, a council decision contains a number of provisions. To date, the most frequent dispositions are community service (43 per cent), Aboriginal agency counselling (42 per cent), attendance at self-help programs

---

[246] Aboriginal people registered under the *Indian Act* are considered 'status', while those who are not are 'non-status'. Since these programs are status-blind, they apply to all Aboriginal people.

[247] "Gathering on Birch Island", cited in note 241, pp. 2-3.

[248] "Demographic and Cases Statistics", cited in note 238. Figures in this and the next three paragraphs are from this quarterly report.

(22 per cent), seeking employment or education opportunities (30 per cent), and continued contact with ALST (49 per cent).

A wide range of charges can be diverted to the council. The most frequently diverted charges are fail to appear/fail to comply (32 per cent), theft (24 per cent), prostitution (19 per cent), assault (18 per cent), mischief (16 per cent), and possession of stolen property (10 per cent). In addition to these charges, the council has also dealt with charges of arson, break and enter, and fraud, among others. Since March 1994 the council has been able to divert narcotics charges[249] as a result of concluding a protocol with federal Crown attorneys.[250] To date, drug charges represent only 4.5 per cent of cases diverted, but this will undoubtedly increase over time.[251]

The council usually sits six or seven times a month with three council members sitting at each hearing. At present there are 27 council members – 17 women and 10 men, all of whom are volunteers serving without remuneration.

Council hearings are not open to the public, although victims of offences are encouraged to attend. The reason for closed hearings is that they tend to reveal very personal information about the offender. Council members and staff are concerned that the presence of people not immediately part of the process might inhibit the offender from speaking freely, which would restrict the council's ability to do its job.

In evaluating the project, Sharon Moyer and Lee Axon were permitted to observe four cases. Their description of the council process is as follows:

> Council members meet over lunch or dinner one hour before the hearing to review information on the case. Some discussion will occur at this time and the [Project] Coordinator may be asked for further information or clarification of specific points. The hearing starts by the Council members introducing themselves to the offender; it is not unusual for Council members to provide personal information about themselves as well as their organizational affiliations, if any. The chairperson, who is chosen during the pre-hearing discussions, then starts to question the offender, sometimes about the offence, but also about personal matters. Other Council members will ask the offender questions, often seemingly at random. The circumstances of the offence, and the

---

[249] All narcotics-related charges are eligible for diversion except cultivation and importation.

[250] Provincially-appointed Crown attorneys are responsible for prosecuting all *Criminal Code* and *Provincial Offences Act* cases, while federal Crown attorneys are responsible for offences under, among other statutes, the *Narcotic Control Act* and the *Food and Drugs Act*.

[251] Since individuals are often charged with more than one offence, these figures may total more than 100 per cent.

offender's perspective on what happened, are obtained near the end of the hearing.

If the offender is known to have a substance abuse problem, very often the Council members will make careful inquiry into the person's motivation for treatment and any past treatment experience...

After questioning, the offender is asked to leave the room and Council members discuss their options. If it has become apparent that the offender has personal or social problems, such as substance abuse, and he or she has indicated an interest in treatment, much of the discussion may revolve around treatment options... The Council's decision is arrived at by consensus.

...The staff member types the decision, which is reviewed by Council members before the offender returns to the hearing room. The chairperson of the hearing formally reads out the decision to the offender. The discussion turns to the offender's view of the order. The offender is asked whether he or she agrees with the decision and is asked to sign a copy...

Some Council members are not reluctant to lecture the person, although quite nicely, about his or her behaviour. From their perspective, the Council members represent the community saying to the client, "you have done something wrong and you should not do that again".... Some hearings become very personal and it is not unknown for offenders (and Council members) to cry.

The total hearing process lasts from about three-quarters of an hour to over three hours. It was noted that there is no relationship between the seriousness of the offence and length of Council hearings because some persons with a very minor offence may have a whole range of problems that the Council can address. In most cases, the Council deals with the person, not the offence.[252]

As noted in this account, the focus of council hearings is the offender, not the offence. This is based on the assumption that the people appearing before the council are not career criminals (although they may have very long criminal records), but people acting out difficulties they have experienced, often since childhood, in a manner that brings them into conflict with the law.

Demographic information on council clients brings this point out very clearly: 68 per cent of those coming before the council have a drug or alcohol problem; 43 per cent were adopted or were in the care of a children's aid society; and 20 per cent have a history of treatment for psychiatric problems. The statistics also appear to indicate that a lack of involvement with the Aboriginal community may well be

---

[252] Moyer and Axon, "An Implementation Evaluation", cited in note 236, pp. 61-63.

a predictor of criminal activity. Thus while only 12 per cent of those who have come before the council could be described as well integrated in the Aboriginal community, 61 per cent of those diverted had no real involvement with the community.[253] In a case study of ALST for the Commission, Don McCaskill found that council members saw the opportunity to link offenders with programs and services in the Aboriginal community and to "acknowledge Aboriginal people [as] part of a larger Aboriginal community" as an important aspect of the council's work.[254]

McCaskill also interviewed a number of people who had appeared before the council. All those interviewed felt that their side of the story had been heard at the council, and all noted that the council process is very different from the non-Aboriginal court system, in that the process is confidential, it puts them at ease, and it allows them to explain their actions. Those interviewed said it was clear that council members wanted to help them. One person said the experience of being before the council was "like a family wanting to help." Seventy-five per cent of those interviewed said they were very satisfied with their council experience, while the remaining 25 per cent described themselves as somewhat satisfied.

Moyer and Axon also interviewed seven people who had appeared before the council. All indicated that they found the experience a good one.

> One person, who had been charged with mischief under $1,000, said that the Council members made her feel ashamed of the offence, which had not occurred to her before. She felt that having the Council members talk to her as an individual had much more impact than would the court system. Another client said, "I didn't lie to the Council because they are my people." A third client went into some detail about her reaction to her Council appearance:
>
> > The Council members made me more relaxed. They made me feel better telling the story even though there were five people there. They understood what I was trying to say. The questions were hard but I felt like I wanted to talk out my problems and some stuff about my behaviour came out. There was a feeling of trust and I felt the elders understood me. They gave me chance to speak up, which I would not have had in court.[255]

The impact of a council hearing on an individual can be quite profound. In 1993, Harold B. (not his real name) appeared before the council on a charge of mischief over $1,000. While drunk, he had broken a glass display window and a large store-front window of a downtown restaurant after being asked to leave because he did

---

[253] "Demographic and Cases Statistics", cited in note 238.

[254] Don McCaskill, "Aboriginal Legal Services of Toronto – Community Study", research study prepared for RCAP (1993).

[255] Moyer and Axon, "An Implementation Evaluation", cited in note 236, p. 64.

not have the money to pay for his meal. When he came to the hearing he was extremely depressed and told the council he was considering suicide. Harold B. was in his late 20s and felt he was a failure. Council members listened to Harold talk about his life and his present state and then told him something of their lives as well – some of them as difficult as his had been. At the end of the hearing council's decision required him to

- attend three AA meetings a week, both open and closed, for three months;
- attend at least one cultural healing circle; the council strongly encouraged to him to continue attending such circles;
- take counselling to deal with sexual abuse he experienced as a child;
- write a letter of apology to the restaurant owner; and
- keep in touch with ALST once a week until the order was complied with.

He was also strongly encouraged to take an educational upgrading course.

Harold B. complied with all the terms of his council order, completed an educational upgrading course and entered a program at a Toronto community college. A number of months after his hearing, Harold wrote to the council members who heard his case. His letter read (in part):

> I realize that their decision regarding my case can be regarded as a form of punishment, but I see it now as a godsend. The requirements of the decision were things I should have been doing years ago but was too afraid or stupid to carry them out on my own. Once again members of the Community Council, I thank you for straightening out my life and hopefully pointing me in the direction of a brighter future.[256]

Next steps

The community council project is now in its fourth operational year. Building on its experience to date, the council hopes to move soon to hearing cases of family violence. Since late 1992, representatives of several Aboriginal social services agencies have been meeting as the Family Violence Working Group. The formation of the group was inspired by a call from the executive director of Anduhyuan – the Aboriginal women's shelter – to the director of the community council project. While she agreed that family violence cases should not yet be diverted to the council, she felt it was important for the community to work toward establishing an amended protocol to deal with these cases. In tandem with this endeavour she also felt it vital to identify the gaps in services for victims and offenders. The working group has held an all-day session for Aboriginal social services agencies

---

[256] Aboriginal Legal Services of Toronto, "Quarterly Report to the Ministry of the Attorney General for the period September to December 1993" (Toronto: Aboriginal Legal Services of Toronto, 1993), pp. 3-4.

to discuss programs now available and service gaps, as well as a day and half conference on family violence issues entitled Community Initiatives in Family Healing.

The conference featured elders and speakers from the Ma Mawi Wi Chi Itata Centre in Winnipeg on dealing with family violence. The working group has now approached the attorney general with an amended protocol for family violence cases that ensures the safety of victims of violence. The group has agreed that progress on this issue cannot occur if new Aboriginal-specific programs are not developed to meet the needs of both victims and offenders.

The success of the council process has also led to discussions about moving into other areas of dispute resolution. Staff at ALST worked with a reference group for almost two years to develop a child welfare community council. This council would act as an alternative to child protection hearings under the provisions of Ontario's *Child Welfare Act*. The child welfare community council heard its first case in December 1994.

There is also a proposal to use the community council concept to resolve landlord and tenant disputes in the Toronto Aboriginal community. ALST's legal clinic now represents Aboriginal tenants in disputes with landlords. At present, there are four Aboriginal non-profit organizations providing housing for Aboriginal people in the city. When a dispute arises between the tenant and the landlord, it is often resolved in court, at significant expense to the landlord and often without a satisfactory resolution of the matter. It is hoped that the council process might provide a way of resolving these disputes in a culturally appropriate manner that will lead to better outcomes for both tenants and landlords.

The community council can thus be seen as the beginning of development of a comprehensive urban Aboriginal justice system. With the commitment of the Aboriginal community and the goodwill of non-Aboriginal actors in the legal process, the council process holds a great deal of promise.

There are challenges ahead for the community council, however. Foremost among them is funding. Funding of the project has always been somewhat tenuous. The project has operated on an annual budget of $100,000 since its inception. This figure covers the cost of a full-time project co-ordinator, a part-time director and a part-time administrative assistant. It also must cover the rent and office costs of the project and the cost of meals and parking for council members. The project is funded on a year-to-year basis, and ALST usually learns of its funding allocation three to seven months into the fiscal year. Continued funding cannot be assumed.

Interest in the community council project has been quite high from Aboriginal and non-Aboriginal organizations across the country and abroad. To date, however, no similar projects have been launched in any other urban centre, although several are in various stages of development. Given the demographic realities of the Aboriginal population in Canada, it is hoped that other urban Aboriginal communities might find a way to build on the Toronto experience and develop their own response to justice issues.

Hollow Water First Nation's Community Holistic Circle Healing Project

History and development

Community holistic circle healing (CHCH) deals with cases of sexual abuse in the northern Manitoba First Nation community of Hollow Water and in the surrounding Métis communities of Manigotagan, Aghaming, and Seymourville. CHCH has fashioned a unique response to the particular needs of people affected by this offence.

The idea behind CHCH took root first in the Ojibwa community of Hollow Water in 1984, when a group of residents and other people involved in providing social services to the community sought to grapple with the legacy of decades of alcoholism and family abuse, suicide and cultural loss. By 1987 a resource group had been formed, and based on their work – and the first trickle of what was to become a stream of disclosures – they became convinced that many of the community's problems could be traced to sexual abuse.[257] The degree to which sexual abuse was a problem undermining the very fabric of the community was illustrated by the fact that the resource group believes that 75 per cent of the community have been victims of sexual abuse and 35 per cent are victimizers.[258]

In 1988 members of the resource group travelled to Alkali Lake to learn about the successful efforts of that community to address the problems of alcohol abuse and sexual abuse.[259] The resource group found the trip to Alkali Lake a moving and profound experience. Upon their return to Hollow Water, the group launched a number of initiatives, among them CHCH.

A sub-committee of the resource group, the assessment team, was responsible for the development of CHCH. Before any initiatives were undertaken specifically to respond to cases of sexual abuse, those interested in participating in the process went through a two-year training program. The program included cultural awareness; alcohol and drug awareness; team building; networking; suicide intervention; family counselling; communications skills; nutrition; and human sexuality.[260]

---

[257] Thérèse Lajeunesse, *Community Holistic Circle Healing, Hollow Water First Nation* (Ottawa: Solicitor General of Canada, Aboriginal Peoples Collection, 1993), p. 1.

[258] Ross, "Duelling Paradigms?", cited in note 93, p. 243. The term 'victimizer' is used rather than offender because it is the belief of the Resource Group that many of those who commit these offences were themselves victims at one point. It is felt that the term may bring out the impact of their experience as victims to those charged with these offences.

[259] Hollow Water First Nation, "The CHCH Approach – Community Holistic Circle Healing", material presented to the Tribal Court Symposium, Federation of Saskatchewan Indian Nations, Saskatoon, 31 March 1994, p. 1.

[260] Lajeunesse, *Community Holistic Circle Healing*, cited in note 257, p. 1.

CHCH focuses on cases of sexual assault, as it is felt that the root problems of the community can be dealt with only when the issue of sexual abuse is addressed. At the same time, resource group members feel it is important that people realize that CHCH is not about addressing a particular problem; rather it is integral to the healing and development of the community.

> CHCH is not a program or project. It is a process with individuals coming back into balance. A process of a community healing itself. It is a process which one day will allow our children and grandchildren to once again walk with their heads high as they travel around the Medicine Wheel of Life.[261]

At its core, CHCH addresses sexual abuse by providing support, counselling and guidance to everyone affected by the crime, including the victim, the victim's family, the victimizer, and the victimizer's family.

The CHCH method of treating sexual abuse contains thirteen steps:

Step 1. Disclosure
Step 2. Protecting the Victim/Child
Step 3. Confronting the Victimizer
Step 4. Assisting the Spouse
Step 5. Assisting the family(ies)/the Community
Step 6. Meeting of the Assessment Team/RCMP/Crown
Step 7. Victimizer Must Admit and Accept Responsibility
Step 8. Preparation of the Victimizer
Step 9. Preparation of the Victim
Step 10. Preparation of All the Families
Step 11. The Special Gathering
Step 12. The Healing Contract Implemented
Step 13. The Cleansing Ceremony[262]

Progress through the entire 13 steps is estimated to take five years.

Project operation

While CHCH is often referred to as a Hollow Water initiative, it actually serves four communities: Manigotagan, Aghaming, Seymourville, and Hollow Water. Using the first initial of each community produces the acronym MASH. The community has taken to this acronym for several reasons:

> 1. We live in a war zone. It's not the guns and bombs kind of war. Ours is a more insidious conflict that has consumed the best

---

[261] "The CHCH Approach", cited in note 259, p. 4.

[262] Lajeunesse, *Community Holistic Circle Healing*, cited in note 257, pp. 2-3.

energies of our best people for several generations. The enemies in this war are alcohol and drug abuse, sexual abuse,
interpersonal and family violence, welfare dependency, dysfunctional family and community relations, and extremely
low self-esteem. We've been at war with these enemies for
quite a while now.

2. MASH is also a good name for us because we are in the business of healing our communities, and the team of us who
work together (sometimes referred to as the Resource Group)
from our four communities are continually struggling to cope
with casualties of the war while at the same time planning and
executing strategies for winning it.[263]

While Hollow Water is a First Nations community, the other three communities
are largely Métis. The total population of the four communities is about 1,500
people.[264] All members of the community can take part in CHCH; it is a status-blind
program. The only time status plays a role in the program is in relation to funding for psychological services. The Medical Services Branch provides this service
for status Indians but not for others.

The overall operation of CHCH is handled by the assessment team, while specific
tasks are undertaken by a management team. The assessment team provides all the
resources necessary to restore balance to those affected by sexual abuse. In particular, the team is responsible for prevention and intervention activities; developing
support systems; providing assessments of those involved in the process; and maintaining liaison with lawyers, Crown attorneys and child welfare agencies.

CHCH is currently staffed by an executive director, seven community and family
violence workers, an administrative assistant, and the volunteers and/or professionals who make up the assessment team. In addition to CHCH staff, the assessment
team calls on volunteers and professionals from virtually all local social services
providers in the community.[265]

The actual process of treating sexual abuse is quite extensive and cannot receive
its full due here. The key to all interventions is the protection, support and healing of the victim. Once a disclosure of sexual abuse has been made, the assessment
team conducts a detailed interview with the victim. Steps are then taken immediately to protect the victim and to ensure her or his long-term safety. Only after these
steps have been taken is the victimizer confronted. In most cases the victimizer is
confronted before the RCMP is notified and charges are laid. The CHCH process is

---

[263] Wanipigow Resource Group, "Down to the Nitty Gritty: A Final Report of the Wanipigow SAFE
(Self-Awareness for Everyone) Program", in Lajeunesse, *Community Holistic Circle Healing*, cited
in note 257, Appendix C, p. 1.

[264] Peter Moon, "Native Healing Helps Abusers", *The Globe and Mail*, 8 April 1995, pp. A1, A8.

[265] Theresa Lajeunesse, *Community Holistic Circle Healing*, cited in note 257, p. 2.

explained to the victimizer at this time. It is emphasized that if the victimizer wishes to enter CHCH he must accept responsibility for the offence and plead guilty in court. The agreement to plead guilty is important because it spares the victim the trauma of testifying in court.[266] The victimizer has five days to decide whether to participate in CHCH. In some cases, victims do not wish to bring formal charges against the victimizer. While the absence of charges limits some of the things CHCH can do, workers nevertheless continue to assist the victim.[267]

Following confrontation of the victimizer, the team meets with the victimizer's spouse to provide support. In her review of CHCH for the federal solicitor general, Theresa Lajeunesse describes the role of team members in dealing with victims, victimizers and their families:

> In some cases, the family of the victim and victimizer will be the same, in other cases they are different. In most cases, they will be from the same community. In all cases, the pain brought about by a disclosure will have a rippling effect throughout the community and members of both immediate and extended families will be affected. As with the victim and the victimizer, individual workers will work with members of all affected families. Often workers must deal with not only the sexual abuse, but past trauma which occurred in the lives of all the participants.[268]

The non-Aboriginal criminal justice system puts the bulk of its energies into securing the conviction of the offender. In cases of sexual assault, it is now recognized that victims too have a legitimate claim on the services of the justice system. There is no comparison, however, between the way the non-Aboriginal justice system understands the impact of sexual assault and the way it is understood in Hollow Water. Rupert Ross describes the energies that go into creating a support network for all those involved:

> At all times, from the moment of disclosure through to the cleansing ceremony, team members have responsibility to work with, protect, support, teach and encourage a wide range of people. It is their view that since a great many people are affected by each disclosure, all of them deserve assistance, and just as important, all of them must be involved in any process aimed at creating healthy dynamics and breaking the inter-generational chain of abuse. I watched them plan for a possible confrontation with a suspected victimizer, and the detailed dispersal of team members through the community to support those whom the disclosure

---

[266] Janet Cook, presentation on CHCH to the Tribal Court Symposium, Saskatoon, 31 March 1994.

[267] Lajeunesse, *Community Holistic Circle Healing*, cited in note 257, p. 5.

[268] Lajeunesse, *Community Holistic Circle Healing*, p. 7.

would touch reminded me of a military operation in its logistical complexity.[269]

CHCH has entered into a protocol with the Manitoba Crown attorney's office to govern the way their intervention is respected. Enough time is taken before sentencing to allow the assessment team to work with the victimizer. Generally, victimizers who plead guilty receive three years' probation. During those three years they are required to continue their work with CHCH. Failure to follow through with the program would result in a charge of breach of probation. No such charges have yet been brought against a victimizer.[270] The three-year probation term is the maximum permitted by the *Criminal Code*. As noted earlier, in the opinion of CHCH staff, five years are required to see a person through the entire program.

An understanding of the process of healing is crucial to an understanding of this initiative in particular and of Aboriginal justice programs in general. With reference to CHCH, Rupert Ross describes the healing process in the following manner:

> This healing process is painful, for it involves stripping away all the excuses, justifications, angers and other defences of each abuser until, finally, confronted with a victim who has been made strong enough to expose his or her pain in their presence, the abuser actually feels the pain he or she created. Only then can the re-building begin, both for the abuser and the abused. The word "healing" seems such a soft word, but the process of healing within the Hollow Water program is anything but.[271]

In a newspaper article about CHCH, Peter Moon discussed the experience of those who participate in the process.

> These circles are wrenching experiences in which all hurt by disclosure talk about their feelings. They dredge up painful suppressed memories. There are tears, anger, sharing and forgiveness. Sometimes offenders and victims participate in the same circles.

> "My body feels strong outside, but not inside," one offender told a recent survey. He wept as he talked in a barely audible voice about the abuse he had suffered as a boy and the sexual assaults he had committed as a man.

> The circles are not an easy path to healing, said Burma Bushie, an Ojibwa child and family worker who coordinates the Hollow Water Healing Programme. But they are crucial...

---

[269] Ross, "Duelling Paradigms?", cited in note 93, p. 245.

[270] Lajeunesse, *Community Holistic Circle Healing*, cited in note 257, p. 10.

[271] Ross, "Duelling Paradigms?", cited in note 93, p. 245.

All circles open and close with a prayer to the Creator, and although people taking part in the program are not compelled to do so, they are given every opportunity to take part in traditional ceremonies.

"The spiritual program is the key," Mr. Hardesty [a member of the Hollow Water band council] said. "It helps people to understand why they have hurt and been hurt and makes them feel better.

"It makes all the difference in the world. The ceremonies, the sweat lodge, even the prayers in the circle. And the burning of the sweetgrass, the sage, cedar and the tobacco. It's all part of the spiritual healing process."[272]

Understanding the healing process at work in Hollow Water helps also to understand the position CHCH now takes on the incarceration of offenders. Initially, CHCH dealt with the sentencing process by providing a pre-sentence report for the court. By 1993, however, dissatisfaction with this role led CHCH to re-evaluate the need for incarceration in the cases they were handling. The issue was important enough that CHCH wrote a paper setting out its position:

CHCH's position on the use of incarceration, and its relationship to an individual's healing process, has changed over time. In our initial efforts to break the vicious cycle of abuse that was occurring in our community, we took the position that we needed to promote the use of incarceration in cases which were defined as "too serious." After some time, however, we came to the conclusion that this position was adding significantly to the difficulty of what was already complex casework.

As we worked through the casework difficulties that arose out of this position, we came to realize two things:

- that as we both shared our own stories of victimization and learned from our experiences in assisting others in dealing with the pain of their victimization, it became very difficult to define "too serious." The quantity or quality of pain felt by the victim, the family/ies and the community did not seem to be directly connected to any specific acts of victimization. Attempts...to define a particular victimization as "too serious" and another as "not too serious"...were gross oversimplifications, and certainly not valid from an experiential point of view, and

- that promoting incarceration was based on, and motivated by, a mixture of feelings of anger, revenge, guilt and shame on our part, and around our personal victimization issues, rather than

---

[272] Moon, "Native Healing Helps Abusers", cited in note 264.

the healthy resolution of the victimization we were trying to address.

Thus our position on the use of incarceration has shifted. At the same time, we understand how the legal system continues to use and view incarceration – as punishment and deterrence for the victimizers...and protection and safety for the victim(s) and community. What the legal system seems not to understand is the complexity of the issues involved in breaking the cycle of abuse that exists in our community.

The use of judgement and punishment actually works against the healing process. An already unbalanced person is moved further out of balance.

What the threat of incarceration does do is keep people from coming forward and taking responsibility for the hurt they are causing. It reinforces the silence, and therefore promotes, rather than breaks, the cycle of violence that exists. In reality, rather than making the community a safer place, the threat of jail places the community more at risk.

In order to break the cycle, we believe that victimizer accountability must be to, and support must come from, those most affected by the victimization – the victim, the family/ies, and the community. Removal of the victimizer from those who must and are best able to, hold him/her accountable, and to offer him/her support, adds complexity to already existing dynamics of guilt and shame. The healing process of all parties is therefore at best delayed, and most often actually deterred.

The legal system, based on principles of punishment and deterrence, as we see it, simply is not working. We cannot understand how the legal system doesn't see this...

We do not see our present position on incarceration as either "an easy way out" for the victimizer, or as the victimizer "getting away." We see it rather as establishing a very clear line of accountability between the victimizer and his or her community. What follows from that line is a process that we believe is not only much more difficult for the victimizer, but also much more likely to heal the victimization, than doing time in jail could ever be.

Our children and the community can no longer afford the price the legal system is extracting in its attempts to provide justice in our community.[273]

---

[273] CHCH position paper (1993), quoted in Ross, "Duelling Paradigms?", cited in note 93, pp. 246-247.

As a result of this shift in perspective, CHCH moved away from providing pre-sentence reports and looked at more community-based ways of providing justice in sexual abuse cases. In December 1993, CHCH took a step toward greater control over the justice process when a sentencing circle was held for two victimizers. The circle, the first in Manitoba, involved 250 residents of the community. The assessment team felt that the sentencing circle approach better met the needs of all those affected by the offence. In outlining their support for this initiative the assessment team wrote:

> Up until now the sentencing hearing has been the point at which all of the parties of the legal system...and the community have come together. Major differences of opinion as to how to proceed have often existed. As we see it, the legal system usually arrives with an agenda of punishment and deterrence of the "guilty" victimizer, and safety and protection of the victim and community; the community on the other hand, arrives with an agenda of accountability of the victimizer to the community, and restoration of balance to all parties of the victimization.
>
> As we see it, the differences in the agendas are seriously deterring the healing process of the community. We believe that the restoration of balance is more likely to occur if sentencing itself is more consistent in process and in content with the healing work of the community. Sentencing needs to become more of a step in the healing process, rather than a diversion from it...
>
> As we see it, the sentencing circle plays two primary purposes (1) it promotes the community healing process by providing a forum for the community to address the parties of the victimization at the time of sentencing, and (2) it allows the court to hear directly from the people most affected by the pain of victimization. In the past the crown and defence, as well as ourselves, have attempted to portray this information. We believe that it is now time for the court to hear from the victim, the family of the victim, the victimizer, the family of the victimizer, and the community-at-large.[274]

By June 1995, CHCH had dealt with 409 clients, including 94 victims (32 of whom have completed the healing program), 180 family members of victims (27 of whom have completed the healing program), 52 victimizers (4 of whom have successfully completed the program), and 83 family members of victimizers.[275] Two victimizers have re-offended since entering the program.

---

[274] Department of Justice, Aboriginal Justice Directorate, "Community Holistic Circle Healing, Hollow Water First Nation Interim Report" (Ottawa: no date), Appendix 3, pp. 15-16.

[275] Moon, "Native Healing Helps Abusers", cited in note 264. These statistics were compiled for Moon by Burma Bushie, a CHCH staff person (Peter Moon, personal communication, April 1995).

Next steps

As with other justice initiatives, the continued funding of CHCH is still unsettled. Funding from the federal Aboriginal Justice Initiative, which has supported the program, is time-limited, and it is not clear where the funds will come from once this funding ceases. Given the intense, holistic approach taken by the project, the per-case cost can appear high for a community of approximately 1,500. But comparisons with the cost of other programs, completely miss the point. CHCH is a program without precedent in Canada – one that truly addresses the needs of all those affected by sexual abuse and attempts to find solutions that deal with the root causes of behaviour and prevent the cycle of abuse from continuing.

Interest in the project from other communities is quite high, and CHCH staff receive a great number of requests to speak about the program and conduct workshops. It is precisely the holistic approach of the program that is generating such interest from other Aboriginal and non-Aboriginal communities.

As the program develops it will undoubtedly come up with new and innovative approaches to the issues arising from sexual abuse in a manner that is grounded firmly in cultural traditions. One area where innovation can be expected is sentencing. Circle sentencing has begun in Hollow Water, but this is not seen as the end point of the process. Ultimately, the resource group sees a move away from the non-Aboriginal justice system altogether, although this can happen only over time. As they say in their report on circle sentencing,

> We realized that, at least until the community mandate was stronger, the community healing process needed the support of the legal system in holding accountable those people who were victimizing others.[276]

Where CHCH moves next in this area will be of interest to everyone with a specific concern for Aboriginal justice issues, as well as for those with a general interest in innovative approaches to solving complex human problems in the criminal law context.

Conclusions

This brief review of current justice initiatives reveals great diversity in the responses developed by Aboriginal communities across the country. At the same time, certain commonalities among the projects allow some generalization about the factors that are important in the development of such initiatives. In particular, we consider five issues: (1) the community-driven aspect of justice projects; (2) the importance of a project development phase before implementing justice projects; (3) the particular resource needs of programs that have a healing rather than a punishment orientation; (4) the irrelevance of artificial distinctions such as status and non-status

---

[276] "Community Holistic Circle Healing, Hollow Water First Nation Interim Report", cited in note 274, p. 16.

in terms of determining a project's jurisdiction; and (5) how these individual community initiatives can become part of the exercise by Aboriginal nations of the inherent right of self-government.

1. The community-driven nature of projects

The fact that the initiatives described in this chapter are community-based is a result of both internal and external factors. On one level, one would expect that programs designed to meet the needs of a particular community would be designed by that community. As well, however, it appears that governments have looked on initiatives at a very local level with more favour than programs designed to operate across a number of Aboriginal communities and aligned on a nation basis.

One of the strongest messages to emerge from the Commission's round table on justice was that successful justice projects must be firmly rooted in the community they are intended to serve. This point was made most explicitly by Judge Robert Cawsey, chief judge of the Provincial Court of Alberta. Judge Cawsey chaired the Task Force on the Criminal Justice System and its Impact on the Indian and Metis People of Alberta. At our round table he stated:

> Everything that has worked when we're dealing with Natives has come from the Natives. I don't know of anything that has worked that has been foisted upon them from above.[277]

This lesson is one that must be kept in mind as new initiatives and projects are developed. Communities themselves know best what justice issues they wish to address and how they wish to address them. There can be no one model of justice development. Any attempt to force Aboriginal nations and communities to develop justice projects along particular lines will fail. This sort of regimentation is totally at odds with the representations made to the Commission.

In Manitoba, for example, the St. Theresa Point First Nation community has chosen to focus its resources on the development of a youth justice committee. In Hollow Water, a comprehensive response to cases of sexual abuse has been designed. Both projects are very successful and could serve as models for similar initiatives in communities that have the same priorities or concerns. There is no basis for saying that these communities have made the wrong choice by focusing their energies in the manner that they have. As communities seek to develop their own justice systems, they will do so in an evolutionary way, beginning with the areas they believe need to be addressed.

In many ways this is a simple point. But it is nevertheless one that is often ignored by federal, provincial and territorial government officials. This freedom is at the heart of self-determination for Aboriginal nations and their communities. It is a

---

[277] Mr. Justice R.A. Cawsey, in "A Time For Action", video produced for RCAP (Stonehaven Productions, 1993).

contradiction in terms to tell a people to exercise a right of self-government or self-determination only in a particular direction. We have been impressed by the diversity of programs developed across the country. It is only through such diversity that other Aboriginal nations and communities can learn about possible directions for their own justice initiatives.

As noted elsewhere in this report – and expanded upon in the next chapter – the exercise of self-government in the justice field is best accomplished at the level of the Aboriginal nation. This does not mean, however, that every community in an Aboriginal nation will necessarily develop the same programs or exercise jurisdiction in the same manner as other communities. Since justice is an issue that is felt most directly at the community level, it is important that as much power as can reasonably be exercised at that level remain there.

Taking control of an aspect of the justice system is a very significant step for a community. Communities have to live daily with the consequences of decisions made in their justice program. Programs that emphasize healing usually require offenders to continue to live in the community rather than being locked up far away for long periods. This reality encourages communities to develop their programs slowly and to ensure that the programs move ahead one step at a time. This evolutionary approach bodes well for the future development of such initiatives.

2. The need for a project development phase in establishing justice programs

An essential component in ensuring the success of Aboriginal justice projects is an appropriate development period to allow for community consultation and training of project staff. Not all Aboriginal justice programs have flourished and not all have been without problems. As noted earlier in this chapter, the South Vancouver Island Tribal Council's justice program was halted because of concerns about the way it functioned. Some of these concerns appear to have arisen from a lack of consultation and discussion among some parties with a vital interest in the development of the project.[278]

Similarly, the Attawapiskat Diversion program, described earlier in this chapter as the first of its kind in Canada, is currently being re-evaluated by the community. An evaluation of the project by Obonsawin-Irwin Consulting for the provincial ministry of the attorney general revealed that some of the problems experienced by the project related to a lack of consultation with community members. Concerns about the types of cases diverted and about those who served as elders on the diversion panel hurt community acceptance of the project. As well, lack of consultation with police on the reserve led to a situation where they acted in an openly non-responsive manner to requests for assistance with the project.

---

[278] Clark & Associates, *Building the Bridge*, cited in note 159.

In addition to evaluating the Attawapiskat project, Obonsawin-Irwin also evaluated the sentencing panel project of the Sandy Lake First Nation for the attorney general. In Sandy Lake, problems with the project led to an interruption of services. Having the opportunity to review both projects, the consultants took time to devise a series of recommendations for the development of future Aboriginal community justice projects. One of the key recommendations was that each project have an explicit project development process consisting of three phases: a needs assessment phase; a project development phase; and a pre-implementation phase.[279]

Neither the Sandy Lake nor the Attawapiskat program had formal project development phases. In Toronto, the first eleven months of the community council's activities were devoted to project development. The evaluation of the community council project supported the Obonsawin-Irwin recommendations that all Aboriginal justice projects have an explicit, funded, project development phase. Referring to the need for project development the evaluators stated:

> Community involvement takes time; it follows the adage, "go slow to go fast." Unless the community is given the required amount of time to take ownership of the program, it may well fail entirely or fail to represent the wishes and objectives of the community.[280]

In the case of the community council project the evaluators found the developmental phase had played a key role in the program's operational success.

Based on the experience to date and the recommendations of the various evaluation studies, a period of between one year and eighteen months of funded development work should be viewed as a necessary part of Aboriginal justice initiatives. It is therefore unrealistic to expect to see such projects up and running in a matter of a few months. As Moyer and Axon point out in their evaluation of the community council, a development phase is not a frill – it is a vital component of any justice project:

> There are no short-cuts to a properly undertaken developmental phase for new programs. Adequate funding of this phase enhances the probability that the process will be done correctly by permit-

---

[279] Obonsawin-Irwin Consulting Inc., *Future Aboriginal Community Justice Project Development Needs: An Addendum to the Sandy Lake and Attawapiskat First Nations Justice Pilot Project Evaluation Reports* (Toronto: Ministry of the Attorney General, July 1992), p. 17.

[280] Moyer and Axon, "An Implementation Evaluation", cited in note 236, pp. 30, 23, 29. In a footnote to this portion of their report, the evaluators emphasize that the importance of a developmental phase has been recognized in other, non-Aboriginal projects. The evaluators also noted that in community consultations, the issue of whether the program would actually be introduced was always left open. If consultation is to be meaningful, one of the options during the development phase must be to discontinue the project.

ting the project manager(s) to take the time to 'do it right'.... in our experience, innovative programs of any sort (Native or non-Native) are frequently undertaken without adequate pre-implementation development with the result that their efficiency and cost-effectiveness is often greatly impaired during the first year or so of operation.[281]

The notion of seeking community input and control is a frightening one to some people. A true consultative process could mean a loss of power and control for police, judges, lawyers, government officials and elected band councillors. Occasionally this concern about loss of control leads to what sociologists refer to as élite accommodation. In this process, bureaucrats or judicial officials approach the leaders they trust and respect in an Aboriginal community and give them responsibility for developing and delivering a justice program. However well-meaning these people might be, such a process rarely works. Even if the individuals chosen are respected in the community, their lack of an express mandate from the community will usually mean the failure of the program. As noted earlier in this chapter, this has already occurred with a number of Aboriginal justice initiatives.

A genuine consultation process is one that allows all those affected by the development of the justice project to have meaningful input to the process. A process undertaken only as a formality and that ignores sectors of the community that want input is obviously not a true consultative process. Ultimately, of course, the process is a sham and will prove counter-productive, since without community support an Aboriginal justice project will not succeed. The hallmark of a meaningful consultative process is one where *not* proceeding with the project is always an option.

The consultative process must include elders, traditional teachers and clan leaders. Their role cannot be simply peripheral or included as a formality. Projects that envisage an outcome different from that provided by the non-Aboriginal system must seek the wisdom and counsel of people who know how to achieve such outcomes. If all that is intended is to create a replica of the non-Aboriginal system with an Aboriginal face, then all that is required are people who understand how to copy. What we have seen in successful Aboriginal justice projects, however, is a search for something different. In this search, the role of elders is crucial.[282]

In addition, however, the consultative process must reach out to the groups that are the most marginal in the community – those whose views are most often ignored when important decisions are made. In many Aboriginal communities, as in the rest of the country, women and young people are often among the most marginalized groups. Because of the significance we attach to ensuring the full

---

[281] Moyer and Axon, "An Implementation Evaluation", pp. 28, 30.

[282] Potential problems associated with the role of elders in justice projects is discussed in the next chapter, in the context of assuring the safety of women and children.

participation of women and young people, we address this issue specifically in the following chapter.

In both Hollow Water and Toronto, the justice projects now in place were the product of extensive community involvement – an involvement that included women directly in the decision-making process. The success of these projects illustrates that significant strides will be made in the development of justice initiatives only when true consultation takes place. Community leaders should not be afraid to discover what members of their community want. Consultation and consensus are hallmarks of the Aboriginal way of dealing with serious issues.[283] There can be few issues more serious or significant than taking control of aspects of the justice system.

3. Differing resource needs for justice projects with a healing orientation

Western notions of governance have encouraged people to look at the issues that affect them in their daily lives in a compartmentalized manner. Thus there is the justice box, which deals with people in conflict with the law, the health box, for people who are physically or mentally ill, the social services box, for people with special needs, and so on. One of the consequences of this approach is to look at programs in terms of locating what box they might fit into, which box should pay for it, and which box will reap benefits. This attempt to compartmentalize human experience is very much at odds with a holistic approach to people and problems.

In the western system, a person who breaks the law is dealt with in the criminal law box. The reason the person may have come into conflict with the law is only an incidental concern of the system. The non-Aboriginal criminal justice system is punishment-oriented, relying on incarceration as the ultimate sanction. This does not mean that all who come before the courts are sent to jail, but it does mean that the system is oriented more toward punishing criminal behaviour than toward approaches that can be characterized as healing. Thus most of the financial resources the system devotes to people found guilty of a crime are put into the construction and maintenance of jails. Judges who find incarceration inappropriate for an offender also find their ability to craft a sentence to address the individual's needs very restricted. In many cases a judge can only hope that offenders learn from their experience and take the responsibility for changing their lives to avoid further contact with the system.

This approach to criminal justice contrasts dramatically with a system that takes a holistic look at the person and emphasizes healing over punishment. The conflict

---

[283] The need for consensus in developing justice projects does not necessarily mean that all decisions must be made by consensus. In some communities and nations, decisions may eventually be made by majority vote on particular challenging issues. However these decisions are ultimately made, it is vital that there be real, substantive consultation among everyone potentially affected by justice initiatives.

between these two orientations is set out concisely in the following passage from a pre-sentence report prepared by the assessment team of CHCH in a 1989 case:

> We understand how the outside system sees punishment as deterrence and uses incarceration for this purpose. A short time ago we ourselves were promoting this. Now we feel differently. Incarceration as we see it now is appropriate only if a person is unwilling or unable to take responsibility for his behaviour, and accordingly, we believe it must be related to the potential for healing rather than the seriousness of the offence.[284]

An emphasis on healing presents different resource needs than a punishment-based system, which requires jails, guards and related resources. A healing orientation requires resources such as treatment facilities, counselling services, elders, and healthy staff. While the impact of appearing before one's peers is a factor in the success of the community council in Toronto, another important component of the program's success is that council members and staff can refer clients to a wide range of Aboriginal-specific services located in the city. Similarly, in Hollow Water, the complete healing and counselling orientation of CHCH allows for those who are guilty of sexual assault to be returned to the community to serve out their term of probation while continuing to move along the 13 steps.

The need for healing resources, both professional and volunteer, was apparent in almost all the justice projects reviewed in this chapter. It is no exaggeration to state that the ability of an Aboriginal justice program to meet its goals depends on the availability of programs in the community to allow offenders to begin their healing. Without such programs, the best intentioned initiatives will have a hard time achieving success.[285]

The experience of the community council in Toronto with respect to family violence is a case in point. The Family Violence Working Group, assembled to look at the conditions under which family violence cases could be diverted to the community council, concluded that the provision of services, particularly to offenders, was a prerequisite for the diversion of such charges. Without these healing resources, the working group concluded, nothing significant could be offered to the offender other than what the current system already provides. No one on the working group favoured incarceration, but there was no debate that the spouse or partner would continue to be in danger until options became available to treat offenders and change their behaviour. Under these circumstances, the working

---

[284] Lajeunesse, *Community Holistic Circle Healing*, cited in note 257, Appendix B, pre-sentence report #2, p. 6.

[285] Pauktuutit, the Inuit Women's Association of Canada, "Setting Standards First", paper presented to a National Symposium on Care and Custody of Aboriginal Offenders, Correctional Service Canada, 1995, pp. 8-10.

group believed it would be irresponsible to divert such charges. Once the resources are in place, then diversion can begin.

4. *Status as an irrelevant factor in determining jurisdiction*

Of interest in the projects reviewed is that most community-based justice initiatives make no distinction in services delivery between status or non-status Indians, Métis or Inuit. Most justice programs define their community geographically. Thus CHCH serves four neighbouring communities, one First Nation community and three largely Métis communities. Even in the North, communities are more interested in dealing with all their residents than attempting to distinguish them on the basis of an external identifying trait. As noted earlier, Judge Heino Lilles in the Yukon had an elders advisory panel assist him in the sentencing of a non-Aboriginal individual who lived in the community.

In the Mohawk Territory of Kahnawake, the jurisdiction of the section 107 court is not limited to status Indians living on the territory, but rather encompasses all individuals who fall within the court's purview. Thus, for example, anyone charged with a driving infraction on the territory, Aboriginal or not, is expected to attend the court at Kahnawake, unless they have reasonable grounds to refuse to enter the reserve.[286]

Some programs extend their jurisdiction beyond their geographic area to encompass other members of the community. Thus the diversion program at Shubenacadie is available to any resident of the reserve and any member of the First Nation arrested anywhere in Nova Scotia. Similarly, the Spallumcheen Band's child welfare by-law was intended to apply to all children on the reserve and to all members of the Spallumcheen First Nation living off the reserve as well.

In Toronto, geographic jurisdiction is not enough to determine eligibility for entry into the community council program. Some method must be used to distinguish Aboriginal people from non-Aboriginal people. As noted earlier, however, the program does not distinguish among Aboriginal people – it is a status-blind program. In fact, for the most part, an individual's self-identification is sufficient to enter the program. During the process to amend the protocol to deal with cases of family violence (described earlier in this chapter), the Family Violence Working Group proposed that the program be open to all Aboriginal families. The protocol defines family as follows:

> For the purposes of this protocol 'family' includes common-law and same-sex relationships. For the purposes of this protocol 'family' also includes traditional Native family or clan arrangements.

> Subject to the other provisions of this protocol, any member of a family unit that identifies itself as a Native family can be diverted

---

[286] See *Guy Favreau* v. *Cour de Kahnawake*, cited in note 149, and accompanying text.

to the Community Council. Ultimately, the decision of whether a family is, or is not a Native family, rests solely with Aboriginal Legal Services of Toronto (ALST).[287]

The Working Group did not believe it was appropriate to restrict entry to the program to cases where only the offender was Aboriginal, since that would have prevented the entry of families where the victim was Aboriginal but the offender non-Aboriginal. The working group could see no rationale for turning away Aboriginal women living with non-Aboriginal men in a family structure that considered itself Aboriginal.

These approaches, which generally ignore status as a criterion for entry and focus instead on geography or personal or family self-identification, represent a sophisticated approach to delivering justice services. However, the jurisdiction of Aboriginal justice initiatives is not solely within the discretion of those operating programs, but is subject to the applicable laws and to negotiation. As a result, the Spallumcheen child welfare by-law is restricted in its operation to members of the First Nation living on-reserve, and respect for the decisions of section 107 courts can be problematic. The issue of jurisdiction is critical and will be looked at in more detail in the next chapter.

5. Moving from Aboriginal justice initiatives to the creation of distinct Aboriginal justice systems

The development of distinct Aboriginal justice systems will take place over time. Indeed, in this report we refer often to a transition period, where increasing numbers of culturally appropriate Aboriginal programs will be put in place to replace those of the non-Aboriginal justice system. Most of the initiatives examined in this chapter have the potential to contribute a great deal to modifications in the current system and to the development of distinct Aboriginal justice systems. For this latter goal to be achieved, however, these initiatives and others like them must move from operating within the bounds of federal and provincial authority and must be recognized as part of Aboriginal peoples' inherent right of self-government. Without such recognition, these initiatives, worthy as they are, will remain isolated and incapable of reaching their full potential.

Once recognition of this Aboriginal right has occurred, the exercise of the right can begin. Initially, most Aboriginal nations and communities will continue to rely on existing justice structures. The difference, however, is that the decision to do so will be, in and of itself, an exercise of self-determination. Over time, as Aboriginal nations turn their attention to justice concerns, the development of these systems and the exercise of law-making powers will become more prevalent. Although it

---

[287] Family Violence Working Group, "Proposed Protocol on the Diversion of Cases of Family Violence to Aboriginal Legal Services of Toronto's Community Council Program" (Toronto: Aboriginal Legal Services of Toronto, 1994), p. 1.

is important to emphasize that self-determination in justice includes the right of Aboriginal nations to exercise control over every aspect of the justice system, few if any nations will be in a position immediately to replace all existing institutions with new culturally appropriate ones. This should not be a source of concern. For one thing, justice is not the only area where Aboriginal people are focusing their attention. Self-government has many facets, and each Aboriginal nation and community will determine the order in which to address these various facets. As well, and as noted often in this chapter, developing justice systems takes time. Even initiatives that seem relatively minor must be subject to significant examination by members of the community. Taking over control of justice issues is a major step, with potentially great repercussions in the community. For this reason, it is something that is best approached with caution.

What this means in practice is that for a period of time – a period more likely to be measured in terms of years and decades than days and months – Aboriginal nations will not be in a position to replace all the institutions of the non-Aboriginal justice system with culturally appropriate ones. In fact, some Aboriginal nations and communities may wish to stay with the present system for an indefinite period and put their energies elsewhere. In any event, it is this transitional stage in the development of Aboriginal justice systems that will see a need for some, if not many, of the aspects of the non-Aboriginal justice system to remain in place.

In some communities this will mean that policing functions will still be done by the RCMP or by municipal police forces. In other communities it may mean that certain cases will be dealt with by the non-Aboriginal court system, assisted perhaps by sentencing circles or elders panels, while other cases will be resolved exclusively by Aboriginal bodies. As this transitional period unfolds, however, it is not necessary to draw rigid lines between the jurisdiction of Aboriginal justice systems and the non-Aboriginal system – some overlap is not only possible but desirable.

4

Creating Conceptual and Constitutional Space for Aboriginal Justice Systems

It is the Commission's position that the foundation for a new relationship between Aboriginal peoples and other Canadians must be
recognition of the inherent right of Aboriginal peoples to self-
government. It is our conclusion that the inherent right of Aboriginal
peoples to self-government is recognized and affirmed in section 35(1) of the
Constitution Act, 1982, and forms the basis for Aboriginal government as one
of three orders of government within Canada. The full implications of this conclusion and the way we see Aboriginal self-government fitting within the Canadian
federal system will be the subject of a chapter in our final report.

In the specific context of this report, it is our conclusion that **the Aboriginal
right of self-government encompasses the right of Aboriginal nations to
establish and administer their own systems of justice, including the power
to make laws within the Aboriginal nation's territory. The Commission is of
the view that federal, provincial and territorial policy in the area of justice
should be formulated and implemented on the foundation of the right of
Aboriginal nations to establish and administer their own systems of justice,
including the power to make laws, within the Aboriginal nation's territory.**

**The right to establish a system of justice inheres in each Aboriginal nation.
This does not preclude Aboriginal communities within the nation from
sharing in the exercise of this authority. It will be for the people of each
Aboriginal nation to determine the shape and form of their justice system
and the allocation of responsibilities within the nation.**

In this chapter we consider the most important questions raised by these conclusions and endeavour to grapple with the principal issues and challenges that arise from establishing and implementing Aboriginal justice systems.

We begin by describing what Aboriginal justice systems might look like, without in any way pre-determining or circumscribing the shape of their ultimate development. As part of this description we review the experience of the tribal court system in the United States, both because it has attracted attention and study by Canadian observers and because experience from the American past and present provides valuable lessons for the future development of Aboriginal justice systems in Canada. The American experience also offers important insights into one of the thorniest issues that will have to be addressed in Canada – jurisdiction. Who will be subject to an Aboriginal justice system, in what kinds of cases, arising in what territories?

We go on to consider how the jurisdiction of Aboriginal justice systems fits into existing constitutional arrangements. Is there constitutional space for such systems in the *Constitution Act, 1867*, which at present divides powers in relation to justice between federal and provincial governments? How is that affected by the provisions of the *Constitution Act, 1982*, in particular sections 25 and 35, which pertain to the recognition, affirmation and protection of existing Aboriginal and treaty rights? Is a constitutional amendment required to provide the necessary foundation for Aboriginal justice systems? As part of our discussion of constitutional arrangements we consider whether the Aboriginal right to make laws in exercising the right of self-government includes the enactment of Aboriginal criminal law. This raises the issue of the role of the *Criminal Code* and whether its existence forecloses Aboriginal law making in the criminal justice area.

A similar question is raised in relation to the *Canadian Charter of Rights and Freedoms*. Does it apply to Aboriginal governments and Aboriginal justice systems? Aboriginal women's organizations are particularly interested in this issue and have argued that the legitimacy of any Aboriginal justice system will be compromised if there are no legal safeguards to assure the protection of vulnerable groups and individuals, particularly those who have been excluded from decision making in recent history. This is not the only challenge that will confront the legitimacy of Aboriginal justice systems. If their decisions are not seen by those affected by them as fair and free from the exercise of abusive and arbitrary power, they will fail in the goal of bringing Aboriginal people within the circle of justice. Is the Charter capable of performing this function, or would Aboriginal charters of rights enacted by Aboriginal governments be more consistent with the right of self-government and the protection of fundamental human rights in culturally appropriate ways?

The need to ensure that Aboriginal justice systems adequately protect women and children is a broader issue than whether the Charter applies to Aboriginal justice systems, and given the importance we attach to the issue, we address it in a separate section of this chapter.

A complete and comprehensive justice system not only has the ability to resolve questions of fact and law at the trial level, but also has room for dissatisfied parties to appeal decisions they believe are wrong. What types of appellate structures are appropriate for Aboriginal justice systems? Is there a role for a pan-national Aboriginal Court of Appeal? What role should the Supreme Court of Canada play in reviewing the decisions of Aboriginal justice systems?

Finally we look at the issue of Aboriginal justice systems operating in urban centres. Can Aboriginal people who live in cities also have access to Aboriginal justice systems and, if so, how would such systems differ from those in place in other regions of the country?

These are all large questions, and we offer a word of caution. **This chapter should not be seen as providing a blueprint for the future containing the answers to all the questions that will ultimately have to be answered. Our intention is rather to provide a framework for the development of Aboriginal justice systems on a more comprehensive basis than has been possible in the case of current Aboriginal justice initiatives, which are small-scale and have developed on an ad hoc basis.** Often these initiatives fight the same battles over and over again with different orders of government and with differing results, and almost always operating with limited budgets and under the shadow of a pilot project mentality. It is hoped that the framework set out in this chapter will provide a more secure foundation for Aboriginal nations to exercise their right of self-determination in the area of justice.

Aboriginal Justice Systems – Back to the Future

Much of the Canadian writing on Aboriginal justice systems has focused on the creation of Aboriginal courts as the centrepiece of such systems. The focus on court-like structures is explained by the fact that the Canadian criminal justice system is characterized by an overriding preoccupation, on the part of the media, the public and criminal justice professionals, with the activities of courts, despite the fact that far larger amounts of public funds are spent on law enforcement, crime prevention and corrections than on the events that take place in courtrooms.[288] To a large extent, what happens in the courtroom shapes the public perception of the criminal justice system. Although crime prevention through community policing is now receiving more attention, processing cases for disposition by the courts remains a significant part of police work. By the same token, the activities of the corrections system hinge upon the court's determination of guilt and imposition of a sentence. Thus, the courts are located institutionally, functionally and symbolically in the public mind at the centre of the system.

---

[288] *Justice on Trial*, cited in note 23, chapter 2, p. 1, citing Statistics Canada figures, reported that policing costs are about three times the cost of the corrections sector and seven or eight times the cost of the courts sector.

As described earlier in this report, Aboriginal societies did not maintain profes-sionalized institutions for the administration of justice in the form of courts, nor did their conceptions of justice hinge upon a necessary connection between crime and punishment. When we envisage the shape that contemporary Aboriginal jus-tice systems might take, therefore, we must not assume that Aboriginal courts will be their centrepiece. Conversely, because Aboriginal societies have changed and have had to respond to the significant problems that manifest themselves through social dysfunction and crime, there is undoubtedly a role for a court-like institu-tion in a contemporary Aboriginal justice system. But it need not look like or act like a non-Aboriginal Canadian court. In exploring Aboriginal justice processes with and without court-like structures, **we emphasize that our aim is not to provide definitive answers or to endorse particular models, but to show that there are viable ways of translating constitutional rights and contemporary justice into practical Aboriginal forms.**

The United States Tribal Court Experience, Past and Present

Many Aboriginal organizations and communities, legal and academic commenta-tors, and several justice commissions and inquiries have felt the pull of the U.S. tribal court experience. This Commission also felt that pull, and in 1992 commission-ers were privileged to be the guests of the Navajo Nation, the Mescalero Apache Nation, and the Zuñi and Santo Domingo *pueblos* for visits to their tribal courts. It is not difficult to understand why the American experience has been the subject of so much Canadian attention. The tribal courts are viewed with pride by U.S. tribal governments as a contemporary demonstration of their inherent right of self-government. Many Aboriginal nations in Canada have strong historical and family connections with American tribes, a connection that the demarcation of the 49th parallel has not severed. For this Commission, a review of the American experi-ence with tribal courts is significant because it sheds important light on issues related to the constitutional right of self-government, the historical injustice under which Aboriginal people in both Canada and the United States have laboured, and the contemporary practice of self-government in relation to the administration of justice. Furthermore, the U.S. experience offers some valuable lessons, both pos-itive and negative, from which Canada can learn.

The U.S. tribal court system is rooted in the early decisions of the United States Supreme Court in the first half of the nineteenth century. In these decisions, Chief Justice John Marshall, building on the foundation of British practice of the seventeenth and eighteenth centuries, reflected on the treaty relationships between Indian nations and the Crown – a subject to which we referred in *Partners in Confederation*.[289] The decisions affirmed that Indian nations in the United States,

---

[289] See *Partners in Confederation*, cited in note 8, chapter 1, "The Original Status of Aboriginal Peoples", pp. 13-19.

while no longer completely sovereign foreign nations, retained their inherent right of self-government. In 1832 in *Worcester* v. *Georgia* the Supreme Court struck down a series of laws enacted by the state of Georgia that would have had the effect of nullifying the Cherokee Nation's constitution and its customary laws and confiscating Cherokee territory. These laws were all in violation of a treaty entered into by the Cherokee Nation and the United States. Drawing on international law and colonial practice, Chief Justice Marshall asserted:

> [T]he settled doctrine of the law of nations is, that a weaker power does not surrender its independence – its right to self-government – by associating with a stronger and taking its protection... The Indian nations had always been considered as distinct, independent political communities, retaining their original natural rights, as the undisputed possessors of the soil, from time immemorial... The very term 'nation', so generally applied to them, means 'a people distinct from others.' The words 'treaty' and 'nations', are words of our own language, selected in our diplomatic and legislative proceedings, by ourselves, having each a definite and well-understood meaning. We have applied them to Indians, as we have applied them to the other nations of the earth. They are applied to all in the same sense.[290]

The principle of retained Indian sovereignty remains important in the contemporary adjudication of issues related to the jurisdiction of Indian tribal courts (an issue addressed in more detail later in this chapter), but some of the facts in *Worcester* v. *Georgia* resonate with more than just historical significance. Over a period of some 30 years in the early nineteenth century, the Cherokee Nation underwent what one American historian has referred to as a "renascence", during which they sought to adjust to a dramatic loss of population, large cessions of their traditional lands, and radical changes in their economic and social life. Adapting their traditional forms of governance to the new circumstances facing them, they developed a bicameral legislature, a district and superior court system and an elective system of representation. The 1820s saw the enactment of new Cherokee laws dealing with the whole spectrum of economic and social life. Although the Cherokee governmental system and laws reflected the U.S. political system and concepts of Anglo-American jurisprudence, many of the laws incorporated Cherokee customary law in an attempt to merge different legal traditions. In 1827 the Cherokee Nation adopted a written constitution asserting the national sovereignty of the Cherokee people. Significantly the constitution adopted a charter of rights that included the guarantee of a jury trial and due process of law.[291]

---

[290] *Worcester* v. *Georgia*, 31 U.S. (6 Pet.) 515 (1832), pp. 559-561.

[291] William G. McLoughlin, *Cherokee Renascence in the New Republic* (Princeton, N.J.: Princeton University Press, 1986), pp. 284, 397-399.

The Cherokee experience of overlaying a western-based system of governance and justice on their own customary law is not necessarily an appropriate model for Aboriginal people in Canada, but it remains a compelling example of how an Aboriginal nation, in the midst of enormous social and economic changes and at a time of much dislocation in their traditional way of life, was able to revitalize and make contemporary a system of governance and the administration of justice.

Notwithstanding judicial affirmation of the inherent right of self-government and the security of its territory from state intrusion, the Cherokee Nation was not permitted to remain in its territory under the protection of its laws and constitution. In one of the darkest moments in American history, the people were removed forcibly to lands west of the Mississippi. Forty-five hundred Cherokee died on this infamous Trail of Tears.

Indian policy in the United States, as in Canada, underwent significant changes late in the nineteenth century under the weight of economic expansionism and theories of social Darwinism. The doctrine of inherent tribal jurisdiction underwent a similar transformation in which the courts upheld a general plenary authority of the federal government over the tribes. It was in this harsh and arid period, when assimilationist policies became the order of the day, that Indian tribal courts were first established in 1883. Their origin and early development has been described this way:

> Far from being an instrument of Indian self-determination, they were conceived as an adjunct to the process of cultural assimilation. The establishment of these Courts was part of the concerted effort to outlaw traditional cultural institutions, eliminate plural marriages, weaken the influence of the medicine men, promote law and order, civilize the Indians and teach them respect for private property by breaking up tribal land holdings into individual allotments. The initial plan was to develop these Courts of Indian Offences for every tribal government. Eventually they were established, at the direction of the Commissioner of Indian Affairs, in roughly two-thirds of all Indian agencies. The Courts were staffed by the local Indian Agent, who applied the law as defined by an abbreviated criminal and civil code drafted by the Commissioner. Customary law was ignored or outlawed as it represented a way of life that the Court was designed to destroy.[292]

Although a number of courts of Indian offences are still functioning, their number has declined over the years, and the great majority of tribal courts functioning today

---

[292] *Locking Up Natives in Canada*, cited in note 37, p. 225. See also Bradford W. Morse, *Indian Tribal Courts in the United States: A Model for Canada?* (Saskatoon: University of Saskatchewan Native Law Centre, 1980); R. Hemmingson, "Jurisdiction of Future Tribal Courts in Canada: Learning from the American Experience", *Canadian Native Law Report* 2 (1989), p. 1; AJI, cited in note 2, volume 1, p. 273.

trace their legal origins to a different era in American Indian policy.[293] In 1934 Congress passed the *Indian Reorganization Act*, sometimes referred to as the 'Indian New Deal'.[294] It was designed to bring to an end a disastrous 50-year period – in which most of the tribes' land holdings were alienated as a result of private allotment – and to restore to tribal governments a measure of control over their economic and social lives. Under the legislation, Indian tribes were authorized to enact their own tribal constitutions, establish tribal governments, define conditions of membership, and enact laws governing their internal affairs, including law and order codes. The legislation also provided that tribal courts could be established as part of the tribal constitution or as a component of the tribal law and order code.

Many tribes created tribal courts pursuant to this legislation. The report of the Aboriginal Justice Inquiry of Manitoba, which studied the tribal court system in some depth, noted that some 108 tribes operate tribal courts that derive their jurisdiction from tribal constitutions or tribal law courts as provided for in the *Indian Reorganization Act* and that the numbers have expanded significantly in recent years.[295]

The *Indian Reorganization Act* was, however, only a limited exercise in the direction of tribal self-government. The legislation authorized development of tribal constitutions, governments, and law and order codes, but the anticipated model for these institutions and codes was non-Aboriginal structures, not traditional Aboriginal ones. The bureau of Indian affairs continued to maintain a heavy hand in tribal affairs, and in 1935 it revised the code for courts of Indian offences; this code for the most part became the model adopted by tribal courts established under the *Indian Reorganization Act*. It was based on state justice of the peace codes and provided essentially misdemeanour criminal jurisdiction (in Canadian terms, summary offence jurisdiction) for tribal courts.

In addition to the courts of Indian offences and other courts established under the *Indian Reorganization Act*, a third kind of tribal court, commonly known as traditional courts, operates primarily among the Pueblo Indians of the southwest. These courts operate under their inherent tribal jurisdiction, restricted only by express federal legislation. They apply tribal customary law supplemented by explicit tribal enactments. Little has been written about the operation of these courts.

Two further pieces of the historical and legislative picture should be put in place before we examine the tribal court system in greater detail. The first is that the criminal jurisdiction of tribal courts was seriously limited by the *Major Crimes Act* of

---

[293] For a more detailed review of the relationship between Aboriginal self-government and U.S. federal law and policy, see Russell Lawrence Barsh, "Aboriginal Self-Government in the United States", research study prepared for RCAP (1993).

[294] Act of 18 June 1934, Public Law No. 73-383, c. 576, 48 Stat. 984.

[295] AJI, cited in note 2, volume 1, p. 275.

1885, which removed from tribal jurisdiction the prosecution of seven (since extended to fourteen) major offences, which must be dealt with in a federal court.[296] Among these crimes are murder, manslaughter, rape and drug offences.

The second piece of federal legislation that impinges on the jurisdiction of tribal courts is the *Indian Civil Rights Act* of 1968, which restricts the operation of tribal courts in two ways.[297] In terms of remedies in criminal cases, the act forbids tribal courts from imposing penalties greater than a $5,000 fine or one year in jail or both. Perhaps more important, the *Indian Civil Rights Act* imports the protections of the U.S. *Bill of Rights* to cases heard by tribal courts. In the case of *Talton* v. *Mayes* the Supreme Court declared that since tribal governments had been in place long before the U.S. Constitution was written, the individual rights in that document could not be extended to members of Indian tribes living on reservations.[298] The 1968 act addressed this situation by giving residents of reservations freedom of speech, freedom of the press, and the various other democratic freedoms found in the *Bill of Rights*. The act also imported criminal law protections from the *Bill of Rights*, including the due process guarantees such as the right to a speedy trial, the right to avoid self-incrimination and the right to counsel. The appropriateness of limiting subject-matter jurisdiction and importing procedural safeguards from the non-Aboriginal system is an issue to which we will return.[299]

Tribal courts established under the *Indian Reorganization Act* and operating under tribal law and order codes or tribal constitutions are the principal vehicle through which Indian governments in the United States exercise their authority in the area of justice. It is therefore the system that has been of primary interest as a possible model for Canada.

A recurring observation of those who have written about *Indian Reorganization Act* tribal courts is that, aside from their Indian personnel, very little about them or about the tribal codes they enforce and administer is uniquely Indian. Their procedures derive from state and federal models of criminal procedure, with the addition of the protections of the *Bill of Rights*, and their tribal codes are modelled essentially after U.S. criminal codes. The difficulties entailed in imposing law and

---

[296] Act of 3 March 1885, c. 341, 23 Stat. 362.

[297] Act of 11 April 1968, 82 Stat. 73.

[298] *Talton* v. *Mayes* (1896), 163 U.S. 376 (United States Supreme Court).

[299] A third piece of legislation had a significant impact on tribal court jurisdiction, although its impact has since been ameliorated by the *Indian Civil Rights Act*. In 1953 Congress enacted *Public Law 280* (Act of 15 August 1953, c. 505, 67 Stat. 588). It was a component of the prevailing congressional policy of terminating federal responsibility for Indians by transferring jurisdiction to state governments. The effect of the law was that in states to which the law applied, most tribal courts disappeared because of the overriding jurisdiction given to the state courts. The legislation was much criticized, particularly in the context of another policy shift in the direction of Indian self-determination, and the *Indian Civil Rights Act* of 1968 allowed for resumption of jurisdiction by tribal governments that had lost it.

order codes and non-Aboriginal procedural requirements are reflected in several commentaries. The American Indian Lawyer Training Program had this to say in its report, *Justice in Indian Country*:

> Tribal courts today face a monumental task. They must comply with the mandates imposed by the federal government, yet main-tain the uniqueness and cultural relevance that makes them 'tribal courts' and not merely arms of the federal government operated by Indians in Indian country. Accomplishment of these goals depends, to a great extent, on the availability of adequate funding and relevant and pervasive training programs. In addition, tribes must address the need for separation of powers in those courts which are not traditional or customary, in order to assure proce-dural due process, fundamental fairness, stability and credibility. Moreover, tribes must demand, and other government entities, both within and outside the tribe, must give recognition to, the judgments of tribal courts.[300]

An Australian lawyer who worked in one of the tribal courts commented on the trade-offs the courts have had to make as the basis for exercising some measure of tribal sovereignty:

> The justification that I see for the tribal courts that operate along similar lines to a European court under a written law and order code is that they are a visible aspect of the tribe's sovereignty. Generally neither the procedures nor the substantive law have any-thing to do with traditional Indian law. The present move is largely toward tightening up the procedures through training to ensure due process. 'Due process' is used entirely in the Anglo sense. I believe that many of the judges and others who were involved in tribal government are aware that 'due process' may not reflect the Indian way of doing things but, especially following the *Indian Civil Rights Act*, it is seen as another imposed value (which may or may not be good) that must be observed if the right to run one's own affairs is to be preserved.[301]

In evaluating the U.S. experience it is important to recognize that tribal courts are not simply static creations of federal legislation but part of a dynamic system. The drive toward greater tribal self-determination, which is now firmly entrenched as a cornerstone of U.S. federal Indian policy, has affected how tribal courts oper-ate. With the benefit of greater legal expertise, often from tribe members, tribes have redesigned their tribal codes, and many now allow expressly for the incor-

---

[300] *Justice in Indian Country* (Oakland: American Indian Lawyers Training Program Inc., 1980), p. 54.

[301] P. Ditton, submission to the Australian Law Reform Commission, quoted in *The Recognition of Aboriginal Customary Laws*, Report No. 31, volume 2, (1986), p. 64.

poration of customary law. Many of the criticisms directed at tribal courts, such as inadequate facilities or support staff, are the result of the lack of adequate resources being provided to support important tribal institutions.

James Zion, a solicitor to the courts of the Navajo Nation, is experienced in a number of tribal court systems and well informed about developments in Canada. In his discussion paper for the Commission's round table on justice issues, he cautioned that a proper understanding of the U.S. tribal court system requires something more than a formal description of the operation of these courts seen from the outside:

> Observers of American tribal courts see court systems that appear to be mirror images of state systems. The tribal Law and Order Code is similar to state statutes, and many tribal courts have a modified form of federal rules of civil and criminal procedure. On the surface, there does not appear to be anything to distinguish tribal courts from state systems....
>
> In 1968, following sensational congressional hearings on abuses of civil rights by tribal governments and courts, the United States Congress enacted the *Indian Civil Rights Act*. It imposed most U.S. *Bill of Rights* protections upon tribal courts and provided for federal court review of criminal convictions by means of *habeas corpus*. The Act prompted further intrusions into tribal court operations, and their actions were measured using non-Indian civil rights standards.... Non-Indian (and some Indian) observers used American criminal civil procedures and substantive provisions to measure tribal court operations. However, they do not see or report what actually takes place.
>
> Many tribal courts conduct proceedings in a native language. Many litigants are related to the judge by blood (usually an extended relationship) or by clan, or they are actually known by the judge. They are members of the community, as is the judge in most cases. What actually takes place in many tribal courts is that customary principles and procedures are applied.... Rather than articulate Indian common law principles in decisions, many tribal judges unconsciously apply tribal values in cases in a way outside observers cannot see.[302]

The process of adapting legal institutions to cultural values is well reflected in the experience of the Navajo justice system:

---

[302] J.W. Zion, "Taking Justice Back: American Indian Perspectives", in *Aboriginal Peoples and the Justice System*, cited in note 7, p. 311 (footnotes omitted).

The Navajo Court of Indian Offenses was created in 1892, and although its Navajo judges had to use the imposed values contained in BIA regulations (many of which were designed to destroy Indian legal values), history shows they often ignored them and used Navajo values. Beginning in approximately 1981, the Courts of the Navajo Nation undertook a conscious program to use Navajo common law as the law of preference. The initiatives of the program include:

- use of Navajo common law in written opinions as the law of preference of the Navajo Nation;
- use of Navajo common law as a means to interpret codes such as the Navajo Nation Bill of Rights (with U.S. *Bill of Rights* and civil rights principles) and the Navajo Nation Criminal Code;
- creation of Navajo Peacemaker Court (1982), an adapted traditional justice method;
- use of Navajo common law principles in court rules and codes (e.g., the 1991 Navajo Nation Code of Judicial Conduct).[303]

The Navajo tribal court system is the largest and most sophisticated of its kind, in part because of the size of the Navajo Nation itself. The Navajo Nation covers an area larger than some U.S. states (and Canadian provinces), with a resident population of close to 200,000 and a tribal justice budget in the millions of dollars. The Navajo judicial system handles more than 40,000 cases a year.[304] The written pronouncements of the Navajo Supreme Court and many Navajo district court decisions are available in commercially produced law reports. A Navajo Bar Association sets its own admission standards, which include knowledge of Navajo law. The Navajo Bar Association also conducts an annual conference on Navajo law to consider law reform proposals and developments in federal law as it affects American Indians.[305]

The sophistication of the Navajo Nation in the development of its justice system is evident in other ways as well. One of the most significant developments has been the introduction of the Peacemaker Court, whose origin and rationale are set out in the preface to the Peacemaker Court's manual:

On April 23, 1982 the judges of the Navajo Nation adopted rules and procedures of establishing the Navajo Peacemaker Court.

---

[303] Zion, "Taking Justice Back", pp. 313-314.

[304] According to statistics provided by the Navajo Nation Judicial Branch for the 1993-94 fiscal year (*Navajo Nation Court Statistics, 1993-95*), a total of 40,114 cases were closed, of which 52 per cent were traffic cases, 37 per cent criminal cases, and 12 per cent civil cases. The 1994-95 figures show a total of 41,283 closed cases.

[305] Robert Yazzie, "Navajo Justice Experience – Yesterday and Today", in *Aboriginal Peoples and the Justice System*, cited in note 7, p. 407.

The new court is based on the ancient practice of the Navajo to choose a 'Naat'aanii,' or 'headman,' who would 'arbitrate disputes, resolve family difficulties, try to reform wrong-doers and represent his group and its relations with other communities, i.e., tribes and governments.' When the Navajo Court of Indian Offenses was founded under the supervision of the Bureau of Indian Affairs in 1903 the Navajo judges of that court continued the tradition of the 'Naat'aanii' by appointing community leaders to work with individuals who had problems and quarrels....

In modern times the emphasis has been to create and maintain Navajo courts based upon an Anglo-European legal model, and that path was followed because of Navajo fears of termination and state control of the Navajo legal system. As a result, tribal attorneys and the Navajo Tribal Council modelled the Navajo courts on a state and federal design, with an assumption there was no justice under Navajo custom. The fact was over-looked that Navajo custom had worked effectively to resolve disputes up to that time.

The current judges of the Navajo Tribal Courts desired to revive the old practice of appointing community leaders to resolve disputes because of the fact that there are many problems in the community which cannot be resolved in a formal court setting. Lawsuits are expensive, time consuming and confusing to the ordinary citizen and often the Anglo-European system of courtroom confrontation simply does not work....

It is very appropriate that Navajo courts have used the term 'Peacemaker Court,' because the Naat'aanii used as the traditional precedent for our court were the 'peace leaders' of the Navajo. The Peacemaker Court system is designed to take the place of formalized, expensive and unharmonious Anglo-European legal systems and to provide a way for the Navajo peacemakers to be new 'peace leaders' to show the way to peaceful community dispute resolution."[306]

Thus we can see how the best known of the U.S. tribal courts is now reaching back and restoring as an important part of its dispute resolution process a contemporary version of its traditional processes. Under the Navajo system, peacemakers are selected by local communities, although the parties to a particular dispute may select someone of their own choosing to act as peacemaker. The peacemaker function combines both mediation and, if the parties agree, the determination of a final decision regarding the dispute. Any decision rendered by the peacemaker can be

---

[306] The Navajo Peacemaker Court Manual (1982), pp. 2-6.

entered as a formal order of the Navajo court system. The process can be initiated by the parties themselves, or the district court, the trial level of the Navajo system, can refer a matter to the Peacemaker Court. There is thus a high degree of flexibility and interaction between the two dispute resolution processes, reflecting the view that the strength of both can be brought to bear in the interests of justice. Although the principal jurisdiction of the Peacemaker Court is civil it also deals with lesser criminal cases.

The Navajo peacemaker concept, characterized appropriately by an associate justice of the Navajo Nation Supreme Court as "going back to the future", bears a strong conceptual relationship to the traditional dispute settlement processes of many Canadian Aboriginal societies, as the following description makes clear:

> The Navajo term *hozhooji naat'aanii* denotes the process of peace-making.... *Hozho* is a fundamental Navajo legal term... According to Thelma Bluehouse, *hozho* measures the state of being in complete harmony and peace. It provides the framework of Navajo thought and justice... *Hozho* is a state of affairs or being where everything is in its proper place, functioning in a harmonious relationship with everything else... The goal of *hozhooji naat'aanii* is to restore disputants to harmony... The peacemaker's role in the justice ceremony is to guide these parties to *hozho*. The peacemaker's authority is persuasive, not coercive... A peacemaker is a guide and a planner. As a guide, a peacemaker helps the parties identify how they have come to the state of disharmony. Non-Indian dispute resolution tends to focus more on the act which caused the dispute. Navajo peacemaking is more concerned with the causes of the trouble. The peacemaking ceremony has stages and devices to instruct and guide disputants in their quest for *hozho*. It begins with an opening prayer to summon the aid of the supernatural. The prayer also helps frame the attitudes and relationships of the parties to prepare them for the process. There is a stage where the peacemaker explores the positions of the parties in the universe, verifying that they are in a state of disharmony, deciding how or why they are out of harmony, and determining whether they are ready to obtain *hozho*. It is similar to diagnosing an illness to find causes. There are lectures on how or why the parties have violated Navajo values, have breached solidarity, or are out of harmony. Lectures are not recitations or exaltations of abstract moral principles, but practical and pragmatic examinations of the particular problem in light of Navajo values. The peacemaker then discusses the precise dispute with the parties to help them know how to plan to end it. The word *hozhoojigo* describes a process of planning – another Navajo justice concept. It means to 'do things in a good way' or 'go in the right way' by identify-

ing practical means to conform future conduct with values. The entire process is called 'talking things out', and it guides parties to a non-coercive and consensual conclusion to restore them to harmony in an on-going relationship within a community. The relationship aspect is central, because the community is entitled to justice and the return of its members to a state of harmony within it. As with the process of ceremonial healing, the method is effective because it focuses on the parties with good will to reintegrate them into their community, and solidarity with it.[307]

Peacemaking in the Navajo way demonstrates that what are often regarded as central features of non-Aboriginal justice processes may not be critical or even relevant to an Aboriginal process of justice based upon different assumptions.

American mediation uses the model of a neutral third person who empowers disputants and guides them to a resolution of their problems. In Navajo mediation, the Naat'aanii is not quite neutral, and his or her guidance is more value-laden than that of the mediator in the American model. As a clan and kinship relative of the parties or as an elder, a Naat'aanii has a point of view. The traditional Navajo mediator was related to the parties and had persuasive authority precisely due to that relationship. The Navajo Nation Code of Judicial Conduct (1991) addresses ethical standards for peacemakers and states that they may be related to the parties by blood or clan, barring objection.[308]

The size and sophistication of the Navajo tribal court system have attracted considerable attention from Canadian observers – to the point where visits to the Navajo courts by Aboriginal groups and commissions of inquiry from Canada have become akin to the search for the Holy Grail. Members of the Navajo Nation involved with the justice system are quick to point out, however, that their system is very much in a state of evolution and that a significant part of that evolution is the re-introduction of Navajo traditional processes to supplement, and in some cases replace, a system that had its origin in the stony ground of the courts of Indian offences and the law and order codes imposed by the bureau of Indian affairs. We, like others, were enormously impressed by what we saw on our visit to the Navajo Nation, and it left us in no doubt about the viability of Aboriginal justice systems and their capacity for growth in accordance with Aboriginal common law.

However, as other commissions have noted, the sheer size of the Navajo Nation makes it exceptional in the U.S. system, and there are no Aboriginal nations in

---

[307] Philmer Bluehouse and James Zion, "Hozhooji Naat'aanii: The Navajo Justice and Harmony Ceremony", *Mediation Quarterly* 10 (Summer 1993, Special Issue, Native American Perspectives on Peacemaking), pp. 327, 331-334.

[308] Bluehouse and Zion, "Hozhooji Naat'aanii", p. 334.

Canada with the population base of the Navajo. For this reason the Commission extended its observations to a number of other tribal court operations on reservations similar in size, population and socio-economic status to those in Canada, in particular a number of the smaller pueblos reservations in New Mexico and Arizona. The Aboriginal Justice Inquiry of Manitoba also observed the operations of the tribal court system in the state of Washington. There the Northwest Intertribal Court System has been established to provide circuit court services to 16 tribes in the Pacific northwest, whose populations range from 200 to 500 people and whose reservations are relatively small. The communities served by the Northwest Intertribal Court System are thus closer in size and population to many Aboriginal communities in Canada. On the basis of their experience, the Manitoba commissioners convened a special session of the inquiry on the subject of tribal courts and held a tribal court symposium. The symposium heard from American tribal court judges, court administrators and tribal lawyers about their work and how they address jurisdictional, legal, administrative and political problems.

Given this extensive review by the Aboriginal Justice Inquiry of Manitoba, this Commission did not attempt to replicate it. The following passages from the Aboriginal Justice Inquiry of Manitoba report is, to our knowledge, the most recent and comprehensive account of the functioning of the contemporary U.S. tribal court system.

Volume

Tribal court systems vary quite dramatically, depending upon the population of the reservations they service, the demand for services, the funding available, the extent of jurisdiction possessed by the courts, and the philosophical orientation of the tribal governments... The latest national figures...indicate case loads ranging from over 70,000 cases for the judicial system of the Navajo tribe, to a low of 3 cases handled by the Jamestown Klallam tribal court... A similar range in population size also is apparent, with...a high of 166,665 Navajos to a low of 65 members of the Shorewater Bay Indian tribe. Only 5 tribes had over 10,000 people in 1985. Some of [the smaller communities] participate in regional justice systems, such as the Northwest Intertribal Court System in Washington and the Western Oklahoma Court of Indian Offenses, while others enter into contract with a larger neighbouring tribe to provide a judge that will enforce their own laws. *Nevertheless, there are a number of tribes with populations very similar to Indian First Nations in Canada who operate their own, fully functioning court system.* The size of the land base also extends over a broad spectrum, with the Navajo again having the largest reservation with over 16 million acres (or some 25,000 square miles) to a low of 2.12 acres.

Judges

There are approximately 360 tribal court judges in the United States. Almost every tribe has its own tribal codes containing civil and criminal laws passed by the tribe's council. There may be other codes, as well, in the particular subject matters. The codes are similar to statutes passed by provincial and federal governments. They form the laws of the tribe that the judges interpret and apply. *It was apparent to us that the fact that tribal court judges apply tribal law renders their work considerably more meaningful to them and to those who appear before them.*

Judges of tribal courts are selected in a variety of ways, depending upon the mechanism preferred by each tribal court district. The method is usually specified in the tribal code. Most tribes do not impose any academic requirements on those seeking judicial office. They usually require judicial candidates to be members of the tribe and to have lived on the reservation for a period of time prior to appointment or election, but this is not always the case. Of the 145 tribal courts for which there is information, the single most popular term of office, as chosen by 65 tribes, is for a period of 4 years for the chief judges. There is some mechanism in each court for the removal of a judge for misconduct. As with courts generally, the grounds for such removal are couched in vague language. There are, however, few reported instances of tribal court judges being discharged for dishonesty or malfeasance.

Personnel

Both legally trained and lay attorneys appear in American tribal courts. *The use of the tribal language or English is permitted during any court proceedings.* While some prosecuting attorneys are lawyers, others are not, but all have some legal training or related experience in other parts of the justice system. A number of tribes formally demand that a lawyer pass a bar examination created by them on tribal and federal Indian law before being able to appear in a tribal court. Eligibility also can differ as many tribes insist upon a degree from a law school approved by the American Bar Association, while many others do not. The apparent intent underlying the latter situation is to allow members of the tribes who are self-taught in their own law, or who have graduated from paralegal programs offered by community colleges, to have the opportunity to become 'tribal advocates,' which is the most commonly used term for defence lawyers and duty counsel... The presence of a tribal bar exam held to ensure that all counsel appearing in court will be fully knowledgeable in the substantive laws that govern life within the community, as well as tribal court procedure. This not only aids the judiciary in reaching proper decisions, but it also fosters respect for tribal law.

In addition to employing over 360 judges, tribal courts employ over 800 other personnel, consisting of court clerks, administrators, bailiffs, prosecutors, secretaries, probation officers, juvenile counsellors, public defenders and detention officers... It also is common to have a tribal prosecutor who not only conducts criminal matters, but also acts for the tribe in legal affairs, advises the council on legal issues and provides legal direction to the tribal police. Some tribes cannot offer probation and counselling services, due to funding restrictions.

Tribal court clerks and administrators have formed a national association to represent their interests, and to organize and provide ongoing training for members. We attended one of the regular conferences organized by the Department of the Interior. *The program was a very impressive indication of how tribal residents, with little formal training, can develop the skills needed to administer all aspects of a court system.*

Financing

Every court system requires adequate financial resources to provide sufficient personnel and physical facilities. The Judicial Services Branch of the Bureau of Indian Affairs is mandated to negotiate annual agreements with federally recognized tribal governments to provide funding in relation to salaries, benefits, administration expenses, training and related matters. A continual complaint from the tribes and tribal judges is that the BIA contributions are insufficient to meet the current costs of operating these unique courts, or to permit their expansion and improvement.

The U.S. government has not extended funding yet for the construction of sufficient and appropriate court facilities on many reservations. While some court facilities compare well to any which we have in Manitoba, most tribal court facilities are inadequate and not conducive to the maintenance of respect for a court.

Concerns Expressed About Tribal Courts

Tribal courts have been criticized for a number of reasons. There is the problem of an inordinate level of judicial turnover. This may be induced, in part, by the rather short tenure granted by tribal codes and constitutions. This may be occasioned by the relatively low salaries and limited benefits that accompany the position.

There is clearly a significant problem with stress. Being a member of a small community and sitting in judgment of neighbours, friends and relatives is inevitably a thankless and personally arduous assignment. Having limited funds available can result in unattractive working conditions and frustration with the lack of creative disposition or alternatives...

The nature of the work load in tribal courts has also changed to such an extent that it requires judges to be more knowledgeable about the relevant law. On the other hand, this has meant that some judges lack the desired level of legal education or training necessary to address some of the more complicated legal questions coming before their courts. On the other hand, there is a danger of over-professionalization facing tribal courts. It can result in the exclusion of members of First Nations, as happened through an increase in the Navajo bar examination standards such that no Navajo candidate was able to pass the bar exams in 1988. Placing a premium on professional training also may result in advocates and judges who are not steeped in traditional values or knowledgeable about customary law. Adopting a Western legal style with formal educational requirements can lead to a loss of Aboriginal uniqueness and much of the strength the tribal courts possess, particularly their informality and acceptance within the community....

Most tribal courts lack a sufficient range of effective sentencing options. While fines and incarceration commonly are used, the difficulty arises in relation to other, more creative strategies, such as fine option programs, community service orders, alcohol and drug abuse programs, detoxification centres, restitution, probation and victim/offender reconciliation. While tribal judges theoretically may be able to choose from this broader list, many cannot do so in reality because there are no such programs, due to a shortage of resources.

The danger, therefore, is that tribal courts may suffer the worst of both worlds. The common law adversarial model may be incompatible, in fact, with long-standing traditional values that promote harmony and reconciliation. Additionally, tribal courts may not be receiving sufficient resources to ensure that advocates are available for all indigent litigants so that they can benefit from the adversarial system, or to operate programs which provide alternatives to incarceration.

Advantages of Tribal Courts

There are many positive features of tribal courts. They provide a very efficient process in both civil and criminal matters. Cases deliberately are heard as quickly as possible so that the dispute does not fester, or an accused does not languish in jail on remand. *Tribal courts are not only more convenient to tribal members, they are perceived by them as being more understanding of their situation, more considerate of their customs, their values and their cultures, more respectful of their unique rights and status, and likely to be more fair to them than the non-Aboriginal justice system has been. In such a situation, where the court has the inherent respect of accused and the community, the impact and effect of its decisions will be that much greater.*

Tribal courts obviously have the capacity to bridge the chasm that now exists between Anglo-American law and Indian cultures... Some tribes have developed modern versions of traditional justice systems.

American tribes are committed to the preservation and expansion of their court system. This fact, perhaps more than anything, demonstrates a faith and belief in their ultimate value... In addition, there is a growing respect shown by federal and state courts towards the importance and authority of this unique system. As one example, a joint annual judicial educational conference, entitled the Sovereignty Symposium, has been under way for the past few years involving the Oklahoma Supreme Court and the tribal courts of that state....

All this leads us to conclude that tribal courts clearly have played a vital role in meeting the needs of American Indians for a fair, just and culturally acceptable legal system.[309]

On the basis of what is probably the most complete examination of the U.S. tribal court system by any recent commissions of inquiry, the Manitoba commissioners concluded:

It is clear that the existence of fully functioning tribal court systems on a variety of Indian reservations in the United States, many of them similar in size and socio-economic status to Indian reserves in Manitoba, and the benefits which those communities derive from them, are strong evidence that separate Aboriginal justice systems are possible and practical.[310]

Based on their review and submissions made by the Aboriginal people of Manitoba, the Aboriginal Justice Inquiry of Manitoba recommended that

...federal, provincial and Aboriginal First Nations governments commit themselves to the establishment of tribal courts in the near

---

[309] AJI, cited in note 2, volume 1, pp. 286-298 (emphasis added).

[310] AJI, volume 1, p. 269.

future as a first step towards the establishment of a fully functioning, Aboriginally controlled justice system.[311]

In light of the small size of most Aboriginal communities in Manitoba and the high
cost of administering separate justice systems for each community, the inquiry also
recommended that

> in establishing Aboriginal justice systems, the Aboriginal people
> of Manitoba consider using a regional model patterned on the
> Northwest Intertribal Court System in the State of Washington.[312]

The inquiry recommended further that

> Wherever possible, Aboriginal justice systems look toward the
> development of culturally appropriate rules and processes which
> have as their aim the establishment of a less formalistic approach
> to courtroom procedures so that Aboriginal litigants are able to
> gain a degree of comfort from the proceedings while not com-
> promising the rights of an accused charged with a criminal
> offence.[313]

There are some obvious advantages to the recommendation to create an Aboriginal
court system as an initial step in the development of Aboriginally controlled justice systems for Aboriginal communities that wish to proceed in that direction. It
is simultaneously a symbolic and a real demonstration of Aboriginal self-government
in action. Submissions to the Aboriginal Justice Inquiry of Manitoba and some of
the submissions to this Commission indicate that some Aboriginal nations and communities in Canada favour the establishment of tribal courts as a major step in taking
back control over justice as part of their self-government agenda.

Aboriginal nations and communities in Canada have the advantage of learning from
the U.S. experience, building on its strengths and seeking to avoid its weaknesses.
The opportunity exists for Aboriginal peoples to develop tribal court systems of
their own shaping and not, as in the early years of U.S. tribal court experience, systems imposed on them. **The purpose of this report is to provide the legal and
policy framework for this kind of development.**

The Canadian Future

Reflecting the diversity of Aboriginal peoples' conceptions of justice systems, not
all Aboriginal nations and communities see tribal courts as a necessary first step
or even as an ultimate goal. As our review in earlier chapters demonstrates, a
number of significant Aboriginal justice initiatives are taking place outside court-

---

[311] AJI, volume 1, p. 266.

[312] AJI, volume 1, p. 317.

[313] AJI, volume 1, p. 315.

rooms – indeed, the goal is to make a court judgement unnecessary. Hollow Water's community holistic circle healing project and the community council of Aboriginal Legal Services of Toronto are examples of this approach. The processes involved in these initiatives, like the recently revived Peacemaker Court in the Navajo system, are more in keeping with traditional Aboriginal values.

We believe it is possible to combine the benefits of traditional approaches to Aboriginal justice, which take place outside the courtroom and court-like processes for appropriate cases that do not simply duplicate non-Aboriginal courts but that, in the words of the Aboriginal Justice Inquiry of Manitoba, use culturally appropriate rules and procedures. Some Aboriginal nations and communities may wish to give priority to justice processes that take place outside the courtroom; others may see the development of an Aboriginal court system as more responsive to the problems facing them; yet others may wish to proceed along both paths simultaneously to ensure that the system works in an integrated and complementary fashion. It is not our purpose to predetermine or circumscribe choice but rather to create conceptual and legal space for these developments to occur.

As our review of justice initiatives revealed, there is already in place (although many rest on insecure jurisdictional and financial bases) a range of community justice processes in which traditional values predominate in the healing of individual and collective disorder and disharmony. **What these initiatives have in common, apart from a shared philosophy, is that the offender has acknowledged responsibility for the offence**. The Hollow Water project requires that the offender accept responsibility for his or her actions and demonstrate a commitment to work within the healing process. The community council project is also based on acceptance of responsibility. For initiatives that operate later in the process, such as sentencing circles, there has been either a plea of guilty or a finding of guilt after a trial conducted in the non-Aboriginal court system. One of the great strengths of Aboriginal justice processes may well be that individuals who deny responsibility in the non-Aboriginal system – because they fear the punitive sanctions underlying that system – will be prepared to accept responsibility for their actions in Aboriginal systems based on goals of restorative justice.

Nevertheless, there will be cases where individuals are not prepared to accept responsibility for one reason or another. For example, someone might be wrongly accused of an offence: a young man previously convicted of breaking and entering is accused of another such offence that he did not commit, the accusation arising from his reputation in the community and a witness's description of someone similar to him at the scene of the crime.

Another example might be a case where the accused person feels unpopular and marginal in the community and lacks confidence that the community process will treat him or her with respect and dignity. In this case, a denial of responsibility might have more to do with doubt about the Aboriginal system than with innocence or culpability. It may well be that over time such individuals will be won over by the way the system actually operates, but until that happens not guilty pleas are likely to be part of the reality of the transitional period.

It is also the case in many Aboriginal communities that social splits have developed where once there was cohesion. Splits often occur along generational lines. Many young Aboriginal people have grown up with a conception and experience of justice based on the non-Aboriginal adversarial system, a perception reinforced by news and entertainment media that reflect values alien to traditional Aboriginal ways. This is part of many young people's reality and part of their expectations about how they will be treated if they are accused of wrongdoing. The creation of Aboriginal justice systems, particularly those based on reconciliation and healing, may in time bring about a new balancing of rights and responsibilities, but it is likely that some accused persons will continue to enter not guilty pleas.

In these examples – and there may be others – an Aboriginal process based exclusively on individuals accepting responsibility and not disputing the allegations against them will not enable the community to address all problems. It will not be a complete and comprehensive justice system.

This poses a range of choices for the community, but it will be a significant measure of the success of Aboriginal justice systems if they can win the respect and confidence of those who have been marginalized and shut out from decision making in the past. As the experience of Hollow Water and the community council demonstrates, Aboriginal justice processes that are fully inclusive are those that appear to be the most successful.

How might an Aboriginal justice system respond to individuals who deny responsibility or claim innocence? One option is to rely on the non-Aboriginal justice system to process the case. At present this is how most serious criminal offences are addressed even where there is an existing Aboriginal initiative. This may be because police and prosecutorial authorities are not prepared to let the Aboriginal system handle such cases, or because the community itself does not feel it has the capacity and the resources to deal with the case. Some Aboriginal nations and their communities, even as they develop their own Aboriginal justice systems, may decide that the most effective use of their energies and resources is to concentrate on cases where the individual is prepared to accept responsibility and to leave other cases to the non-Aboriginal system, relying on other reforms to that system to make it more sensitive to Aboriginal people. The great majority of recommendations from the many inquiries that preceded ours are directed to that objective.[314]

---

[314] Another possible response when an individual refuses to acknowledge responsibility – and an option resorted to all too often in some Aboriginal communities – is to leave such cases to informal processes of social control. The problem is that this may leave those who are most subject to victimization vulnerable and unprotected. For example, Carol La Prairie, in her study of eight Cree

However, for Aboriginal nations and communities that wish to exercise the fullest authority in relation to the administration of justice, an authority that is integral to their inherent right of self-government, there will be a need to develop a process that can fulfil the adjudicative function in the face of not guilty pleas.

The historical and anthropological literature we reviewed is relatively silent on how such cases were dealt with in traditional Aboriginal practice. In "Law Ways of the Comanche Indians", E.A. Hoebel found that "denial of guilt by an accused...was so uncommon that there are not cases enough to draw sound conclusions."[315] In their study of the Cheyenne, Hoebel and Llewellyn addressed the issue of adjudication in the context of disputed questions of fact and the problem this poses for close-knit communities:

> True dispute of fact, secrecy of the relevant truth, tries ingenuity. Consider then the extraordinary number of devices recorded in the Cheyenne cases which were invented from occasion to occasion to deal with some doubtful point of fact – and this although the culture showed no sign of working toward a single general pattern for the purpose. A horse had been borrowed and was long overdue; what are the borrower's intentions? An aborted fetus was aborted by whom? Was there truth in jealous suspicion of a wife? Had a suspected warrior actually been aiding the enemy whites? Had there been an adequate degree of intention in a drunken, accidental, killing? Who was the attempting rapist? Was the accusation of bootleg hunting true?... This, without more, is a fairish range of fact-questions faced by the Cheyennes. All but two got answered to satisfaction; and in almost as many different ways as there were questions.[316]

The Canadian historical and anthropological material also sheds little light on adjudicative processes in these situations. There may be good reasons for this. As with the Cheyenne, the issues may have lent themselves to particular forms of resolution, the subtlety of which may have escaped the non-Aboriginal observer, particularly if the observer had not mastered the Aboriginal language. A further reason may be that for Aboriginal legal systems where the critical issue was whether

---

communities concluded that "the nature of the offence, community pressures, gossip, ridicule, fears about punishment of offenders, beliefs that reporting offences results in court and jail, or conversely, cynicism about police and the belief that nothing will happen anyway, conspire to inhibit reporting." (Carol La Prairie, *Justice For the Cree*, cited in note 49, p. 72.) The James Bay research indicated that lack of reporting was particularly prevalent in relation to spousal and intrafamily abuse.

[315] E. Adamson Hoebel, "Law Ways of the Comanche Indians", in *Law and Warfare*, ed. Paul Bohannon (New York: National History Press, 1967), p. 187.

[316] K. Llewellyn and E. Adamson Hoebel, *The Cheyenne Way* (Norman, Oklahoma: University of Oklahoma Press, 1941), pp. 306-307.

harm was caused, rather than whether harm was accidental or intentional, the circumstances in which disputation was necessary were much reduced.

Even if the adjudicative function in disputed fact situations had less significance in Aboriginal systems than in common and civil law systems, Aboriginal nations designing their own justice systems do not have to replicate the adjudicative process of the non-Aboriginal trial process. That process, set out in the *Criminal Code* and supplemented by the rules of evidence, is itself the creature of long development. Many of its features, now deemed essential to ensure a fair trial, did not exist a century ago. It is worth recalling that an accused did not have a full right to counsel until 1836, the ability to compel the attendance of witnesses until 1867, or the 'privilege' of testifying under oath until 1898. There were few, if any, rules of evidence before the eighteenth century.[317] Furthermore, in Canada it is only really since the advent of the Charter in 1982 that there has been significant development in relation to exclusionary rules designed to protect the integrity of the trial process and the administration of justice.[318] Thus, the common law system, like other legal systems, is a dynamic one that has changed over time; similarly, Aboriginal justice systems, building on different legal traditions, can be expected to develop to address issues that might not have arisen in earlier times and to adapt their processes to contemporary circumstances.

An Aboriginal trial process: some possible directions

Embarking on the challenging task of reconstituting and developing a contemporary adjudicative process, Aboriginal nations and their communities have a variety of models from which to choose, only one of which is the existing criminal trial process. They also have the advantage, gained through bitter and alienating experience, of seeing how the existing trial process, with its heavy emphasis on confrontation and cross-examination, runs counter to important Aboriginal values. It is reasonable to expect that Aboriginal nations would strive mightily to make sure that their own process does not perpetuate this cultural insensitivity.

It is not our purpose to be prescriptive with regard to designing a trial process that is consistent with Aboriginal values. That is a task for Aboriginal peoples. For the benefit of those who remain sceptical, however, about the possibility of doing so, we offer some possible directions.

The approach we have found most useful in thinking about the contours of an adjudication process within an Aboriginal justice system has two related aspects. **The first is to build on traditional Aboriginal processes of decision making that**

---

[317] See G. H. Baker, *An Introduction to English Legal History*, second edition (London: Butterworths, 1979), pp. 411-419.

[318] See, for example, the discussion by McLachlin J. in *R. v. Hebert*, [1990] S.C.R. 151 (Supreme Court of Canada), tracing the development of the common law rules governing confessions and the privilege against self-incrimination and the impact of the *Canadian Charter of Rights and Freedoms*.

are perceived as reflecting contemporary Aboriginal values; the second is to identify and avoid the features of the existing criminal justice process that are perceived as the most alienating and culturally inappropriate. The obvious connection is that aspects of the criminal law system are likely to be alienating and culturally inappropriate precisely because they run counter to Aboriginal values and patterns of decision making.

Judge Murray Sinclair has given us some useful examples of the various approaches Aboriginal people would likely bring to the central task of adjudication.

> In Aboriginal societies "truth determination" would, in my view, be very different from "truth determination" in Western society. Methods and processes for solving disputes in Aboriginal societies have, of course, developed out of the basic value systems of the people. Belief in the inherent decency and wisdom of each individual implies that any person might have useful opinions on any given situation and, if they wish to express them, should be listened to respectfully. Aboriginal methods of dispute resolution, therefore, would allow for any person to volunteer an opinion or make a comment. The "truth" of an incident would be arrived at through hearing many descriptions of the event. Because it is impossible to arrive at "the whole truth" in any circumstances, Aboriginal peoples would believe that more of the truth can be determined when everyone is free to contribute information. In such a system, the silence of an accused in the face of a mounting consensus as to what happened would be taken as an acknowledgment that the consensus is correct.
>
> This differs substantially from a system where the accused not only has the right to remain silent and not to have that silence held against him or her, but where he or she is invariably discouraged by counsel from testifying; where only the victim or a small number of people are called to testify; where the questions to be responded to are carefully chosen by adversarial counsel; where questions can be asked in ways that dictate their answer; where certain topics are considered irrelevant; and where certain very important information about the accused or the accuser or their families is deemed inadmissible.[319]

As we have come to understand them, traditional Aboriginal perspectives favour a dispersal of decision making authority, coupled with an emphasis on reaching consensus. By contrast, in western legal systems authority and decision making are exercised within hierarchical structures. The criminal trial process is a classic

---

[319] Sinclair, "Aboriginal Peoples, Justice and the Law", cited in note 58, pp. 180-181.

example. As described by Judge Barry Stuart of the Yukon Territorial Court in the case of *R. v. Moses*,

> In any decision-making process, power, control, the overall atmos-
> phere and dynamics are significantly influenced by the physical
> setting, and especially by the places accorded to participants... In
> the criminal justice process the physical arrangement in the court-
> room profoundly affects who participates and how they participate.
> The organization of the courtroom influences the content, scope
> and importance of information provided to the court. The rules
> governing the court hearing reinforce the allocation of power
> and influence fostered by the physical setting....
>
> The judge presiding on high, robed to emphasize his authorita-
> tive dominance, armed with the power to control the process, is
> rarely challenged. Lawyers, by their deference, and by standing
> when addressing the judge, reinforce to the community the judge's
> pivotal influence. All this combines to encourage the community
> to believe judges uniquely and exclusively possess the wisdom
> and resources to develop a just and viable result... Counsel, due
> to the rules, and their prominent place in the court, control the
> input of information. Their ease with the rules, their facility with
> the particular legal language, exudes a confidence and skill that lay
> people commonly perceive as a prerequisite to participate.
>
> The community relegated to the back of the room, is separated
> from counsel and the judge either by an actual bar or by placing
> their seats at a distinct distance behind counsel tables. The inter-
> play between lawyers and the judge creates the perception of a
> ritualistic play. The set, as well as the performance, discourages
> anyone else from participating.[320]

In a co-operative initiative with the Aboriginal community of Mayo in the Yukon, Judge Stuart was able to help fashion a process through which the court and the community addressed Moses's long and entrenched pattern of dysfunctional and violent behaviour, which had led him again and again to court and to prison. That process involved convening the hearing in the form of a circle, an approach that has come to be called 'circle sentencing'. In his reasons for judgment in the *Moses* case, Judge Stuart explained how restructuring the process in accordance with the form and philosophy of an Aboriginal circle changed the dynamics of the hearing and enhanced the quality of decision making, encouraging much broader com-munity participation in issues affecting its members.

> By arranging the court in a circle without desks or tables, with all
> participants facing each other, with equal access and equal expo-

---

[320] *R. v. Moses*, cited in note 169, pp. 355, 357.

sure to each other, the dynamics of the decision making process were profoundly changed.

Everyone around the circle introduced themselves. Everyone remained seated when speaking. After opening remarks from the judge, and counsel, the formal process dissolved into an informal, but intense discussion of what might best protect the community and extract Phillip from the grip of alcohol and crime.

The tone was tempered by the close proximity of all participants. For the most part, participants referred to each other by name, not by title. While disagreements and arguments were provoked by most topics, posturing, pontification, and the well worn platitudes, commonly characteristic of courtroom speeches by counsel and judges were gratefully absent.

The circle setting dramatically changed the roles of all participants, as well as the focus, tone, content and scope of discussion....

The circle significantly breaks down the dominance that traditional courtrooms accord lawyers and judges. In a circle, the ability to contribute, the importance and credibility of any input is not defined by seating arrangements. The audience is changed. All persons within the circle must be addressed. Equally, anyone in the circle may ask a direct question to anyone... The circle denies the comfort of evading difficult issues through the use of obtuse, complex technical language.

The circle setting drew everyone into the discussion. Unlike the courtroom, where the setting facilitates participation only by counsel and a judge, the circle prompted a natural rhythm of discussion....

In traditional courtroom settings, all inputs, all representations are directed to the judge. Not surprisingly, all participants, including the community, expect the judge after hearing all submissions to be responsible for rendering a sage and definitive edict. The circle re-directed the flow of discussion from a single channel leading to the judge to a flow that followed the natural rhythms of interest around the circle... The circle by engaging everyone in the discussion, engaged everyone in the responsibility for finding an answer. The final sentence evolved from the input of everyone in the circle. The consensus-based approach fostered not just shared responsibility, but instilled a shared concern to ensure the sentence was successfully implemented....

Their creative search produced a sentence markedly different from customary sentences for such crimes and radically departed from the pattern of sentences previously imposed upon Phillip for similar offences. The circle forged a collective desire for something different, something unlike the sentences imposed in the past ten years, something everyone could support, something they believed would work. Fuelled by the expanded and responsive flow of information, the circle participants worked towards a consensus, towards a unique response to a problem that had plagued the community for ten years and had stolen ten years of productive life from Phillip.[321]

Although the use of the circle in criminal cases in the non-Aboriginal system has thus far been limited to sentencing, in the context of an Aboriginal justice system this traditional process could be used as the principal process of decision making, including the adjudication of responsibility.[322]

To those trained in western legal systems, this suggestion raises a number of problems. What if a member of the community participating in the circle wanted to talk about other offences that he believed the accused might have committed but with which the accused had not been charged? Under the existing rules of evidence this would be neither relevant nor admissible except under the very limited rules of 'similar fact' evidence. What if members of the community in the circle disclosed what they had heard others say about the accused, statements that would be ruled hearsay and inadmissible under the existing rules of evidence? Consider also the situation of a member of the tribal police force who wanted to tell the circle of a statement the accused had made when arrested for the offence, a statement that amounted to a confession. Such statements are admissible under existing rules of evidence only under certain conditions, principally that they are made voluntarily and that Charter rights and protections are respected.

In the existing system these issues are addressed in the framework of an adjudication process controlled by lawyers and judges. Lawyers determine what evidence will be presented to the court and they do so guided by the rules of evidence. To the extent that a lawyer seeks to introduce evidence that may not be admissible, the lawyer on the other side has a responsibility to challenge its admission, and the judge then rules on whether it will be admitted. In other words, lawyers and judges are the gatekeepers for the evidence that will form the basis for the adjudication. The question that arises, therefore, is who will be the gatekeeper if adjudication occurs within a circle.

Several answers occur to us. The first is that the need for a gatekeeper stems from the rules of evidence, which are designed to restrict the facts that can be placed in evidence. Some of these rules have to do with relevance, some have to do with pro-

---

[321] *R. v. Moses*, pp. 356-360.

[322] See our comments, however, on the evolution of the circle process in the Yukon and northern Quebec in our discussion of circle sentencing in Chapter 3.

tecting the rights of the accused, and yet others are designed to assure the integrity of the judicial process by not admitting evidence that would bring the administration of justice into disrepute. It should not be assumed that these rules would necessarily be appropriate in an Aboriginal justice system, particularly one based on restorative goals.[323] If the goals of the system are healing and reconciliation and the threat of imprisonment does not anchor the system, the need for restrictive rules of evidence may be less compelling. An Aboriginal justice system might therefore adopt a much broader concept of what is relevant evidence and a very different sense of what would bring its administration into disrepute. The need for lawyers as gatekeepers might be greatly reduced in such a system.

Even if an Aboriginal system, either in a transitional period or in its fully developed form, determined that the existing rules of evidence were appropriate to its adjudication process, those rules could still be applied in the context of a circle. Although there might be a need for gatekeepers to screen evidence before its presentation, as well as an adjudicator if objections were raised to such evidence being admitted, this could take place quite easily in a different framework. That framework, in accordance with the philosophy of the circle, would assign certain responsibilities to lawyers and judges but would not do so in a way that excluded other members of the community from participating in the process.

In considering how the rightful participation of community members might be accommodated in an Aboriginal adjudication process, there are some established precedents of shared decision making. The jury process is an exemplary model of community involvement in criminal justice. The right to trial by a jury of one's peers has its common law roots in *Magna Carta* and is heralded as one of the most important safeguards of the liberty of the subject, but in the contemporary Canadian criminal justice system juries are involved only in a very small percentage of cases. The overwhelming majority of cases are decided by judges. Even in cases with juries, the evidence suggests that Aboriginal people are under-represented as jurors, in stark contrast to their over-representation as accused persons.[324]

In an Aboriginal justice system the jury concept might receive a new lease on life. Where an offender denies responsibility for an offence, an Aboriginal criminal jus-

---

[323] McElrea, "Restorative Justice", cited in note 194; and Consedine, *Restorative Justice*, cited in note 103.

[324] In its chapter on juries, the Aboriginal Justice Inquiry of Manitoba concluded:

> We believe that the jury system in Manitoba is a glaring example of systemic discrimination against Aboriginal people. Studies conducted for our inquiry confirm that Aboriginal people are significantly under-represented on juries in Northern Manitoba and are almost completely absent from juries in the City of Winnipeg.... Our studies clearly show that Aboriginal people are not properly represented on juries, even on juries trying an Aboriginal person accused of committing an offence against another Aboriginal person in an Aboriginal community. (AJI, cited in note 2, volume 1, pp. 378-379; see also *Justice on Trial*, cited in note 23, chapter 4, pp. 45-46.)

tice system might provide for the first time what Aboriginal people could truly regard as trial by a jury of peers. Moreover, the principle of requiring a jury's unanimity to convict an offender fits comfortably with the Aboriginal value of consensus decision making. It would be an interesting turn of fate if Aboriginal communities were to adopt a process of adjudication that is losing its central place in the non-Aboriginal system and make it an important part of a contemporary Aboriginal system.

This does not mean that the jury's role in an Aboriginal system would have to mirror that in the non-Aboriginal system. The latter system draws sharp distinctions between issues of fact and issues of law, distinctions that even the most experienced lawyers sometimes have difficulty applying. The Aboriginal system may choose to give the jury greater responsibility, including issues determined exclusively by judges in the non-Aboriginal system. One area might be in the questioning of witnesses. In some provinces the procedures for coroner's inquests allow jury members to question witnesses to clarify their understanding of the evidence. In criminal trials this is not permitted, mainly because of the rules of evidence and lawyers' exclusive control over the presentation of evidence. In an Aboriginal adjudication process in which the role of lawyers was reduced, there could be room for an expanded role for the jury. Depending on the rules of evidence to be applied, there might still be a need to determine whether particular questions were relevant and hence the need for someone to decide such issues. However, the redefinition and redistribution of responsibilities could produce a very different and distinctively Aboriginal shape for both procedural and substantive due process.

The adversarial nature of the criminal justice process might be the feature most likely to change under the guiding hand of Aboriginal people. We have been told that the confrontational nature of the process – pitting not only Crown and

---

Archibald Kaiser also addressed this issue in a study for the Law Reform Commission of Canada:

> The current statutes provide no real ability for accused persons to influence the profile of a jury particularly with respect to its racial or cultural representativeness, except in so far as the general techniques of jury selection, such as peremptory challenges and challenges for cause, enable him or her to move the composition in one direction or another. The problem really exists even prior to these selection processes being invoked, in that it is most unlikely that the jury's panel will be composed of a high proportion of members of the accused's racial origin, assuming the accused is Aboriginal. This is a function of provincial *Juries Acts* and the restricted nature of challenges to jury panels which are now available under s. 629 [of the *Criminal Code*]. Judicial decisions seem to have continued this restrictive analysis of jury selection, in saying that the absence of members of a particular race does not constitute proof of discrimination. Canadian courts are simply reluctant to admit that the racial or cultural features of a jury would in any way be capable of affecting the outcome. (H. Archibald Kaiser, "The Criminal Code of Canada, A Review Based on the Minister's Reference", *U.B.C. Law Review* (1992, Special Edition: Aboriginal Justice), pp. 120-121; see also *R. v. Kent, Sinclair and Gode* (1986), 27 C.C.C. (3d) 405 (Manitoba Court of Appeal).)

defence against each other but also witness against witness as a means of establishing 'the facts' – is, in the eyes of Aboriginal people, disruptive of interpersonal relations and destructive of social harmony. The primary method of establishing credibility – the examination and cross-examination of witnesses – ignores the proscription in many Aboriginal societies against saying anything that might be harmful to your family, clan or community. As Rupert Ross pointed out in *Dancing with A Ghost*, in Aboriginal societies it may be ethically wrong to say hostile, critical, implicitly angry things about someone in their presence – precisely what our adversarial trial rules require.[325] Other features of the existing trial process have been identified as problematic for Aboriginal people. The concept of accused persons having to speak through another person – a lawyer – when they are present in the courtroom and perfectly able to speak for themselves is alien, and the rules of evidence, which prevent people in the community with intimate knowledge of the circumstances from testifying, are in conflict with Aboriginal consensual practice.

Some of these features would not be difficult to change if Aboriginal people are the principal actors in the hearing process. An Aboriginal lawyer, knowledgeable of the values of the people in whose system he or she is practising, can be expected to bring to the task of representation attitudes and behaviours different from those encouraged in the non-Aboriginal system. For example, advising a client not to participate in a circle where the community expectation is that accused persons should respond to allegations against them would not further the credibility of the client. Similarly, asking questions in a manner considered insensitive and inappropriate by other members of the circle would neither further the client's case nor be a useful contribution to resolving a matter of importance to the community.

An Aboriginal trial process may not be able to avoid all aspects of the adversary system in situations where accused persons dispute the case against them. There will continue to be cases in which witnesses are mistaken or lie about evidence. It may be necessary to mount a serious challenge to particular evidence, and Aboriginal counsel may feel that rigorous cross-examination to bring out an ulterior motive for the witness's evidence or inconsistent statements may be the best or even the only method of establishing credibility. But the strategy of choice in the non-Aboriginal system might be the last resort in an Aboriginal system. We should not underestimate the ability of Aboriginal counsel, particularly those trained in both Aboriginal and non-Aboriginal systems, to develop more culturally appropriate ways of getting at the facts.

In our hearings and research we were struck by the distinctively Aboriginal way in which facts and opinions were presented. The practice of making a point not by simply asserting it but by presenting a narrative, perhaps drawn from another time and place, to illustrate the point or lesson, has deep roots in Aboriginal societies. Aboriginal counsel might well develop a style of questioning witnesses that draws on this narrative tradition. Narratives might be drawn from the extensive

---

[325] Ross, *Dancing with A Ghost*, cited in note 135, chapter 3.

repertoire of 'Trickster' stories so common among Aboriginal peoples in Canada. As explained by John Borrows, a member of the Anishnabe Nation and a professor at Osgoode Hall Law School,

> In First Nations discourse a literary character known as the Trickster is used to convey what it might be like to think or behave as someone or something that you are not. This assists First Nations peoples in understanding different perspectives because it allows for the contrast and comparison of disparate understandings. The Trickster has various personas in different cultures. The Anishnabe (Ojibwa) of central Canada called the Trickster Nanabush; the First Nations people of British Columbia know him as Raven; he is known as Glooscap by the Micmac of the Maritimes; and as Coyote, Crow, Badger or Old Man among the other First Nations peoples in Canada. The Trickster is alive today as he survives in our ancient stories told anew... Lessons are learned about other people's self-understanding as the Trickster engages in conduct which is on some particulars representative of the listener's behaviour, and on other points uncharacteristic of their comportment. The Trickster encourages an awakening of consciousness about the complexities of difference because the listeners are compelled to interpret and reconcile the possibility that their perspective may be partial. As such, the Trickster helps the listeners conceive of the limited viewpoint they possess.[326]

Incorporating this Aboriginal perspective, a witness might be asked to reflect on the narrative and give his interpretation of it as a way of opening up an opportunity for the witness to admit that he or she might be mistaken or for others in the circle to draw that conclusion. This approach has limitations, but so does cross-examination. Ultimately it will be up to Aboriginal people to determine the adjudicative balance that best serves the goals of their justice systems.

The emergence of an Aboriginal adjudicative process based on the philosophy of the circle, with broad participation from the community, not just legal professionals, and an evidentiary framework that is not limited to questions and answers but encompasses the narrative style of relating experiences, may not only result in a process consistent with Aboriginal concepts of justice, but may also open up some new windows for the non-Aboriginal trial process. There is already a body of research supporting the theory that non-Aboriginal juries reconstruct the evidence in narrative forms in reaching a verdict. Nancy Pennington and Reid Hastie, two American psychologists who have done extensive research on decision making by juries, have written:

---

[326]John Borrows, "Constitutional Law From a First Nation Perspective: Self-Government and the Royal Proclamation", *U.B.C. Law Review* 28 (1994), pp. 7-8.

The story model is based on the hypothesis that jurors impose a narrative story organization on trial information... The constructive nature of comprehension is especially relevant in the context of legal trials in which characteristics of the trial evidence make it unwieldy and unstory-like. First there is a lot of evidence, often presented over a duration of several days. Second, evidence presentation typically appears in a disconnected question and answer format; different witnesses testified to different pieces of the chain of events, usually not in temporal or causal order; and witnesses are typically not allowed to speculate on necessary connecting events such as why certain actions were carried out, or what emotional reaction a person had to a certain event. The attorney's opportunity to remedy the unstory-like form of evidence presentation occurs during the presentation of opening and/or closing arguments, but this opportunity is not always taken.[327]

The authors also found that jurors were least likely to convict an accused when the prosecution evidence was presented in witness order and the defence evidence was presented in story order (31 per cent reached a guilty verdict) and they were most likely to convict when prosecution evidence was in story order and defence evidence was in witness order (78 percent reached a guilty verdict).[328] It may well be, therefore, that the narrative approach to presenting evidence could provide further insights into alternative models for the non-Aboriginal trial process.

In contemplating what Aboriginal justice systems might look like, we have contrasted the non-Aboriginal process, typically in a courtroom, with an Aboriginal process in a circle. These should not be seen as either/or alternatives. The way proceedings are conducted in a non-Aboriginal process are not cast in stone.

Equally important, the circle is a highly dynamic and flexible approach. The circle has no predetermined composition; one community may decide that the circle should consist of representative members of the community (for example, in the form of a jury) and individuals with responsibilities as advocates or keepers of the process. Another community may decide that the circle should involve as many community members as possible, particularly if aspects of the case affect the whole community (for example, vandalism to a school or other public building). The degree of community involvement is likely to change over time. At the beginning the community may want to have broad participation for educative purposes, to establish the legitimacy of the Aboriginal system and demonstrate how it differs from the non-Aboriginal system. Administering justice will not be the only thing on the self-government agenda, however. The need to attend to other matters of

---

[327] Nancy Pennington and Reid Hastie, "A Story Model of Juror Decision Making", in *Inside the Jury*, ed. R. Hastie (Cambridge, Massachusetts: Harvard University Press, 1993) p. 195.

[328] Pennington and Hastie, "A Story Model of Juror Decision Making", p. 211.

vital concern to the community will likely lead to distinctions being drawn between cases that can be resolved without involving the whole community and those that cannot. It is inevitable that the diversity of Aboriginal peoples will result in a broad diversity of approaches to Aboriginal justice.

Indeed, it is a reflection of diversity that some Aboriginal nations and communities will not adopt the circle as the most culturally appropriate process. The Coast Salish, the Kwakiutl, the Gitksan, the Nisga'a, and other nations of the west coast, as well as the Haudenosaunee in the east, are peoples of the longhouse or the big house. Traditionally, and in their contemporary form, proceedings in the longhouse and the big house follow distinctive formal arrangements and protocol, although they do have philosophical and spiritual dimensions similar to proceedings held in circles. In some longhouses the members of the various clans sit along the walls of the longhouse in accordance with particular and formalized seating arrangements that reflect people's relationships and responsibilities with and to each other. We can anticipate that the power and strength of longhouse and big house ceremonies and proceedings will be harnessed in the shaping of contemporary Aboriginal justice systems. Indeed, this is already happening.

In a precedent-setting case, the Coast Salish Nation on Vancouver Island demonstrated the effectiveness of its traditional laws and institutions in resolving one of the most difficult kinds of contemporary dispute. Although the case was not one involving the criminal law, it was a good illustration of Aboriginal dispute resolution.[329]

The case concerned the custody of a child whose mother had died. One of the mother's last requests was that her child, Jeremy, be brought up by her sister, a member of the Nuu-chah-nulth Nation, so that he could be taught the traditions that would give him privileged status in her band. The boy's father, a member of the Coast Salish Nation, claimed that the child was entitled to similar rights through his family. Both the father and the aunt wanted custody, and the case ended up in the provincial family court. Achieving privileged status would require teachings from a very early age, and the question before the court was whether the court should recognize this as being in the boy's best interests and, if so, whether the mother's family was more important than the father's. Jeremy's aunt applied for custody under the provincial *Family Relations Act*. The South Island Tribal Council obtained intervener status in the provincial court hearings and proposed that the matter be referred to a council of elders to mediate the dispute. The case was adjourned for six weeks and terms of reference for the mediation were agreed to by the parties. They included the following elements:

> The Council of Elders was to be acceptable to both families and was to be chaired by the chairman of the Tribal Council; the

---

[329] The account in the next few pages, as well as the quotations and the excerpts from the agreement, are drawn from Michael Jackson, "In Search of the Pathways to Justice", cited in note 103, pp. 204-207.

mediation was to take place in a neutral Big House, the traditional meeting place of the Coast Salish Nation. The proceedings were to take place in the evening hours in order that the families on both sides could be properly represented. The families could call forward spokespersons to address the Council of Elders in the traditional way to address their concerns and act on their families' behalf. Elders or elected members of council could act as witnesses to the proceedings from each of the two families' villages; the families had the right to the presence of legal counsel as observers during the mediation. The mediators' alternatives and recommendations to the families were not to be binding except if the families were so decided in common agreement.

The council of elders convened and met with the parties. The case history and the precedents in Coast Salish Aboriginal law were discussed, and the parties agreed to the council's proposed resolution of the dispute. Although traditionally such resolution was not formally transcribed in writing, in this case, to enable the court to incorporate the terms of the resolution, a formal agreement was drawn up and signed by all parties and the legal representatives. The agreement contains the following provisions:

> Whereas differences did arise between Allan John Jones [the father] and Audrey Thomas [the mother's sister], in the manner of disposition, custody, and welfare of the child, Jeremy...
>
> And Whereas it is desirous of both families that the child develop with the benefit of love and harmony of both families;
>
> And Whereas the teachings, traditions, and culture and heritage of both families are Jeremy's birthright and gift from the Creator;
>
> Therefore Be It Resolved that in accordance with the precedent of Indian Family Law and the recommendations of the Council of Elders and the grandparents of both families that tradition be honoured and respected, and that as per the customs of our Aboriginal communities that custody of the child to Allan John Jones is so recognized... and further be it resolved that Allan John Jones shall respect the role, advice, and the influence of the grandparents of both families in regard to raising the child and respect to our customs and traditions regarding Indian Family Law and the courtesies regarding the extended families;
>
> And Further Be It Agreed that Audrey Thomas, sister to the late Lucy Thomas, does have special interest in the raising of Jeremy and that she be accorded due consideration in accordance with our teachings;
>
> And Be It Further Agreed that the child shall be raised in respect of the customs and traditions of both families and the cultures of

the great nations of the peoples of the Nuu-chah-nulth and the Coast Salish;

And Be It Further Agreed that Allan John Jones shall allow access and visitations to the relatives and members of both families in accordance with the courtesies and customs of the Aboriginal peoples in general and in particular shall ensure that the child does spend a respectful and sufficient time with the grandparents of both families and be further agreed that the same privileges accorded the grandparents shall be accorded to Audrey Thomas;

And Be It Further Agreed that both families shall maintain an open heart and open door in regard to access and influence to the child Jeremy in accordance with the courtesies and customs of our Aboriginal peoples;

And Further Be It Agreed that Allan John Jones does now have special obligation in accordance with the customs and traditions of Indian Family Law to his son Jeremy and to both families in this regard;

And Therefore Be It Further Resolved that Allan John Jones and Audrey Thomas in conjunction with the grandparents and the Council of Elders do petition his Honour Judge E.O. O'Donnel of the Provincial Court...to render a decision accordingly with respect to the wishes of both families which reflects the best interests of the child in accordance with the customs and traditions of Indian Family Law;

All parties do agree by their signature to this document to raise the child Jeremy with regard to our traditional customs with love, respect and education so that he may be properly prepared for life within our Aboriginal society and the non-Indian community that shall be a part of his world in the future.

Proceedings resumed before the provincial family court, and a consent order giving the father custody, with access by the aunt and the grandparents of both families, was entered. Attached to the order was the written agreement, which was made part of the court's order. In his written judgement, Judge O'Donnel made the following comments:

Before dealing with the form of the actual Order, I personally would like to add a few words because of the historical significance of this process by which this agreement and this court judgment has been arrived at.... This method of resolving disputes has shown that traditional native methods and institutions can and do operate effectively in this day and age. The entire process has demonstrated that it is possible for the native institutions and our courts to cooperate and work together for the benefit of all parties.[330]

In this case the application of Coast Salish law and its dispute resolution process avoided the hostility and pain usually associated with custody battles. As a result, both families will have an opportunity to contribute to the development of the child, who will enjoy and benefit from the heritage and traditions of both families without having to choose between them. In his commentary on the case Michael Jackson points out that the same result probably could not have been achieved by relying on court proceedings and having each party call elders to give expert evidence on Coast Salish law, leaving it to a judge to determine the best interests of the child.

> The successful outcome of this case is integrally related to the fact that all essential elements of the Aboriginal system of justice were invoked. The parties were able to accept the recommendations of the Council of Elders because they have legitimacy as law-givers; the forum – the Big House – in which their deliberations regarding the law and its application to this case took place, architecturally reflected the inter-connectedness of Coast Salish families and its carvings, totem poles and crests encapsulates their shared history; the procedures in the Big House, the making of speeches which are listened to with respect and without interruption in the search for a consensus, draw upon time honoured traditions of Coast Salish decision making.
>
> If the matter had been dealt with through the giving of expert evidence in court proceedings, the legitimacy of *our* judicial office, the symbolism of *our* court architecture and protocol, and *our* procedural style of examination and cross-examination would have been brought to bear on the case and the ultimate decision would rest with one individual outside the community. Had the parties continued with adversary court proceedings the result would have been an imposed resolution which would likely have further divided the families and not only further fragmented the community but ultimately worked to the detriment of the child.[331]

As Judge O'Donnel said in his judgement, Aboriginal decision making and the court process were able to work in harmony. This was achieved in large measure because the tribal council has been working with the judiciary to develop cross-cultural awareness and judges like Judge O'Donnel have been receptive to their efforts.

---

[330] "Family Relations Act and Audrey Thomas and Allan John Jones", unreported judgement of His Honour Judge E.O. O'Donnel, 13 July 1988.

[331] Jackson, "In Search of the Pathways to Justice", cited in note 103, pp. 206-207.

Michael Jackson also raises the following questions, however, which he suggests are central to any discussion of achieving justice in Aboriginal communities.

> Why should it be necessary for Aboriginal communities like the First Nations of South Island to educate and persuade non-Aboriginal judges that they should respect the Aboriginal system in making their decisions? To the extent that Aboriginal peoples have their own ways of resolving disputes such as this in a manner more conducive to social harmony and individual development, why should we not recognize their authority to determine such matters in accordance with their own principles and procedures?[332]

Our answer to the last question is clear. The inherent right of self-government includes the right of Aboriginal nations to resolve disputes such as these, which are integral not only to maintaining social harmony, but also to transmitting values from one generation to another, in accordance with their own laws and procedures.

Aboriginal justice systems: some broad contours

Having said that the Commission will not prescribe the shape Aboriginal justice systems should take, setting out the possible contours of such systems, beyond the trial process, may nevertheless contribute to understanding the diversity of Aboriginal approaches to justice. This is particularly important because the existing criminal justice system, anchored in a philosophy of punishment and an architecture of imprisonment, can blind us to alternative means to achieve peace and order within a framework of justice.

Our review of Aboriginal concepts of justice showed clearly that Aboriginal justice systems are premised on principles of restorative justice, with reconciliation and healing assuming primary importance. Flowing from a restorative justice approach is the need to develop processes that involve everyone whose participation is necessary to effect reconciliation and healing, together with the human and physical resources to achieve this goal. In our review of Aboriginal justice initiatives we saw how Aboriginal people of various nations have invoked their own distinctive processes to address cycles of crime and victimization. These initiatives contain important lessons for the future direction of Aboriginal justice systems.

If peacekeeping and reconciliation are central to the goals of Aboriginal police forces, for example, the recruitment and training of Aboriginal police will likely be somewhat different from training for the RCMP and provincial police forces. This does not mean that Aboriginal police will need no training in dealing with dangerous situations, where control has to be asserted before reason and reconciliation can be attempted. However, Aboriginal police forces, acting under the authority of Aboriginal governments, will be able to develop a range of techniques that draw upon skills and traditions different from those used by non-Aboriginal police forces.

---

[332] Jackson, "In Search of the Pathways to Justice", p. 207.

For matters that cannot be resolved through the intervention of peacekeepers we have also seen, in initiatives such as Hollow Water, how Aboriginal people have developed processes that hold offenders accountable, empower victims, recognize the historical and social roots of violence and sexual abuse, and engage the whole community in healing and renewing individual and collective strength. As those involved in the Hollow Water initiative are quick to point out, theirs is not necessarily the model other Aboriginal nations and their communities should adopt; it is the model that makes sense and works for them. Nevertheless, it contains powerful lessons from which others can learn as they develop their own distinctive processes, which may take the form of justice or healing circles or may reflect and respect the relationships of the longhouse or other Aboriginal meeting places. It is also clear, from initiatives such as those being put in place by the Gitksan and Wet'suwet'en nations, that where extended families and clans are the bedrock of social and economic organization, they will play pivotal roles in contemporary Aboriginal justice systems. Whether they are designed to resolve cases where the accused accepts responsibility or to adjudicate cases of disputed fact, a justice system that builds on the traditions and strengths of an Aboriginal nation's forms of social organization is inherently more likely to achieve its goals than one based on alien and alienating forms. For the Gitksan and Wet'suwet'en, the feast hall, not the courthouse, is the hall of justice.

The growing experience with sentencing circles also illustrates how models of decision making can be developed that empower communities in the search for constructive responses to individuals and families whose lives are the source of pain for themselves and harm to others.

In Chapter 3 we also reviewed the experience in New Zealand/Aotearoa, where the family group conference has been heralded as a major legal and policy shift to deal with young offenders using a restorative justice approach. Similar conferences could also become part of Aboriginal justice systems in Canada, their composition reflecting patterns of Aboriginal social organization. Aboriginal nations in Canada will no doubt draw on other experiences from abroad as well. The U.S. tribal court system provides important lessons for the development of Aboriginal courts, particularly in terms of what such systems require. One of those requirements, a recognized and sufficiently broad jurisdiction, is discussed later in this chapter. We would anticipate that more recent developments, such as the Navajo Peacemaker Court, could become important features of Aboriginal justice systems in Canada.

The journey of Aboriginal prisoners toward spiritual renewal may also provide a bridge in the development of Aboriginal justice systems. Aboriginal people did not build iron houses, and contemporary Aboriginal justice systems would likely devote greater efforts than the non-Aboriginal system to developing alternatives to imprisonment. Even with alternatives in place, however, some individuals will not be able to stay in the community if they present a continuing danger, or because of the nature of the offence. These cases will require solutions offering greater control than can be provided in communities. Does this mean that

Aboriginal nations exercising their jurisdiction over justice must now build their own prisons or make arrangements for the detention of these individuals in non-Aboriginal prisons? In addressing this issue, Aboriginal nations will have the benefit of experience with existing programs organized around Aboriginal spirituality and what will be learned with the opening of the healing lodge at Maple Creek, Saskatchewan. As discussed in Chapter 3, this new facility is not only architecturally inspired by Aboriginal structures, but its philosophical foundation is the principles and processes of the healing journey. To the extent that there will be a need for places where Aboriginal people can address violence and abuse outside their own communities, we would see a future for healing lodges rather than penitentiaries in Aboriginal justice systems.

Jurisdiction

Types of Jurisdiction

In this section we examine the jurisdictional issues that must be resolved if Aboriginal nations are to establish their own justice systems. By Aboriginal justice systems we mean systems that both administer justice and make laws. The development of Aboriginal justice systems will have to take place under a constitution that divides powers in relation to justice between the Parliament of Canada and the provincial legislature and a constitution that recognizes and affirms existing Aboriginal and treaty rights. It is therefore necessary to begin by examining the current constitutional framework to see how Aboriginal justice systems can fit into it. It will also be necessary to examine the extent to which the exercise of law-making authority by Aboriginal governments may be constrained by current constitutional provisions or practices. In particular, we will look at the exercise by Aboriginal nations of law-making powers in the area of criminal law.

We then examine how potential jurisdictional conflicts between Aboriginal justice systems and the non-Aboriginal system might be resolved. Among the issues are those relating to jurisdiction with respect to the person and the subject-matter, territorial jurisdiction, and mutual recognition and respect on the part of Aboriginal and non-Aboriginal decision-making bodies for each other's decisions.

Before examining these issues in detail, however, it is useful once again to look at the experience of the United States. Many of the jurisdictional issues that concern us here have been addressed in one form or another in the development and evolution of the tribal court system. We should not miss the opportunity to learn from that experience.

Tribal Court Experience

The tribal court system is rooted in the constitutional history of the United States. Thus the significance of the U.S. Supreme Court decision in *Worcester* v. *Georgia* in 1832 was that it affirmed the notion of tribal sovereignty over actions of individual states.

The relevance of this decision to jurisdiction is that, for the most part, criminal law in the United States is a matter for each state to determine. The conflict between state criminal law power and tribal sovereignty arose on a number of occasions over the 90 years after *Worcester*. In *Ex Parte Crow Dog*,[333] in 1883, the U.S. Supreme Court ruled that only tribal courts had jurisdiction over criminal matters arising in Indian territory, and thus a Sioux who killed another Sioux on Indian land could not be tried by state courts. It was in response to this decision that the U.S. Congress passed the *Major Crimes Act*.

While Indian nations thus had complete freedom from interference by state governments in the area of law-making and enforcement, the federal government, the courts determined, retained an ability to intervene in Indian affairs. This notion was confirmed in the Supreme Court decision in *Talton v. Mayes* in 1896;

> ...although possessed of these attributes of local government, when exercising their tribal functions, all such rights are subject to the supreme legislative authority of the United States.[334]

While Supreme Court decisions of the nineteenth century did not prescribe the form that Indian dispute resolution systems had to follow, the federal government essentially controlled the development of tribal courts from 1883 on.[335] With the passage of the *Indian Civil Rights Act* in 1968, the federal government ensured that tribal courts, in form and function, would resemble the courts in the rest of the country.

Determining the jurisdiction of tribal courts over individuals is a very difficult task and, even for U.S. tribal court lawyers, quite confusing. With respect to criminal matters, tribal courts have jurisdiction over members of the tribe for all criminal offences except those covered by the *Major Crimes Act*. They have no jurisdiction over non-Indians who commit crimes on the reservation except for minor traffic offences. Crimes committed by non-Indians must be tried in federal or state courts. Until 1990 it was thought that tribal courts had jurisdiction over crimes (other than those covered by the *Major Crimes Act*) committed by Indians living on a reservation although members of another tribe. In 1990, however, the Supreme Court muddied the waters further in *Duro v. Reina*.[336] The *Duro* decision illustrates the problematic nature of jurisdiction when it is left to the vagaries of ad hoc non-Aboriginal judicial determination.

---

[333] *Ex Parte: In The Matter of Kang-Gi-Shun – Otherwise Known as Crow Dog* (1883), 109 U.S. 556 (United States Supreme Court).

[334] *Talton v. Mayes*, cited in note 298, p. 384.

[335] Jonathan Rudin and Dan Russell, "Native Alternative Dispute Resolution Systems: The Canadian Future in Light of the American Past" (Toronto: Ontario Native Council on Justice, 1993), pp. 7-8.

[336] *Duro v. Reina* (1990), 110 S. Ct. 2053 (United States Supreme Court).

On 15 June 1984, Albert Duro, a California Mission Indian, allegedly shot and killed a 14-year-old boy on the Salt River Pima-Maricopa reservation in Arizona. Duro was charged with murder and thus, under the *Major Crimes Act*, his case was heard in federal court. The federal prosecutor dropped the charges against Duro. He was then charged on the reservation with unlawful discharge of a firearm, a misdemeanour offence within the jurisdiction of the tribal court. Duro challenged the jurisdiction of the tribal court to hear charges against him, and the matter eventually made its way to the Supreme Court. The Supreme Court agreed with Duro that tribal court jurisdiction was restricted to members of the tribe where the court was sitting.[337]

The decision in *Duro* resulted in a jurisdictional void on Indian reservations (one acknowledged by the Supreme Court) and raised the problem of how tribes could maintain law and order when significant numbers of the reservation population were beyond the reach of tribal justice. Indeed, not only were they beyond the reach of tribal justice, but there were serious concerns about whether state and federal authorities were prepared to fill the gap in all cases.

In the wake of *Duro*, an already confused jurisdictional picture became a nightmare. Eldridge Coochise, president of the American Indian Court Judges' Association made a presentation before the house of representatives committee on interior and insular affairs in 1991, which was meeting to consider the implications of the *Duro* decision. In his presentation, Coochise showed a chart providing an overview of how jurisdiction was exercised by tribal courts. The chart was full of blanks indicating either jurisdictional loopholes or unresolved jurisdictional issues.[338] As a result of representations from Indian nations across the country, Congress passed legislation essentially overturning *Duro* and giving back to tribal courts authority to hear cases involving any Indian person on the reservation subject to the continuing restrictions of the *Major Crimes Act*. This decision by Congress restored the jurisdictional morass in the tribal courts to the pre-*Duro* situation of simple confusion.

In the civil law area tribal courts have largely unlimited jurisdiction over matters that arise on the reservation and have resolved very complex cases involving millions of dollars. This jurisdiction includes cases involving tribal members and Indians from other tribes. The law is much more complex when it comes to civil jurisdiction in relation to non-Indian litigants, and over the past 40 years an extensive jurisprudence has developed regarding this issue. In *Williams* v. *Lee*[339] the

---

[337] United States Congress, House of Representatives Committee on Interior and Insular Affairs, *The Duro Decision: Criminal Misdemeanour Jurisdiction in Indian Country* (Washington: U.S. Government Printing Office, 1991), p. 3.

[338] Eldridge Coochise, written statement, in House Committee on Interior and Insular Affairs, *The Duro Decision: Criminal Misdemeanour Jurisdiction in Indian Country*, p. 119.

[339] *Williams* v. *Lee* 358 U.S. 217, 223, 3 L. Ed. 2d 251 (1959) (United States Supreme Court).

Supreme Court concluded that exclusive jurisdiction rested with the Navajo tribal court rather than the Arizona Supreme Court in an action brought by a non-Indian to enforce a debt under a contract entered into on the Navajo reservation with an Indian person. In its decision, the court declared that the essential test for resolving the issue of whether a matter was one of tribal, rather than federal or state jurisdiction was whether the matter was an essential feature of the tribe's right of self-government. Using this test the Supreme Court has upheld a tribal cigarette tax on sales to non-Indians and a mineral tax on companies operating on reservation lands. The court has also sustained business taxes on non-Indian corporations while striking down state taxes on tribal royalty interests in mineral leases to non-Indians.[340]

Before leaving the issue of tribal courts, we must emphasize two points made earlier in this chapter. First, it would be a mistake to see tribal courts as necessarily the preferred method of adjudication of disputes. The choice of tribal courts as the forum for dispute resolution on reservations emerged not after any significant community consultation or discussion; rather it was imposed by the government of the United States. Similarly, resolution of the conflict between due process concerns and Aboriginal traditions of dispute resolution also came from the outside. The passage of the *Indian Civil Rights Act* determined the issue according to the wishes of the U.S. Congress. The act provides no opting-out procedures; thus communities have no choice but to adhere to the ICRA. The tribal court model thus represents the imposition of what Rudin and Russell refer to as a 'one size fits all' approach to Aboriginal justice.[341]

The second point that must be emphasized is that the limits imposed by federal legislation have not totally restricted the growth of alternative justice systems on reservations. Indeed, as our discussion of the Navajo Peacemaker Court demonstrates, a process in some ways similar to the development of alternative Aboriginal justice projects in this country is taking place in some tribal court jurisdictions.

The Jurisdictional Basis for Establishing Aboriginal Justice Systems

The constitutional framework

We discussed the place of Aboriginal peoples in Canada's constitutional framework in some detail in *Partners in Confederation*, and it is not our purpose to review all the material cited in that document.[342] However, one of the issues that must be addressed in the context of this discussion is whether the right to make laws and to adminis-

---

[340] For a summary of the civil jurisdiction of U.S. tribal courts, see AJI, volume 1, pp. 278-279.

[341] Rudin and Russell, "Native Alternative Dispute Resolution Systems", cited in note 335, pp. 31-32.

[342] See *Partners in Confederation*, cited in note 8, chapter 2, "A Constitutional Watershed: The *Constitution Act, 1982*", pp. 29-45.

ter and develop justice systems is one that belongs to the inherent jurisdiction of Aboriginal peoples. If so, the next question is whether the laws in question fall within the core of Aboriginal criminal jurisdiction or the periphery. If the latter, such legislation would require the agreement of the other orders of government.

The *Constitution Act, 1867* contains several provisions allocating responsibilities in relation to justice between the federal and provincial governments. Broadly speaking, the Parliament of Canada is responsible for the criminal law and its procedures while the provincial legislatures are responsible for the adminstration of justice. These responsibilities flow from the division of powers under sections 91 and 92 of the *Constitution Act, 1867*. Section 91(27) gives the Parliament of Canada exclusive legislative jurisdiction in relation to "The criminal law, except the constitution of the courts of criminal jurisdiction, but including the procedure in criminal matters." Section 92(14) gives that the provincial legislatures exclusive legislative jurisdiction in relation to "The adminstration of justice in the province, including the constitution, maintenance and organization of provincial courts, both of civil and of criminal jurisdiction, and including procedure in civil matters in those courts."

Wayne Mackay has described how these provisions are normally interpreted absent any consideration of the effect of section 35 of the *Constitution Act, 1982*.

> From a literal reading of these two sections it is apparent that the federal government will decide what the substantive law will be, including the rules of evidence. The federal power also encompasses criminal procedure. This federal power includes the processing of the criminal matter from the laying of a charge to the final outcome but the provincial governments also have an important role to play in policing, prosecution and the general adminstration of justice. The practical result is an exercise in cooperative federalism – a cooperation that has rarely included Aboriginal people. Left to the provincial government is the power to set up a court system that will adjudicate these matters.[343]

Section 35(1) of the *Constitution Act, 1982* states:

> 35 (1) The existing aboriginal and treaty rights of the aboriginal peoples of Canada are hereby recognized and affirmed.

Before the courts pronounced on the issue, the meaning of section 35(1) was the subject of great speculation. What was meant by "aboriginal and treaty rights", and what was the significance of the word "existing" at the beginning of the section?[344]

---

[343] A.W. Mackay, "Federal-Provincial Responsibility in the Area of Criminal Justice and Aboriginal Peoples" *U.B.C. Law Review* (1992, Special Edition: Aboriginal Justice), p. 315.

[344] The word 'existing' did not appear in the original draft of section 35. The provinces that wanted the word added though that it would limit section 35 rights to Aboriginal rights in effect at the time the *Constitution Act* was passed.

Some of the uncertainty was cleared up in 1990 with the Supreme Court of Canada decision in *R. v. Sparrow*.[345]

While *Sparrow* broke very significant ground, care must be taken in interpreting this case. The Supreme Court noted in its reasons for judgement that the case turned specifically on the issue of the extent of the Aboriginal right to fish for food, and the court was concerned that this context not be forgotten in subsequent interpretations of its decision.

The court concluded that an "existing" right contemplated by section 35(1) was one that had not been extinguished through the requisite government action. Regulation was not seen as synonymous with extinguishment, however. To establish extinguishment, the court said, there must be a clear and plain intention on the part of the government to extinguish the Aboriginal right.

What then is the situation of the right of Aboriginal self-government in the broadest sense and, in particular, the right to administer justice and develop laws in the context of section 35(1)? In *Partners In Confederation* we wrote,

> it does not appear that federal Indian legislation purported to deprive Indian peoples of all governmental authority, even if it severely disrupted and distorted their political structures and left them with very limited powers. There are persuasive reasons to conclude that their inherent right of self-government was still in existence when the *Constitution Act, 1982* was enacted. As such it qualifies as an "existing" right under section 35(1)... a similar approach can be taken to the governmental rights of Inuit and Métis peoples under section 35(1) [as well].[346]

However, the exercise of the rights contemplated in section 35(1) is not without restriction. While in general the protections of the Charter are, to quote from section 1, "subject only to such reasonable limits prescribed by law as can be demonstrably justified in a free and democratic society", section 35 is not part of the Charter, and thus section 1 cannot be used to defend government actions infringing section 35(1) rights. Before *Sparrow*, any government legislation that infringed a section 35(1) right would arguably have to be struck down, as the only other section dealing with conflicts between the constitution and government action was section 52, which stated that any law "inconsistent with the provisions of the Constitution is, to the extent of the inconsistency, of no force or effect."

Despite the absence of what has been referred to as a 'reasonable limits test' in section 35, the court indicated in *Sparrow* that Aboriginal rights are not absolute. To override a section 35(1) right, the court said, the government would first have to identify a valid legislative objective in relation to the challenged regulation or

---

[345] *R. v. Sparrow* [1990] 1 S.C.R. 1075 (Supreme Court of Canada).

[346] *Partners in Confederation*, cited in note 8, chapter 2, p. 35.

law. Having done that, the government would then have to justify the regulation by showing that the need for it is compelling and substantial. In justifying a limit on a section 35(1) right, the court emphasized that

> ...the honour of the Crown is at stake in dealings with aboriginal peoples. The special trust relationship and the responsibility of the government vis-à-vis aboriginals must be the first consideration in determining whether the legislation or action in question can be justified.[347]

Taking all this into account, we commented on the scope of the right of self-government as contemplated by section 35(1) in *Partners in Confederation* and outlined three guiding principles:

> First, the potential Aboriginal sphere of authority under section 35(1)...has roughly the same scope as the federal head of power over "Indians, and Lands reserved for the Indians" recognized in section 91(24) of the *Constitution Act, 1867*. Within this sphere, Aboriginal governments and the federal government have concurrent legislative powers; that is, they have independent but overlapping powers to legislate....
>
> Second, where a conflict arises between an Aboriginal law and a federal law, and both laws are otherwise valid, Aboriginal laws will take priority, except where the federal laws meet the standard laid down in the *Sparrow* case. Under this standard, federal laws will prevail where the need for federal action can be shown to be compelling and substantial and the legislation is consistent with the Crown's basic trust responsibilities to Aboriginal peoples.
>
> Third, the interaction between Aboriginal and provincial laws is regulated by rules similar to those that govern the interaction of federal and provincial laws in this area.[348]

Where does this leave Aboriginal governments in terms of establishing and administering their own justice systems? Our earlier discussion of section 107 courts illustrates that, at least in some form, the federal head of power under section 91(24) contemplated distinct forms of Aboriginal justice delivery. If the rights under section 91(24) are shared by Aboriginal governments and the federal government, then it would seem that Aboriginal peoples have at least concurrent powers with the federal government in this area, subject of course, to the possibility of federal supremacy in cases of compelling and substantial need.

---

[347] *R. v. Sparrow*, cited in note 345, p. 1114.

[348] *Partners in Confederation*, cited in note 8, pp. 38-39 (footnotes omitted). We will return to this issue in our final report.

222

In determining the scope of the inherent right of self-government, specifically in the area of the administration of justice, it is also necessary to acknowledge the argument of Indian nations that have signed treaties with the Crown that include justice provisions. It is the contention of those nations that their treaties are a confirmation of their right of self-government in this area.[349]

The first treaty between the British and the Haudenosaunee in 1664 provided for the punishment of trans-national crimes and recognized the mutual jurisdiction of each party over such crimes committed by its subjects or peoples under its protection. Thus crimes committed by British subjects against the Iroquois were to be punished by the British authorities, while those committed by Iroquois against British subjects or Indians subject to British protection were to be punished by the Iroquois.[350]

The 1726 restatement and renewal of a 1725 treaty between the Mi'kmaq Nation and the British also contained clauses on jurisdiction over justice. The Indian nations of the Wabanaki confederacy agreed that "if there happens any robbery or outrage committed [against His Majesty's subjects within the province] by any of the Indians, the tribe or tribes they belong to shall cause satisfaction and restitution to be made to the parties injured". The Mi'kmaq Nation interprets this article to mean that the chiefs were to be responsible for their members' acts against British subjects, rather than accepting the jurisdiction of civil or criminal courts or provincial legislative bodies.[351]

The numbered treaties negotiated after Confederation by the Indian nations of what is now Manitoba, Saskatchewan and Alberta also had provisions that are interpreted by the Indian nations that were parties to the treaties as affirming their retained jurisdiction over justice. Through their oral history, the Indian nations of western Canada maintain that it was understood in the treaty negotiations that neither party to the treaty would interfere in the internal government of the other. In particular they understood that the Indian nations would continue to maintain their own justice systems and that they would deliver to the North West Mounted Police any person who needed to be brought to justice under the Crown's jurisdiction.[352] In their presentation to the Aboriginal Justice Inquiry of Manitoba,

---

[349] A proper understanding of the treaties referred to here cannot come solely from an examination of the written text. The oral tradition is also essential to a full understanding of the documents. This issue will be addressed more fully in our final report.

[350] "Articles of Agreement Between the Five Nation Indians and Colonial George Cartwright, 1664", in *Early American Indian Documents, Treaties and Laws, 1607-1789*, ed. A. Vaughan (Washington, D.C.: University Publications of America), volume 7, p. 294.

[351] The Mi'kmaq interpretation of the Wabanaki compact is set out in the submission by Marie Battiste on behalf of the Grand Council of the Mikmaq Nation to the Royal Commission on the Donald Marshall, Jr., Prosecution, cited in note 31, volume 3, appendix 2, p. 81.

[352] The interpretation of the numbered treaties will be discussed at length in our final report.

the Assembly of Manitoba Chiefs submitted that the numbered treaties not only affirmed their jurisdiction to administer and maintain justice over the retained lands but also envisaged a role for Indian tribes in the adminstration of justice even on lands that had been ceded under treaty.[353]

It is the Commission's view that the recognition and affirmation of existing Aboriginal and treaty rights in section 35(1) of the *Constitution Act, 1982* gives constitutional scope for Aboriginal self-government in matters relating to the establishment of justice systems.

Recommendation 1

The Commission recommends that federal, provincial and territorial governments recognize the right of Aboriginal nations to establish and administer their own systems of justice pursuant to their inherent right of self-government, including the power to make laws, within the Aboriginal nation's territory.

Providing a foundation for Aboriginal justice systems within the constitution: the division of powers

In light of our interpretation of section 35(1), what legal framework can best accommodate this? To guide our thinking we reviewed work on this issue by the Aboriginal Justice Inquiry of Manitoba, the Law Reform Commission of Canada and our own commissioned research. Within the existing constitutional and legal framework several means are available to provide a foundation for these systems. The first two options can be summarized as follows. Either the federal government or a province could legislate for the establishment of an Aboriginal justice system, including the establishment of an Aboriginal court system. The federal government would have such authority by virtue of either section 91(24) or section 101 of the *Constitution Act, 1867*. Section 91(24) gives Parliament authority over "Indians, and Lands reserved for the Indians" (which the Supreme Court of Canada determined also applies to Inuit[354]), and section 101 states that the Parliament of Canada may "provide for the constitution, maintenance, and organization of a general court of appeal for Canada and for the establishment of any additional courts for the better administration of the laws of Canada." The jurisdiction of a federally established Aboriginal court could include disputes governed by federal statute, including the *Indian Act*, as well as matters governed by federal common law, including the common law of Aboriginal title. It could also include jurisdiction to adjudicate crim-

---

[353] AJI, cited in note 2, volume 1, p. 313.

[354] *Re Term "Indians"*, [1939] S.C.R. 104 (Supreme Court of Canada). It is our view that the section also covers the Métis people. We will return to this issue in our final report.

inal matters and disputes governed by provincial laws of general application that are incorporated by reference under section 88 of the *Indian Act*.[355]

Provincial legislative competence would stem from section 92(14) of the *Constitution Act, 1867*, which confers on provincial legislatures the authority to pass laws in relation to the adminstration of justice and the constitution, maintenance and organization of provincial courts. Jurisprudence with respect to section 91(24) provides that although in certain circumstances a province can regulate Aboriginal people by laws of general application, a provincial law cannot, generally speaking, single out Aboriginal people. In *Kruger and Manuel* v. *The Queen*, the Supreme Court of Canada, held that "the fact that our law may have greater consequence to one person than to another does not, on that account alone, make the law other than one of general application."[356] However a provincial initiative establishing an Aboriginal court, by necessity, would not be a law of general application and thus could be construed as a law in relation to Indians and their lands.

Despite this possibility, there are arguments in favour of provincial authority to establish an Aboriginal court. In particular, the courts have held that section 92(14) entitles a province to create a court designed specifically for a class of persons who fall under exclusive federal jurisdiction without invading federal legislative power. Thus in *Reference re Young Offenders Act (PEI)*, the Supreme Court of Canada upheld a federal/provincial scheme to establish a separate court system to deal with young offenders. At issue was an arrangement whereby federal legislation conferred jurisdiction on provincial youth courts to administer federal law governing young offenders. The Supreme Court affirmed the constitutional validity of provincial participation in the following terms:

> With regard to the institutional aspect of the administration of the Young Offenders Act, the power lies within the provincial legislatures under s. 92(14) to constitute, maintain and organize the courts required for the application of the Act.[357]

Thus, the decision provided that a province is competent to establish a court intended for a specific class of persons who fall within federal legislative jurisdiction, namely, young persons charged with a criminal offence. On the strength of this case, it seems possible that a province would be entitled to establish Aboriginal courts, despite the fact that Aboriginal peoples fall within federal legislative competence.[358]

---

[355] See Patrick Macklem, "Aboriginal Justice, the Distribution of Legislative Authority, and the Judicature Provisions of the *Constitution Act, 1867*", in *Aboriginal Peoples and the Justice System*, cited in note 7, p. 326. See also Mackay, "Federal-Provincial Responsibility", cited in note 343.

[356] *Kruger and Manuel* v. *The Queen*, [1978] 1 S.C.R. 104 (Supreme Court of Canada), p. 110.

[357] *Reference re the Young Offenders Act (PEI)*, [1991] 1 S.C.R. 252 (Supreme Court of Canada), p. 263.

[358] In a discussion paper prepared for our round table on justice issues, Patrick Macklem observed, with respect to the difference between provincial establishment of a youth court and an Aboriginal court,

Provincial legislative competence to establish an Aboriginal justice system will hinge upon whether the provincial initiative can be characterized as a law in relation to the administration of justice. A provincial law establishing an Aboriginal court would present both federal and provincial aspects. Its federal aspect would be that it singles out Aboriginal people. Its provincial aspect would be that it is intended to administer justice within the province. If the provincial aspect of the law is relatively more important than the law's federal aspect, then it will be within the legislative competence of the province.[359] While it is difficult to assess the constitutionality of legislation in the abstract, a provincial law establishing an Aboriginal court would likely single out Aboriginal people in the interests of administering justice in the province. The federal aspect would merely be a means to achieve a valid provincial legislative objective, and thus it would be relatively less important than the law's provincial aspect.

The province could confer jurisdiction on Aboriginal courts to adjudicate matters involving Aboriginal people that fall under provincial legislative competence and may also be able to confer jurisdiction to adjudicate matters that fall under federal legislative authority. In *A-G Ontario* v. *Pembina Exploration of Canada Ltd.*, a unanimous Supreme Court held that

> The provincial power over the adminstration of justice in the province enables a province to invest its Superior Courts with jurisdiction over the full range of cases, whether the applicable law is federal, provincial or constitutional.[360]

The analogy between a youth court and an Aboriginal court cannot be taken too far. One difference between the establishment of a youth court and the establishment of an Aboriginal court is that, unlike 'Indians', young persons charged with a criminal offence do not constitute a class of persons explicitly named by the *Constitution Act, 1867*. Federal legislative competence over young offenders is a consequence of Parliament's authority to pass laws in relation to criminal law. Moreover, Parliament does not possess legislative authority to pass laws in relation to all aspects of the lives of young persons charged with a criminal offence, whereas Parliament, subject to the *Canadian Charter of Rights and Freedoms*, and section 35(1) of the *Constitution Act, 1982*, does possess such authority with respect to 'Indians'. However, it is not immediately apparent why these differences possess any constitutional significance for the purposes of determining the scope of provincial legislative authority in relation to the administration of justice. If provincial authority over the administration of justice supports provincial establishment of a court aimed specifically at young offenders, a class of persons who fall within federal legislative competence, it ought to also support the establishment of an Aboriginal court. ("Aboriginal Justice, the Distribution of Legislative Authority, and the Judicature Provisions of the *Constitution Act, 1867*", cited in note 355, pp. 328-329.)

[359] *Multiple Access Ltd.* v. *McCutcheon*, [1982] 2 S.C.R. 161 (Supreme Court of Canada), p. 181.

[360] *A-G Ontario* v. *Pembina Exploration Canada Ltd.*, [1989] 1 S.C.R. 206 (Supreme Court of Canada), p. 217.

Writing for the court, Justice La Forest also held that a province could confer general jurisdiction on a provincially established inferior court, "including actions arising out of federal matters." Unless the federal government had expressly conferred exclusive jurisdiction over the subject matter on a federally established court, a province is competent to confer jurisdiction over federal matters on provincial courts. Federal/provincial co-operation, as was the case in *Reference Re Young Offenders Act (PEI)*, would reduce the risk of a provincial initiative being ruled unconstitutional.[361]

As a third option, federal/provincial negotiations could be directed to achieving recognition of the right of Aboriginal people to establish and maintain Aboriginal justice systems as an aspect of the existing Aboriginal and treaty rights of Aboriginal peoples recognized and affirmed by section 35 of the *Constitution Act, 1982*. This was in fact the route recommended by the Aboriginal Justice Inquiry of Manitoba, which concluded:

> ...the manner of resolution that appears to provide the greatest potential for the successful establishment of Aboriginal justice systems for...First Nations, Métis and Inuit peoples involves a process of trilateral negotiations, leading to an agreement that contains within it an express provision that the right to establish and maintain Aboriginal justice systems is an 'existing treaty or Aboriginal right' within the meaning of section 35 of the Constitution Act, 1982. Whether that leads ultimately to a constitutional provision does not deter us from our conclusion that the establishment of Aboriginal justice systems can, with effort and cooperation, be accomplished.[362]

A fourth option would be for Aboriginal justice systems to be established pursuant to the Aboriginal right of self-government under section 35(1) of the *Constitution Act, 1982*. Although interpretation of section 35 is in its infancy, there are strong reasons to believe that as an Aboriginal right, and possibly as a treaty right flowing from provisions of particular treaties, Aboriginal peoples retain an inherent right to establish their own justice systems. The problem, of course, with this asserted basis for jurisdiction is that, absent federal and provincial agreement, any Aboriginal initiative would be vulnerable to constitutional challenge in the courts.

Providing a foundation for Aboriginal justice systems within the constitution: the judicature provisions

One other issue has to be considered in determining which of the available options, either singly or in combination, would best accomplish the goal of providing a con-

---

[361] The issue of provincial legislative competence is dealt with in greater depth in Macklem, "Aboriginal Justice, the Distribution of Legislative Authority", cited in note 355, pp. 327-332.

[362] AJI, cited in note 2, volume 1, p. 313.

stitutional foundation for Aboriginal justice systems. This issue relates to the judicature provisions of the *Constitution Act, 1867*. Contained in sections 96-100, the provisions enable the governor general to appoint the judges of the superior, district and county courts in each province (section 96) and provide that the judges of the courts of those provinces shall be selected from the respective bars of those provinces (section 97); such judges are removable by the governor general on address of the Senate and House of Commons (section 99(1)); they are subject to mandatory retirement at the age of 75 (section 99(2)); and they are to be paid by the federal government (section 100). If these provisions are constitutionally applicable to Aboriginal justice systems, it is not difficult to see how this would unduly constrain the shape of such systems and undermine the objective of restoring Aboriginal control in the area of justice. Aboriginal people will not have the necessary degree of control over matters of Aboriginal justice if the federal government has the constitutional authority to select Aboriginal candidates for the judiciary and the Parliament of Canada has constitutional authority to dismiss Aboriginal judges. Given the important role elders are likely to play in many Aboriginal justice systems and the reasons for seeking their experience, it would make no sense to require that they be members of a provincial bar, and it would be perverse to limit their participation after they have reached 75 years of age.[363]

The legal issue of when the judicature provisions apply to a provincially created court or tribunal is complex. Essentially, if the court or tribunal is exercising jurisdiction broadly analogous to the jurisdiction exercised by superior, district or county courts at the time of Confederation, then the provisions apply. Jurisdiction over indictable criminal offences falls into this category, and the judicature provisions would therefore seem to apply to the appointment and tenure of judges of an Aboriginal court that was given such jurisdiction. The issue is further complicated, however, by the fact that the courts have developed relatively complex tests to determine whether jurisdiction exercised by a provincial body falls within the ambit of the judicature provisions. In one of the leading cases, *Labour Relations Board of Saskatchewan* v. *John East Ironworks*, the judicial committee of the privy council adopted a purposive approach to the judicature provisions. Lord Simonds stated:

> It is as good a test as another of 'analogy' to ask whether the subject matter of the assumed justiciable issue makes it desirable that the judges should have the same qualifications as those which distinguish the judges of superior or other courts.[364]

The judicial committee dismissed a challenge to the constitutionality of the Saskatchewan Labour Relations Board on the grounds that the jurisdiction of the board found no analogy in issues that would have been familiar to the courts of 1867. The court held that because of the nature of industrial relations, "It is essen-

---

[363] On the meaning of the term elder, see note 160, Chapter 3.

[364] [1949] A.C. 134, p. 151.

tial that...[the board's] members should bring an experience and knowledge acquired extra-judicially to the solution of their problems."

In a subsequent case involving the Ontario Residential Tenancies Commission, the Supreme Court of Canada developed the test further and held that even where jurisdiction does conform to that exercised by superior courts at Confederation, if

> 'judicial powers' are merely subsidiary or ancillary to general administrative functions assigned to the tribunal...or the powers may be necessarily incidental to the achievement of a broader policy goal of the legislature...the grant of judicial power to provincial appointees is valid. The scheme is only invalid when the adjudicative function is a sole or central function of the tribunal...so that the tribunal can be said to be operating 'like a section 96 court'.[365]

Applying these tests to Aboriginal justice systems suggests the following tentative conclusions. To the extent that Aboriginal justice initiatives are based on a philosophy of justice as healing, in which restoration of harmony rather than punishment is the primary objective, and that they accept only offenders who acknowledge responsibility, they would seem not to be exercising jurisdiction analogous to that exercised by superior courts at Confederation. If such systems also have an adjudicative component to deal with cases where the accused person pleads not guilty, then, although the adjudicator would be exercising a judicial function, this component could be seen as ancillary to the primary function of achieving reconciliation or necessarily incidental to the achievement of the broader policy goal of developing resolutions or dispositions infused with the specific values and traditions of particular Aboriginal nations and their communities.

The case for applying the judicature provisions would become more compelling the closer an Aboriginal justice system came to replicating the functions exercised by non-Aboriginal criminal courts. Thus, if an Aboriginal court were to operate on the same procedures and principles as a non-Aboriginal court, adopting the same philosophy in relation to sentencing, with the only difference being that the judges were Aboriginal, it would become more difficult to argue that the appointment of those judges should not be subject to the judicature provisions.

Thus far we have been talking about the application of the judicature provisions to Aboriginal courts created pursuant to provincial legislation. Would the situation be different if such a court were created by Parliament? The courts have made it clear that section 96 binds the Parliament of Canada as much as provincial legislatures when Parliament seeks to vest jurisdiction in provincial courts to adjudicate federal matters. In *McEvoy* v. *A.G. New Brunswick*, at issue was a federal/provincial agreement whereby the criminal jurisdiction of provincial superior courts to try all indictable offences under the *Criminal Code* was to be transferred to a new unified criminal court staffed by provincially appointed judges. The

---

[365] *Reference re Residential Tenancies*, [1981] 1 S.C.R. 714 at 736, per Dickson J.

Supreme Court of Canada held that such a proposal violated section 96 because Parliament would be surrendering the power of the governor general to appoint judges who try indictable offences while the province would be exercising an unconstitutional appointing power. The Supreme Court said, "Section 96 bars Parliament from altering the constitutional scheme envisaged by the judicature sections of the *Constitution Act, 1867*, just as it does the provinces from doing so."[366]

Left unsaid by the Supreme Court in *McEvoy* was the extent to which section 96 limits the federal government's ability to transfer superior court jurisdiction to an entity created not by a province but by Parliament. If Parliament established an Aboriginal court and vested it with criminal jurisdiction, would the provisions of sections 96-100 regarding the appointment, qualifications and retirement of judges be applicable?

One view is that the judicature provisions do not apply to courts or tribunals established and vested with jurisdiction by the federal government.[367] The alternative view is that the provisions bind Parliament in exactly the same way as they bind the provinces, with the result that federally established courts that exercise superior, district or county court jurisdiction as it stood in 1867 must conform to the judicature provisions.[368] The Supreme Court of Canada recently declined to rule on this question.[369]

The resolution of this issue turns on how the courts will characterize the underlying purpose of the judicature provisions. There are two competing perspectives on the subject. One perspective is that the judicature provisions are an expression of the value of judicial independence. This perspective supports the conclusion that the judicature provisions bind Parliament in the same manner and to the same extent as they bind the provinces. The competing perspective is that given that superior, district and county court judges are constitutionally authorized to exercise jurisdiction over federal as well as provincial law, the judicature provisions reflect and secure a valid federal interest in the appointment and tenure of those judges against countervailing provincial power. Such a purpose would not be undermined if Parliament ignored the judicature provisions in establishing a federal court or tribunal to administer federal law, as there would be no risk of a province trying to usurp federal authority in this regard.[370]

---

[366] *McEvoy v. A.G. New Brunswick*, [1983] 1 S.C.R. 704 (Supreme Court of Canada), p. 720.

[367] See Peter W. Hogg, *Constitutional Law of Canada*, third edition (Scarborough: Carswell, 1992), pp. 423-424. This was also the view of the late chief justice of Canada, Bora Laskin. See, for example, *Reference re Section 6 of the Family Relations Act*, [1982] 1 S.C.R. 62 per Laskin C.J., dissenting in part.

[368] See Robin Elliot, "Case Comment: Is Section 96 Binding on Parliament?", *U.B.C. Law Review* 16 (1982), p. 313.

[369] See *Chrysler Canada Limited v. Canada (Competition Tribunal)*, [1992] 2 S.C.R. 394 (Supreme Court of Canada).

[370] These competing perspectives are reviewed in Macklem, "Aboriginal Justice, the Distribution of Legislative Authority", cited in note 355, pp. 349-350.

Even if the judicature provisions are in principle applicable to the federal government, the extent to which a court would deem them relevant to a federally created Aboriginal justice system would depend on the extent to which the process and philosophy drew its inspiration from Aboriginal traditions and values rather than duplicating the non-Aboriginal system.

The remaining question, which takes us into uncharted waters, is whether the judicature provisions would be applicable to Aboriginal justice systems established by Aboriginal nations pursuant to their inherent right of self-government under section 35(1) of the *Constitution Act, 1982*. In light of the different perspectives on the underlying purposes of these provisions, there are arguments that, depending on the nature and function of Aboriginal justice systems, these provisions ought not to apply. Robin Elliot, articulating the perspective that sections 96-100 secure judicial independence, has written that "the most important of our rights and obligations [ought to be] determined and enforced by persons learned in the law and independent of government and public pressure."[371] The provisions of sections 96-100 are intended to ensure that only persons learned in the law and independent of government are appointed. In Aboriginal justice systems, the qualifications for those who are respected as learned in the law are likely to be quite different from those set out in the judicature provisions. The respect accorded the judgement of certain elders does not derive from their being members of a provincial bar, and to the extent that their judgements are based on precedents, they are not found in non-Aboriginal law reports. If, as we believe, the Aboriginal right of self-government includes the right to establish justice systems that reflect distinctive Aboriginal values, it makes little sense, as a matter of either constitutional law or policy, to apply provisions that would undermine that purpose.

If an Aboriginal nation determines that the adjudication function should be performed by a body that includes members of both the offender's and the victim's family or clan – because this is consistent with the primary goal of restoring harmony – it would again subvert the Aboriginal right of self-government to apply provisions based upon a concept of independence developed in a non-Aboriginal context. The integrity of decision making is equally critical to Aboriginal and non-Aboriginal justice systems, and we address this issue later in this chapter. For purposes of this discussion, we are of the view that it is possible and indeed desirable in interpreting the application of the judicature provisions to Aboriginal justice systems developed pursuant to section 35, to find the necessary constitutional space to allow these systems to develop.

There are arguments that would support the non-applicability of the judicature provisions to Aboriginal justice systems, whether established by provincial, federal or Aboriginal governments, but the issue remains complex; moreover, its ultimate resolution would be decided not by Aboriginal people but by the Supreme Court of Canada. Depending on that resolution, the development and growth of

---

[371] Elliot, "Is Section 96 Binding on Parliament?", cited in note 368, p. 328.

Aboriginal justice systems in ways different from the non-Aboriginal system could be either encouraged or thwarted.

The jurisprudence with regard to the constitutional division of powers in criminal justice has taken place in the context of all powers being allocated between federal and provincial governments and in a framework that assumes a common justice system. The existence of distinctive Aboriginal systems has not been part of that equation. Constitutional recognition of an Aboriginal jurisdiction in relation to justice as part of the Aboriginal right of self-government requires an expansion of both legal and conceptual horizons as Aboriginal people embrace the challenges of bringing justice to their nations and communities.

This part of our report has been particularly technical, engaging as it does some of the more complex aspects of constitutional law. Our conclusions can be summarized as follows.

Although the Commission believes that it is constitutionally possible for various elements of Aboriginal justice systems to be established by federal and provincial governments, the preferred option is for these to be established pursuant to the inherent Aboriginal right of self-government recognized and affirmed in section 35(1) of the *Constitution Act, 1982*. If, as we believe, the right to establish a justice system is part of the inherent right of self-government, that system should be based fairly and squarely on the authority of Aboriginal governments and not have its foundation in federal and provincial legislation. We do not believe that the establishment of Aboriginal justice systems has to depend on the exercise of federal or provincial legislative authority, but the transition to Aboriginal justice systems, based on the legislative authority of Aboriginal governments, will clearly be smoother and avoid many of the constitutional challenges that might otherwise be made if negotiations take place with federal and provincial governments aimed at finding both conceptual and practical accommodations for the exercise of the right of self-government in the area of justice.

Recommendation 2

The Commission recommends that the federal, provincial and territorial governments of Canada include the establishment of Aboriginal justice systems on the agendas of current negotiations regarding land claims, treaty making and self-government and consider re-opening existing treaties and agreements to address justice issues, if the Aboriginal parties so desire.

Aboriginal justice systems and law-making powers

Our discussion of Aboriginal justice systems and the constitutional and legal bases for their establishment has focused so far on the scope of these systems, what form they might take, and the jurisdiction they might exercise. We have also reviewed how traditional Aboriginal justice systems and their contemporary expressions in various initiatives emphasize healing and restorative goals rather than punishment. However, a justice system consists of more than dispute resolution; it also comprises the rules or laws that set out the rights and responsibilities that determine people's relationships to each other, to their families, to their communities and to their environment.

The power to make laws is a necessary and integral part of an Aboriginal nation's right of self-government. In our final report, which will explore the full dimensions of the right of self-government, we build on the foundations laid in *Partners in Confederation* to develop the framework within which we see Aboriginal nations, as one of three orders of government, exercising law-making authority and how we see this co-existing with federal and provincial law-making authority. For purposes of this report, which addresses mainly criminal justice, it has been necessary to grapple with the difficult issue of Aboriginal law-making authority as part of the right of self-government, including the power to make criminal law, which is a head of power assigned exclusively to the Parliament of Canada under section 91(27) of the *Constitution Act, 1867*.

The relationship between the federal criminal law-making power and the right of Aboriginal governments to pass laws raises the broader issue of the place of legal pluralism in Canada. Legal pluralism has been described as the existence of more than one distinct type of laws or legal systems in a single country. In *Partners in Confederation* we showed how Canadian and U.S. jurisprudence of the nineteenth century recognized the continuing validity of Aboriginal laws, co-existing with those of the new colonial regimes. The decision of Mr. Justice Monk in *Connolly* v. *Woolrich*, recognizing that "the Indian political and territorial right, laws, and usages remained in full force" in the northwest, illustrates that legal pluralism has an honourable place in this country's history.[372] We also advanced the argument that legal pluralism is not just a historical precedent but has had an important role in shaping contemporary relationships between Aboriginal and non-Aboriginal people.

In the particular context of the criminal law, the crucial questions raised by legal pluralism have been identified by Bryan Keon-Cohen in reviewing the Canadian, U.S. and Australian experience.

> In assessing social activity and the resolution of disputes, whose standards are to be applied, those of the native community involved, or those of the majority community? When assessing what is right or wrong, condoned or condemned, humane or inhumane, legal or illegal, or just or unjust, should one be ethnocentric and apply Western notions; should one attempt to see things as natives see them and judge accordingly; should one have

---

[372] *Connolly* v. *Woolrich* (1867), 17 Rapports Judiciaires Révisés de la province de Québec 75 (Quebec Superior Court).

"a bet each way" according to circumstances; or is the only realistic approach to accept that you have no choice in the matter? These are intransigent problems, but they are vital, for once a stance is adopted, all else follows....

These questions are perhaps most acutely raised, in the three jurisdictions under study, in the context of indigenous minority populations and the "Anglo-based" criminal justice system. The response to date of the three jurisdictions has been very much concerned with limiting, or avoiding altogether, legal pluralism in the sense of accepting parallel, separate systems of law, as between native and non-native populations. This analysis, it is suggested, also applies to what might be perceived as a major exception, the American Indian Reservation justice systems, for these systems are considered to be no more than a pale mirror-image of the regular American justice system. Some reforms and inquires...are underway, but there remains a deeply ingrained reluctance in all three countries to cut the Gordian knots and allow separate, parallel native justice systems to develop. This tension between social theory and legal administration continues to cause problems. It is suggested when dealing with indigenous peoples, policies of social pluralism should be complemented by legal separatism. It is also suggested that the brutal and bloody facts of history show that the alternative has rarely achieved native justice.[373]

In considering the place of legal pluralism in a re-ordering of the relationship between Aboriginal and non-Aboriginal people there are powerful competing arguments about a unified *Criminal Code* applicable to all Canadians, Aboriginal or non-Aboriginal. Before reviewing these arguments it is important to be clear about the functions of the *Criminal Code*. In a research paper for the Law Reform Commission of Canada (LRCC) as part of its reference on Aboriginal peoples and criminal justice, Archibald Kaiser provided this useful summary:

> The *Criminal Code* performs several important functions in the criminal justice system. First, it specifies what kind of conduct will ultimately be considered blameworthy according to the criminal law. This requires the *Code* to discuss general principles of liability in defences and to specify certain types of conduct as invoking the criminal sanction. Second, the *Criminal Code* provides for many aspects of criminal procedures, from the laying of information to search and seizure to the conduct of a trial and so on, setting forth the steps which the state and its agents must follow

---

[373] Bryan A. Keon-Cohen, "Native Justice in Australia, Canada and the U.S.A.: A Comparative Analysis", *Canadian Legal Aid Bulletin* (1982), pp. 189-90.

in order to prove an allegation of criminality. Third, the *Criminal Code* specifies what the maximum punishment is for any particular crime and provides for a variety of sanctions which may apply for offences.[374]

These three functions – defining what is a criminal offence, setting out the procedures for invoking the criminal process to determine guilt or innocence, and determining sanctions – are interrelated, but they raise different issues in terms of making space for distinctive Aboriginal criminal justice systems.

The other preliminary point is that in evaluating the competing arguments we must be careful to recognize that the *Criminal Code* is hardly a model of perfection. Kaiser summarized some of the more recent criticism as follows:

> [T]he Law Reform Commission of Canada...in its 1986 study, *Recodifying Criminal Law* [stated]:
>
>> The present *Code* has served us well for nearly a century, but it is now obsolete. Enacted originally in 1892, revised in 1955 and amended on many occasions over the decades, it shows the wear and tear of many years of heavy use....
>
> The revised and enlarged edition of this study, which was published in 1987 by the LRCC, was somewhat more expansive in its criticism:
>
>> The present *Criminal Code*...is no longer adequate to our needs....It is poorly organized. It uses archaic language. It is hard to understand. It contains gaps.... It includes obsolete provisions. It over-extends the proper scope of the criminal law. And it fails to address some current problems.
>
> *Our Criminal Procedure* in 1988 was, if anything, even more caustic in its assessment of the state of Canadian criminal procedure.
>
>> Canadian procedural law has arrived in the late 20th century in a somewhat dishevelled state.... The result is labyrinthine complexity and often baffling incoherence.
>
>> Consistency, uniformity, philosophical coherence and even pragmatism are not presently general attributes of our criminal procedure.
>
>> The procedural parts of the *Code* are scattered and incoherent.... The absence of guiding principles is a particularly telling defect in our law.

---

[374] Kaiser, "The Criminal Code of Canada", cited in note 324, p. 96.

By 1991, the LRCC's verdict on the *Code* was beginning to sound familiar:

> But the passage of time and a process of incremental amendment have diminished its usefulness. As a result it now has few of the virtues of a true Code.
>
> ...it no longer serves us well.[375]

What then are the arguments in favour of Aboriginal people having the power to create their own criminal codes? The first line of argument is that as a matter of principle the right of self-government encompasses the right of an Aboriginal nation to determine the laws governing those subject to its jurisdiction. Going beyond this first level of general principle, it is possible, as a second line of argument, to identify other principles related to the specific functions of criminal codes. Addressing first the function of a criminal code – defining what behaviour is viewed as wrong or blameworthy so as to justify sanctions by the authorities – there is a strong argument that the criminal law plays a critical role in defining the values that reflect the distinctive features of any society. The argument was expressed forcefully by Lord Patrick Devlin, a former judge in England's highest court the House of Lords. In one of the classic lectures of modern British jurisprudence, Lord Devlin wrote:

> What makes a society of any sort is a community of ideas, not only political ideas but also ideas about the way its members should behave and govern their lives; these latter ideas are its morals. Every society has a moral structure as well as a political one: or rather, since that might suggest two independent systems, I should say that the structure of every society is made up both of politics and morals.
>
> ...[W]ithout shared ideas on politics, morals, and ethics no society can exist.... [T]he law must protect also the institutions and the community of ideas, political and moral, without which people cannot live together.[376]

Aboriginal nations formed distinct societies before the arrival of European settlers. Despite centuries of colonization and the legacy of dispossession, repression and attempts at forced assimilation, Aboriginal nations continue to be distinct societies. Earlier in the report we described some of the philosophies, values and processes that inform Aboriginal perceptions of justice. They are, without doubt, different from the philosophies, values and precepts that inform non-Aboriginal perceptions of justice. In our final report we will be commenting on the Aboriginal world view, how

---

[375] Kaiser, "The Criminal Code of Canada", pp. 59-60.

[376] Patrick Devlin, *The Enforcement of Morals* (London: Oxford University Press, 1965), pp. 9, 10, 22.

236

it has shaped Aboriginal life experience and how it has succeeded in maintaining a contemporary vitality. It is arguable therefore that Aboriginal nations are entitled to make their own criminal laws to reflect the values that define who they are.

However, Aboriginal peoples share many of the values embraced by non-Aboriginal people. The *Criminal Code* provisions prohibiting assault, physical and sexual abuse, armed robbery, theft and unlawful destruction of property are basic to any society's sense of peace and dignity. But it should not be assumed that there is complete convergence between what the *Criminal Code* designates as an offence and what Aboriginal nations might consider an offence. Take, for example, the issue of protecting the environment. For many Aboriginal peoples, the environment has a very high priority, and those who violate their responsibilities of stewardship are severely censured.[377] Although the *Criminal Code* contains hundreds of offences dealing with violations of the integrity of persons or property, very few offences are directed to protecting the integrity of the environment. There are, of course, growing numbers of federal and provincial environmental protection laws, and many of these create offences punishable by short terms of imprisonment and, in some cases, substantial fines. For the most part, however, these offences are characterized as regulatory offences and attract less moral condemnation than criminal offences. Inclusion of offences against the environment in an Aboriginal criminal code would reflect the seriousness of this behaviour in the Aboriginal nation's scheme of values.

Another example of a significant difference is in the area of obligations and duties to other people. The *Criminal Code* reflects the common law position that individuals are not responsible for a failure to act unless they are under a legal duty to do so. Thus the failure to provide food or to render help to a person in need is not an offence unless you stand in a particular relationship to that person, such as that of spouse or a parent or guardian of a person under 16, or you have undertaken specifically to perform certain acts.[378] By contrast European penal codes, drawing on the civil law tradition, have provisions that impose a broader obligation to render assistance.[379] The civil law tradition is reflected in the Quebec *Charter of Human Rights and Freedoms*, article 2, which provides that "Every person must come to the aid of anyone whose life is in peril, either personally or calling for aid, by

---

[377] See Gisday Wa and Delgam Uukw, *The Spirit of the Land*, cited in note 6, pp. 23, 34. See also Diamond Jenness, "The Indian's Interpretation of Man and Nature", in *Sweet Promises: A Reader on Indian-White Relations in Canada*, ed. J.R. Miller (Toronto: University of Toronto Press, 1992), pp. 444-445.

[378] See *Criminal Code*, sections 215-218.

[379] See, for example, the French penal code, article 63 (Paris: Éditions Dalloz, 1992), which reads as follows:

> Sans préjudice de l'application, le cas échéant, des peines plus fortes prévues par le présent code et les lois spéciales, sera puni d'un emprisonnement de trois mois à cinq ans [et d'une amende] ou de l'une de ces deux peines seulement, quiconque,

giving him the necessary and immediate physical assistance, unless it involves danger to himself or a third person, or he has another valid reason."[380]

Many Aboriginal nations have a broad concept of obligation based on social reciprocity, often derived from the clan-based nature of their societies. In implementing fundamental principles of criminal responsibility it would be reasonable to expect that Aboriginal nations would reflect in their criminal law this broader concept of obligation, which seems to have more in common with the civil law than with the common law tradition.

Turning to the second function performed by the *Criminal Code* – setting out the procedures for invoking the criminal process and determining guilt or innocence – we have discussed how the rules governing non-Aboriginal criminal procedure developed in the context of an adversary system. There is therefore a strong case that if legal pluralism is to have real meaning in the context of recognizing distinctive Aboriginal justice systems, room must be made for rules of Aboriginal criminal procedure that are tailored to a non-adversary type of system. However, as discussed earlier, comprehensive Aboriginal justice systems would have to deal with not-guilty pleas, and therefore some elements of an adversary process would have to be included in an Aboriginal code. Many of the provisions in the *Criminal Code* may be appropriate to ensure a proper balancing of the interests of the Aboriginal nation and the rights of the accused. In addition, many of the legal issues in criminal procedure – such as protections against unreasonable search and seizure

---

pouvant empêcher par son action immédiate, sans risque pour lui ou pour les tiers, soit un fait qualifié crime, soit un délit contre l'intégrité corporelle de la personne, s'abstient volontairement de le faire.

Sera puni des mêmes peines quiconque s'abstient volontairement de porter à une personne en péril l'assistance que, sans risque pour lui ni pour les tiers, il pouvait lui prêter, soit par son action personnelle, soit en provoquant un secours.

[*Translation:* Without prejudice to the application in a proper case of severer penalties prescribed by the present Code and by special laws, anyone who could, by his prompt action, without risk to himself or to third persons, prevent either a crime or a delict against the bodily security of a person, and who wilfully abstains from so acting, shall be punishable by imprisonment of from three months to five years [and by a fine]...or by only one of these penalties.

The same penalties shall be applicable to one who voluntarily abstains from bringing to a person in danger such assistance as he could lend him without risk to himself or to third parties, either by his own action or by obtaining help.]

[380] Quebec, *Charter of Human Rights and Freedoms*, R.S.Q., chapter 12. The obligation set out in the Quebec Charter is now reinforced by provisions of the new Quebec *Civil Code* (S.Q. 1991, chapter 64, which came into force 1 January 1994), article 1471 of which provides:

Where a person comes to the assistance of another person or, for an unselfish motive, disposes, free of charge, of property for the benefit of another person, he is exempt from all liability for injury that may result from it, unless the injury is due to his intentional or gross fault.

– raise constitutional issues under the *Canadian Charter of Rights and Freedoms*. We address this issue later in this chapter.

Other rules of criminal procedure, while consistent in principle with Aboriginal values, have operated unfairly in practice. A case in point is the bail provisions; as discussed in Chapter 2, systemic discrimination has resulted in higher rates of pre-trial detention for Aboriginal than for non-Aboriginal accused. The problem is not with the provisions themselves but with the way they are applied to Aboriginal people. In Chapter 3 we reviewed some of Rupert Ross's suggestions for greater community participation in bail hearings to ensure that bail conditions are not only more culturally appropriate but better integrated with the community's need for protection and healing. In an Aboriginal criminal code, the rules for bail would in all likelihood incorporate this aspect of community involvement.

This brings us to the third function of the *Criminal Code*, sentencing those convicted of offences. Given the public significance of sentencing, it may come as a surprise to learn that the *Criminal Code*, while establishing a punishment for each offence expressed as a maximum term of imprisonment, until very recently contained no legislative statement of the purposes or principles underlying sentencing. It was only in 1995 that Parliament amended the Code to provide such a statement.[381] Before that, the task of developing sentencing principles had been left to the appellate courts of each province, with only a very limited role for the Supreme Court of Canada.[382]

The principles of sentencing as developed by appellate courts have reflected primarily punishment and deterrence rather than reconciliation. In its historical review of the *Criminal Code*, the Canadian Sentencing Commission wrote: "In assigning onerous penalties, the Code of 1982 embodied a rationale of retribution and deterrence."[383] Although the courts have affirmed that the purposes of sentencing embrace not only deterrence and denunciation but also rehabilitation and restitution, it is fair to say that the overall emphasis of the system has been on the first two purposes. The best evidence of this is Canada's high rate of incarceration – one of the highest per capita in the western world and a phenomenon that has had and continues to have a discriminatory and devastating impact on Aboriginal people.[384] As we showed in Chapter 2, this emphasis on punishment runs counter

---

[381] Bill C-41, An Act to Amend the Criminal Code (sentencing) and other capital Acts in consequence thereof, S.C. 1995, chapter 22 (assented to 13 July 1995), sections 718, 718.1 and 718.2.

[382] For a discussion of the historical development of sentencing and the lack of legislative guidance, see *Sentencing Reform: A Canadian Approach*, Report of the Canadian Sentencing Commission (Ottawa: Supply and Services, 1987), chapter 3. The limited role of the Supreme Court of Canada in this area derives from the fact its rules do not, except in very exceptional cases, allow appeals of sentences.

[383] *Sentencing Reform: A Canadian Approach*, p. 32.

[384] At 130 per 100,000, the Canadian rate of incarceration is the fourth highest in the world, after Russia (558), the United States (519) and South Africa (368). The Canadian rate is significantly higher than

to the restorative justice concepts of many Aboriginal nations and the justice-as-healing approach that underlies many Aboriginal justice initiatives.

The 1995 amendments to the *Criminal Code* provided a legislative statement of purpose and principles for the first time. Though long overdue, these amendments represent a codification of existing sentencing principles developed by the courts rather than a fundamental shift in emphasis. Section 718 provides that

> The fundamental purpose of sentencing is to contribute, along with crime prevention initiatives, to respect for the law and the maintenance of a just, peaceful and safe society by imposing just sanctions that have one or more of the following objectives:
>
> (a) to denounce unlawful conduct;
>
> (b) to deter the offender and other persons from committing offences;
>
> (c) to separate offenders from society, when necessary;
>
> (d) to assist in rehabilitating offenders;
>
> (e) to provide reparations for harm done to victims or to the community; and
>
> (f) to promote a sense of responsibility in offenders and acknowledgment of the harm done to victims and to the community.

Section 718.2 provides:

> A court that imposes a sentence shall also take into consideration the following principles:...
>
> (e) all available sanctions other than imprisonment that are reasonable in the circumstances should be considered for all offenders, with particular attention to the circumstances of Aboriginal offenders.

This statement of purposes and principles certainly does not preclude imposing a sentence that emphasizes restorative and healing goals, but these are not given priority nor are they seen as anchoring the sentencing process.

An Aboriginal statement of purposes and principles would likely read quite differently. Primacy would likely be given to restoring harmony and peaceful relationships through the healing of both offenders and victims and the provision

---

that of comparable western European countries; for example, it is more than 40 per cent higher than that of the United Kingdom, at 92 per 100,000, and three times that of the Netherlands, at 44. See Council of Europe, "Americans Behind Bars, The International Use of Incarceration, 1992-93", *Prison Information Bulletin* (1992).

of restitution and compensation for harms done. In other words, healing and restitution would be at the centre rather than on the margins of the process.

The statement of purposes and principles proposed by the House of Commons committee on justice and solicitor general in its 1988 report on sentencing reform, *Taking Responsibility*, came much closer to shifting the primary purpose of sentencing from retributive to restorative goals and thereby reflecting Aboriginal perspectives.[385]

The statement of sentencing purposes incorporated in the *Criminal Code* by Bill C-41 reflects a different emphasis from *Taking Responsibility*, tipping the balance in favour of retributive rather than restorative justice for reasons that have much to do with a political climate that increasingly favours tougher sentences and longer imprisonment. Perhaps one of the most compelling reasons for Aboriginal nations taking their own approach to justice is that the measure of justice for Aboriginal people would no longer be dependent on and driven by the politics and policies of non-Aboriginal governments.

We can get some idea of what an Aboriginal code of offences might look like by reviewing two examples, one a proposed code of offences for the Mohawk Territory at Akwesasne, the other an existing code in Greenland.

In 1989 a Code of Offences and Procedures for Justice for the Mohawk Territory at Akwesasne was presented to the Mohawk Nation Council of Chiefs. The code has not been implemented, as it requires negotiations with two federal governments,

---

[385] According to the committee,

> The purpose of sentencing is to contribute to the maintenance of a just, peaceful and safe society by holding offenders accountable for their criminal conduct through the imposition of just sanctions which:
>
> (a) Require, or encourage where it is not possible to require, offenders to acknowledge the harm they have done to victims in the community, and to take the responsibility for the consequences of their behaviour;
>
> (b) Take account of the steps offenders have taken, or propose to take, to make reparations to the victim and/or the community for harm done or to otherwise demonstrate the acceptance of responsibility;
>
> (c) Facilitate victim-offender reconciliation where victims so request, or are willing to participate in such programs;
>
> (d) If necessary, provide offenders with opportunities which are likely to facilitate their habilation or rehabilitation as productive and law-abiding members of society; and
>
> (e) If necessary, denounce the behaviour and/or incapacitate the offender.

Among the committee's recommended principles of sentencing was the following:

> ...A term of imprisonment should not be imposed without canvassing the appropriateness of alternatives to incarceration through victim-offender reconciliation programs or alternative sentence planning. (Report of the Standing Committee on Justice and Solicitor General, *Taking Responsibility* (Ottawa: 1988), pp. 55-56.)

two provincial governments and a state government (the Territory overlaps Quebec, Ontario and New York). The proposed code is only 40 pages long, but it lays out a comprehensive list of criminal offences. It divides offences into three broad categories: Offences Against One Another; Offences Against the Community; and Offences Against Nature. Offences are also ranked in terms of severity as minor, grievous and serious. Those convicted of serious offences can be sentenced to fines not exceeding $5,000, a penalty of twice the profit made from the illegal activity, probation or community service not to exceed five years, or banishment. The code also sets out a "procedure of justice" in which hearings are conducted by a tribunal of justices whose decisions and sentences must be reached by consensus. The code also makes provision for allegations of misconduct against a justice to be reviewed by a Mohawk justice conduct society.

The Mohawk Code of Offences includes many that are also offences under the *Criminal Code*. Article 1, for example, which deals with Offences Against One Another, prohibits, among other things, murder, rape and sexual abuse, kidnapping, assault, theft, possession of stolen property, and malicious damage. Article 12 also makes it an offence "to make any false statement against another." Although the *Criminal Code* prohibits the publication of blasphemous, seditious and defamatory libels (sections 59-60, 296-301) the offence specified in the Mohawk code is clearly intended to provide more general protection for a person's good reputation. Offences Against the Community include disorderly conduct, public intoxication, and embezzlement of public funds. Under the third broad group, Offences Against Nature, it is an offence "for any person or group of persons to change or alter any terrain or water course which would be detrimental to natural life cycles, or which would have an adverse effect on nature." This is clearly designed to reflect the high value placed by Aboriginal people on the protection of the natural environment.

The Greenland criminal code was introduced by the government of Denmark in 1954. At that time Greenland had a population of about 35,000, 5,000 of whom were Danes; the other 30,000 were Inuit. From the time of the initial colonization of Greenland by Denmark in 1721, Danish and other settlers in Greenland were, with certain qualifications, subject to Danish law, while the indigenous population was subject to its own customary practices supplemented by certain regulations enacted by the Danish government.[386]

---

[386] Gerhard Muller, ed., *The Greenland Criminal Code*, Comparative Criminal Law Project, New York University School of Law (London: Sweet & Maxwell Ltd., 1970). The code has been amended several times, and its present text is contained in Danish Ministry of Justice, Promulgation no. 49, 1979. The principal provisions dealing with the administration of justice are found in *Danish Adminstration of Justice Act for Greenland*, Promulgation no. 99, 21 March 1984. In 1994 Denmark's justice ministry established the Greenland Commission for Adminstration of Justice to consider what changes should be made in the Greenland criminal code and the *Administration of Justice Act for Greenland* in light of social change in Greenland in the past 40 years. At an international conference in Vancouver in July 1995, one of the members of the commission, Finn Larsen, reported

Verner Goldschmitt, a professor of law at the University of Copenhagen and one of the drafters of the Greenland criminal code, summarized the customary law system that operated in Greenland.

> The basic principle in the administration of justice in Greenland was found to be...the individualized treatment of criminals, substantially unaffected by the gravity of the crime. The outstanding characteristic of the informal system of sanctions...was its flexibility and its rejection of the prison.[387]

The new Greenland criminal code was an attempt to codify existing customary law. Thus, unlike the normal civil law tradition, the 1954 code was designated a criminal code instead of a penal code in order to emphasize that punishment, as it is traditionally conceived, is only one of the sanctions authorized by the code. The substantive provisions of the code, while similar to those in the Danish penal code, do include some offences unique to Greenland. In particular the code provides that "a person shall be convicted of abuse of alcohol who intentionally or by gross negligence brings himself or another person into a state of drunkenness and therefore endangers the person or substantive property of another."[388]

Reflecting the customary law of Greenland, offences are not ranked according to severity, and any of the sanctions authorized by the code can be imposed singly or in combination for any offence. Section 87 of the code sets out the principles governing sentencing:

> The decision shall give proper consideration to the nature of the crime and society's interest in counteracting such action. Special regard shall be given to the personality of the criminal and to what is deemed necessary to prevent him from committing further crimes.

The code applies to everyone in Greenland, but it makes a specific exception for those not domiciled in Greenland and those whose connection with Greenland is very loose. In those cases, the Danish criminal code applies. Goldschmitt has explained the rationale for this exception:

---

that although some amendments will likely be introduced, the basic shape of the code is likely to remain unchanged. (Finn Larsen, "Local Involvement in Legal Policy and Justice Delivery in Greenland", paper presented at 'Putting Aboriginal Justice Devolution Into Practice: The Canadian and International Experience', Vancouver, 5-7 July 1995. See also Henrik G. Jensen, "Justice in Greenland", in *Preventing and Responding to Northern Crime*, ed. Kurt, Taylor and Griffiths (Burnaby: Northern Justice Society and Simon Fraser University, 1990), p. 121.

[387] Muller, *The Greenland Criminal Code*, p. 3.

[388] Greenland criminal code, section 24, cited in note 386. This provision is more far-reaching than the provision in the Danish penal code but was considered necessary in light of problems with alcohol in Greenland, in particular the danger of alcohol-related accidents such as drowning and freezing to death.

> [It] allows for cases in which it would either be a burden to apply punitive measures against persons not really linked to the life of Greenland, or it would be unjust to seek to adapt the criminal to Greenland rather than Danish social conditions. Thus Danish domiciliaries who are seasonally employed in Greenland and commit offences there will be tried by a Danish court under the *Danish Penal Code*. It is also clear that the punitive measures of the *Criminal Code* cannot be expected to have their intended effects on one who, for example, has been repeatedly imprisoned in Denmark.[389]

The Greenland code is an example of how a traditional approach to sanctions can be reflected in a contemporary form. In Canada, Aboriginal criminal codes would likely give similar priority to restorative principles rather than punitive ones. As in the Greenland code, the underlying philosophy would be to protect society through the reintegration of offenders rather than their isolation.

These examples suggest that Aboriginal criminal codes could provide legal expression for the underlying values of Aboriginal nations and reflect their distinctive philosophies and processes for ensuring peace and order in their communities. What then are the arguments in favour of a single criminal code applicable to all Canadians, Aboriginal and non-Aboriginal? One argument is framed in the language of equality. In a paper prepared for our round table on justice, Jeremy Webber cast the argument in the following terms:

> These objections insist on identical treatment simply because, according to this view, in a country, all citizens should be governed by the same law, they should obey the same rules. Obeying that law is part of the common identity of citizenship. It is part of what it means to have a country. Insisting on different treatment suggests that the common run of rules are not good enough for you, that you are better than your fellows. This objection is almost visceral, then, having more in common with nationalism – an idea of the degree of identity necessary to a country – than a concern with individual rights.[390]

Considered at the most general level, this argument does not carry much force in a federal country such as Canada, where the constitution is designed expressly to permit diversity in the laws applying in the various regions of the country. Few Canadians think that their basic equality as citizens is seriously compromised because the laws in Nova Scotia differ in many respects from those in Saskatchewan, not to mention those in Quebec.

---

[389] Muller, *The Greenland Criminal Code*, cited in note 386, p. 8.

[390] Jeremy Webber, "Individuality, Equality and Difference: Justifications for a Parallel System of Aboriginal Justice", in *Aboriginal Peoples and the Justice System*, cited in note 7, p. 152.

Nevertheless, the equality argument can also be presented in a more specific form. Unlike some other federal countries, Canada has a uniform *Criminal Code* that applies to the entire country. The Code has been in place for more than a century, and Canadians take it for granted that, for the most part, behaviour that is criminal in British Columbia is criminal in Ontario and Prince Edward Island. By contrast, the United States and Australia have a multiplicity of criminal codes, because the states making up the federation have the power to legislate in the criminal law area. Thus, runs the argument, even though Canada embraces two distinctive legal traditions – the civil law in Quebec and the common law in the rest of the country – the *Criminal Code* serves as a unifying institution, helping to forge a common Canadian identity through shared fundamental values. One of the implications of this argument is that there must be uniform minimum standards of behaviour to ensure respect for the basic values underlying both these legal traditions.

In assessing this argument, it is important to recognize that existing Canadian constitutional arrangements in the criminal justice area seek a balance between uniformity and diversity by conferring legislative jurisdiction on Parliament in relation to criminal law and procedure and on the provinces in relation to the administration of justice. In this way, constitutional space is provided for provincial control over policing, prosecution, the establishment of courts, some elements of the corrections system and the development of alternative measures for young offenders. Moreover, some provisions of the *Criminal Code* clearly contemplate regional variation. For example, the sections dealing with gambling allow for provincial regulatory schemes, which may differ from province to province. Recent amendments to the *Criminal Code* with respect to alternative measures for adult offenders also leave the development and implementation of these measures to provincial attorneys general.

It is also important to recall that, although the provinces cannot enact criminal laws as such, they have the power to enforce other laws by way of fine, penalty or imprisonment.[391] The courts have taken a generous view of this power and have upheld provincial offences, such as careless driving and furnishing false information in a prospectus, that resemble offences in the *Criminal Code*. The result is that in practice the federal and provincial governments have concurrent legislative powers over a considerable portion of the field loosely considered 'criminal law'.[392]

However, recognition of the right of Aboriginal nations to develop their own justice systems pursuant to their inherent right of self-government introduces a totally new dimension of diversity into existing constitutional arrangements, a dimension that, unlike the federal and provincial dimensions in many respects, is not based on shared values and a common identity but on different values reflected

---

[391] *Constitution Act, 1867*, section 92(15).

[392] Hogg, *Constitutional Law of Canada*, cited in note 367, pp. 492-495.

in unique Aboriginal cultures and identities. Most Aboriginal people do not see the *Criminal Code* as representing their values and reflecting their identity. As the reports of the many justice inquiries preceding this one show, they see it as quite alien in many respects.

As a result, it is not just a matter of rethinking the balance between uniformity and diversity within a single criminal justice system reflecting shared values (that is, the existing system), but how to re-order the system to make room for a distinct system based on different values. This is not an easy task. The establishment of Aboriginal criminal justice systems, operating on Aboriginal territories, parallel to the non-Aboriginal system will require a high measure of co-operation and cross-cultural awareness and understanding to make it work. If successful, this re-ordering will articulate, in a framework appropriate to the twenty-first century, the respective contributions of Aboriginal and non-Aboriginal people so that their traditions of justice can be respected through justice systems that function in harmony.

In *Partners in Confederation* we discussed the nature of the inherent right of self-government recognized and affirmed in section 35(1) of the *Constitution Act, 1982*. We described that right as organic and as having several dimensions. Some aspects of self-government are considered core matters, and in these areas Aboriginal nations can pursue self-starting initiatives without the need for negotiated agreements with federal, provincial or territorial governments.[393] Other aspects of self-government we described as peripheral, and action in these areas can begin only following the conclusion of agreements with the relevant governments. We described core aspects of self-government as including "matters of vital concern to the life and welfare of the community that, at the same time, do not have a major impact on adjacent jurisdictions and do not rise to the level of overriding national or regional concern."

To state this definition with greater precision, by the phrase 'matters of vital concern to the life and welfare of the community' we mean 'matters of vital concern to the life and welfare of a particular Aboriginal people, its culture and identity'. Similarly, by 'do not rise to the level of overriding national or regional concern' we mean 'are not otherwise the object of transcendent federal or provincial concern'. We will examine these issues in more detail in our final report.

Accordingly, the test for matters falling within the core of Aboriginal self-governing jurisdiction is that (a) they are of vital concern to the life and welfare of a particular Aboriginal people, its culture and identity; (b) they do not have a major impact on adjacent jurisdictions; and (c) they are not otherwise the object of transcendent federal or provincial concern.

The issue is thus whether the right to determine which acts constitute violations of a nation's fundamental values, and how such acts should be dealt with, consti-

---

[393] See *Partners in Confederation*, cited in note 8, p. 38. We emphasized, however, that as a practical matter agreements should be sought as far as possible.

tutes *prima facie* a matter of vital concern to the life and welfare of the nation, its culture and identity. If it does, then law-making powers in the area of criminal justice would fall within the core of Aboriginal self-governing jurisdiction and, subject to the other two parts of the test, Aboriginal nations would be able to enact, if they so wished, their own criminal law operative within their territories, including rules of criminal procedure and principles of sentencing.

Although the jurisdiction to define which acts violate a nation's fundamental values would appear to be *prima facie* core, there will be situations where, through the application of the second and third parts of the test, the power to legislate in relation to particular matters is removed from the core area and therefore requires the agreement of other governments before an Aboriginal government can legislate.

The Commission's conclusions about the scope of the powers of Aboriginal nations in relation to criminal law can be summed up as follows.

First, Aboriginal governments have jurisdiction to deal with a wide range of matters in the area of criminal law and procedure operative within their territories pursuant to their inherent right of self-government recognized and affirmed in section 35 of the *Constitution Act, 1982*.

Second, aspects of criminal law and procedure that fall into the *core* of Aboriginal jurisdiction can be dealt with by Aboriginal governments at their own initiative. Matters falling outside the core, that is, *peripheral* matters, require the agreement of the other relevant orders of government before jurisdiction can be exercised.

Third, the test for distinguishing between core and peripheral matters is that core matters (a) are of vital concern to the life and welfare of a particular Aboriginal people, its culture and identify; (b) do not have a major impact on adjacent jurisdictions; and (c) are not otherwise the object of transcendent federal or provincial concern.

Fourth, Aboriginal jurisdiction in relation to criminal law and procedure operative on Aboriginal territories is *concurrent* with federal jurisdiction over criminal law and procedure generally. Where a conflict arises between an Aboriginal law and a federal law passed pursuant to section 91(24) of the *Constitution Act, 1867*, the Aboriginal law will take precedence except where the need for federal action can be shown to be compelling and substantial and the federal legislation is consistent with the Crown's basic trust responsibilities to Aboriginal peoples.

Fifth, while Aboriginal governments may in principle take action in their core areas of jurisdiction without agreements with other orders of government, we believe that in the area of criminal law making such an approach is not advisable as a practical matter because of considerations of comity and the avoidance of litigation.

Readers might find it helpful to have some illustrations of matters in the core and the periphery of Aboriginal criminal law-making jurisdiction. Because the definition of core matters is determined by what is fundamental to the culture and identity of Aboriginal nations, however, core matters may well vary from nation to nation; it is not appropriate for the Commission to make such determinations. Determining what is core and what is peripheral is a matter for each Aboriginal nation to decide.

Recommendation 3

Although Aboriginal nations can enact their own criminal law and procedure in their core areas of jurisdiction without agreements with the other orders of government, the Commission recommends that, in the interests of comity and the avoidance of litigation, they should enter into negotiations to secure such agreements before doing so.

We anticipate that negotiations will in many cases shape the content not only of Aboriginal laws but of federal legislation as well. Indeed, it may well be that as a result of these negotiations the need for Aboriginal legislation in relation to a particular subject-matter may become less pressing and that Aboriginal governments may be able to adopt federal criminal laws as their own. This will be their choice, however. The primary goal of negotiations would be to give Aboriginal nations the requisite certainty that their legal regimes will operate as fully respected elements in the overall framework of Canadian criminal justice.

The exercise of Aboriginal law-making power would normally take place over a period of time. We are not suggesting that constitutional recognition of the right of self-government prevents the *Criminal Code* from applying to Aboriginal people. We envisage the *Criminal Code* as continuing to apply to Aboriginal people until Aboriginal nations prepare their own legislation, if they so desire, in areas where they have jurisdiction. Such legislation might adopt the *Criminal Code* in part or in whole. The process of considering the need for more culturally appropriate criminal laws for Aboriginal people will focus attention on precisely what parts of the existing Code are inconsistent with fundamental Aboriginal values, what acts or omissions not in the Code should be embodied in Aboriginal legislation, and what procedures and sanctions are needed to reflect Aboriginal values and approaches to dealing with criminal behaviour.

We would also emphasize that the power to make laws in the area of criminal justice belongs to the Aboriginal nation alone, not to its individual communities. The people of a nation may choose to allocate certain aspects of the criminal justice process to individual communities, but the right in its entirety can be exercised only at the level of the nation.

Finally, we would point out that the *Criminal Code*, when first introduced in 1892, was hardly a distinctively Canadian institution. The Code borrowed heavily from the *Draft Code* of 1879, prepared by the distinguished English judge and jurist James

Fitzjames Stephen. Stephen's draft was transformed, with slight modifications, into the British *Commissioners' Draft Code* of 1879, which in turn provided the base for the English *Draft Code* of 1881. Ironically, although this last code was never enacted in England, its influence on the drafting of the Canadian *Criminal Code* was extensive.[394] Seen in this historical perspective, the development of Aboriginal criminal codes a century after the introduction of the first *Criminal Code* would constitute the first codifications that are truly made in Canada and, appropriately, by the Aboriginal nations of Canada.

To sum up, Aboriginal nations have the right to establish criminal justice systems that reflect and respect their cultural distinctiveness pursuant to their inherent right of self-government. This right is not absolute, however, when exercised in the framework of Canada's federal system. The contemporary expression of Aboriginal concepts and processes of justice will be more effective than the existing non-Aboriginal system in responding to the wounds inflicted by colonialism and meeting the challenges of maintaining peace and security in a changing world.

Resolution of jurisdictional conflicts

The nature of the potential problems

There are basically four ways to characterize the jurisdictional issues that will face Aboriginal justice systems. The first three, which may overlap in practice, are jurisdiction over subject-matter – what types of issues the justice system can adjudicate; jurisdiction over the person – who is entitled or required to use the justice system; and territorial jurisdiction – where the justice system holds sway. The fourth area is comity – the mutual recognition by justice systems of each other's decisions. A number of responses to these issues are available. The choices an Aboriginal nation makes in this area will likely depend on a balancing of concerns related to principles and pragmatism.

The starting point for discussing these issues must be the notion of territorial jurisdiction. It should be assumed that, absent any other compelling arguments, an Aboriginal nation should have jurisdiction over all persons within its territory. This is not a particularly radical response, as it mirrors the situation in the rest of the country. There is no question that the jurisdiction of a province over all within its territory is supreme. An individual charged with a criminal offence in Alberta is tried by judges who live in the province, prosecuted by the provincial Crown, and defended by lawyers licensed to practise in the province according to the terms and conditions of the Law Society of Alberta.[395] Accused persons do not have the option of asking that the trial be held in another province.

---

[394] *Sentencing Reform: A Canadian Approach*, cited in note 382, p. 32.

[395] As noted in Chapter 3, some criminal or quasi-criminal offences, e.g., counterfeiting and drug trafficking, are prosecuted by the federal Crown. Lawyers selected by the federal government for this role must all be qualified to practise in the province where they are to work.

By the same token, Aboriginal accused persons, wherever they are charged in Canada, must abide by the jurisdiction of the relevant court even though its practices and procedures may go against their values or culture. If Aboriginal accused persons must appear before a court system that does not recognize fundamental cultural differences when they are within a province's boundaries, why should it be any different in principle for a non-Aboriginal person in the territory of an Aboriginal nation? This approach would be simple, consistent and easy to apply.

There will, however, be real differences between the Aboriginal and non-Aboriginal justice systems. These differences may not be merely ones of form, but may well be rooted in very different approaches to achieving justice. In the non-Aboriginal system, the criminal courts, in both form and function, are basically the same across the country. This will not necessarily be the case with justice systems developed by Aboriginal nations. One major difference will be that within certain limits, Aboriginal nations will have the power to make their own criminal laws and develop their own ways of addressing the needs of victims and offenders. For this reason, even if an Aboriginal nation continues to use the *Criminal Code*, their fact-finding procedures, their sentencing policies, indeed, the entire way they address criminal behaviour may differ markedly from those in the provinces and territories.

In addition, as discussed later in this chapter, Aboriginal nations may be able to use section 33 of the *Canadian Charter of Rights and Freedoms* – the notwithstanding clause – if they consider it necessary to achieve the goals of their justice systems. Provinces also have the right to use section 33, but they do not have that right with regard to criminal law and procedures, because the constitutional division of powers assigns this area exclusively to Parliament.

These factors lead to consideration of another difference between Aboriginal and provincial/territorial justice systems. The assumption behind the *Criminal Code* is that the cultural values it reflects are universally shared by Canadians. As noted throughout this report, in some fundamental aspects this assumption does not hold true for many Aboriginal people. There are no doubt other Canadians who do not share all the values either, but Aboriginal peoples have historical rights as the original peoples of this country, rights that are constitutionally recognized and that entitle them to develop laws in core aspects of their criminal law jurisdiction to reflect the particular values of their nations. One of the challenges in doing so, however, will be the presence of non-Aboriginal residents on their territories.

In their work for the Ontario Native Council on Justice, Jonathan Rudin and Dan Russell addressed this difficulty in the context of an Aboriginal justice system functioning on a reserve:

> Let us assume that a non-Native person is accused of committing an offence on the reserve... It could be argued, that to the extent that the system is culturally appropriate to the Native residents of the reserve, it is just as inappropriate to the non-Native accused. If the system is grounded on the values, customs and beliefs of the

community, then what meaning or relevance will it have to a person who does not share those values, customs or beliefs. As alien as the dominant culture's justice system is to Native people, so a Native justice system would be to a non-Native. This argument could even be offered by a Native person who was not a member of the reserve's tribe. Such an individual might contend that their culturally appropriate justice system does not resemble the system they now must face and thus it would be unfair and unjust to require him or her to be dealt with by such a system.[396]

This situation is by no means far-fetched or speculative. Rather, as we saw in our discussion of the tribal court system, Aboriginal justice systems in the United States have faced just such problems. Even with the inherent right to make laws and administer justice in their own territories, the tribal court system still faces significant problems. The first relates to jurisdiction over people. In the opinion of the U.S. Supreme court in *Duro*, the right of Indian nations extends only to regulating the affairs of those members of the nation living on the reservation. This is a very restricted right. In her testimony before the congressional committee looking at the *Duro* decision, Gay Kingman, executive director of the National Congress of American Indians, noted that on many reservations, while the majority of the population is Indian, a great number are not formally members of the reservation's tribe.[397] So that tribal courts could regain jurisdiction over all Indians on reservations, Congress passed specific legislation in the wake of *Duro*. As for jurisdiction over non-Indians, this does not exist in the criminal law area except in very minor traffic-related offences.

In the United States, the procedural protections of the *Bill of Rights* apply to tribal courts through the operation of the *Indian Civil Rights Act*. In our view, the *Canadian Charter of Rights and Freedoms* applies to Aboriginal nations, but Indian nations in the United States cannot avail themselves of a provision similar to the notwithstanding clause, an option that we believe is available to Aboriginal nations in Canada. Under these circumstances, an assertion of jurisdiction over non-Aboriginal persons within an Aboriginal nation's territory in a situation where the full range of Charter protections was not available because of recourse to the notwithstanding clause would invite a challenge to the Supreme Court of Canada. The court might well determine that there is no recourse for the aggrieved individual, it might order that the justice system in that nation amend some of its procedures, or it might, as the U.S. Supreme Court did in *Duro*, make sweeping changes to the legal regimes of all Aboriginal nations.

A further issue relates to recognition of the decisions of Aboriginal adjudicative bodies by the non-Aboriginal justice system. Since the right of self-government

---

[396] Rudin and Russell, "Native Alternative Dispute Resolution Systems", cited in note 335, p. 55.

[397] Testimony of Gay Kingman, in *The Duro Decision*, cited in note 337, p. 110.

is inherent and extends to a host of justice issues, Aboriginal governments could begin immediately to assume control over justice matters in core areas. A serious difficulty would arise, however, if the decisions of an Aboriginal decision-making body were not recognized as binding by outside courts. Individuals charged with criminal offences and tried or otherwise dealt with in an Aboriginal justice system would want some assurance that they would not be subject to prosecution in the non-Aboriginal system after the matter had been heard in the Aboriginal forum.[398] The same concern would exist with respect to family or civil law matters. Without agreements between Aboriginal and non-Aboriginal governments with respect to the mutual recognition of the decisions of each other's tribunals, individuals will have gained little but confusion about the disposition of their cases.[399]

For these reasons, it is not sufficient simply to assert that the existence of the inherent right of self-government in section 35(1) of the *Constitution Act, 1982* resolves all the dilemmas that arise in terms of the interaction between two justice systems. It is necessary to look for other possible resolutions.

In the United States, one system or the other – the tribal court or the non-Aboriginal system – must exclusively serve those within its jurisdiction. This premise has led to many of the problems faced by tribal courts. Because of the *Major Crimes Act*, tribes are unable to deal with certain offences, much as they might wish to do so.

This bifurcated notion of jurisdiction, resolved in many cases solely on the basis of whether the individual is a member of the tribe, has led to the jurisdictional disputes tribal courts find themselves in today. This jurisdictional model has constrained development of the tribal court system unnecessarily. The restrictions placed on tribal courts by the *Indian Civil Rights Act* have also impeded the creativity of Indian nations to move toward more culturally appropriate methods of dispute resolution. Because of section 25 of the Charter and the ability of Aboriginal nations to develop their own charters, there is no need for Canada to replicate this

---

[398] This issue is not simply theoretical. In 1988, three young people from Kahnawake were charged with arson and a number of other criminal offences by the Sûreté du Québec. Rather than subject themselves to the non-Aboriginal justice system, the youths asked that their case be decided by the Longhouse. The Longhouse was convened and judgements were given. Although the Quebec Crown acknowledged that the sentences the young people received in the Longhouse were not only more culturally appropriate, but also tougher than what they might have expected in Quebec courts, the Crown nevertheless insisted that the young people be tried in the Quebec courts. The young people refused to appear, and warrants were issued for their arrest. For more detail on this case see M. David, "Two Justice Systems for One Nation?", *Tribune Juive* 6/4, p. 16, and "Decision of the Longhouse in the Case of Ryan Deer, Dean Horne and another" (Kahnawake, unpublished).

[399] Our focus in this report is criminal law, but it is our view that activities in the civil law area – both law making and administration of justice – also fall within the inherent right of Aboriginal peoples to develop their own justice systems.

experience; instead, we can develop a jurisdictional model that, rather than inhibiting, provides space for the growth of Aboriginal justice systems.

In contrast to the situation in the United States, the jurisdiction of Aboriginal justice systems should not be determined unilaterally by non-Aboriginal courts or legislatures. Rather, once the areas of Aboriginal jurisdiction over justice have been negotiated with the other orders of government, the nation itself should determine the extent to which it wishes to take on that jurisdiction.

Choice by the Aboriginal nation in respect of offences and offenders

Aboriginal nations should not be constrained in the types of offences they can deal with. Instead Aboriginal peoples themselves should determine when they are ready to deal with particular offences. Offences that fall within their jurisdiction but that they are not prepared to deal with will continue to be handled by non-Aboriginal courts.

Aboriginal justice systems should also be able to determine which alleged offenders can come before them. Whether the individual is an Aboriginal person should not determine the issue; Aboriginal justice systems should be open to all. Most of the justice initiatives surveyed in the previous chapter focused on the notion of healing. Offenders seeking to enter these programs are required to accept responsibility for their actions as a precondition of entry; the programs do not determine guilt or innocence. If an Aboriginal justice program adopts a healing orientation, it must be able to refuse entry to people who have demonstrated over time that they have no interest in this approach.[400] Of course, Aboriginal justice systems may well also have a fact-determination process; in this case, whether the accused person accepted responsibility for his or her actions would not be as significant.

In practice this could mean that individuals charged with identical criminal offences in the same geographic territory might have their cases heard in different forums. But, unlike the situation in tribal courts in the United States, the choice of forums should not depend on whether the individual is a member of the tribe or on the offence. Rather, the choice of forums would be determined by the willingness and readiness of the Aboriginal justice system to address the particular needs of the individual.

It is essential that Aboriginal justice systems be able to exercise choice with respect to offences and offenders. Requiring Aboriginal justice systems to handle every type of offence and every offender as soon as they are established will prevent the development and evolution of such systems in accordance with their capacities.

---

[400] Thus in the Toronto community council program, a person is not allowed to come before the council on a subsequent criminal charge if he/she has failed to appear for the original council hearing or failed to follow the original council decision.

Recommendation 4

The Commission recommends that Aboriginal justice systems be able to exercise choice with respect to the types of offences they will hear and the particular offenders who are to come before them. Offences and offenders not dealt with by Aboriginal justice systems would continue to be dealt with by the non-Aboriginal system.

Choice and the alleged offender

If an Aboriginal justice system can choose which alleged offenders it wishes to deal with, should a similar right be extended to offenders who are not Aboriginal? While giving alleged offenders a choice about which system will hear their case would be unique in Canada, there are strong arguments that non-Aboriginal people living on the nation's territory should have a choice between the Aboriginal justice system and the mainstream system.

Giving non-Aboriginal persons a choice will ensure that they are not forced to appear before a system based on cultural assumptions they do not share. From a pragmatic point of view, allowing a choice of forums is also likely to forestall the potential crippling effects of a *Duro*-type challenge to the jurisdiction of Aboriginal justice systems – a challenge that would be inevitable if every person living within the nation's boundaries were required to participate in the nation's justice system.

Providing a choice of forum may not be appropriate, however, if the individual is charged with violating a law that is unique to the Aboriginal nation. Not all laws enacted in Aboriginal nations will be criminal laws; many will be what are referred to as regulatory offences. Writing on this subject for the Commission, Peter Hogg and Mary Ellen Turpel suggest that dispute resolution in the following areas should always lie within the exclusive jurisdiction of Aboriginal nations: the management of land; the regulation of activity on the land, including hunting, fishing, gathering, mining and forestry; the licensing of businesses; planning, zoning and building codes; and environmental protection.[401]

In addition, it would be strange for the prosecution of laws unique to an Aboriginal nation to be undertaken by Crown prosecutors in the non-Aboriginal system with no particular understanding of the offence. It would be equally strange to leave the sentencing of offenders under these laws to judges of the non-Aboriginal system with no real appreciation of the purpose of the legislation or intimate knowledge of the particular range of sentencing options available in a specific case. Indeed, the entire idea that the unique laws of one jurisdiction could possibly be enforced in a different jurisdiction makes little sense.

---

[401] P.W. Hogg and M.E. Turpel, "Implementing Aboriginal Self-Government: Constitutional and Jurisdictional Issues", in *Aboriginal Self-Government – Legal and Constitutional Issues* (Ottawa: RCAP, 1995), pp. 391-392. Also published in *Canadian Bar Review* 74 (1995), p. 187.

At the same time, however, if conviction of an offence under one of these laws entailed punitive sanctions, an Aboriginal nation might wish to ensure that accused persons had available all the legal and Charter defences they would have if tried in the non-Aboriginal system.It is precisely in cases where people face punitive sanctions without recourse to a full range of constitutional and procedural guarantees that the likelihood of *Duro*-type decisions restricting the jurisdiction of Aboriginal legal systems on tribal or racial grounds is greatest.

It can be argued that if non-Aboriginal persons are to have a choice of forum because they do not share the culture and values of the Aboriginal nation on whose territory they reside, why not a choice for Aboriginal persons who belong to a different nation? Their culture and values may also differ from those of the nation on whose territory they live. Why should they not be able to choose to be dealt with by their own nation's system? There may be merit in such an argument, but we think a nation would be justified in rejecting it on two grounds: first, that the fundamental aspects of culture and the basic values of the two nations are likely to be shared; and, second, that Aboriginal people who choose to live in another nation's territory should respect the systems in place in that territory. Indeed, history discloses that a considerable degree of comity existed traditionally among Aboriginal nations and that they would therefore be highly motivated to recognize and respect each other's institutions in the future.[402]

There is no doubt that the ideal would be to have all persons within the nation's territory subject to the nation's justice system without exception. It will take some time, however, before distinctively Aboriginal criminal justice systems win the confidence of all residents, particularly non-Aboriginal residents. They will have to see the system in action in order to appreciate its workability and its merits. This will occur over time, and the ultimate goal of universal territoriality will be achieved as non-Aboriginal residents become more familiar with and more attuned to the values that underpin the system.

Territorial jurisdiction and comity

In terms of territorial jurisdiction, members of Aboriginal nations who commit criminal offences outside the territorial reach of their nations should expect to be dealt with by the judicial system in the place where the offence occurred. Section 479 of the *Criminal Code* allows persons charged with criminal offences to plead guilty to those charges in any court in the province where the events giving rise to the charges took place, as long as they have the consent of the Crown attorney's office in the jurisdiction where the charge was laid.[403] This is called traversal of charges.

---

[402] See, for example, Paul Williams, "Kaswentha – Relations Between the Haudenosaunee and the Crown, 1664-1993", research study prepared for RCAP (1993); and Olive P. Dickason, *Canada's First Nations: A History of Founding Peoples from Earliest Times* (Toronto: McClelland & Stewart Inc., 1992), chapter 4.

[403] In practice, accused persons are also able to avail themselves of this right even where the offence occurred in a different province.

There is no reason why similar provisions could not be put in place to allow members of Aboriginal nations to have matters dealt with in their home communities if they agree to accept responsibility for the offences with which they are charged. This right cannot be unfettered, however, or at the sole discretion of the accused. Before any decision to traverse charges, the individual's home community would have to be contacted to see whether it was willing to accept a traversal. The decision to accept or reject such a request would be based on the nature of the charge and the community's readiness to hear the case of the particular individual.

Finally we come to the issue of comity. As noted earlier, the best efforts of Aboriginal nations to establish distinct justice systems will be largely for naught if their decisions are not recognized as binding by the courts of the non-Aboriginal system. A jurisdictional framework based on negotiated agreements between an Aboriginal nation and relevant governments, and one that gives non-Aboriginal accused a choice of venue, should mean that non-Aboriginal justice systems will have little difficulty respecting the decisions of Aboriginal decision-making bodies. Indeed, assuring this recognition should be a major part of negotiations to establish Aboriginal justice systems. At the same time, it would be expected that Aboriginal decision-making bodies would recognize the decisions of non-Aboriginal courts involving Aboriginal residents on non-Aboriginal territory who commit offences on that territory.

By clearly recognizing the right of Aboriginal nations to determine which offences and which offenders they are willing and ready to handle, and by giving non-Aboriginal accused who are not members of the Aboriginal nation a choice about which system will deal with them, most of the major stumbling blocks besetting discussions of the transfer of jurisdiction can be removed. Aboriginal nations that do not give non-Aboriginal accused a choice may have difficulty negotiating and achieving recognition of the decisions of their adjudicative bodies by non-Aboriginal governments and courts.

Recommendation 5

The Commission recommends that, in designing their criminal justice systems, Aboriginal nations give non-Aboriginal residents accused of offences within their territory a choice about where their cases will be dealt with – in the Aboriginal nation's criminal justice system or in the non-Aboriginal system – except in cases where the offence involved is unique to the nation's system and is designed to protect values that are fundamental to the nation's culture.

Conclusion

Rupert Ross has seen many attempts to establish Aboriginal justice initiatives run aground on a preoccupation with categorizing the types of offences best suited for disposition by Aboriginal bodies and those that should remain in the non-Aboriginal system. These negotiations usually attempt to categorize offences in terms of seriousness, with the intention of reserving to the non-Aboriginal system the 'serious' cases. The problem is that the seriousness of an offence cannot be determined simply by reference to the *Criminal Code*. A genuine understanding of the seriousness of an offence can be reached only after examining the facts of the case and the background of the accused and his or her relationship with the victim and the community. Almost inevitably negotiations aimed at categorizing offences go nowhere, and all parties end up frustrated. As Ross says, "At the end of each day, participants seem to leave with a sense that the agenda for change has not only failed to progress, but has been made even more daunting still."[404]

We see the impasse Ross identifies as a consequence of non-Aboriginal justice professionals reserving to themselves the right to determine the scope of Aboriginal jurisdiction. Their agreement to permit an Aboriginal justice initiative is the exercise of *their* discretion. Aboriginal jurisdiction is thus conceived of as a privilege, not a right. Our approach is different. Aboriginal jurisdiction in relation to justice should be treated as a right; the exercise of that right should, however, be progressive and incremental, dependent upon the choice, commitment and resources of each Aboriginal nation.

This approach should help to prevent the clash of cultures that could arise when different systems operate within a single country. Given that Aboriginal nations and communities will be able to choose the offences to be addressed and the offenders to be dealt with in their systems, it is to be expected that Aboriginal justice systems will differ markedly from those of non-Aboriginal society. This recognition of the need for diversity, coupled with the availability of choice in justice forums, should alleviate pressure on the federal government to introduce a law such as the U.S. *Major Crimes Act*, as well as influence the courts in the direction of giving greater flexibility, through the interpretive shield of section 25 and Aboriginal charters, in their application of the *Canadian Charter of Rights and Freedoms*.

Application of the *Canadian Charter of Rights and Freedoms* to Aboriginal Justice Systems

The Issue

The *Canadian Charter of Rights and Freedoms* provides many guarantees for individuals coming before the courts. The legal rights sections of the Charter (sections 7-14) afford those charged with criminal offences such protections as the presumption of innocence; the right to counsel; protection against double jeopardy; the right to trial within a reasonable time; and so on. As well, section 7 guarantees the right to fundamental justice – a term that is still evolving as the Supreme Court maps out the dimensions of this right. Finally, section 15 guarantees equal-

---

[404] Ross, "Managing the Merger", cited in note 185, pp. 4-6.

ity before and under the law and in particular prohibits discrimination on the basis of race, national or ethnic origin, colour, religion, sex, age, and mental or physical disability.

Documents such as the Charter are intended to provide a solid foundation for the development of free societies and are seen as representing values common to everyone who espouses this goal. The Charter is not a value-free document, however, but represents a particular vision of the relationship between the individual and governments, a vision that looks primarily to western liberal traditions for its justification. Indeed, in fleshing out the scope of the Charter, the Supreme Court of Canada often refers explicitly to western liberal notions. As Chief Justice Lamer stated in delineating the scope of the term "principles of fundamental justice" in section 7, "the principles of fundamental justice are found in the tenets of our legal system."[405]

The Charter's vision of the relationship between the individual and the collectivity is specific and relates to ideals that are not necessarily shared universally. Madam Justice Bertha Wilson made this point in *R. v. Morgentaler*: "The Charter is predicated on a particular conception of the place of the individual in society." She went on to flesh out what that particular conception is:

> Thus, the rights guaranteed in the Charter erect around each individual, metaphorically speaking, an invisible fence over which the state will not be allowed to trespass.[406]

This statement may indeed summarize the vision of societal interaction provided by the Charter, but this vision is not one that is shared universally by the Aboriginal peoples of Canada. This point has been made repeatedly by representatives of Aboriginal organizations and by many individuals as well. Aboriginal concerns regarding the Charter were evident when the notion of an entrenched constitutional rights document was first introduced. In an appearance before a parliamentary subcommittee on Indian women and the *Indian Act* in 1982, the Assembly of First Nations stated:

> As Indian people we cannot afford to have individual rights override collective rights. Our societies have never been structured in that way, unlike yours, and that is where the clash comes... If you isolate the individual rights from the collective rights, then you are heading down another path that is even more discriminatory. The Charter of Rights is based on equality. In other words, everybody is the same across the country...so the Charter of Rights automatically is in conflict with our philosophy and culture and organization of collective rights. There would have to be changes.

---

[405] *Reference Re Section 94(2) of the Motor Vehicle Act*, [1985] 2 S.C.R. 486 (Supreme Court of Canada), p. 503.

[406] *R. v. Morgentaler*, [1988] 1 S.C.R. 30 (Supreme Court of Canada), p. 164.

> We could not accept the Charter of Rights as it is written because that would be contrary to our own system of existence and government.[407]

Concern about Charter protections being available in Aboriginal justice systems is that making good on these guarantees could mean that such systems end up resembling the non-Aboriginal system in both form and function. This has been the experience of the tribal courts in the United States under the *Indian Civil Rights Act*, and some fear that the same thing would happen in Canada if the Charter applied to Aboriginal justice systems.

Some of the protections provided by the *Bill of Rights* in the United States and the Charter in Canada may well run counter to the precepts of many Aboriginal justice systems. Take, for example, the protection against self-incrimination. Many Aboriginal justice initiatives require the accused person to speak – often without a lawyer to speak on the person's behalf. This is based on the idea that healing cannot begin if the offender is not prepared to speak about what he or she has done.

Another example is in the area of sanctions or sentences. As we saw in our review of the Greenland criminal code, Aboriginal justice systems may not necessarily include defined penalties for specific offences. As a result, individuals who admit to committing robbery, for example, may be treated in dramatically different ways by an Aboriginal justice system, depending on their particular needs and their history in the community.[408] In fact, decisions of Aboriginal justice systems do not necessarily hinge on a finding that individuals have committed specific offences. For example, in 1988, when the Longhouse at Kahnawake considered the cases of three young people charged with arson and other offences, the most serious punishment was reserved for the offence of falsely informing the community that the Sûreté du Québec was trying to frame them. For this offence of deception, the young people were given their first of three warnings. After three warnings they would be banished from the community.[409] The *Criminal Code* contains offences

---

[407] Quoted in Menno Boldt and J. Anthony Long,"Tribal Philosophies and the Canadian Charter of Rights and Freedoms", in *The Quest for Justice, Aboriginal Peoples and Aboriginal Rights*, ed. Menno Boldt, J. Anthony Long and Leroy Little Bear (Toronto: University of Toronto Press, 1985), p. 171.

[408] As indicated earlier, there is also some flexibility in the non-Aboriginal justice system. See discussion in the section beginning on page 249.

[409] The decision of the Longhouse in this matter read in part,

> This warning will follow you for life. This system was given to us by the Peacemaker in order to rid ourselves of disharmony. It is a formula used by our ancestors to decide when an individual or individuals can no longer co-exist in our society and still have peace and security. In the event of a second warning, you will again be reminded of your ties and obligations to the people and a more severe penalty will have to be levied. The third warning is the last and final chance for someone to correct their erring ways. If this is not heeded, the only choice is banishment for life. ("Decision of the Longhouse", cited in note 398, p. 2.)

similar to deception (for example, public mischief), but there is no precise comparison. As well, the Longhouse does not have a specific definition of what constitutes deception – indeed, it does not have a set definition of any offence. It is very possible, then, that given the severe consequences that could result from breaching the unwritten rules of the Longhouse, punishing a person for the offence of deception with a warning, or ultimately by banishment, would violate the principles of fundamental justice referred to in section 7 of the Charter.

Similarly, we referred earlier to the possibility that Aboriginal justice systems might leave decisions about the admissibility of evidence to the fact-finding body to decide on case by case. If the evidentiary rules governing issues such as hearsay and similar fact evidence are seen as "principles of fundamental justice", then Aboriginal justice initiatives could face Charter challenges as well.

Not all the problematic aspects of the Charter are issues of trial procedure or fact adjudication. Some of the protections afforded by the Charter – for example, against unreasonable search and seizure (section 8) – would have an impact at the investigation stage of proceedings. An example of the conflict between individual and collective rights that could arise is the decision of Mr. Justice Stach of the Ontario Court, General Division, in *R. v. Hatchard*. The facts of the case are as follows:

> The Big Trout Lake First Nation is a remote, fly-in reserve community in Northwestern Ontario. The community airport is off-reserve and a bus takes those arriving in the community from the airport to the community. As part of a concentrated campaign against drugs and alcohol abuse, the community had passed a prohibition by-law pursuant to section 85(1) of the Indian Act...which permitted the searching by a "special constable, a band constable or any other authorized peace officer," of any person and the baggage of any person entering the reserve in order to search for intoxicants. The First Nation, as part of the campaign, had instituted a regular system of community patrols which stopped persons as they entered the reserve in order to search for drugs and alcohol.
>
> The First Nations officials received a tip from a drug and alcohol employee, that the accused was returning to the community with drugs for the purpose of trafficking. The Ontario Provincial Police were absent from the community at the time and did not have the manpower to assist the First Nations officials. There was no resident justice of the peace in the community and the First Nation officials had not obtained a search warrant.[410]

A search of the bags of the accused was carried out, and alcohol and drugs were found. At his trial on the charge of trafficking, the accused argued that the search

---

[410] *R. v. Hatchard*, [1993] 1 C.N.L.R. 96 (Ontario Court of Justice).

violated section 8 of the Charter which guarantees freedom from unreasonable search or seizure.

On the particular facts of the case the evidence was found to be admissible. The court made special reference to the fact that

> The search was part of the collective effort of a remote Aboriginal community to remove from its midst the social destructiveness of intoxicants and admission of the real evidence obtained in the search will not bring the administration of justice into disrepute.

The case was not appealed. It is very possible that if the matter went further, or a similar situation arose in another community, the results might be very different.

If a court were to find that such actions did contravene the Charter, the problems that would be created are apparent. Attempts by a community to control activities it regards as detrimental to its overall health would be seriously impaired if it were required to conform to a balancing of individual and collective rights that did not take into account that community's culture, traditions and needs.

Since the enactment of the Charter, the Supreme Court of Canada has placed significant emphasis on protecting the rights of those charged with criminal offences. There is no reason to think that this orientation will change in the near future. Cases involving Charter challenges to Aboriginal justice systems might be framed as conflicts between the rights of the Aboriginal individual and those of the Aboriginal collectivity. If this happened, the court might, in light of its track record, come down on the side of protecting the rights of the individual accused. A series of such decisions could have a crippling effect on the development of Aboriginal justice systems.

On the other hand, there are those who suggest that Charter protections are as vital for Aboriginal justice systems as they are for non-Aboriginal systems. For example, there is no reason to think that Aboriginal governments will be any less disposed than non-Aboriginal governments to abuse their powers.[411] One form of protection from such abuses, whether intentional or unintentional, is a document such as the Charter. In addition, it has been argued that the isolated nature of many Aboriginal communities makes them more vulnerable to possible abuses of individual rights. This is not because Aboriginal communities are necessarily less concerned about the rights of individuals, but rather because smaller communities, Aboriginal and non-Aboriginal, tend to be more conservative and less tolerant of difference.[412]

---

[411] On the issues of conflict of interest and ethics in government as they concern Aboriginal people, see Mary Ellen Turpel, "Enhancing Integrity in Aboriginal Government: Ethics and Accountability for Good Governance", research study prepared for RCAP (1995).

[412] Roger Gibbins, "Citizenship, Political, and Intergovernmental Problems With Indian Self-Government", in *Arduous Journey, Canadian Indians and Decolonization*, ed. J. Rick Ponting (Toronto: McClelland & Stewart Inc., 1986), p. 375.

Aboriginal women's organizations, particularly the Native Women's Association of Canada (NWAC), are very concerned that Aboriginal governments be constrained by entrenched legislation that assures protection of the rights of Aboriginal women.[413] Section 35(4) of the *Constitution Act, 1982* addresses this issue in part by stating:

> Notwithstanding any other provision of this Act, the aboriginal and treaty rights referred to in sub-section (1) are guaranteed equally to male and female persons.

While the importance of constitutional recognition of the rights of Aboriginal women cannot be overstated, it is equally important to recognize that constitutional recognition does not, in and of itself, necessarily translate into meaningful protection. The fact that Aboriginal women are marginalized in many communities, despite the existence of constitutional guarantees, bears strong witness to this fact. The issue of protecting women's rights in the development of Aboriginal justice systems goes well beyond the question of whether the Charter should apply to Aboriginal governments. We have therefore devoted a separate section to the issue later in this chapter.

One of the difficulties involved in resolving the question of the application of the Charter to Aboriginal governments is that the *Constitution Act, 1982* does not address this issue.[414] Section 32(1) of the Charter states that

This Charter applies

(a) to the Parliament of Canada and government of Canada in respect of all matters within the authority of Parliament including all matters relating to the Yukon Territory and the Northwest Territories; and

(b) to the legislature and government of each province in respect of all matters within the authority of the legislature of each province.

It is therefore clear that the Charter applies to the acts of federal, provincial and territorial governments. The Charter also covers any body delegated by those governments to carry out governmental functions. Thus, if the federal or a provincial government, by way of ordinary statute, gave authority to Aboriginal nations to administer justice, Aboriginal nations would be exercising a delegated power and would therefore be bound by the Charter in the exercise of that power.[415] However, our view is that the right of Aboriginal nations to exercise governmental powers

---

[413] See Teressa Nahanee, "Dancing With a Gorilla: Aboriginal Women, Justice and the Charter", in *Aboriginal Peoples and the Justice System*, cited in note 7, pp. 359-382.

[414] We will return to this issue in more detail in our final report.

[415] Hogg and Turpel, "Implementing Aboriginal Self-Government", cited in note 401, pp. 414-419.

is not a delegated power but an inherent right that is given constitutional recognition in section 35 of the *Constitution Act, 1982*. Does the Charter apply, then, to Aboriginal governments exercising their inherent right?

Since section 32 does not mention Aboriginal governments, it can be argued that the Charter has no application to their activities. This position is arguably reinforced by the fact that section 35, which recognizes and affirms the Aboriginal and treaty right of self-government, is located outside the Charter, which is in Part I of the act. Section 35 is in Part II of the act, entitled "Rights of the Aboriginal Peoples of Canada".

Kent McNeil presents this argument in a paper he prepared for the Commission. At the end of the paper he writes,

> Courts may, however, be tempted to downplay these arguments [that the Charter does not apply to Aboriginal governments] out of the fear that fundamental rights and freedoms will not be protected if Aboriginal governments are permitted to function outside the scope of the Charter. That kind of judicial activism must be avoided. The issue of whether the Charter should apply is a political one that should not be decided until the matter has been thoroughly investigated and publicly debated, and the consequences of applying the Charter to Aboriginal governments adequately understood. We are a long way from achieving anything like an adequate understanding of this matter at present.[416]

On the other hand, section 32(1), rather than exhaustively cataloguing the governments covered by the Charter, can be seen as standing for the broader principle that the Charter applies to the acts of governments rather than to the acts of private individuals. According to this view, which the Commission shares, the fact that section 32 does not state that it applies to Aboriginal governments is not necessarily determinative of the matter. Indeed, it would be anomalous to see the *Constitution Act, 1982* recognizing, through section 35(1), the inherent right of Aboriginal self-government in other than express language, yet require the presence of express language to ensure that the Charter applies to such governments.

The tacit recognition of an Aboriginal order of government in section 35(1) leads us to take a broad view of section 32(1). If section 35(1) is interpreted as recognizing an inherent right of Aboriginal self-government, we think that section 32(1) should be read in a way that takes this recognition into account. If this were not the case, there would be a serious imbalance in the application of the Charter, one that should be avoided in the absence of explicit language to the contrary. In other words, the progressive unpacking of the broad rights referred to in section

---

[416] Kent McNeil, "Aboriginal Governments and the *Canadian Charter of Rights and Freedoms*: A Legal Perspective", research study prepared for RCAP (1994).

35(1) should be achieved in a manner that takes into account the central position of the Charter in Canada's overall constitutional scheme.

This argument is bolstered by the fact that the creation of Charter-free zones, where individuals would lose Charter protections against governmental violations of protected rights only to regain those rights when they left the territory, would trivialize the declaration, in section 52, that the constitution, including the Charter, is the supreme law of the country and that all laws that are inconsistent with its provisions are of no force or effect.

That the Charter applies to the laws and acts of Aboriginal governments does not mean that Aboriginal justice systems must be carbon copies of the non-Aboriginal system. As we will see in the next section, Aboriginal nations have several options for ensuring that distinct justice systems can thrive even under the Charter.

Differing Means of Protecting Individual Rights in Aboriginal Nations

The issue regarding the role of the Charter in Aboriginal justice systems is not whether individual rights require protection in such systems, but rather how to provide such protections and the balance to be struck between individual and collective rights. Given that the Charter applies to Aboriginal governments, several options are available to Aboriginal nations in this regard. The first is reliance on the Charter, mediated by the impact of section 25. Another is the development of Aboriginal charters of rights to supplement and add to the protections in the Charter and to guide courts in interpreting existing protections in the Charter. Yet another option builds on the first two – reliance on the Charter, mediated by section 25 and by Aboriginal charters of rights – and adds the use of section 33, the notwithstanding clause of the Charter. We examine each of these options in turn, keeping in mind that the issue is – and always will be – which option will secure protection of their fundamental human rights as Aboriginal people for members of Aboriginal nations.

The starting point for each nation must be continued reliance on the Charter. However, the Charter itself contemplates that its provisions will be examined in light of Aboriginal rights guaranteed elsewhere in the *Constitution Act, 1982.* Section 25 of the Charter states:

> The guarantee in this Charter of certain rights and freedoms shall not be construed so as to abrogate or derogate from any aboriginal, treaty or other rights or freedoms that pertain to the aboriginal peoples of Canada including
>
> (a) any rights or freedoms that have been recognized by the Royal Proclamation of October 7, 1763; and
>
> (b) any rights or freedoms that now exist by way of land claims agreements or may be so acquired.

The interaction between sections 25 and 35 has been the subject of much speculation but has not yet been addressed by the courts. In *Partners In Confederation*, we adopted the prevalent, but not universally held view that although section 25 shields the Aboriginal right of self-government from Charter review, individuals subject to the actions of Aboriginal governments enjoy the protection of the Charter. Thus, while an individual could not successfully challenge the establishment of a justice system by an Aboriginal government – since establishment of such systems is part of the right of self-government – if the functioning of the justice system violated the individual's rights under the Charter, that violation could be subject to review by the courts.

Section 25 thus gives Aboriginal nations and their communities an additional way of justifying actions that might otherwise run afoul of the Charter. Federal and provincial governments must rely solely on section 1 of the Charter to justify otherwise unconstitutional acts (subject to their use of section 33, described later), but the application of the Charter to Aboriginal governments is tempered by the mandatory provisions of section 25, which ensures that the Charter will receive a flexible interpretation that takes into account the distinctive philosophies, traditions and cultural practices that animate the inherent right of self-government. Peter Hogg and Mary Ellen Turpel believe that the existence of section 25 severely curtails the pressures that might otherwise make Aboriginal justice programs conform to western ideals:

> The important point here is that the application of the Charter, when viewed with section 25, should not mean that Aboriginal governments must follow the policies and emulate the style of government of the federal and provincial governments. Section 25 allows an Aboriginal government to design programs and laws that are different, for legitimate cultural reasons, and have these reasons considered relevant should such differences invite judicial review under the Charter. Section 25 would allow Aboriginal governments to protect, preserve and promote the identity of their citizens through unique institutions, norms and government practices.

In the opinion of Hogg and Turpel,

> Interpretations of the Charter that are consistent with Aboriginal cultures and traditions would likely be found when the court is faced with a situation where different standards apply and the difference is integral to culturally-based policy within an Aboriginal community.[417]

Overall then, section 25 should be capable of protecting culturally appropriate justice systems from Charter challenge. Taking as examples initiatives discussed in this

---

[417] Hogg and Turpel, "Implementing Aboriginal Self-Government", cited in note 401, pp. 418-419.

report, a fact-determination process that gave authority to a jury-like assembly to determine the admissibility of evidence could be constitutionally valid. Similarly, a requirement that, in certain circumstances, accused persons speak for themselves could also be justified. Finally, a process involving elders or clan leaders as decision makers, even where they had personal knowledge of the situation of accused persons, could also be protected.

On the other hand, section 25 would not be as readily available to Aboriginal justice systems that chose to model themselves on non-Aboriginal systems. In a system where incarceration was the preferred method of punishment and deterrence and evidence was presented in the manner of criminal courts, deviations from principles of fundamental justice, as developed by the Supreme Court, would likely not be justifiable by referring to section 25. Even where section 25 was not available to Aboriginal governments, however, an Aboriginal government could still rely on section 1 of the Charter, the 'reasonable limits' clause.

The use of section 25 by the courts should go a long way toward restoring confidence that application of the Charter need not spell an end to the development of distinct Aboriginal justice systems. One of the problems inherent in relying on section 25, however, is that non-Aboriginal judges, who are often unfamiliar with Aboriginal ways, would be determining which practices of an Aboriginal justice system are consistent with Aboriginal traditions and culture and which are not. The potential difficulties of having non-Aboriginal judges as the final arbiters of these issues is apparent. One way of addressing this issue would be to provide non-Aboriginal judges with relevant information from Aboriginal nations about what constitutes their vision of justice. One significant way of accomplishing this would be for Aboriginal nations to develop their own Aboriginal charters of rights.

The idea that Aboriginal nations could develop their own charters of rights has been considered for a number of years but received particular emphasis during discussions on the Charlottetown Accord. As the concept was developed during those negotiations, it was thought that if an Aboriginal nation enacted its own charter of rights, that document would give its citizens rights in addition to those in the Canadian Charter. In this sense an Aboriginal charter would supplement the Canadian Charter but not displace it. Citizens of the Aboriginal nation concerned about acts of their nation could then rely on the provisions of the Aboriginal charter where applicable and seek relief based on the provisions of the Canadian Charter as well.[418]

The Aboriginal charter would also serve as an interpretive tool for the courts of the non-Aboriginal justice system in applying the Canadian Charter to the laws and acts of Aboriginal governments. In this way, the concern about having judges of the non-Aboriginal system pronounce on the validity of an Aboriginal nation's

---

[418] See Hogg and Turpel, "Implementing Aboriginal Self-Government", p. 419.

laws or acts would be largely alleviated, since the values underpinning such legislation or acts should be readily discernable in its charter.

Where an Aboriginal charter is part of a self-government treaty between an Aboriginal nation and the Crown, the interpretive influence of the Aboriginal charter would be amplified. This is because section 25 shields treaty rights from the impact of the Canadian Charter. Where a self-government treaty includes an Aboriginal charter among its provisions, it would appear that courts would be bound to seriously consider the terms of this charter in interpreting any related provisions of the Canadian Charter.

There is no question that the *Canadian Charter of Rights and Freedoms* reflects a particular approach to balancing individual and collective rights. The unmodified application of the Charter to Aboriginal nations might well make development of Aboriginal justice systems that are responsive to the needs of the people difficult if not impossible. Fortunately, we do not have to choose between having the Charter apply to Aboriginal nations in precisely the same way as in the rest of Canada or not having it apply at all. The provisions of the Charter itself, particularly section 25, operating in conjunction with the development of unique Aboriginal charters, means that Aboriginal nations have a degree of flexibility within the provisions of the *Constitution Act, 1982* to set their own course in the justice field.

Recommendation 6

The Commission recommends that Aboriginal nations develop their own charters of rights to supplement the protections in the *Canadian Charter of Rights and Freedoms* and provide guidance to courts in interpreting existing protections in the Canadian Charter.

Section 33 of the Canadian Charter of Rights and Freedoms

Although section 52 of the *Constitution Act, 1982*, declares that the constitution is the supreme law of Canada and that all laws must be in consistent with it, the Charter itself contains a significant exception to this rule. Section 33 states:

> (1) Parliament or the legislature of a province may expressly declare in an Act of Parliament or of the legislature, as the case may be, that the Act or a provision thereof shall operate notwithstanding a provision included in section 2 or sections 7 to 15 of this Charter.

Commonly known as the notwithstanding clause, this section allows governments to escape the scrutiny of the courts by declaring that specific laws or sections of laws will operate notwithstanding certain provisions of the Charter.

The first question in discussing the effects of section 33 on the ability of Aboriginal nations to escape the impact of particular aspects of the Charter is whether

Aboriginal nations have the right to rely on section 33 at all. The argument against giving Aboriginal nations that right is that the wording of section 33 speaks only of Parliament and the legislature of a province and therefore does not include Aboriginal governments.

Aboriginal governments are not mentioned expressly in section 33, but nor are they mentioned in section 32(1). If Aboriginal governments are to be considered governments for the purposes of section 32(1) to ensure that the Charter applies to their actions, how can they be excluded from section 33? It is difficult to justify the position that an Aboriginal government is a government for purposes of section 32 but not for purposes of section 33, the section immediately following. The close connection between the two sections suggests that they should be interpreted in the same way.

Having recourse to section 33 would allow Aboriginal governments to enact legislation striking a different balance between individual and collective rights in areas regarding freedom of expression (section 2), legal rights (sections 7-14), and equality rights (section 15). With regard to equality rights it should be noted that Aboriginal governments would not be able to use section 33 to enact legislation that discriminated on the basis of sex, for two reasons. First, section 28 of the Charter states that

> Notwithstanding anything in this Charter, the rights and freedoms referred to in it are guaranteed equally to male and female persons.

This guarantee is reiterated as it relates to Aboriginal people in section 35(4):

> Notwithstanding any other provision of this Act, the aboriginal and treaty rights referred to in subsection (1) are guaranteed equally to male and female persons.

It must also be noted that any legislation passed under the provisions of section 33 expires after five years unless expressly re-enacted (sections 33(3) and (4)). This provision would also apply to the laws of Aboriginal nations.

Authority to use section 33 would belong only to the Aboriginal nation. The governments of local Aboriginal communities that make up the nation would not have the right to use the notwithstanding clause.

The Commission concludes that the *Canadian Charter of Rights and Freedoms* applies to Aboriginal governments, including their justice systems, and regulates their relations with individuals under their jurisdiction. However, under section 25, the Charter must be given a flexible interpretation that takes account of the distinctive philosophies, traditions and cultural practices of Aboriginal peoples. Moreover, under section 33, in their core areas of jurisdiction, Aboriginal governments can include in legislation notwithstanding clauses to suspend the operation of certain Charter protections for

a five-year renewable period. Nevertheless, by virtue of sections 28 and 35(4) of the *Constitution Act, 1982*, Aboriginal women and men have equal access to the inherent right of self-government and are entitled to equal treatment by their governments.

Ensuring the Safety of Women and Children in Aboriginal Justice Systems

We touched on the need to ensure that Aboriginal justice systems protect women and children in our discussion of consultation in the development of such systems and of the role of the Charter. The concerns discussed here relate specifically to family violence. By discussing this issue separately, we are not suggesting that these concerns are afterthoughts or that the needs of women and children should be addressed only after those of the rest of society have been met. On the contrary, assuring the safety of women and children is central to any Aboriginal justice system. A system that fails to protect women and children is a system that fails. We address this issue separately because it was raised on so many occasions by witnesses appearing before the Commission, and we are persuaded that it deserves special attention.

In general, one would expect Aboriginal justice systems to move carefully in dealing with criminal acts committed by community members because, for the most part, offenders would likely remain in, or in close proximity to, the home community rather than being incarcerated far away. Communities do not usually rush to welcome those who have caused disruption or harm, so a community that chooses a justice system designed to heal and rehabilitate offenders within the community will have thought long and hard about the implications of such an approach and the consequences for the community.

This has not always been so with respect to family violence, however. These offences are not always viewed with the seriousness they warrant by all community members. Thus, if the community does not recognize the seriousness of wife assault, for example, a program to keep offenders in the community may be adopted without a full appreciation of the serious threat to the safety of victims. As objectionable as incarceration is to most Aboriginal societies, the one thing jail does accomplish is removal of the offender, even if for only a short time, thus giving the victim at least a temporary sense of security.

If family violence is addressed without proper concern for the needs of victims, two dangerous messages are sent. The first is that these offences are not serious. This message puts all who are vulnerable at risk. The second and more immediate message is that the offender has not really done anything wrong. This message gives the offender licence to continue his actions and puts victims in immediate danger.

By far the bulk of the submissions received on these issues from Aboriginal women's organizations did not recommend incarceration to deal with such offences but rather emphasized the need for holistic community healing. Lillian Sanderson of the La Ronge Native Women's Council told the Commission, "Our men as well as our women need to go through the healing process to become healthy, functional individuals."[419] In summarizing the problems facing the community of Baker Lake, Northwest Territories, Joan Scottie echoed the feelings of many who testified before us:

> We have had a lot of problems in Baker Lake in the last few years with sexual assaults and child sexual abuse – a lot of problems. Many of the people who are committing these and other crimes are repeat offenders. They get sentenced for a crime, go to jail, get released, and then a month or two later you see them back in court again.
>
> Many of the people who phone me to talk about these problems feel that putting people away in jail is not the answer. They are being punished, but they aren't being helped. They are not getting counselling, and no one is looking at the reasons why they commit these crimes...
>
> I can think of someone in Baker Lake who has been in constant trouble for six years. There are people in the community who know why he is doing what he is doing who believe that steps could be taken to deal with the root causes of his behaviour. But when people approach social services, no one there wants to listen. They think they know how to handle everything – usually by having more charges laid.[420]

These submissions suggest the need for programs and services along the lines of those developed at Hollow Water. The Hollow Water program is much more intensive, however, than most other Aboriginal justice programs. Moreover, in cases of physical or sexual abuse, initiatives such as sentencing circles often fail to meet the goals alluded to by Joan Scottie.[421]

Pauktuutit, the Inuit Women's Association of Canada, has been particularly concerned about this issue. Pauktuutit advocates programs developed in accordance with traditional Inuit concepts of justice, but many of the initiatives to date fall short of this mark. Pauktuutit's report on a sentencing circle in an Inuit community identifies some of the problems with this approach. The circle was convened to deal with a man who assaulted his wife. In addition to ignoring the power relationship

---

[419] Lillian Sanderson, La Ronge Native Women's Council, RCAP transcripts, La Ronge, Saskatchewan, 28 May 1992, p. 157.

[420] Joan Scottie, RCAP transcripts, Baker Lake, N.W.T., 19 November 1992.

[421] We will address the issue of family violence in greater detail in our final report.

in evidence between the man and woman, which was partly responsible for silencing the woman during the circle, the report noted another problem:

> Not only was the victim silenced by her husband, the sentencing circle may have imposed an even greater silence. This circle was the first of its kind being supported by the Judge and Inuit leaders. If she spoke out about further abuses or her dislike for this sentence what would she be saying about this process everyone supported? Now in addition to fearing her husband's retribution, she may fear by speaking out she would be speaking out against the community. The sentence created in this circle is one endorsed not only by the mayor and other participants but by the judge and a highly respected Inuk politician. The pressure to not speak out against a sentencing alternative supported by so many is great. The victim may be afraid to admit she is being beaten because such an admission, she may fear, may be interpreted as a failure of this process. She may hold herself to blame and once again continue to suffer in silence.[422]

This situation arose in a sentencing circle presided over by a judge, but there is no reason to think that this situation could not also occur in an Aboriginal-controlled system. In light of the experience in that circle, Pauktuutit offered several recommendations for future initiatives in this area:

1. There must be full community discussion of the cases that should be eligible for such programs.

2. Where Circles are organized, there must be adequate preparation of the community for the Circle – people need to know what is expected of them.

3. Membership in the Circle cannot be decided unilaterally, the entire community must have full input into this process.

4. The victim must have a meaningful say in the deliberative process whether that be in person or through some type of impact statement.

5. Communities themselves must acquire greater awareness about wife abuse issues in general.

6. Sentencing alternatives must look beyond the needs of the offender.

As Mary Crnkovich wrote in her report for Pauktuutit and the federal justice department on a sentencing circle,

> ...in the sexual assault and wife assault cases, the sentencing alternative must not only be designed to deal with rehabilitation of the

---

[422] M. Crnkovich, "Report on the Sentencing Circle in C", in Pauktuutit, Inuit Women's Association, IPP brief to RCAP (1993). The village was not identified so as to protect the identity of the woman.

offender, it must also deal with the rehabilitation and protection of the victim and family, independently of what is decided for the accused.... What is missing from this focus of "healing" is the assurance that if the wrongdoer stays in the community the victim is protected from further assaults. Without such protection, it is unlikely the victims will ever "heal".

7. Couples should not be required to attend counselling together. The needs of each party may be very different. Requiring both parties to attend counselling suggests that both parties are equally responsible for the assault.[423]

The scope and limitations of healing should be understood, as the Pauktuutit recommendations point out. The Family Violence Working Group in Toronto spent some time on this issue in the context of discussions about diverting family violence cases to Aboriginal Legal Services. The group was firm in stating that it is a mistake to equate healing with the re-establishment of the family unit; in some cases this will not be possible and should not be sought. Rather the notion of healing should mean that the parties learn to resolve their conflicts and, if necessary, part on good terms. For the working group, healing encompasses a healthy separation and the ability of the individuals to begin new relationships on a stronger foundation.[424]

In constituting circles or sentencing panels, the strengths and limitations of elders must also be recognized. An issue that must be faced here is the extent to which differences in values may have developed along generational lines. In this regard, the report of the special adviser on gender equality to the minister of justice of the Northwest Territories stated:

> There must also be an awareness of the fact that there can be differences that develop along generational lines and that older people may evidence a tolerance of violence against women that is no longer acceptable to younger women. In seeking advice and input from communities these differences must be recognized.[425]

A similar point has also been made by Carol La Prairie as a result of her work in the Yukon:

> The potential for discrepancy between the values of the younger and the older community members in justice hearings and deci-

---

[423] See Pauktuutit, *Inuit Women and Justice: Progress Report Number 1*, cited in note 54, part 4, pp. 24-25. The report was prepared as part of the Inuit Women and Justice Project, which received funding from the justice department's Aboriginal Justice Directorate.

[424] Minutes of the Family Violence Working Group (Toronto), 25 October 1993, pp. 9-10. For a discussion of the work of the Family Violence Working Group, see Chapter 3.

[425] K. Peterson, *The Justice House*, Report of the Special Advisor on Gender Equality to the Minister of Justice of the Northwest Territories (Yellowknife: Government of the Northwest Territories, 1992), p. 72.

sion-making is considerable. Few communities are untouched by events of the past two decades where women's issues, victims' rights and alternate life-styles have gained respectability and recognition. The social changes evolving from these events may be more in the psyche of the younger than the older members of the community. The use of elders in justice systems, to the exclusion of other age groups, may reflect values not representative of contemporary community values.[426]

One of the things we learned from the evidence before us is that in Aboriginal communities where intergenerational chains of sexual abuse and family violence have occurred, few members of the community remain unaffected. Elders have often experienced violence and abuse, perhaps as a result of residential schooling and its aftermath. There is growing recognition in communities such as Hollow Water, where the healing journey is well under way, that those who wish to become involved in the healing of others must first undertake their own healing. A report prepared by the Grand Council of Treaty 3 in northwestern Ontario addresses this point explicitly.

> There have been a number of goals and recommendations that state that some persons would like to return to traditional ways through the guidance of the elders. With due respect to the elders and with recognition of the great contributions they make, it must be brought out that elders themselves are victims of abuse. It is important that the elders embark on a program of personal healing. A commitment such as this by the elders would provide an example to other people and it would be a necessary and beneficial undertaking for their personal well-being.[427]

Testimony before the Commission also revealed that in some cases elders have been perpetrators of sexual assault, just as members of the non-Aboriginal community who hold positions of respect and authority, including priests and school teachers, have dishonoured themselves and their professions by perpetrating physical and sexual assaults on their charges. Involving victimizers as decision makers in Aboriginal justice systems before they have been through their own healing and have been restored to positions of trust in the community is one of the important issues that Aboriginal nations and their communities will have to address.

It is one thing to set standards for the development of Aboriginal justice systems – it is another to see that they are achieved. The problem facing women and chil-

---

[426] Carol La Prairie, "Exploring the Boundaries of Justice, A Report Prepared for the Department of Justice, Yukon Territory, First Nations of the Yukon Territory and Justice Canada" (1992), p. 112.

[427] Grand Council of Treaty 3, "Final Report on Community Consultations", p. 38, quoted in Ross, "Duelling Paradigms?", cited in note 93, p. 258. The report was prepared by the Grand Council of Treaty 3 as an initial step in developing an Aboriginal family violence strategy for its 25 member communities (Ross, p. 243).

dren in many Aboriginal communities is that they have little power to influence important decisions about their own lives. To quote again from the report of the special adviser on gender equality in the N.W.T.,

> In consultations at the community level, many aboriginal women voiced concerns that their voices are not heard. There appears to be a willingness to hear from male elders and not from women. There were also strongly voiced concerns that the issue of violence against women is not treated with the degree of seriousness that it may deserve and in some cases is overtly tolerated. Women must have the confidence that, in hearing from "the community" the position of women is also heard. The message that violence against women is not culturally acceptable, excusable or justifiable was very clearly delivered during the course of community workshops. Therefore, in developing means of receiving a broader range of input from communities into the administration of justice there must be a large degree of sensitivity utilized. In the event that community justice committees are a vehicle utilized for receiving this input, the voice of women on such committees must be guaranteed.[428]

As we have seen, initiatives to address family violence and sexual abuse in Hollow Water and Toronto feature a strong role for women. Their participation helps to ensure that the process does not further victimize women and children. But how can we be sure that all such programs take the needs of women and children fully into account?

One option is for a body at the level of the Aboriginal nation to review criminal justice initiatives in its constituent communities with respect to their approach to family violence. Aboriginal women's groups active in the nation – or where such groups are not in place, Aboriginal nations may need to encourage their formation – could review and approve such programs before implementation.

One thing is clear. Aboriginal society is not free of the sexism and violence that permeate the rest of Canadian society. The root causes of this problem may be somewhat different in Aboriginal society than in non-Aboriginal society, but this does not change the nature or the extent of the problem. Unless this is acknowledged and concrete steps are taken to address violence, women and children will continue to be at risk in Aboriginal justice systems. On the positive side, programs such as the one in Hollow Water indicate that it is possible to design systems that emphasize holistic healing of all the parties affected by crimes of family violence and sexual assault. These represent a significant improvement over the way such cases are dealt with in the non-Aboriginal justice system.

---

[428] K. Peterson, *The Justice House*, cited in note 425, p. 72.

Recommendation 7

The Commission recommends that the safety and security of Aboriginal women and children be given a high priority in the development of Aboriginal justice systems and program initiatives.

Recommendation 8

The Commission recommends that all nations rely on the expertise of Aboriginal women and Aboriginal women's organizations to review initiatives in the justice area and ensure that the participation of women in the creation and design of justice systems is both meaningful and significant.

Assuring the Integrity of the Decision-Making Process

One important factor that could work against the successful establishment of Aboriginal justice systems is a perception that decision makers are exercising their authority in a biased or unfair manner. It is therefore important to protect and assure the integrity of this process.[429]

In the non-Aboriginal justice system these concerns have been addressed by the gradual emergence of what are now referred to as the rules of natural justice. These rules protect the integrity of the decision-making process in three ways: (1) they ensure that the individual has a right to be heard by the decision maker before the decision is made; (2) they require that justice not only be done but be seen to be done; and (3) they ensure that the individual's case is decided by decision makers who have not pre-judged the case as a result of information received before the hearing or personal relationships with those involved in the case.

The rules of natural justice are relatively easy to state, but their application is not always simple. For example, courts have determined that the right to be heard does not always include a right to cross-examine individuals with relevant information on the matter at hand or even to speak directly to decision makers. As well, determining whether a decision maker is biased can be difficult. The courts decide each case on its merits, with particular attention to the role of the decision-making body and the consequences of its decisions for the individual. Thus criminal courts are held quite strictly to the rules of natural justice while regulatory bodies are permitted more flexibility in meeting the duty to act fairly.

Concerns about the fairness of decisions reached in Aboriginal justice systems must be taken seriously. The Aboriginal Justice Inquiry of Manitoba noted that accusations that judges of U.S. tribal courts are susceptible to the influence of local politicians, while not common, have certainly been made.[430]

---

[429] The broader issue of ensuring the legitimacy and integrity of Aboriginal governments will be addressed in our final report.

[430] AJI, cited in note 2, volume 1, p. 295.

In response to these concerns, community pressure has resulted in tribal councils taking steps to protect judges from political interference.[431] Some tribal constitutions now set the appointment period for judges beyond the term of tribal council members. Some tribal codes also specify the grounds for removing judges from office.[432]

Certainly it is essential that Aboriginal nations and communities that wish to adopt a tribal court-like structure put in place similar provisions to protect decision makers from political interference. The situation of Aboriginal communities in Canada, however, raises other concerns about pressure on decision makers. Most reserves are small; it is not unusual for reserves to have just a few hundred members, most of whom belong to a small number of families. How can community decision makers be insulated from pressure in this situation?

If communities reconstitute their nations on a historical or regional basis, this will enable them to achieve the economies of scale and the independence from community pressure necessary to establish a functioning justice system. This approach would see decision makers go into communities on a regular basis to deal with justice issues. Unlike the fly-in courts, these individuals would understand the reality of life in the Aboriginal communities they serve and would dispense justice in the manner the communities themselves mandate. This approach is currently in place in the western portion of Washington state. Justice services to reservations in this area are provided by Northwest Intertribal Court Systems (NICS). NICS centralizes the location of justice service providers but sends them out on a regular basis to administer justice on the reservations.

Some communities within nations may wish to bypass a court-like structure entirely and vest decision-making powers in band councils or other elected or traditionally appointed bodies. In these cases, many of the same concerns would have to be addressed. For example, under the Spallumcheen child welfare by-law, decisions are made by chief and council. Recognizing that council members could be related to families being dealt with under the by-law, council members do not sit on cases where a relative is involved; instead, an alternate member sits on the case.[433]

---

[431] For a discussion of these ethical problems, and possible solutions, see Turpel, "Enhancing Integrity in Aboriginal Government", cited in note 411.

[432] Rudin and Russell, "Native Alternative Dispute Resolution Systems", cited in note 335, p. 31. In response to this issue the Aboriginal Justice Inquiry of Manitoba noted that

> many tribal court leaders whom we met are addressing [the issue of political pressure] through tribal constitutional provisions which guarantee the separation of the judiciary from the legislative and executive arms of tribal government, and which are intended to provide for the appointment and tenure process for judges which is secure and fair. Such developments, as tribal court officials are pursuing with their tribal councils, appear to be the most obvious and effective ways to deal with such criticisms. (AJI, cited in note 2, volume 1, p. 295.)

[433] Godin-Beers and Williams, "Report on the Spallumcheen Child Welfare Program", cited in note 140, p. 65.

All the responses looked at to this point have been developed to address deficiencies that would lead to violations of the rules of natural justice. This does not mean that all the rules of natural justice as they are understood in the non-Aboriginal system must apply to all aspects of Aboriginal justice systems. Simply adopting the norms of the non-Aboriginal system will not necessarily assure development of an Aboriginal justice system capable of responding to the needs of the nation and its communities.

There is no question that the first rule of natural justice, the right to be heard, will be a cornerstone of Aboriginal justice systems. Indeed, many Aboriginal justice initiatives require the individual to speak for him or herself. The other rules – that the decision maker be unbiased and that justice be done and be seen to be done – are certainly appropriate and necessary for Aboriginal justice systems modelled on the non-Aboriginal system. But systems that do not have this orientation may not find it easy to adhere to all the rules of natural justice.

For instance, many Aboriginal justice initiatives rely heavily on the involvement of clan leaders and elders and on the participation of the community at large. The reason for their involvement is precisely because they have personal knowledge of the individual and her or his family. As noted earlier, the application of rules of natural justice depends a great deal on the tasks to be accomplished by a decision-making body. To the extent that Aboriginal justice systems are healing-based systems, they would naturally want to involve those who know and understand the offender. It is precisely these individuals who can craft decisions that meet the person's needs and develop options that lead to healing and change.

We have emphasized repeatedly in this report that the success of Aboriginal justice systems will not be the extent to which they measure up to yardsticks developed to serve an offence-based, punishment-oriented system; rather, it will be their ability to meet the needs of the nations and communities they serve. This will require extensive consultation and continuous monitoring and evaluation. Thus, for example, decision makers may not necessarily have to demonstrate that they are neutral in the sense that they do not know the parties involved in the dispute; rather what is needed is a process that all participants see as fair, regardless of decision makers' relationship to the parties. Just because a program meets the criteria for formal objectivity, there is no reason to assume that the program will benefit those it serves or that it will be seen as just. An object lesson on this point can be gained simply by looking at how the non-Aboriginal system – with all its formal procedural protections – has been unable to address the real needs of Aboriginal people.

Appeal Structures

The focus of this chapter until now has been decision making in the initial stages of dispute resolution and healing. Especially when Aboriginal justice systems include fact-determination forums – bodies that perform a role analogous to that of trial courts – the need will arise for an appeal mechanism for decisions by these bodies. What form should they take? Also, if such bodies are created, is there a role for the non-Aboriginal system's appeal courts in determining issues arising from decisions in Aboriginal systems?

The Aboriginal Justice Inquiry of Manitoba listed four approaches to appeals in tribal court systems in the United States:

> Where there are more than three judges in a court, the three who did not sit on the case as the trial judge comprise the court of appeal. On occasion a judge from another tribal court may be asked to take one of the appeal positions.

> Where there are three or fewer judges, a judge or judges from another tribal court will be asked to attend to sit with the others who did not hear the case, and they will comprise the court of appeal.

> People from outside the community are appointed as members of an appellate branch to sit from time to time as needed. In the Hopi system the court of appeal is made up of three legally trained tribal members who no longer live on the reservation. One is a judge in a state court, one is a practicing lawyer and the other is a university professor.

> In the Navajo court, a separate court of appeal with three full time judges sits to hear all appeals.[434]

In the United States, appeal bodies tend to hear few appeals, at least in criminal law cases, because of the tribal courts' limited jurisdiction (owing to the effects of the *Major Crimes Act*) and the limited nature of sentences that can be imposed under the *Indian Civil Rights Act*. If Aboriginal justice systems in Canada resist the temptation to follow the U.S. model, appeal bodies may well have a more significant number of cases to decide.

Given our emphasis on enabling Aboriginal nations and their communities to develop justice systems appropriate to their needs, it makes little sense to suggest that a single appellate structure will suit all Aboriginal justice systems.

In cases where the justice system resembles the non-Aboriginal court system, appellate structures would mirror their counterparts in the non-Aboriginal system. Appeal bodies might be organized on a nation basis, or several nations might jointly establish such bodies to permit development and pooling of expertise and achieve economies of scale.[435] As a further level of appeal, the development of a pan-

---

[434] AJI, cited in note 2, volume 1, p. 289.

[435] This is being done in the southwestern United States, where a number of tribal courts have banded together to create an appellate level. See Rudin and Russell, "Native Alternative Dispute Resolution Systems", cited in note 335, p. 30.

Canadian Aboriginal appeal body should also be considered. The purpose of this body would be to render decisions on cases from across the country so as to ensure that Aboriginal concepts of justice would be reflected in appellate decisions in all relevant cases. One readily apparent role would be interpreting Aboriginal charters of rights. In addition, the decisions of an Aboriginal appeal body would likely carry significant weight when the Supreme Court of Canada considered cases (probably small in number) coming from Aboriginal justice systems through the pan-Canadian appeal body. In the absence of a pan-Canadian Aboriginal appeal body, appeals from decisions of the appeal body of a specific nation should be to the relevant provincial court of appeal. If the nation's territory covers more than one province, appropriate legislation would specify which provincial court of appeal would have jurisdiction. Appeals from that court would be to the Supreme Court of Canada.

Where decision-making bodies are structured differently from non-Aboriginal courts, then clearly the appeal structure would also differ. Some traditional Aboriginal systems, such as that of the Haudenosaunee, have a history of appeal-like processes that have been used to deal with problems that cannot be resolved at the local level. Under the Haudenosaunee system there are four levels of dispute resolution – the relatively informal intra-clan level, the inter-clan level, the inter-village level, and a final tier reserved for resolving disputes crossing the nation's boundaries.[436] Recently discussions have taken place among members of the Mohawk Nation with respect to renewing a longhouse justice system that would build upon this traditional framework.

Whatever appellate structures are developed, they will have to develop expertise in addressing the unique issues that might arise from the operation of Aboriginal justice systems. As a result, these bodies should, as much as possible, have exclusive jurisdiction over appeals. At a minimum, no right of appeal to the courts of the non-Aboriginal system should be permitted until all avenues of appeal within the Aboriginal system have been exhausted.

Recommendation 9

The Commission recommends that Aboriginal nations' justice systems include appellate structures that could be organized on a nation basis or on the basis of several nations coming together. As a further level of appeal, the creation of a pan-Canadian Aboriginal appeal body should be considered. In the absence of a pan-Canadian Aboriginal appeal body, an appeal of the decision of an appeal body of a specific nation should be to the relevant provincial court of appeal. Appeals from that court, and from a pan-Canadian Aboriginal appeal body, would be to the Supreme Court of Canada.

---

[436] See Elizabeth Dixon-Gilmour, "Resurrecting The Peace: Separate Justice and the Invention of Legal Tradition in the Kahnawake Mohawk Nation", PH.D. thesis, London School of Economics and Political Science, February 1994, p. 139.

In our discussion of the impact of section 96 of the *Constitution Act, 1867*, we noted the complexity of determining the jurisdiction of federal, provincial and Aboriginal governments to create court-like structures. In general, the less these bodies resemble courts of the non-Aboriginal system in form and function, the more scope Aboriginal nations have to create them.

The need to ensure that Aboriginal appellate bodies reflect distinctively Aboriginal approaches to justice requires the appointment of uniquely qualified individuals to such bodies. Although section 96 gives the federal government the exclusive right to appoint superior court judges, where Aboriginal appeal bodies are established pursuant to treaties between the Aboriginal nation and the government, these treaties could provide a framework for appointments by mutual agreement of the parties. These treaty rights would be constitutionally protected under sections 35 and 25 of the *Constitution Act, 1982*.

Recourse to the non-Aboriginal appeal system should occur only in cases where the non-Aboriginal system might have a useful role to play. In practice this should mean that the only matters heard by the non-Aboriginal system, other than by way of judicial review, would be those involving interpretation and application of the Constitution Acts, including the Charter. All other matters should remain exclusively within the jurisdiction of the Aboriginal appellate system. The existence of a pan-Canadian Aboriginal appeal body would minimize recourse to the non-Aboriginal court system.

The appeal structures discussed here are not, of course, the only possible structures, and it is not the Commission's intention to be prescriptive in this regard. It will be for Aboriginal governments to devise the appeal framework they consider most appropriate.

Aboriginal Justice Systems and Urban Aboriginal Communities

There is often an unspoken assumption that Aboriginal justice systems will develop in rural or northern communities and that urban Aboriginal people, because they have chosen to live in the city, have no choice but to deal with the non-Aboriginal system if they come into conflict with the law. This ignores the facts about Aboriginal people today, however, and makes the promise of culturally appropriate justice systems an illusion for almost half of all Aboriginal people in Canada – the half that live in towns and cities.

The realities of life in many reserves and northern communities mean that people often have to leave to pursue education or find employment. Some, particularly women, have left to escape violent situations; others, such as people with disabilities, leave because of the lack of services on reserves. Leaving their reserves or communities does not mean that these people have abandoned their culture, their traditions or their understanding of who they are.

A focus on the reserve or rural community as the place where Aboriginal justice systems will develop effectively shuts out many status and non-status people, Métis people and some Inuit. As we saw in our review of justice initiatives, the distinction between status and non-status Aboriginal people is not one communities consider relevant when designing justice projects.

All the evidence before the Commission makes it clear that the non-Aboriginal justice system has failed Aboriginal people. This failure is not restricted to reserve, rural and northern communities. On the contrary, the jails in Canada's urban centres, particularly in the west, provide abundant proof that the justice system treats Aboriginal people in the city as inappropriately as it does elsewhere.

Under these circumstances, what justification can there be for not developing urban Aboriginal justice programs? In many ways, urban communities are better suited than reserves to develop such programs. For example, the Aboriginal population of Toronto was about 40,000 in 1991, according to Statistics Canada, while Aboriginal service providers in the city estimate the population at between 60,000 and 70,000.[437] Concentrations of Aboriginal people are also found in Vancouver, Winnipeg, Regina, Saskatoon and Calgary, among other cities. The Aboriginal population of many urban centres is the equivalent of a small city – Red Deer, Alberta, for example, or Fredericton, New Brunswick. If small cities are capable of administering justice, why not the Aboriginal population of a city?

In many urban areas, Aboriginal people have a quite well developed network of social and cultural agencies. Toronto has a multiplicity of Aboriginal social services agencies as well as organizations providing educational and cultural programs. In the social services field, for example, Native Child and Family Services provides child welfare services, Anduhyuan is a women's shelter, Anishnawbe Health provides a range of traditional and conventional health services, Pedahbun Lodge offers a residential treatment program for drug or alcohol dependency, Aboriginal Legal Services offers a wide array of legal services, and NaMeRes provides shelter for homeless men. In the area of social and cultural programs the Native Women's Resource Centre and Two Spirited People of the First Nations offer programs designed for segments of the Aboriginal population. The Native Canadian Centre and Council Fire offer a wide range of programs for community members, while the Native Earth Theatre Company presents an annual season of award-winning plays.[438] This web of independent Aboriginal-controlled agencies provides almost all the services one would expect of a government.

---

[437] In the 1991 census, 40,000 people in the Toronto census metropolitan area (CMA) stated that they had some Aboriginal ancestry. However, Statistics Canada reports that 14,205 persons living in the Toronto CMA in 1991 identified themselves as Aboriginal. This figure represents single responses and is not adjusted to account for undercoverage of the population arising from methodological constraints. (Statistics Canada, *1991 Aboriginal Peoples Survey*, cited in note 232, Table 2, p. 6.)

[438] This list is by no means comprehensive. It is estimated that Toronto is home to more than 40 Aboriginal-specific agencies.

In speaking of Aboriginal government to this point, we have referred to nations having exclusive jurisdiction over everyone living in their territory (although we did recommend that non-Aboriginal accused have a choice about which system they will be tried in). This model of governance does not make sense in an urban context, but this does not mean that urban Aboriginal communities cannot develop self-governing institutions. In our final report we address the issue of urban Aboriginal governance in detail.

Briefly, we see a governance model based on a community of interest as the most appropriate for urban Aboriginal communities. This would involve governmental structures serving only Aboriginal people who agreed voluntarily to associate with the urban government but would not be territorially-based in the same manner as Aboriginal nations. Membership in a community of interest model would be open to all Aboriginal people and would not exclude those who maintained an affiliation with a home nation. This type of government would concentrate on program and service delivery, proceeding from a basis of stable and secure funding.

Taking Toronto as an example once again, the structures necessary for the exercise of a community of interest model of self-government already exist. At this time, however, the continued existence of virtually all Aboriginal services in the city depends primarily on the vagaries of government funding – federal, provincial and municipal. A more secure funding base is required, one tied to recognition that the exercise of Aboriginal self-government in the urban context could lead to greater and more significant innovation. The development of the community council to address child welfare and landlord and tenant disputes and the work of the Family Violence Working Group illustrate that with co-operation among agencies, a great deal can be accomplished in the urban setting to meet the needs of a diverse Aboriginal community.

Reserves and rural or northern communities dealing with alcohol or drug abuse problems often have to send people hundreds or thousands of miles away for treatment. Anger management programs and the like are also rare in these types of Aboriginal communities. Urban centres, by contrast, tend to have more Aboriginal-specific services available. As noted earlier, one of the important criteria for the success of Aboriginal justice programs is the existence of services to help people in the healing process.

Since 1992, Toronto has had an Aboriginal adult criminal diversion program – the community council. This program takes in a wider array of offences than non-Aboriginal diversion programs do and is also open to a wider range of offenders. Although conclusive statistical analyses have not yet been completed, preliminary evidence indicates that the program has succeeded, in ways the non-Aboriginal system has not, in meeting the needs of Aboriginal offenders, helping them move to a healing path, and thus ultimately reducing recidivism.

The development of justice systems is a vitally important aspect of Aboriginal self-government in the urban context. The development of urban justice sys-

tems will require a great deal of co-operation and co-ordination between the non-Aboriginal justice system and Aboriginal systems. Urban Aboriginal governments based on community of interest will be concerned with matters of justice delivery and the administration of justice, not with the exercise of law-making powers.

Jurisdictional matters, for instance, will likely have to be determined on a basis different from that for reserve or rural communities. The fact that different communities require different responses, however, should in no way be seen as an impediment to establishing this vitally important aspect of Aboriginal self-government in the urban context.

5
Reforming the Existing Justice System

We have already made the point that in charting a path for reform we must be careful not to create unnecessary dichotomies; in particular in calling for recognition of distinctive Aboriginal justice systems, we must not signal the abandonment of reforms in the non-Aboriginal system. As has been clear from our discussion, the development and implementation of Aboriginal justice systems will be evolutionary, and there will be a continuing need for bridges between the two systems. Thus, although our primary focus has been on creating space for Aboriginal justice systems, we also deem it important to set out our thinking on strategies for reform of the existing system to make it more respectful of Aboriginal people and more responsive to their experiences.

Reform of the existing system has been the focus of many inquiries preceding ours. We therefore determined early in our mandate that it would make little sense for this Commission to replicate their research or reproduce their recommendations; indeed, simply reciting them would occupy a volume of significant length.

During its research phase, the Alberta task force on the criminal justice system assembled a list of 708 recommendations for reform from all the Aboriginal justice reports between 1967 and 1990. In its own 1991 report, *Justice on Trial*, the task force made 340 recommendations of its own. Several hundred additional proposals have since been made in other reports, bringing the total to as many as 1800 recommendations for reform. Yet despite this wealth of good ideas, the essence of the evidence we received from Aboriginal nations, communities, organizations and scholars is that there has not been significant change in the day-to-day realities facing Aboriginal people in their involvement with the criminal justice system, except where Aboriginal initiatives have taken hold. It is clear that the reason is not the lack of sound recommendations but a lack of concrete implementation. Our recommendations therefore focus on this lack of implementation – precisely because it is the primary stumbling block to reform of the existing system.

Implementing the Recommendations of Justice Inquiries

Little point would be served in listing all the recommendations in other justice reports, but grouping the most common and often repeated recommendations, may be useful. In its analysis of more than 700 recommendations, the Alberta task force identified the 10 most common:

1. cross-cultural training for non-Aboriginal staff working in the criminal justice system;

2. more Aboriginal staff in all areas of the justice system;

3. more community-based alternatives in sentencing;

4. more community-based programs in corrections;

5. more specialized assistance to Aboriginal offenders;

6. more Aboriginal community involvement in planning, decision making and service delivery;

7. more Aboriginal advisory groups at all levels;

8. more recognition of Aboriginal culture and law in service delivery;

9. additional emphasis on crime prevention programs for Aboriginal offenders;

10. self-determination must be taken into account in planning and operation of the criminal justice system.[439]

The Alberta task force report noted that many of its recommendations fell into one of these categories and had been made in earlier reports. But the task force decided to make them again because "in our opinion, they have not been implemented fully or appropriately and are still applicable".[440] Its terms of reference called for the task force to "formulate a process for the ongoing monitoring and upgrading of programmes and initiatives implemented pursuant to the recommendations of the task force."[441] Commenting on these words, the task force wrote,

> the wording...is unfortunate because it permits Government to
> select favoured recommendations, with the result that only those

---

[439] *Justice on Trial*, cited in note 23, volume 3, chapter 4, p. 7.

[440] *Justice on Trial*, volume 1, chapter 1, p. 5.

[441] *Justice on Trial*, volume 1, appendix 2, p. 2.

recommendations will be monitored by the ongoing process. Many of the recommendations made in this Report depend upon other recommendations being implemented.[442]

To ensure implementation of all its recommendations, the task force recommended a short- and a long-term monitoring mechanism. For the first 18 months following the report, a five-person task force monitoring committee was to have authority to make inquiries of government and investigate components of the criminal justice system to ensure implementation of the recommendations. The committee would report quarterly to federal and provincial justice and solicitor general departments, with a report to be filed in the provincial legislature within one year with further implementation recommendations. The committee was to consist of four appointed members, one each from the federal and provincial governments, and the Indian Association of Alberta, and the Métis Association of Alberta. The chairperson was to be chosen by the committee and failing that by the government of Alberta. Preferably the chair would be an Aboriginal person.[443]

The long-term mechanism, a five-person Aboriginal justice commission, was to have the same membership appointment procedure as the task force monitoring committee and would assume its functions. It would also facilitate communication between Aboriginal peoples, governments and components of the criminal justice system; negotiate a framework agreement among all parties regarding jurisdiction and cost-sharing; assist Aboriginal persons to direct their concerns regarding the administration of justice to the appropriate government department; and generally facilitate communications and assist government in developing Aboriginal justice policy. Significantly, the commission was to employ an Aboriginal advocate to receive, forward and follow up on official complaints lodged by Aboriginal persons regarding criminal justice administration. As with the short-term mechanism, the commission would table in the provincial legislature within one year, and annually thereafter, a report of its proceedings and recommendations.[444]

Neither the short-term task force monitoring committee nor the long-term Aboriginal justice commission was established. Instead, the original Alberta task force steering committee, which had overseen the task force and was still in place, was asked to report to the Alberta attorney general and solicitor general on an implementation strategy for the recommendations, and a working committee was struck to oversee further consultations with Aboriginal groups and communities regarding implementation.

During the Aboriginal Justice Inquiry of Manitoba, Rufus Prince, an elder of the Long Plain First Nation, addressed commissioners as follows concerning his fears

---

[442] *Justice on Trial*, volume 1, chapter 10, p. 1.

[443] *Justice on Trial*, volume 1, chapter 10, p. 3.

[444] *Justice on Trial*, volume 1, chapter 10, p. 4.

about the fate of the commission's report, based on the experience of previous reports:

> *We ask that the Province extend the power of this Commission to mon-*
> *itor the implementation of its recommendations... you've got to do this*
> *or...the bureaucrats are going to find a nice high shelf for your report* and
> recommendations and a generation later, if they have another
> commission on the same subject, they will find that they are cov-
> ered with dust.
>
> All the time and effort and sacrifice you have devoted to this
> Commission will go to nothing and be all in vain. We will only
> have dug the ruts a little deeper.[445]

In response to repeated expressions of concern such as this, the 1991 Report of the Aboriginal Justice Inquiry of Manitoba devoted an entire chapter to "A Strategy for Action" on its recommendations, part of which involved establishing two bodies: the Aboriginal justice commission and Aboriginal justice college. The Aboriginal justice commission was considered central to implementation and was to have a broad mandate to monitor implementation and report publicly from time to time on progress in implementing the inquiry's recommendations. The com-mission was to have several other tasks as well, including entering into discussions with Aboriginal peoples to determine their wishes with respect to the various rec-ommendations; recommending the form and method of implementation of recommendations; assisting in the establishment of Aboriginal justice systems; and monitoring the progress of affirmative action programs. The commission was to be independent, with a board of directors made up of equal numbers of Aboriginal persons and non-Aboriginal government representatives and an inde-pendent chairperson. The Aboriginal representatives were to include status Indians, Métis people, non-status Indians and representatives of Aboriginal women and urban Aboriginal people.[446]

The second body, the Aboriginal justice college, was conceived primarily as a training and continuing education body for Aboriginal people assuming positions of responsibility in the existing justice system and Aboriginal justice systems. The report also saw the college organizing cross-cultural training for non-Aboriginal judges, lawyers, court staff, police, correctional officers, and other persons involved in the administration of justice.[447]

Neither of these recommendations has been acted on by the Manitoba government, which has instead proposed further consultations between government and

---

[445] AJI, cited in note 2, volume 1, pp. 639-640 (emphasis added).

[446] AJI, volume 1, pp. 657-658.

[447] AJI, volume 1, pp. 638-639.

Aboriginal peoples regarding implementation. The high shelf to which Elder Rufus Prince referred seems to have been found yet again.

A similar fate has befallen the recommendations of the Law Reform Commission of Canada (LRCC) in its 1991 report, *Aboriginal Peoples and Criminal Justice*. In the report the LRCC commented that its mandate to examine the *Criminal Code* met with little enthusiasm among Aboriginal people consulted because "in their eyes, no new catalogue of the particular deficiencies in the *Criminal Code* or in the practice of the criminal law was required. What they believed was needed was not more study but more action."[448] The LRCC also pointed out that many of its own recommendations were not new, having been made in other reports over the years. Its conclusion, not surprisingly, was that "*a major difficulty in solving Aboriginal criminal justice problems lies not in finding solutions, but in instituting them.*"[449]

The LRCC's proposals for ensuring progress were twofold. The first was to ascertain the costs of change through identifying and evaluating the current level of resources devoted to Aboriginal justice issues, including provincial resources. The second was to create an Aboriginal justice institute to oversee implementation of its recommendations and perform other functions, including conducting empirical research, collecting data, providing assistance to Aboriginal communities in establishing programs, and developing policy options regarding Aboriginal justice issues. As described by the LRCC,

> The Institute could conduct or commission research into customary law. It could help train Aboriginal Justices of the Peace. It could help establish cross-cultural training programmes or training programmes for legal interpreters. It could advise on holding court sittings in Aboriginal communities. It could develop criteria for granting bail or parole that take the special situation of Aboriginal persons into account.
>
> The Institute could also evaluate existing measures such as diversion, fine option or community services programmes. The Institute could formulate programmes of its own, provide expert assistance to communities wishing to create such programmes and assist in making funding applications. Another possibility is to give the Institute the ability to fund those programmes itself.[450]

The LRCC made no detailed recommendations concerning the composition of an Aboriginal justice institute, but it did call for staffing, operation and control by Aboriginal persons "to the fullest extent possible".[451] Shortly after the release of the

---

[448] LRCC, *Report on Aboriginal Peoples and Criminal Justice*, cited in note 29, p. 3.

[449] LRCC, *Report on Aboriginal Peoples and Criminal Justice*, p. 85 (emphasis added).

[450] LRCC, *Report on Aboriginal Peoples and Criminal Justice*, p. 88.

[451] LRCC, *Report on Aboriginal Peoples and Criminal Justice*, p. 89.

report, the LRCC was disbanded by the federal government, and there was no direct follow-up on its recommendations.[452]

In retrospect, it seems clear that efforts to ensure implementation of the reform agenda have been frustrated. Instead of independent, institutional support mechanisms to ensure progress in Aboriginal justice reform, in most instances there have been further consultations followed by more discussion. After more than 30 reports on Aboriginal justice, it is difficult not to draw the conclusion that there is a lack of political will and significant bureaucratic resistance to real change, both prompted in part by the fact that the establishment of Aboriginal justice systems has never been addressed in tandem with exercise of the inherent Aboriginal right of self-government.

In light of this history, we believe it is incumbent upon this Commission to provide a framework for implementing the specific recommendations of provincial and federal justice inquiries. It is particularly important to provide for government accountability regarding implementation of these recommendations.

Recommendation 10

The Commission recommends that the federal, provincial and territorial governments report to their respective legislatures annually regarding implementation of the recommendations of Aboriginal justice inquiries and commissions. These reports should address

(a) **the nature and extent of cross-cultural programs offered to government employees and to the judiciary, the number of employees and judges who take them, the delivery agencies involved in these programs, and whether and to what extent national, provincial and regional Aboriginal organizations and local Aboriginal communities have been consulted or otherwise involved in the delivery of these programs. As well, government reporting should indicate whether and to what extent follow-up programs have been put in place to measure the effectiveness of these programs and whether and to what extent disciplinary procedures are in place to deal with employees or members of the judiciary who exhibit racist or other discriminatory attitudes;**

(b) **the number of Aboriginal people employed in all capacities in government departments with an interest in justice issues; the number of Aboriginal judges at all levels and of Aboriginal justices of the peace, and the percentage of all personnel in these departments who are Aboriginal people. In addition, the report should outline the difficulties facing gov-**

---

[452] Bill C-106, An Act respecting the Law Commission of Canada, was tabled in the House of Commons by the minister of justice on 6 October 1995. It is expected to re-establish a renamed and altered version of the law reform commission by the spring of 1996.

ernment in recruiting Aboriginal people for these positions and the steps being taken to address issues of under-representation;

(c) the extent to which national, provincial and regional Aboriginal organizations and Aboriginal communities have been consulted in the development of justice policies and whether and to what extent such organizations have been involved in the direct delivery of justice services to Aboriginal communities, including urban and reserve, northern and rural. Government reporting should also state what plans are in place to increase the level of Aboriginal involvement;

(d) the extent to which reform of or amendments to the Criminal Code or related criminal matters under federal jurisdiction, to provincial offences, or to regulatory offences under either federal or provincial jurisdiction have been subject to appraisal from an Aboriginal perspective by Aboriginal nations, Aboriginal communities, or national, provincial or regional Aboriginal organizations; and

(e) efforts made to involve Aboriginal nations and communities at all stages of the criminal justice process, whether these efforts have involved consultation or negotiation with Aboriginal nations and communities regarding the role they can play, and to what extent federal, provincial and territorial governments are providing resources and training to Aboriginal nations and communities willing to assume justice responsibilities.

In addition to concern about implementation of the recommendations of previous justice inquiries, we think it important that the recommendations in this report – a report that considers Aboriginal justice issues from a broader perspective than simply reform of the non-Aboriginal system – be given careful and serious thought.

Recommendation 11

The Commission recommends that the government of Canada, within one year of the release of this report,

(a) convene an intergovernmental conference of federal, provincial and territorial ministers of justice and attorneys general, solicitors general, ministers of correctional services, and ministers responsible for Aboriginal affairs to address the issues and recommendations in this report;

(b) invite to this conference representatives of Aboriginal peoples and national Aboriginal organizations; and

(c) ensure that people working directly in developing and implementing Aboriginal healing and restorative justice projects participate in the conference.

Recommendation 12

The Commission recommends that the regular meetings of federal, provincial and territorial ministers of justice and attorneys general include an agenda item addressing Aboriginal justice issues. Solicitors general, ministers of correctional services, and ministers responsible for Aboriginal affairs should participate in the discussion of this agenda item, and appropriate representatives of Aboriginal peoples should be invited to attend the discussion of this agenda item.

The Canadian Bar Association stated in its 1988 report, *Locking Up Natives in Canada*, that lawyers have a particular responsibility in advancing the cause of justice for Aboriginal people.

Recommendation 13

The Commission recommends that, within a year of the release of this report, the Canadian Bar Association, provincial bars or law societies, and the Indigenous Bar Association convene a joint meeting to address the issues and recommendations in this report.

The Cost of Justice

Considering reform of the non-Aboriginal system and development of Aboriginal justice systems requires some attention to the issue of resources. Although additional resources will undoubtedly be required, it should not be assumed that vast amounts of new money will have to be found. If one message comes through loud and clear in the evidence before the Commission, it is that we as a society are already spending enormous amounts of money to process and in many cases warehouse a small segment of the population.

The Aboriginal Justice Inquiry of Manitoba observed that the justice system costs about half a billion dollars annually in Manitoba, taking into account Manitoba's share of federal expenditures on justice, the Manitoba department of justice, municipal police forces, the cost of enforcing fishing and hunting regulations and operating the child welfare system, and expenditures by non-governmental organizations such as those that assist offenders after they are released from prison.

> With Manitoba's Aboriginal population representing 12% of the total population of the province and more than 50% of the jail population, it is clear an enormous amount of money is being spent dealing with Aboriginal people.[453]

---

[453] AJI, cited in note 2, volume 1, p. 11. The Alberta task force referred to Aboriginal people in Alberta as accounting for 20 to 35 per cent of the "client base" of the justice system, despite being less than 5 per cent of Alberta's population. The task force estimated that at projected rates of growth in Aboriginal incarceration and population, by the year 2011 the increase in Aboriginal offender

In his submission to the Commission, the minister of justice and attorney general of Saskatchewan, Robert Mitchell, cautioned that it is difficult to attribute expenditures precisely (because they often serve multiple clients – accused persons, victims and communities), but he estimated nevertheless that "Saskatchewan Justice spent about $81 million of its $117 million 1992-93 criminal justice budget (policing, prosecutions, courts and correctional services) in relation to Aboriginal peoples. Of this total, roughly $59 million was spent in relation to Indians, and $22 million in relation to Métis."[454]

The Osnaburgh/Windigo committee also concluded that a great deal of money is being spent to deal with a relatively small part of the population in northern Ontario. Moreover, the money is being spent largely to deal with problems related to alcohol and solvent abuse, which, far from being helped, are being aggravated by the existing criminal justice processing. The committee concluded that these expenditures are of significant economic benefit to non-Aboriginal society in surrounding areas since it enables many non-Aboriginal persons to have employment in the justice system. The commissioners referred to Aboriginal offenders as a "commodity" – the raw material processed by the justice system.

> In Osnaburgh, based on an analysis of the court cases from Pickle Lake in 1989, approximately 80% of all appearances for offenses involved alcohol or solvent abuse (i.e. the accused had been abusing alcohol or solvents at the time when the offense was allegedly committed). The residents of Osnaburgh feel that there is inefficient allocation of resources by non-Native government in addressing the problem. For example, more money appears to be spent on moving people back and forth from Osnaburgh to the Kenora jail – where they are fed and housed and salaries are paid to non-Native correctional officers – than is spent on the treatment of alcohol and substance abuse. They believe that the present system of fines, leading to non-payment, the issuance of committal warrants and jail sentences totally fails to deal with the underlying socio-economic problems and simply provides work for non-Native police, court and custodial personnel. From this perspective, the First Nations "drunk" can be seen as important "commodity" in the non-Native wage economy of Northern Ontario.[455]

---

admissions alone would cost an extra $23 million over and above existing expenditures. This figure did not take into account the effects of inflation. (*Justice on Trial*, cited in note 23, volume 1, chapter 8, p. 17.)

[454] Mitchell, submission to RCAP, cited in note 34, p. 12.

[455] Report of the Osnaburgh/Windigo Tribal Council Justice Review Committee, cited in note 22, p. 62.

Faced with this sort of information the Law Reform Commission of Canada recommended that more precise information about the costs of the current system be obtained:

> Funding for various Aboriginal justice programmes is currently drawn from several sources. The federal departments – Indian Affairs and Northern Development, Justice, Solicitor General, Secretary of State – all provide resources, as do many provincial government departments and other bodies such as Bar Associations and universities. We suggest that the level of resources currently devoted to Aboriginal justice issues, including provincial resources, should be precisely identified and evaluated. Expenditure priorities should be established in consultation with Aboriginal peoples to decide the best ways to deploy resources and eliminate unnecessary duplication. This process should include not only "Aboriginal-specific programmes", but also the portion of spending that in large part concerns Aboriginal people, such as funding for correctional facilities or policing. Comprehensive cost-feasibility studies should be immediately undertaken in respect of all proposals carrying resource implications that are advanced in this report.
>
> *The historical disadvantage suffered by Aboriginal persons in the justice system has been too long ignored. If needed reforms have not been made in timely fashion, we cannot now plead poverty as an excuse for continued inaction.*[456]

The Law Reform Commission went on to make a further point that we see as fundamental in assessing how much society can afford to devote to Aboriginal justice:

> Further, although funds must be allocated immediately, a short-term perspective is not appropriate. Aboriginal justice systems may be expensive in the short-term, but in the long-term, there would be a return on the investment. The expense can be rationalised by looking at the saving that would come partly from the fact that the rest of the justice system, the correctional system in particular, would be required to deal with fewer Aboriginal persons. But beyond that, restoring social control to communities could help to reverse the process of colonization that has created the problems Aboriginal persons face in the justice system. Their increased social control should result in lower crime rates and a lesser need for the use of any justice system.[457]

---

[456] LRCC, *Report on Aboriginal Peoples and Criminal Justice*, cited in note 29, p. 86 (emphasis added).

[457] LRCC, *Report on Aboriginal Peoples and Criminal Justice*, p. 87.

The recommendation of the Law Reform Commission that there be a precise and comprehensive accounting of the resources now devoted to Aboriginal justice issues has not been acted upon by the federal government. As a result, five years after the release of the Law Reform Commission's report, we still lack an official figure to serve as a baseline against which to measure the cost of reform.

The absence of a baseline is not limited to the administration of justice. For this reason we commissioned a study to provide more specific information regarding the extent of federal, territorial and provincial expenditures related to Aboriginal people. In calculating expenditures the study takes into account the Aboriginal population's share of such expenditures, as well as the estimated average level of use of particular programs by Aboriginal persons (as compared to levels of use by non-Aboriginal persons). The study does not capture all the costs associated with the criminal justice system and Aboriginal people, but it does give some measure of their magnitude.

Federal expenditures for the 1992-93 fiscal year amounted to $129.6 million, divided between spending on Aboriginal policing ($44.7 million) and correctional services ($84.9 million). The policing component includes $12.3 million to the RCMP and a little over $30 million for First Nations-specific programs employing 690 First Nations police officers. The correctional component includes costs for the 2,300 self-identified Aboriginal offenders in federal correctional institutions in 1992, together with some $3 million for institutional programs such as Aboriginal spirituality, inmate liaison and substance abuse programs.[458]

In terms of provincial expenditures, a total of $31.9 million was spent in the justice sector in Ontario in 1991-92, including $11.6 million associated with the First Nations Policing Agreement, $8.2 million in relation to correctional facilities, $4.3 million for Aboriginal court staff-related activity, $5.4 million for Aboriginal-specific support for inmates and probationers, $0.8 million for sexual assault/wife assault prevention, and $1.6 million for other projects, including family healing policy development. For the province of British Columbia, total expenditures in the justice sector attributable to Aboriginal people amounted to $99.7 million. This included $19 million for adult institutional services, $3.8 million for youth institutional services, $7.2 million for community services, $18.2 million for justice support, $21 million for police services, $17.8 million for court services, and $3.1 million for legal services. For the province of Alberta the figure of $84.6 million made up of $13.6 million for court services, $5.5 million for legal aid, $41.4 million for correctional services, and $24.1 million for law enforcement.[459]

It is clear from this study, figures in the report of the Aboriginal Justice Inquiry of Manitoba, and submissions we received from the government of Saskatchewan,

---

[458] Goss Gilroy Inc., "Federal, Territorial and Provincial Expenditures Relating to Aboriginal People", research study prepared for RCAP (1995).

[459] Goss Gilroy Inc., "Federal, Territorial and Provincial Expenditures".

that expenditures run into the hundreds of millions of dollars a year, even if we limit the calculation to direct costs for the administration of criminal justice, such as policing, courts and corrections.

The figures from the study we commissioned represent our best effort to extrapolate from total expenditures in the justice sector the expenditures attributable to Aboriginal people. Governments, however, are in a better position to determine these expenditures more precisely.

Recommendation 14

The Commission recommends that federal, provincial and territorial governments conduct a complete review and audit of the current justice system and provide detailed figures on the costs of the administration of justice as it affects Aboriginal people at all stages, including crime prevention, policing, court processing, probation, corrections, parole, and reintegration into society.

Security of funding is an important issue. In Chapter 3 we referred to several submissions to the Commission that explained the difficulties of planning and implementing Aboriginal justice initiatives in the absence of a secure financial base. Although in some cases substantial amounts of money have been made available for Aboriginal justice initiatives, by the time the money is distributed across the country the individual amounts allocated are too often inadequate to the task. Furthermore, the pilot project mentality often limits funding to relatively short periods, making long-term planning and expansion difficult if not impossible. The Canadian experience parallels what has occurred in some other countries. Kayleen and Cameron Hazlehurst, examining the Australian experience, referred to the "confetti approach" to government funding:

> Over many years of government experience, the cutting up into small pieces, and the dispersal to the winds, of Aboriginal funding had proved to be a fundamentally flawed strategy. A multitude of inadequately funded and poorly developed projects very quickly came to nothing – failing as their funding evaporated or when their over-burdened and under-skilled staff resigned.

> The harm of these disappointments has been far reaching. As another project was terminated, as another community felt the pang of yet another failure, negative beliefs about the 'usefulness' of Aboriginal people and the 'hopelessness' of the situation were reinforced. The social and psychological damage may even outweigh the year or so of community service which the particular projects provided to youth in need, women's groups, and so forth.[460]

---

[460] Kayleen Hazlehurst and Cameron Hazlehurst, "Sober, Successful, and in Control: Proposing an Aboriginal Community Recovery Strategy to the Queensland Government" (7 April 1995, unpublished).

The limitations of pilot project thinking were stated succinctly by Brent Cotter, deputy minister and deputy attorney general of Saskatchewan at the Saskatoon Conference on Aboriginal Peoples and Justice:

> Federal ministries have had the unfortunate tendency to limit funding for innovative or pilot programming to two- or three-year projects. It seems to me this has to stop. There has to be money made available to give Aboriginal self-government the opportunity to succeed. Particularly in the justice sector, Aboriginal peoples have to have full access to stable sources of long-term funding.[461]

We agree that the parsimony that has thus far characterized the funding of Aboriginal justice initiatives must come to an end.

In our review of Aboriginal justice initiatives we commented on the fact that thus far the great majority of financial resources have been devoted to indigenization of the existing justice system. We do not suggest that these initiatives be cut back and the moneys reallocated to Aboriginal justice systems. Rather, to ensure that effective change takes place, it is necessary to proceed simultaneously with reform of the existing system and the investment necessary to enable Aboriginal nations to build the infrastructure for their own systems of justice.

Recommendation 15

The Commission recommends that in the allocation of financial resources greater priority be given to providing a secure financial base for the development and implementation of Aboriginal justice systems.

Recommendation 16

The Commission recommends that federal, provincial and territorial governments provide long-term funding for criminal justice initiatives undertaken by Aboriginal nations or communities. At a minimum, funding for new initiatives should be guaranteed for at least the period required for serious and proper evaluation and testing; in the event of a positive evaluation, long-term funding should continue.

In discussing the cost of change, it is critical to take a long-term perspective. We know the enormous and increasing cost of processing and essentially warehousing disproportionate numbers of Aboriginal men, women and young persons. In the Commission's view, establishing Aboriginal justice systems, with distinctive Aboriginal ways to address the underlying causes of Aboriginal crime, will be a far

---

[461] Brent Cotter, "The Provincial Perspective on the Split in Jurisdiction", in *Continuing Poundmaker and Riel's Quest*, cited in note 35, p. 134.

more positive and productive undertaking than building more prisons. The cost of financing Aboriginal justice systems must be seen as a long-term investment in the future of Aboriginal people and one that will ultimately bear fruit, not only in terms of Canada's record of human rights with respect to Aboriginal people, but also in terms of reducing the financial cost, which will continue to escalate in the absence of genuine and sustained change.

The Agencies of Change

A common thread in the recommendations of the Alberta task force, the Aboriginal Justice Inquiry of Manitoba, and the Law Reform Commission of Canada is that an integral part of effecting change is the establishment of agencies or institutions charged with overseeing the implementation of recommendations and to act as a co-ordinating and facilitating body in relation to Aboriginal justice issues.

Although the Aboriginal justice institute proposed by the Law Reform Commission of Canada was not established, the federal government did establish and fund an Aboriginal justice directorate in the department of justice in 1991. In formulating our own recommendations for agencies or institutions of change, we considered both the mandate and the work undertaken by the Aboriginal justice directorate, so as to avoid duplication or overlap. We are satisfied that our recommendation for a new Aboriginal justice council (see page 305) is qualitatively different, in terms of jurisdiction, administration and financial base, from anything that exists now, including the Aboriginal justice directorate.

The Aboriginal justice directorate was established as part of the federal Aboriginal justice initiative, which was developed after the release of the Law Reform Commission's report and the federal government's discussion paper, *Aboriginal People and Justice Administration*. The following extracts from that paper describe the parameters of the initiative:

> Improved Aboriginal justice is a key element of the federal government's overall Aboriginal policy, referred to as the Native Agenda. This overall policy is built on the frank recognition that Aboriginal people have too often been treated unfairly, with lack of respect, and with insensitivity to their language and culture, and that the current difficulties confronting many Aboriginal people reflect that history...
>
> Aboriginal justice reform is...essential to achieving the objectives of the overall government policy and particularly to establishing a new relationship between Aboriginal people and government. Accordingly, in describing the third pillar of the policy [changing the relationship between Aboriginal people and governments primarily by enlarging the capacity of Aboriginal people for self-government] the Prime Minister stated the intention of the federal government to "find practical ways to ensure that

Aboriginal communities can exercise greater control over the administration of justice." Eight months later in Victoria he enlarged upon this commitment with the pledge "to enter into discussions with the provincial governments and Aboriginal people on a new approach to Aboriginal justice."

This document is the first step in the development of that new approach. It is based on the principle that solutions must be found within the Constitution of Canada, present and future, as interpreted by the Supreme Court of Canada. In this sense, *it does not envisage an entirely separate system of justice for Aboriginal peoples although community justice systems, for example as connected to Aboriginal self-government, are both possible and desirable...*

The purpose of the Aboriginal justice policy is to support the federal government's overall policy by enhancing its contribution:

- to the equitable participation of Aboriginal peoples in the overall system of justice and to their effective participation in shaping justice policy and delivering justice programmes;
- to the reduction of the economic and social costs of crime by and against Aboriginal peoples, and to the preservation of peace, safety and order in Aboriginal communities;
- to the equitable and fair treatment of Aboriginal persons by the justice system in a manner that respects Aboriginal culture and the unique history and circumstances of Aboriginal people and which responds to the special needs and aspirations of Aboriginal people; and
- to increasing responsibilities of Aboriginal communities before justice administration, compatible with and supportive of government policy and negotiations on self-government.[462]

The federal discussion paper also proposed a number of policy principles. Organized under four broad headings, they are as follows:

Level and Quality of Service

(a) Aboriginal people should have: access to justice programmes and services equal to that enjoyed by all Canadians; fair treatment by the justice system, respectful of the individual and the needs and circumstances of Aboriginal peoples; and equitable participation in all aspects of the administration of justice.

---

[462] Justice Canada, "Aboriginal Peoples and Justice Administration: A Discussion Paper" (Ottawa: September 1991), pp. 19-24 (emphasis added).

(b) Aboriginal communities should have access to at least the same optional models of justice administration that are available to similar communities in the region.

(c) Any special measures or arrangements developed to meet the unique needs and aspirations of Aboriginal communities should meet standards with respect to the quality and level of service that would be comparable to similar communities in the region...

Culture and Responsiveness

(d) Justice Officials should receive appropriate training to ensure respect for the individual and for the diverse cultures and aspirations of Aboriginal peoples.

(e) Aboriginal persons should have access to culturally appropriate information about the legal and justice systems...

Tripartite Approach

(f) All policy and programming initiatives should respect, without prejudice to Constitutional negotiations, the current roles and responsibilities of the levels of government, and the unique history and circumstances of Aboriginal peoples.

(g) All policy and programme initiatives should be based on tripartite consultations.

(h) The funding arrangements for developmental projects and justice programmes and services provided to Aboriginal communities should reflect the shared obligations and responsibilities of the federal and provincial governments and the communities on the basis of consistent and equitable funding arrangements and the mutually acceptable formula that serves to support the aforementioned principles...

Alternative Arrangements

(i) Consideration should only be given to special measures or alternative arrangements that fall within Canadian constitutional arrangements in effect at the time, and the relationship between any proposed Aboriginal programmes and the existing federal and provincial justice system should be clear and agreed.

(j) Any alternative Aboriginal justice arrangements should be administratively and financially practical, taking into account the size of the community, community infrastructure, and the resources available.

(k) The development of new Aboriginal-Administrative arrangements should provide for a phased (multi-year)
implementation. Provision should be made for community
involvement in planning and for increasing community
responsibility.

(l) The development of any alternative Aboriginal justice
arrangements should keep sight of the principles of fundamental fairness, taking into account community standards.
Aboriginal communities should have a clearly defined role in
the administration of justice through appropriate accountability mechanisms which at the same time insure the requisite
level of independence.

(m) Arrangements for Aboriginal communities should ensure the
availability of mechanisms of review and individual grievance
and redress.[463]

In announcing the Aboriginal justice initiative, which was "to improve the administration of justice as it affects Aboriginal people", the minister of justice of the day,
Kim Campbell, said that a total of $26.4 million over five years had been allocated
to enable the minister of justice and the solicitor general "to work with Aboriginal
people, the provinces and the territories, and the Minister of Indian Affairs and
Northern Development and other colleagues to make justice administration more
responsive to Aboriginal aspirations, needs and concerns."[464]

The $26 million earmarked for the Aboriginal justice initiative has shrunk by
about 10 percent because of budget reductions. Of the original $26 million, $3.9
million was allocated to the solicitor general for Aboriginal corrections initiatives, and the balance went to the department of justice. The largest block of
funding (some $18 million) was allocated to the Aboriginal justice directorate, which
has a five-year mandate and has been responsible for the funding of a variety of
Aboriginal justice projects since 1991. Of the directorate's $18 million original allo-
cation, $10 million was allocated to pilot projects and community support (since
reduced to $9 million as a result of budget cuts).

As described by the directorate, the projects it has funded fall into five major
categories:

1. policy consultations and co-ordination;

2. cross-cultural training;

3. public legal education and information;

---

[463] "Aboriginal Peoples and Justice Administration", pp. 25-30.

[464] "Message from the Justice Minister", in "Aboriginal Peoples and Justice Administration", p. i.

4. resource centre; and

5. pilot projects, including comprehensive legal services; alternative dispute resolution; diversion; involvement of Aboriginal people in the justice process;
   customary law; alternative approaches within the existing constitutional framework; crime prevention; and improved services to women, victims and youth.

Funding for pilot projects is approved by the minister of justice and is limited by
Treasury Board to a maximum of three years for each project.[465]

Some of the Aboriginal initiatives described in Chapter 3 received funding from the
directorate. The Hollow Water First Nation received $60,000 to support the first
phase of the community holistic circle healing project and a further $240,000 for
the later phases of the project, ending in 1996. The adult diversion initiative of the
Shubenacadie Band was supported over a three-year period from 1992 to 1995 with
funding of $136,000, and the South Island Tribal Council Diversion Project received
$50,000 for a two-year period from 1991 to 1993. The St. Theresa Point First
Nation received $100,000 to support implementation of a community-based Indian
government youth court designed to serve young offenders who contravene band
by-laws, provincial statutes and some provisions of the *Criminal Code*.

For the period 1992-94, Pauktuutit, the Inuit Women's Association, received
$176,000 from the directorate to prepare a policy paper on how to ensure the par-
ticipation of Inuit women in the establishment and evolution of Aboriginal justice
systems. Further funding in the amount of $273,000 has also been granted for the
period 1994-96 to enable Pauktuutit to continue its research and consultations with
Inuit women and to promote dialogue on issues related to the administration of
justice.[466]

Clearly, the Aboriginal justice directorate has played an important and valuable role
in funding these and other projects. Serious limitations are built into the Aboriginal

---

[465] Justice Canada, Aboriginal Justice Directorate, "Projects Approved 1991/1992-1994/1995"
(May 1995).

[466] Other projects funded by the Aboriginal Justice Directorate range from $5,000 for a public legal
education needs assessment carried out by the Shuswap Nation Tribal Council to $950,000 to sup-
port the development of the Nishnawbe-Aski Legal Services Corporation, which delivers legal and
para-legal and related services to 48 Aboriginal communities in northern Ontario. The funding has
also been extended to universities; for example, the Northern Justice Society of Simon Fraser
University received $29,000 to support publication of *Native North Americans: Crime, Conflict and
Criminal Justice, A Research Bibliography*, and the Faculty of Law of the University of Alberta also
received $29,000 to provide academic assistance to Aboriginal first-year students. A number of con-
ferences on Aboriginal justice issues have been supported; for example, the Deh Cho Tribal Council
of Fort Simpson in the Northwest Territories received $15,000 for a community justice educational
forum in 1992, and the Metis Association of Alberta received $6,000 for a youth conference held
in Calgary in 1993 to examine preventive solutions to abusive situations affecting young people.
The Metis Society of Saskatchewan received $50,000 for the Metis Justice Development Conference,
held in Saskatoon in 1992 to establish a framework for the development of culturally appropriate
justice-related structures and programs in Métis communities in the province of Saskatchewan.

justice initiative, however, as it is administered by the directorate. The first relates to the pilot project mentality. Pilot projects funded through the department of justice are limited to three years. Roland Crowe, former chief of the Federation of Saskatchewan Indian Nations, identified the problem with this approach and the double standard involved.

> Many times we see pilot projects begin and, just when they're going great guns suddenly we run out of money. When we build a highway or federal buildings or provincial buildings, if we run out of money, do these buildings and highways stop? They don't. If you allocated a certain number of dollars to the correctional system or the justice system and suddenly half way through you run out of money do you say "That's alright, we'll shut the system down?"[467]

The absence of long-term stable funding is not the only problem with the pilot project approach under which the Aboriginal justice directorate operates. Leonard Mandamin, an Aboriginal lawyer from Alberta who spoke at our round table on justice, recognized that pilot projects have some advantages but identified their limitations, particularly the absence of a recognized Aboriginal jurisdiction in the administration of justice.

> Use of the mainstream system as an incubator for Aboriginal justice systems has two beneficial effects.
>
> First, different starting points may be used to initiate the development of an Aboriginal justice system. From a starting point of policing, sentencing panels or corrections, the Aboriginal initiative may expand into other areas and develop into a complete system. Beginning with a developed Aboriginal system is possible, but the flexibility offered by a developing system is more likely to serve the needs of different Aboriginal communities.
>
> Second, this approach lends itself to a phased development with the Aboriginal communities, given time to assimilate new developments and plan the next logical step.
>
> The drawback to the incubator approach to development is that it is dependent on the mainstream criminal justice personnel involved and the objectives of the government of the day. The transfer of a Crown prosecutor, the retirement of a judge, or a change in government priorities from prevention and rehabilitation to stricter law enforcement can rapidly wipe out Aboriginal justice gains. Without more, it is likely that the long-term result

---

[467] Roland Crowe, "First Nations Perspective on Justice and Aboriginal Peoples," in *Continuing Poundmaker and Riel's Quest*, cited in note 35, p. 35.

would be to revert to the conventional criminal justice system and the status quo.

One last point which is very important: every Commission that has come out has said that this should be negotiated with the possible exception of Manitoba, which went further on it. *You cannot negotiate if you do not have something to negotiate with. If you do not have the authority or the jurisdiction or the de facto position, then it is extremely difficult to negotiate, because the only thing you have left is your own people's misery, and that's a fine negotiating position.*

If one talks about a negotiated process then one had better take a serious look at ensuring that Aboriginal people have cards to play in negotiation. Otherwise, it will be a fine exercise here and I will go back to Alberta and listen to justice department opinions that say you cannot do that, or go into court, after listening to the RCMP describe the fine list of measures that they are taking, and defend Aboriginal people who are charged after a donnybrook between the Natives and Whites and only the Natives are charged. That is what happens today.

These are fine words here, but until we actually see results, we have not got anywhere.[468]

These points have relevance to the mandate of the Aboriginal justice directorate and the federal policy under which it operates. The directorate is an agency of the federal department of justice and operates within the constraints of the objectives and policy principles set out in the discussion paper quoted earlier. Aboriginal nations and communities make applications for funding that are evaluated in terms of these objectives and principles. Funding is entirely discretionary, and there is no Aboriginal participation in evaluating applications or setting funding priorities. From our review of the projects funded by the directorate we believe it is fair to say that most of the money has gone to projects intended to improve the existing system rather than initiatives designed to provide a framework for distinctive Aboriginal justice systems. This is not entirely surprising, since the discussion paper states that the policy "does not envisage an entirely separate system of justice for Aboriginal peoples".[469] A further problem is that the evaluation of proposals for initial funding and renewal of funding is conducted largely by non-Aboriginal policy advisers and researchers.

The five-year mandate of the Aboriginal justice initiative comes to an end in 1996. That is also when funding channelled through the Aboriginal justice direc-

---

[468] Leonard Mandamin, "Aboriginal Justice Systems: Relationships", in *Aboriginal Peoples and the Justice System*, cited in note 7, pp. 289-290; and transcripts, National Round Table on Aboriginal Justice issues, Ottawa, 27 November 1992 (emphasis added).

[469] "Aboriginal Peoples and Justice Administration", cited in note 462, p. 20.

torate will terminate. The climate of uncertainty this creates is of great concern to many who have devoted their energies to bringing justice to their communities. While extending the initiative would alleviate these immediate concerns, in the transition to self-government, we believe that the process for funding Aboriginal justice initiatives requires fundamental change and that change must be consistent with recognition of an Aboriginal jurisdiction in relation to justice.

Under the jurisdictional model we envisage, in which Aboriginal governments are one of three orders of government, Aboriginal nations would determine the shape of Aboriginal justice systems and the allocation of resources within their overall budgets. Until that fundamental restructuring of relationships between Aboriginal and non-Aboriginal governments takes place – and in our final report we will develop recommendations to achieve that end – we believe it is necessary to establish a mechanism to facilitate Aboriginal self-determination in the area of justice.

This mechanism could take the form of an Aboriginal justice council, whose mandate would combine several elements of the Aboriginal justice institute proposed by the Law Reform Commission and the Aboriginal justice commission and college proposed by the Aboriginal Justice Inquiry of Manitoba. The role we see for the Aboriginal justice council would extend beyond those proposals, however. The present responsibilities of the Aboriginal justice directorate would eventually be transferred to the Aboriginal justice council as an arm's-length federal agency to facilitate the development, financing and implementation of Aboriginal justice systems. Thus, the council would determine which Aboriginal initiatives are funded and the level of funding they receive.

In proposing establishment of an Aboriginal justice council we are not suggesting that administrative responsibilities simply be shifted from one federal agency to another. Establishing an Aboriginal justice council is not simply indigenization. The council itself would be broadly representative of First Nations, Métis people and Inuit, Aboriginal people from urban areas, and Aboriginal women and youth. It would determine funding policy and priorities as between reform of the existing system and development of Aboriginal systems. There would be no policy constraints on the council in the form of the federal policy reflected in the discussion paper, and development of policy principles would proceed from an Aboriginal perspective. Thus establishment of distinctive Aboriginal justice systems, far from being precluded, could be the centrepiece of funding policy.

The overall direction for the Aboriginal justice council would be set by a board of directors. The initial group of directors would have to be selected by the federal government, but one of the board's first tasks should be to recommend to the government an arm's-length process for further appointments. To ensure continuity of membership, we suggest that appointments to the board be staggered so that not all directors are replaced in any one year.

Recommendation 17

The Commission recommends the establishment, by legislation, of an Aboriginal Justice Council, operated and staffed primarily by Aboriginal people, to facilitate the development, financing and implementation of Aboriginal justice systems.

Although we see an Aboriginal justice council taking over the responsibilities of the Aboriginal justice directorate, there will obviously be a transition period. With funding slated to end in 1996, the survival of several Aboriginal justice initiatives will be imperilled.

Recommendation 18

The Commission recommends that as a transition measure the Aboriginal Justice Initiative be extended until the Aboriginal Justice Council has been established and is ready to carry out its mandate.

We have heard repeatedly that the time for identifying problems is over, and the time for action is at hand. We see the Aboriginal justice council as an action-oriented body, facilitating and making things happen. That does not rule out the need for continuing research, not so much to identify the problems, but to foster imaginative responses that are consistent with Aboriginal principles and processes of justice and designed to translate ideas into concrete change.

A research agenda for the Aboriginal justice council would not be difficult to design. Many of the issues discussed in Chapter 4 call for research that is best done by Aboriginal legal scholars and practitioners working together with Aboriginal communities. Examples of the kind of research we see the Aboriginal justice council sponsoring are the development of Aboriginal charters of rights and the design of adjudication processes that respect the rights and responsibilities of the accused and ensure that the rights and responsibilities of the victim are at the centre, not the edge, of the circle of justice. The Aboriginal justice council could also play a vital role in developing new forms of legal education appropriate for Aboriginal justice systems. Even though Canadian law schools have taken important steps to increase the enrolment of Aboriginal law students, it appears that the law school experience is as alienating for many of them as the criminal justice system is for Aboriginal people involved as accused or victims. Patricia Monture-OKanee, now a professor at the University of Saskatchewan, has reflected on her experience as a law student:

> Just as the expectations of my grandmothers were never met, I always felt during my law school days that I was waiting for my legal education to begin. I always felt that something was "missing" or perhaps that I was missing something. Nor am I certain that I am now able to define clearly what exactly this "something" is.[470]

---

[470] Patricia Monture-OKanee, "Now that the Door is Open: First Nations and the Law School Experience", *Queen's Law Journal* 15 (1990), p. 185.

Shannon Cumming, who recently graduated from law school, has tried to articulate what that "something" is. In a paper entitled "Ghosts in the Machine: The Law School Experience and Aboriginal Peoples on the Road to Community Justice", he wrote,

> This paper is unlike any other I have written at Law School. It is a very personal account, written at a place – Law School – where academic discourse rewards detached analysis of facts and law and personal observations have little value... Like many other Aboriginal law students, I have dutifully carried out the tasks of briefing cases, researching papers and writing tests in much the same manner as do non-Aboriginal law students. Like many other Aboriginal law students, I have struggled to articulate the concerns of my community to a community which know little of our concerns. Like many other Aboriginal law students, I have questioned at times whether we can truly change the system from within, or whether we must take more pro-active measures to assert our inherent right to self-government...
>
> My ancestors have been restless lately. I can sense their discomfort, and during the last three years in which I have attended law school, I have found it difficult to hear their voices above the din. They are best heard in quiet places, such as when we are on the land.... There are many aspects of Aboriginal community which the traditional research community – mostly non-Aboriginal and non-resident in the communities – either downplays in significance or misses completely... For many Aboriginal students, the process of attending law school is unsettling, because they are required, in short order, to reject their notions of community justice, and instead, gather knowledge of a different sort. The process, therefore, is much like building a house with tools which you have never used before, and that you would prefer not to use at all... The "something" referred to [by Patricia Monture-OKanee] may be the inability of the present law school structure to accommodate Aboriginal discourse on models of Aboriginal justice systems.[471]

Re-imagining legal education, so that it becomes a gateway rather than a barrier to integrating life and law for the benefit of community, will be critical to the development of Aboriginal justice systems. Bringing together those who can participate in this endeavour is one of the exciting activities the Aboriginal justice council could promote.

---

[471] Shannon Cumming, "Ghosts in the Machine: The Law School Experience and Aboriginal Peoples on the Road to Community Justice", paper prepared for a seminar on Aboriginal justice, University of British Columbia Law School, 19 April 1995, pp. 1-5.

The Aboriginal justice council could create a climate in which Aboriginal people could share their visions of justice and explore ways to give them contemporary expression, and also bring to bear the experience of other indigenous peoples. Aboriginal people are already involved in a wide range of international exchanges and are increasingly aware of each other's legal and political development. There has already been much sharing through forums such as the Working Group on Indigenous Populations. In areas such as intellectual and cultural property and personal and community healing, a vibrant international Aboriginal perspective has developed. At an international conference in Vancouver in 1995, Kayleen Hazlehurst described recent initiatives in the state of Queensland and acknowledged the significant contribution of Aboriginal people from Canada in the development of the healing movement in Aboriginal communities in other countries.

> The healing process has largely taken its lead from the 'healing circle' concept shared with us by Canadian Native people through our various communications, by our participation in Healing Our People conferences and other exchanges since 1988... These indigenous processes are not unfamiliar to Australian Aboriginal people and visits from Native Canadian workers have helped steel confidence in experimentation and new skills development.[472]

We would anticipate that this international Aboriginal perspective in the area of justice could play an important role in the development of Aboriginal justice systems in Canada. The value of this comparative experience and its incorporation into contemporary solutions for common problems is captured by Moana Jackson, writing about the development of a contemporary Maori justice system.

> As the Pakeha law has drawn on such diverse trains of thought as those of the Aristotelians and the Stoics, so a developing Maori jurisprudence would undoubtedly draw on the ideals of other indigenous peoples and other legal systems. But in developing those ideals into actual legal practices a Maori system would pass them through the filter of its own needs and its own perspectives.[473]

A further function for an Aboriginal justice council would build on Canadian and international experience. We have referred to ground-breaking work in Aboriginal communities across the country dedicated to individual and community healing. Informal and formal networks of knowledge and resources are helping to shape these developments. An Aboriginal justice council could play an important role in

---

[472] Hazlehurst, "Community Healing and Revitalization and the Devolution of Justice Services", cited in note 76, p. 6. See also Kayleen Hazlehurst, *A Healing Place, Indigenous Visions for Personal Empowerment and Community Recovery* (Rockhampton, Queensland: Central Queensland University Press, 1994).

[473] Jackson, *The Maori and the Criminal Justice System*, cited in note 21, p. 269.

enhancing both formal and informal exchanges. This role could include the foundation of national or provincial/regional Aboriginal healing lodges to provide training and support for community workers, a subject to which we will return in our final report.

Finally, the Aboriginal justice council could monitor changes in the existing justice system recommended in so many other justice reports. Earlier in this chapter, we recommended that governments be required to report annually to their legislatures regarding the implementation of such recommendations. These reports could also be submitted to the Aboriginal justice council so that the Aboriginal perspective and the Aboriginal experience of implementation could be brought to bear at the nation and community level.

6

Summary of Major Findings, Conclusions and Recommendations

Major Findings and Conclusions

1. The Canadian criminal justice system has failed the Aboriginal peoples of Canada – First Nations, Inuit and Métis people, on-reserve and off-reserve, urban and rural – in all territorial and governmental jurisdictions. The principal reason for this crushing failure is the fundamentally different world views of Aboriginal and non-Aboriginal people with respect to such elemental issues as the substantive content of justice and the process of achieving justice.

2. Aboriginal people are over-represented in the criminal justice system, most dramatically and significantly in provincial and territorial prisons and federal penitentiaries.

3. Over-representation of Aboriginal people in the criminal justice system is a product of both high levels of crime among Aboriginal people and systemic discrimination.

4. High levels of Aboriginal crime, like other symptoms of social disorder such as suicide and substance abuse, are linked to the historical and contemporary experience of colonialism, which has systematically undermined the social, cultural and economic foundations of Aboriginal peoples, including their distinctive forms of justice.

5. Responding to and redressing the historical and contemporary roots of Aboriginal crime and social disorder require the healing of relationships, both

internally among Aboriginal people and externally between Aboriginal and non-Aboriginal people.

6. At the heart of a new relationship between Aboriginal and non-Aboriginal people must be recognition of Aboriginal peoples' inherent right of self-government. This right encompasses the authority to establish Aboriginal justice systems that reflect and respect Aboriginal concepts and processes of justice.

7. Aboriginal nations have the right to establish criminal justice systems that reflect and respect the cultural distinctiveness of their people pursuant to their inherent right of self-government. This right is not absolute, however, when exercised within the framework of Canada's federal system. The contemporary expression of Aboriginal concepts and processes of justice will be more effective than the existing non-Aboriginal system in responding to the wounds that colonialism had inflicted and in meeting the challenges of maintaining peace and security in a changing world.

8. Aboriginal peoples' inherent right of self-government is recognized and affirmed in section 35 of the *Constitution Act, 1982* and forms the basis for Aboriginal government as one of three orders of government within Canada. In the specific context of this report, it is our conclusion that the Aboriginal right of self-government encompasses the right of Aboriginal nations to establish and administer their own systems of justice, including the power to make laws within the Aboriginal nation's territory.

9. The right to establish a system of justice inheres in each Aboriginal nation. This does not preclude Aboriginal communities within the nation from sharing in the exercise of this authority. It will be for the people of each Aboriginal nation to determine the shape and form of their justice system and the allocation of responsibilities within the nation.

10. The inherent right of self-government recognized and affirmed in section 35 of the *Constitution Act, 1982* includes the right to exercise jurisdiction over core and peripheral areas. In the core area, Aboriginal nations can pursue self-starting initiatives without the need for negotiated agreements with federal or provincial governments. In peripheral areas, Aboriginal nations can take action only after negotiating agreements with the other relevant governments. The test for determining whether matters fall within the core of Aboriginal self-governing jurisdiction is that (a) they are of vital concern to the life and welfare of a particular Aboriginal people, its culture and identity; (b) they do not have a major impact on adjacent jurisdictions; and (c) they are not otherwise the object of transcendent federal or provincial concern.

11. Aboriginal jurisdiction in relation to criminal law and procedure operative on Aboriginal territories is *concurrent* with federal jurisdiction over criminal law and procedure generally. Where a conflict arises between an Aboriginal law and a federal law passed pursuant to section 91(24) of the *Constitution Act, 1867,*

the Aboriginal law will take priority except where the need for federal action can be shown to be compelling and substantial and the federal legislation is consistent with the Crown's basic trust responsibilities to Aboriginal peoples. While Aboriginal governments can in principle take self-starting initiatives in their core areas of jurisdiction without the need for agreements with other relevant orders of government, we believe that in the area of criminal law such an approach is not advisable as a practical matter because of considerations of comity and the avoidance of litigation.

12. Since Aboriginal peoples' inherent right of self-government is recognized and affirmed in section 35(1) of the *Constitution Act, 1982*, the *Canadian Charter of Rights and Freedoms* applies to the legislation and acts of Aboriginal governments, including their justice systems, under section 32 of the Charter, and Aboriginal nation governments have access to section 33 of the Charter.

13. The impact of the *Canadian Charter of Rights and Freedoms* on the development of Aboriginal justice systems will be influenced primarily by two factors. The first is section 25 of the Charter, which guarantees that the Charter will not abrogate or derogate from Aboriginal and treaty rights. The second is the right of Aboriginal nations to create their own Aboriginal charters of rights, which should ensure that the Canadian Charter receives a flexible interpretation that takes account of the distinctive concepts and processes of Aboriginal justice.

14. The *Canadian Charter of Rights and Freedoms* applies to Aboriginal governments, including their justice systems, and regulates relations with individuals under their jurisdiction. However, under section 25, the Charter must be given a flexible interpretation that takes account of the distinctive philosophies, traditions and cultural practices of Aboriginal peoples. Moreover, under section 33, in their core areas of jurisdiction, Aboriginal nation governments can include in legislation notwithstanding clauses to suspend the operation of certain Charter protections for a five-year renewable period. Nevertheless, by virtue of sections 28 and 35(4) of the *Constitution Act, 1982*, Aboriginal women and men have equal access to the inherent right of self-government and are entitled to equal treatment by their governments.

15. The development of justice systems is a vitally important aspect of Aboriginal self-government in the urban context. The development of urban justice systems will require a great deal of co-operation and co-ordination between the non-Aboriginal justice system and Aboriginal systems. Urban Aboriginal governments based on community of interest will be concerned with matters of justice delivery and the administration of justice, not with the exercise of law-making powers.

Recommendations

The Commission recommends that

Recognition and Comity

1. Federal, provincial and territorial governments recognize the right of Aboriginal nations to establish and administer their own systems of justice pursuant to their inherent right of self-government, including the power to make laws, within the Aboriginal nation's territory. *(Recommendation 1, page 224)*

2. Aboriginal justice systems be able to exercise choice with respect to the types of offences they will hear and the particular offenders who are to come before them. Offences and offenders not dealt with by the Aboriginal justice system would continue to be dealt with by the non-Aboriginal justice system. *(Recommendation 4, page 254)*

3. In designing their criminal justice systems, Aboriginal nations give non-Aboriginal residents accused of offences within their territory a choice about where their cases will be dealt with – in the Aboriginal nation's criminal justice system or in the non-Aboriginal system – except in cases where the offence involved is unique to the nation's system and is designed to protect values that are fundamental to the nation's culture. *(Recommendation 5, page 256)*

4. Although Aboriginal nations can enact criminal law and procedure in their core areas of criminal jurisdiction without agreements with the other two orders of government, in the interests of comity and the avoidance of litigation, they should enter into negotiations to secure such agreements before doing so. *(Recommendation 3, page 248)*

5. The federal, provincial and territorial governments of Canada include the creation of Aboriginal justice systems on the agendas of current negotiations regarding land claims, treaty making and self-government, and consider reopening existing treaties and agreements to address justice issues, if the Aboriginal parties so desire. *(Recommendation 2, page 232)*

Development of Aboriginal Charters

6. Aboriginal nations develop their own charters of rights to supplement the protections in the *Canadian Charter of Rights and Freedoms* and provide guidance to courts in interpreting existing protections in the Canadian Charter. *(Recommendation 6, page 267)*

Aboriginal Women and Children 7. The safety and security of Aboriginal women and children be given a high priority in the development of Aboriginal justice systems and program initiatives. *(page 275)*

8. All nations rely on the expertise of Aboriginal women and Aboriginal women's organizations to review initiatives in the justice area and ensure that the participation of women in the creation and design of justice systems is both meaningful and significant. *(page 275)*

Appellate Structures 9. Aboriginal nations' justice systems include appellate structures that could be organized on a nation basis or on the basis of several nations coming together. As a further level of appeal, the creation of a pan-Canadian Aboriginal appeal body should be considered. In the absence of a pan-Canadian Aboriginal appeal body, an appeal of the decision of an appeal body of a specific nation should be to the relevant provincial court of appeal. Appeals from that court, and from a pan-Canadian Aboriginal appeal body, once in existence, would be to the Supreme Court of Canada. *(page 279)*

Governments' Role in Implementation 10. Federal, provincial and territorial governments report to their respective legislatures annually regarding implementation of the recommendations of Aboriginal justice inquiries and commissions. These reports should address

(a) the nature and extent of cross-cultural programs offered to government employees and to the judiciary, the number of employees and judges who take them, the delivery agencies involved in these programs, and whether and to what extent national, provincial and regional Aboriginal organizations and local Aboriginal communities have been consulted or otherwise involved in the delivery of these programs. As well, government reporting should indicate whether and to what extent follow-up programs have been put in place to measure the effectiveness of these programs and whether and to what extent disciplinary procedures are in place to deal with employees or members of the judiciary who exhibit racist or other discriminatory attitudes;

(b) the number of Aboriginal people employed in all capacities within government departments with an interest in justice issues; the number of Aboriginal judges at all levels and of Aboriginal justices of the peace, and the percentage of all personnel in these government departments who are Aboriginal people. In addition, the report should outline the difficulties facing government in recruiting Aboriginal people for these positions and the steps being taken to address issues of under-representation;

(c) the extent to which national, provincial and regional Aboriginal organizations and Aboriginal communities have been consulted in the development of justice policies and whether and to what extent such organizations have been involved in the direct delivery of justice services to Aboriginal communities, including urban and reserve, northern and rural. Government reports should also state what plans are in place to increase the level of Aboriginal involvement;

(d) the extent to which reform of or amendments to the *Criminal Code* or related criminal matters under federal jurisdiction, to provincial offences, or to regulatory offences under either federal or provincial jurisdiction have been subject to appraisal from an Aboriginal perspective by Aboriginal nations, Aboriginal communities, or national, provincial or regional Aboriginal organizations; and

(e) efforts to involve Aboriginal nations and communities at all stages of the criminal justice process, whether these efforts have involved consultation or negotiation with Aboriginal nations and communities regarding the role they can play, and to what extent federal, provincial and territorial governments are providing resources and training to Aboriginal nations and communities willing to assume justice responsibilities. *(page 289)*

11. The government of Canada, within one year of the release of this report,

(a) convene an intergovernmental conference of federal, provincial and territorial ministers of justice and attorneys general, solicitors general, ministers of correctional services and ministers responsible for Aboriginal affairs to address the issues raised and recommendations in this report;

(b) invite to this conference representatives of Aboriginal peoples and national Aboriginal organizations; and

(c) ensure that people working directly in developing and implementing Aboriginal healing and restorative justice projects participate in the conference. *(page 290)*

12. Regular meetings of federal, provincial and territorial ministers of justice and attorneys general include an agenda item address-

ing Aboriginal justice issues. Solicitors general, ministers of correctional services, and ministers responsible for Aboriginal affairs should participate in the discussion of this agenda item, and appropriate representatives of Aboriginal peoples should be invited to attend the discussion of this agenda item. *(page 291)*

Legal Profession's Role in Implementation 13. Within a year of the release of this report, the Canadian Bar Association, provincial bars or law societies, and the Indigenous Bar Association convene a joint meeting to address the issues and recommendations in this report. *(page 291)*

Financial Resources 14. Federal, provincial and territorial governments conduct a complete review and audit of the current justice system and provide detailed figures on the cost of administering justice as it affects Aboriginal people at all stages, including crime prevention, policing, court processing, probation, corrections, parole, and reintegration into society. *(page 295)*

15. In the allocation of financial resources greater priority be given to providing a secure financial base for the development and implementation of Aboriginal justice systems. *(page 296)*

16. Federal, provincial and territorial governments provide long-term funding for criminal justice initiatives undertaken by Aboriginal nations or communities. At a minimum, funding for new initiatives should be guaranteed for at least the period required for serious and proper evaluation and testing; in the event of a positive evaluation, long-term funding should continue. *(page 296)*

Aboriginal Justice Council 17. An Aboriginal Justice Council be established by legislation, operated and staffed primarily by Aboriginal people, to facilitate the development, financing and implementation of Aboriginal justice systems. *(page 305)*

18. As a transition measure, the Aboriginal Justice Initiative be extended until the Aboriginal Justice Council has been established and is ready to carry out its mandate. *(page 305)*

For further information:
Royal Commission on Aboriginal Peoples
P.O. Box 1993, Station B
Ottawa, Ontario
K1P 1B2

Telephone: (613) 943-2075
Facsimile: (613) 943-0304